ZOUAVE THEATERS

ZOUAVE THEATERS

TRANSNATIONAL MILITARY FASHION
and PERFORMANCE

CAROL E. HARRISON AND
THOMAS J. BROWN

LOUISIANA STATE UNIVERSITY PRESS

BATON ROUGE

Published by Louisiana State University Press
lsupress.org

DESIGNER: Michelle A. Neustrom
TYPEFACE: Freight Text Pro

JACKET ILLUSTRATION: "Armée française, Zouaves (no. 265)."
Imprimerie Pinot et Sagaire, Epinal, 1860–72. Authors' collection.

LIBRARY OF CONGRESS CATALOGING-IN-PUBLICATION DATA

Names: Harrison, Carol E., author. | Brown, Thomas J., author.
Title: Zouave theaters : transnational military fashion and performance /
    Carol E. Harrison, Thomas J. Brown.
Description: Baton Rouge : Louisiana State University Press, 2024. | Includes
    index.
Identifiers: LCCN 2023035522 (print) | LCCN 2023035523 (ebook) |
    ISBN 978-0-8071-8118-8 (cloth) | ISBN 978-0-8071-8211-6 (pdf) | ISBN
    978-0-8071-8210-9 (epub)
Subjects: LCSH: Military uniforms—History—19th century. | France. Armée.
    Infanterie. Zouaves. | France. Armée—Uniforms—History—19th century.
Classification: LCC UC480 .H355 2024 (print) | LCC UC480 (ebook) | DDC
    355.1/409034—dc23/eng/20231122
LC record available at https://lccn.loc.gov/2023035522
LC ebook record available at https://lccn.loc.gov/2023035523

for Kay and Doug Harrison

and Helen Brown

and in remembrance of Lou Brown

CONTENTS

ILLUSTRATIONS

ZOUAVE THEATERS

FIG. 1. Jean-Marie Bérot, carte de visite of Louis Joseph Badout.
Collection of Jérôme Discours, www.military-photos.com.

INTRODUCTION

The Zouave Moment

*Z*ouave uniforms were the most important military fashion fad of the nineteenth century. Developed in the French occupation of Algeria as a fantasy of native prowess, the baggy trousers, collarless short jacket, and fez with turban created a look that spread around the world, taken up by both soldiers and stage performers. For a brief period in the 1850s and 1860s, soldiers of many nations enthusiastically adopted Zouave dress: the volunteers who defended Papal Rome, both sides of the U.S. Civil War, the British West India Regiments, guardsmen of the last king of Hawai'i, Polish insurgents against Russian rule, and free Black Brazilian units in the war against Paraguay all wore the look. The outfit was a costume as much as a uniform. Zouave performances featuring human pyramids, precision rifle maneuvers, and plots that turned on crossdressing sold out theaters in Europe and the United States. Some of these Zouave performers were veterans of Zouave military units, some were con artists, and many were women. During this Zouave moment, wearing the ensemble meant embracing ethnic, racial, and gender crossing, even as nineteenth-century society reified those identities and reinforced the lines between them.

The Zouave pictured in this carte de visite is Louis Joseph Badout, a member of the Imperial Guard, an elite troop that Emperor Napoleon III established to serve under his personal command and to add luster to his capital city. The Zouave fad coincided with the vogue for cartes de visite, and soldiers, generally, were good clients. Badout had his photograph taken in the mid-1860s in the Parisian studio of Jean-Marie Bérot, who was best known for portraits of prominent journalists.[1] Badout's pose emphasizes his distinguished service: the chevrons on his sleeve indicate his seniority, and his decorations, including the Legion of Honor and service medals for the Crimean War and the Italian Campaign, are clearly visible. Born in Calais in 1823 to an unmarried mother, Badout had been a Zouave since the age of twenty, when he enlisted as a replacement for someone who had bad luck with the conscription lottery but enough money to pay for a replacement. He made a career out of the army, and in this photograph, with about twenty years of service under his belt, including a decade in Algeria, he is at ease in his striking uniform. Like a typical Zouave he wears a full beard, with his cap and turban pushed precariously to the back of his head.[2]

Zouave presence in Paris gave substance to Napoleon III's claim to rule as an emperor, and Zouaves were often on display, frequently accompanying the sovereign. Members of the Guard were required to be above average height, enhancing the effect of their bright red trousers and blue jacket with gold braiding. Their presence brought the spectacle of conquest to the capital, reminding Parisians that they lived at the heart of a modern, colonial empire. His confident gaze and relaxed posture suggest that Badout has come a long way from his provincial past, and he appears fully aware of his role as a representative of both imperial cosmopolitanism and urban sophistication.

The French army's establishment of Zouave units in 1830 was an institutional manifestation of Orientalism: French soldiers engaged in the conquest of North Africa assumed a fantastic version of the dress of their antagonist.[3] Wearing his garb, Frenchmen would know their enemy from the inside out. The lore associated with the Zouave soldier focused on his ability to out-native the native, and Zouaves exulted when they were mistaken for Arabs.[4] The officers of France's African army prided themselves on knowledge about North Africa that they sought to harness for imperial ends, and they established a lasting organizational framework for French engagement with the Arabic-speaking world. Zouave cartes de visite form part of an enormous corpus of photographic documentation of colonial Algeria seen through an Orientalist lens. That body of work includes shots of Algerian towns contrasting "native quarters" with modern, French neighborhoods, pictures of ancient ruins, and ethnographic images of Algerian "types," and it is today both a rich source base for scholars and a deep reservoir of material for postcolonial nostalgia.[5] Although taken in a Paris studio, the photograph of the young European in native dress makes a similar statement about Western knowledge and mastery of North Africa.

The Zouave fad coincided with a specific Orientalist moment—the rise of imperial liberalism alongside the modern nation-state—and it illuminated dynamics of imperialism and cross-national transmission of culture in the West. In the first half of the nineteenth century, liberal thinkers in Europe were increasingly convinced that imperialism was compatible with—even necessary for—their political aims. Their confidence in European superiority banished late Enlightenment doubts about the justice of empire and led to a new period of colonial expansion.[6] Zouave dress was a uniform for liberal empire. It made its French debut in 1830 with the conquest of Algeria and entered the British Empire in 1858 as a new look for the soldiers of the West India Regiments. It appealed to expansionist sentiment in the United States and appeared on both sides of the Civil War in the following decade.

The Zouave uniform liberated the men and women who wore it from many strictures of bourgeois society—another feature of European Orientalism.[7] The uniform legitimized everything from risqué jokes to murderous violence. The reputation of the French Zouave soldier derived from everyone knowing that he fought "like a savage"—and they approved of his adoption of allegedly primitive battlefield ethics. Zouave dress also licensed forms of exhibitionism in a social world that otherwise prized modesty: our Zouave of the Imperial Guard was a showman as well as a fighter. Others—including actresses—went much further, building stage careers out of feats of athleticism and suggestive dancing, all performed in Zouave costume. Zouave Orientalism, then, was simultaneously an instrument of conquest and liberation.

The diffusion of Zouave dress is an example of a global history of France that focuses especially on Franco-American dialogue. No other country embraced the French Zouave with as much enthusiasm or developed the look with as much gusto as the United States. Approximately thirty thousand soldiers fought as Zouaves in the American Civil War— several times the number of French soldiers then in Zouave regiments. The American Zouave craze illustrated a transatlantic process of adaptation, redefinition, and occasional misunderstanding as well as an institutional contrast between the French army and American reliance on militia and U.S. Volunteer units distinct from the regulars. French observers on the eve of the U.S. Civil War were bemused by American eagerness to go to war in Zouave dress. One reporter for *Le Moniteur des armées* explained that "[a] Parisian businessman in New York will dress as a Turk to free the negroes of Louisiana in South Carolina, where he will meet a negro dressed as a Turk who will kill him without asking if he's a real Zouave." In the eyes of this Frenchman, national identity had broken down completely, the two sides in the American war were indistinguishable, and everyone was playacting. French expatriates in the United States would sign up for the fight, however, because "every Frenchman, when he's abroad, is a bit of a Zouave."[8] Like French reverberations in American art and literature or the 1824–25 return visit of the Marquis de Lafayette or the gift of the Statue of Liberty, the career of the American Zouave measured disconnections between the two countries as well as French influence within the military sector of American culture.[9]

Ascendant principles of liberal democracy that French and American citizens shared shaped praise for Zouave outfits as freeing rank-and-file soldiers from the discipline of traditional infantry attire. Champions of the Zouave look perceived it as a uniform for soldiers who were capable of showing initiative on the modern battlefield. Zouave outfits offered a stark contrast with uniforms designed to control the soldier's body by encasing it in a tight, high-buttoned jacket and crisp trousers; often a stiff leather stock forced him to hold up his head. Soldiers in those uniforms were supposed to maintain their position in a tight formation. Zouaves, in contrast, could spread out over the battlefield and find their own way to enemy lines. The short, collarless, open jacket and wide, knee-length pants permitted freedom of movement and prepared Zouaves to fulfill new ideals of athleticism. It was an outfit suitable for offensive warfare, which French military thinkers believed was key to their success and even part of the national character. Commentators on Zouave uniforms regularly invoked the *furia francese*, the legendary impetuosity of French fighting men.[10] Expected to thrive in raids and skirmishes rather than remain always within a shoulder-to-shoulder mass, the common soldier in his Zouave uniform demonstrated individual verve and self-sufficiency.

Military leaders who saw practical benefits in Zouave dress would have been offended by the charge that the uniform pandered to military vanity rather than extending military efficiency. Observers today tend to see the Zouave uniform as massively impractical. Why would anyone wear red trousers on a battlefield, much less enormously wide, baggy trousers that seem like an easy target? This attitude has shaped the view of American scholars of the U.S. Civil War in particular: surely, such self-defeating behavior cannot be taken seriously in military terms. The virtues of the Zouave uniform were real, however, and the fad hit as military organization was becoming increasingly professional and, as officers liked to say, "scientific." Zouave dress was part of this turn toward a rationalized military, and it demonstrated that political and aesthetic values inflected every facet of warfare, including what counted as "practical."[11]

For most of the nineteenth century, soldiers' invisibility to one another was a bigger problem than their visibility to the enemy. Because rank-and-file infantrymen were rarely targets of aimed fire at any substantial distance, what soldiers wore made little difference to their vulnerability. Until the 1880s, it was difficult to see much of anything on a battlefield because gunpowder filled the air with black smoke, so uniforms that were easily recognizable by their color and their silhouette presented a battlefield advantage. World War I—not coincidentally, the moment at which French Zouaves relegated their distinctive uniform to parade dress—was the first major conflict in which camouflage, a coinage of that era, became a major concern.[12] At mid-century, however, strikingly dressed soldiers could find one another easily in the field. They took confidence from their outfits, and their enemies knew that they faced a particularly fierce foe.

Zouave dress also had practical uses as a recruitment tool because aesthetic preferences shaped enlistment patterns. An army that wanted soldiers to join voluntarily needed to give recruits reasons to sign up, and the possibility of individual distinction that attached to Zouaves was appealing. In the mid-nineteenth-century world of drab, peasant colors, vibrant reds and blues set the soldier apart from his neighbors and family.[13] The Zouave uniform also brought to enlisted troops a level of panache customarily restricted to higher ranks. Lest we think that using sharp uniforms as a recruitment tool is a feature of a naive past, we should consider the aesthetic appeal of military camouflage today. Camo fatigues worn in a modern urban setting are anything but camouflaging, but they do gesture toward a warrior identity whose appeal is important to modern volunteer armies.[14] Zouave dress worked in a similar manner, suggesting to the potential recruit a fully realized narrative of an exciting soldiering life.

That Zouave script encompassed personal qualities in addition to dress and battlefield tactics. The Zouave was dashing. He approached battle with a daredevil élan and a sense of fun. His attitude toward military hierarchy was casual, and he respected competence rather than rank. He appreciated the comforts of life, and he was endlessly resourceful in obtaining them even in wartime. Above all, his jokester reputation belied his ferocity: he was a ruthless and efficient fighter. His superiors forgave his laxity where regulations were concerned because he was such an asset to the army. *Zouaverie* was the full panoply of Zouave qualities, the uniform plus its personality, a complete package that made the Zouave a recognizable character type and gave recruits a role to live up to.

This soldiering script marked a departure from the military imaginary of an earlier era. Napoleonic soldiers often imagined war through the emerging form of the novel. War was the turning point of Napoleon's personal *Bildungsroman,* the challenge that he vaulted over, knowing that he might instead fail tragically. His contemporaries similarly regarded the battlefield as the site where thoughtful young officers tested their capabilities and discovered their most authentic selves.[15] This romantic vision of war as the truest test of individual character remains influential; war movies have often combined the trial of personal development with the challenge of forming a cohesive combat unit.[16] It is not, however, the only way to conceptualize military service or to imagine the soldier's story.

The Zouaves instead configured war as a performance in which ordinary people played leading roles. The genre of their war was the music-hall theater, not the novel, and the Zouave was as much at home on the stage as in the field. Instead of a romantic individual realizing his unique genius, the Zouave was an actor, ready to change costume, learn new lines, think up new lyrics for old tunes, and appeal to a broad audience. Success required wit and artifice, not any particular quality of the heart. The Zouave did not strive for authenticity: *zouaverie* was always a performance, and the goal was to make it convincing, not necessarily true.

The Zouave fad was as much the product of the popular theater as it was the result of military achievement.[17] Real Zouaves put on plays at the front, and some veterans went on to performing careers. Zouave characters appeared in plays, and actors regularly wore Zouave dress on stage. In the United States, in particular, Zouave theater flourished and produced extravagant new forms of showmanship that belong in the ancestry of both the Broadway musical and cheerleading. On both sides of the Atlantic, however, Zouaves moved easily from stage to battlefield, from one theater to another.

Racial and ethnic cross-dressing were central to Zouave theatricality from the early development of the uniform in French Algeria. That impulse went in many directions. French soldiers who presented plays in the Crimea satirized their British allies and Russian enemies. Through their emulation of French Zouaves, Britain's West Indian soldiers took their sartorial cues from North Africa, and Pontifical Zouaves dressed as Muslims to defend the Roman Catholic Church. Blackface minstrels in the United States saw an apt mirror in the European imitation of African practice, and their parodies colored American ideas about Zouaves much as Parisian boulevard theater informed French ideas about Zouaves. French Zouaves relished the moment when their performance was so convincing that they fooled observers—perhaps their British allies, or Turks on the Black Sea. The reveal was everything, however: the point was not to maintain the deception but to unmask oneself and accept applause for a convincing impersonation.

Locating Zouave performance in the theater as well as on the battlefield meant that the role was open to women. The romantic idea that soldiering was the crucible that tested individual mettle implied a great gulf between men and women. *Zouaverie*, in contrast, was an occasion to perform both. Gender cross-dressing became as dynamic as racial cross-dressing and made Zouaves a revealing focus for interrogation of gender conventions defined by military service. Crimean War soldiers' performances in drag on stage underscored the effeminacy of the Zouave silhouette and preoccupation with dress and ornament. Zouave-style jackets became a staple item of women's wardrobes first in Paris and then everywhere that followed the fashion capital. The vogue took a sharper edge in the American political and sartorial context. Burlesque female dance-drills in Zouave costume achieved popularity in the United States even before Zouave soldiering gained traction, and the militia company that turned Zouaves into a national sensation logically specialized in precision exhibitions. Such showpieces remained a Zouave specialty in Civil War armies in which large-scale troop reviews instituted a disciplinary program of spectacle. Meanwhile, women continued to play transgressive Zouaves on the stage and develop routines that challenged the male monopoly over martial virtue.

Both Zouave dress and the full panoply of *zouaverie* fly in the face of the so-called "great masculine renunciation," "a central (and mostly uncontested) tenet of men's fashion history" since J. C. Flügel introduced the idea in 1930.[18] Men, according to Flügel, gave up ornament, color, and display in exchange for the presumption of bourgeois rectitude and seriousness of character. The dark business suit, which emerged in its modern form at roughly the same time as Zouave dress, was a form of "inconspicuous consumption" that proclaimed that aesthetic and sensuous pleasure found in clothing was essentially feminine—or effeminate.[19] Zouave dress suggests that, at the very least, the great masculine renunciation always had an escape clause available to men who wanted to enjoy dressing up.

The most influential interpretation of military dress, James Laver's account of seduction and utility as organizing principles of uniform design, is a version of the masculine renunciation thesis. According to Laver, colorful, elaborate uniforms whose principal goal is "to heighten . . . mascu-

linity and 'martial' bearing" inevitably give way to drab utility.[20] Seduction
is a passing phenomenon, while utility remains the lodestar of military
dress, and soldiers, like other men, must abandon aesthetic pleasure in order to fulfill their mission. Colonial military uniforms allegedly follow the
same pattern, with khaki, originating in the British Indian Army, as the ur-
example. A style that begins as genuine "native dress" develops into "styl-
ized native dress" in European armies and, eventually, "becomes simply
a military style," bereft of its exotic associations. Khaki entered Western
armies on the backs of native troops in India; it became a sort of colonial
costume as both British and native troops wore it, and it quickly ended
up as the most unremarkable element of any military uniform.[21] Native-
inspired dress retained its utilitarian features while losing its distinctiveness. Military professionalism steamrolled seductive romantic fantasy.

Zouave fashion, however, was a poke in the eye to anyone who demanded that soldiers renounce beauty or abandon seduction in their
mode of dress.[22] The diffusion of the Zouave look raises different questions about seduction and utility. First, we have to ask who is seduced and
by whom? The claim that uniforms follow a path from seduction to utility
assumes that soldier boys seduce girls, but that is not always how Zouave
seduction worked. The sex appeal, available both to men and to women,
derived from the gender ambiguity of the Zouave look rather than any
hypermasculinity. The seduction of a Zouave uniform involved the pleasures of cross-dressing rather than the reification of gender difference.
The opportunity to play with national, racial, and gender identity fed the
popularity of the look on both sides of the Atlantic.

The theatricality of Zouaves made them favorite subjects of visual artists, and their iconography reveals important trends in genre and media.
Horace Vernet, Adolphe Yvon, Edouard Détaille, and Alphonse de Neuville featured their battlefield exploits in the last waves of heroic war
paintings. Winslow Homer, Paul Alexandre Protais, and Giuseppe Castiglione in contrast situated Zouaves in characteristic recreational activities, which culminated in Vincent Van Gogh's acid portraits of a fellow
brothel patron. Paintings shaped and also drew inspiration from newer
art forms. The rise of illustrated magazines was crucial to the journalis-

tic foundations of the Zouave moment. Periodicals on both sides of the Atlantic reported wartime and peacetime military news, covered stage performances, and promoted consumer fashions. Zouave popularity converged as well with the emergence of photography. Roger Fenton, Gustave Le Gray, and Matthew Brady led exploration of the motif at the most ambitious edge of the profession, and countless photographers worked with soldier-models to fashion representations like Bérot's carte de visite for Louis Joseph Badout. The history of Zouaves combines the trajectories of institutions and the permutations of an image.

Zouave Theaters presents an analytic narrative that advances chronologically, geographically, and thematically. The first two chapters chart the rise of French Zouaves. In the period from the initial 1830 invasion of Algeria through the fall of Constantine in 1837, the invention and deployment of Zouaves expressed France's modern vision of empire. The establishment of the Zouaves and the native *tirailleurs algériens,* known as Turcos, produced the Army of Africa, which, separate from the metropolitan army, became the instrument of empire. Under the leadership of career officers who found North Africa an auspicious posting for advancement, Zouaves developed a reputation as extraordinarily resourceful, ferocious, and spirited soldiers. The second chapter documents the arrival of the "Zouave moment" when they won international fame for their service in European operations during the Crimean War. Acclaim only intensified with the Italian Campaign of 1859. Zouaves were among the most prominent representatives of the Second Empire in peace as well as war. They personified the carnival regime of Napoleon III that aimed to entertain citizen-spectators in the capital of the nineteenth century.[23]

The next three chapters turn to Zouaves in the United States and the Papal States during the 1860s. Naturalization of Zouaves in America did not erase remembrance of their French origin but generated distinctive characteristics and established fresh relations between military and civilian incarnations. The popularity of Zouave units in the North and South was a prime feature of volunteer enlistment in the Civil War. Attention to Zouave units helps to supplement extensive scholarship on *why* Americans left home to fight by exploring *how* Americans left home to fight.

Contrary to some scholars' claims that Zouaves faded quickly after the war got underway, Zouaves remained a vigorous part of the Union army throughout the conflict and thrived in popular culture. In the early post-war era, Black militia companies embraced Zouave dress as the emblem of an African military tradition most recently updated by the West India Regiments and Bahian volunteers in the Brazilian war against Paraguay.

The transplantation of Zouaves to the Papal States also involved modifications of the French template. The paternalism of officers and camaraderie of soldiers cultivated in Africa deepened into a more utopian religious egalitarianism binding aristocrats and ordinary volunteers. The commitment to military efficacy, on the other hand, became a pursuit of martyrdom. Papal Zouaves flourished in transatlantic Catholic memory for decades after the fall of Rome, and their defeat merged with broader French and Quebecois frustrations to make the Zouave a symbol of intransigent Catholic rejection of the modern world of nation-states and citizen armies.

The final chapter charts the decline of Zouaves after their moment of celebrity. The paradigmatic imperial soldiers of the Third Republic, they sustained a reputation as embodiments of France that lasted until the Great War created a vastly different national military identity. In the United States, in contrast, the end of their military significance in the decades after the Civil War destabilized their cultural resonance. Zouaves on stage in the heyday of the railroad circus and the vaudeville circuit evolved into a frenetic spectacle without the social satire advanced in earlier burlesques and variety acts. American celebration of warfare as the most authentic form of the strenuous life left little space for visions of the military as costumed performance. By the 1920s, Zouaves had largely disappeared in the United States. They faded more slowly in France, and the end of the Algerian War prompted quiet termination of the Zouaves as an element of the national army.

Zouaves are an exceptionally playful but nonetheless disturbing historical topic. Embracing comedy as they fused war and theater, they tended toward a self-deprecatory humor that exposed political hierarchies and gender norms embedded in military service. Their insistence on the supremacy of appearance countered dangerous forms of martial essentialism. They were, however, born as agents of oppression, and they inflicted immense physical suffering in addition to epitomizing a particular arrogance of cultural masquerade. Despite their unorthodox relations with the military establishments of France and the United States, they demonstrated that any uniformed soldier might become an instrument of misguided patriotism. The picturesque Zouaves have drawn attention from many eminent artists, writers, composers, and performers. These works offer not only evidence but also inspiration for an attempt to interpret Zouaves through scholarship.

1

PROJECTIONS OF EMPIRE

The French Army created Zouave units as instruments of a supposed civilizing mission in its Algerian colony, but it was the uniform's de-civilizing potential that caught the public imagination. French officers designed the distinctive Zouave look for native troops they recruited shortly after the invasion of 1830. The brightly colored wide trousers and open jacket were an extravagant, folkloric gesture to the new, postrevolutionary empire they imagined themselves to be building. Unlike France's lost Old Regime colonies of the plantation Caribbean, North Africa would be a colony of free men, both French and native. When soldiers put on the Zouave uniform, French military planners hoped, the best qualities of the two groups would fuse. The ethnic ambiguity of the Zouave was key to the look from the beginning: was he a native reshaped by colonial European military discipline or a Frenchman whose costume endowed him with primitive ferocity? The possibility that native soldiers might acquire the market-oriented discipline of the Frenchman proved much less alluring, ultimately, than the prospect that civilized, disciplined Frenchmen might develop some of the native's alleged recklessness and embrace of violence. Zouave dress became a means and an opportunity for Frenchmen to transgress the rules of bourgeois society.

The Zouave persona developed on both sides of the Mediterranean in a variety of sites. Algeria itself was, of course, fundamental. Plans for the unit and recruitment of native soldiers took place in the colony under the direction of a corps of officers whose subsequent careers would depend on their reputation as "African" officers. They defended the soldiering capabilities of these new troops, and they led them into action, where Zouaves proved themselves in battles to take Algerian territory and in raiding expeditions to break the resistance of native society. Paris, however, was equally important in the story of the first Zouaves. The exotically garbed soldiers first arrived in the metropole as figures in popular representations of French military glory and as characters in staged reenactments of Algerian battles. Parisians' first encounters with Zouaves involved costume and performance, a characteristic that would remain central to *zouaverie* throughout the course of its history.

New Soldiers for France's New Colony

French armies had no sooner landed in North Africa and overthrown the Dey of Algiers than the government that had ordered the invasion itself fell. Charles X, France's Bourbon monarch, abdicated following the Parisian uprising of July 1830. The new king, Louis-Philippe, the Duke of Orléans and Charles's cousin, inherited both the throne and the situation in Algeria.

Louis-Philippe's task, in France as in Algeria, was a difficult one. He was assuming the throne and founding a dynasty in the wake of a popular revolution in which French citizens had taken to the streets to demand the overthrow of his predecessor and cousin. His reign would be more liberal than Charles X's, but he would still be a hereditary monarch—in a key formulation of the summer of 1830, he would be king of the French rather than king of France. The Orléanist July Monarchy was caught from the beginning in this awkward position between monarchical rule and popular sovereignty. Louis-Philippe began his reign by replacing the dynastic Bourbon flag—golden *fleur de lys* on a white ground—with the revolutionary tricolor. He recognized a Constitutional Charter that specified the rights of French citizens, and he expanded, very slightly, the number of citizens entitled to vote. He also established a royal court and began grooming his eldest son to succeed him.[1] The effort to reconcile meritocracy with monarchy shaped the eighteen years of his rule.

What to do with Algeria was a key dilemma for Louis-Philippe's project of establishing a liberal government under royal rule. It was tempting to abandon the colonial project right away—to denounce the invasion as Bourbon overreach and return French troops to their homeland. Indeed, many supporters of the new king argued that the invasion had been Charles X's misguided effort to distract attention from fundamental problems in France that required a king's full attention, and they naturally recommended that the new king abandon the effort. The cost of the invasion certainly encouraged Louis-Philippe to consider changing course: why should a new king's finances be held hostage to his predecessor's military adventures?

Ultimately, however, Louis-Philippe opted to retain possession of Algeria and even expand French territorial control. Instead of an embarrassing legacy of a despotic and despised king, Algeria should become a showplace for the military, economic, and civilizational capacities of the July Monarchy. Frenchmen, including most notably Louis-Philippe's sons, would pacify North African territory and civilize its inhabitants. July Monarchy colonial policy thus distanced itself from the military adventures of the deposed Bourbon monarchy while committing itself to empire. The initial invasion might have been an act of royal overreach, but the Orléans family and the resources of the French nation would redeem it and make Algeria a model, modern colony. By the mid-1830s, then, July Monarchy officials were firmly committed to the French presence in North Africa.[2]

The army was the key to the July Monarchy's colonial strategy in North Africa, and the first Zouave battalions emerged as the army began to adapt to its new, Orléanist mandate. Louis-Philippe and his officers recognized that France's conscript army could not effectively garrison an overseas colony: the posting would simply be too unpopular to sustain. Finding an alternative source of troops was thus fundamental to any long-term French presence in North Africa. General Louis-Auguste-Victor de Bourmont, who had commanded the initial expeditionary force for the Bourbon monarchy, had already proposed recruiting auxiliaries from the populous, mountain regions east of Algiers whose inhabitants, he claimed, had a taste for battle. General Bertrand Clauzel, who assumed command of French forces on behalf of the July Monarchy, was fully committed to colonization, and he immediately adopted Bourmont's plan in order to send French soldiers home as quickly as possible.[3]

Enlistment of native troops began in October 1830, and by 1831 Clauzel claimed that he had replaced two-thirds of the initial French invasion force.[4] Only ten thousand French troops remained in North Africa, and two Zouave battalions had joined them in securing the colony. With the creation of these native units, France began the process that over the course of the nineteenth century bifurcated its army. The metropolitan army, tasked with protecting France's European borders, drew on conscripts who were rarely posted far from home, while the African army built France's colonial empire, fought in all distant conflicts, and, by the time of the First World War, emerged as the real backbone of France's military forces.[5]

Clauzel's plan for native recruitment went beyond simply hiring cheaper soldiers. Indigenous units were a key element in a larger project of establishing a new kind of colony, one that was more suitable for the nineteenth century and for a power that had learned the lessons of the Old Regime with the loss of its early modern American empire. Clauzel, who had been governor of the city of Le Cap during Napoleon Bonaparte's effort to retake Saint-Domingue in 1802, was fully aware of what France had lost with its Caribbean colonies. In the new empire, he imagined, military conquest would lead to agrarian settlement, and veterans, some natives but mostly European settlers, would become farmers and create a hard-working, productive society. Algeria would be a superior replacement for France's lost Caribbean empire because it was, Clauzel claimed, "destined to be the first example of a colony without slaves."[6] In place of slavery, he imagined a rationalized system of land ownership that would produce a large body of cheap native labor. Once the army had stabilized the colony, Algeria would attract settlers from many European countries who wanted to make a living while participating in the repression of the "shameful trade" in slaves along the Mediterranean coast. Some soldiers from France's regular army would no doubt also wish to settle, especially if they received land in exchange for their service. Simultaneous with native enlistment, Clauzel set up an experimental farm that, he hoped, would identify suitable crops, establish best practices for agriculture in the region, and encourage small farmers to settle in North Africa. The experimental farm would serve as a conduit between the army and a new, colonial civil society, encouraging soldiers—ambitious young natives and Frenchmen alike—to take up farming in recently pacified territory.[7]

Clauzel's proposal for native battalions, then, was an element of a larger, moralizing approach to colony-building in the nineteenth century. He imagined that recruiting native troops would create "a type of fusion" based on "sympathy" between colonizer and colonized. Under French command, natives would "accept our way of life [and] our standards of hygiene whose superiority they will soon recognize."[8] Clauzel was describing what by the late nineteenth century would be France's "civilizing mission," with the army as its primary instrument. Military service was to be the first step toward sedentary, market-oriented agricultural life for native men, and the skills they would learn as French soldiers would make them fine representatives of the colonial mission in later civilian life.

The plan to shift the costs of colonization away from the metropole by raising native troops was not original. Clauzel and his colleagues had multiple examples on which to draw. The British East India Company, for instance, began recruiting native military units in the late eighteenth century, and by the end of the nineteenth century the British Indian Army fought not only on the subcontinent but across the empire.[9] Closer to home, the Ottoman Empire was also accustomed to raising troops in ethnically varied regions, including the North African territories that France was trying to govern. Clauzel claimed to be drawing on this local tradition, as the men he targeted for recruitment were accustomed to serve Barbary princes or Ottoman sultans. They were the "Swiss of Africa," commentators asserted, prepared to serve the French as long as they received decent wages and professional leadership.[10] In the long run, however, once natives recognized that the French were in Algeria to stay, French officers hoped, they would cease being mercenaries and permanently transfer their loyalties to their colonial overlords.

Clauzel counted on natives' respect for military prowess as the foundation for the mutual understanding he hoped to create. He recruited most of the members for the first two battalions from a Berber people whom the French described as the "confederation of the Zouâoua," a version of whose name they adopted. These men, Clauzel reported back to Paris, were the "most bellicose . . . of their nation," and he was confident that he could quickly enlist over a thousand of them.[11] Clauzel's recruits were predominantly Kabyle, an ethnic group whom the French understood to be more hardworking and less "fanatical" than their Arab neighbors. Kabyles were allegedly more individualistic and egalitarian than Arabs, and Ottoman overlords had never fully succeeded in subduing them. Their sedentary habits and a supposedly more moderate version of Islam made them susceptible to civilization, French observers asserted. They were colonized subjects with whom French military officials believed they could work.[12]

The creation of two predominantly Kabyle Zouave battalions in late 1830 and 1831 encouraged the development of what scholars describe as a "Kabyle myth" in the first decade of French colonization.[13] The division of native people into Arabs and Kabyle facilitated French rule, identifying one ethnic group as potential partners in the project of subduing and civilizing the other. Some French observers even argued that Kabyle customs indicated that they had at one time been Christian subjects of the Roman Empire and that the isolation of their mountain homes had saved them from "the irremediable laxity" of the Arab Mediterranean.[14] Kabylia became the object of a series of brutal French campaigns in the late 1840s and 1850s that culminated in a final assault in 1857. Even Kabyle resistance could be integrated into the myth of their suitability as a subaltern colonial partner, however: they were clearly worthy opponents. The first quarter-century of imperial rule in North Africa convinced many French observers that the Kabyles were "a proud, fearless, industrious race whose submission to the Turks was never more than nominal."[15] Once the French succeeded in bringing them to heel, as the Ottomans never did, the Kabyle, they insisted, would be loyal colonial subjects.

The Zouave was the appropriate role for Kabyle participation in French colonization because Zouave soldiering built on Kabyles' warlike nature to encourage their proclivity for civilization. Instructed in French military practice, they demonstrated "a natural taste and remarkable dexterity" that augured well for their future.[16] The minister of war, Nicolas Soult, referring to Kabyles' warrior qualities, warned General Pierre Berthezène, on the ground in Algiers, against using money as the sole recruiting inducement. Kabyles' warrior pride demanded that they serve a cause greater than personal profit.[17] The Zouaves required careful handling, French officers reminded one another, because they would not serve inept commanders. Having conquered the valiant Kabyle and earned their respect, however, the French would find them as loyal as they were fierce. The Zouaves would soon be, one general asserted, as valuable to the French in Africa as Black Numidian soldiers had been to the Romans.[18]

Within months of their initial constitution, however, the Zouaves became an ethnically mixed unit, and the first Frenchmen to fight in native garb contributed the famous grit and ingenuity of the Parisian working class to the Zouave image. In December 1830 the minister of war wrote to General Clauzel to announce that he was sending five hundred Parisians who had served in the French army in various capacities to the southern city of Toulon where they would embark for North Africa. Clauzel should verify their rank—some had been officers—and make whatever use of them he could. The minister suggested the new Zouave unit as a potential destination.[19] Clearly, the French government was already using its colony to dispose of potential troublemakers. Many of these men, often called "constitutional volunteers," had participated in the July uprising that brought Louis-Philippe to the throne, but the new regime was wary of their politicization and their disaffection. Military discipline, the minister felt, would be good for these potentially disruptive Parisians, not least because it would keep them in Algeria, far away from the streets of Paris. Clauzel's instructions from the minister specified that he should be on the lookout for any insubordination and should remind his volunteers that soldiers could not leave the army at their own discretion.[20] Having joined the African army, they were to make their careers and their future lives in the colony, far from France's revolutionary center.

Clauzel was hardly pleased with the arrival of these Parisians. He complained bitterly about being asked to conquer Algeria while simultaneously absorbing "all who live in misery" and seemed likely to "upset tranquility and public repose."[21] The arrival in North Africa of several dozen Spanish refugees, followed by instructions to integrate them into Zouave battalions as well, did nothing to mollify him. The Spaniards were mostly political opponents of the Carlist monarchy in Madrid, although there were "smugglers and fornicators" among them as well, colonial officers complained.[22] Consigning them to the Zouaves was clear evidence that the government in Paris did not give these new native battalions the respect that General Clauzel thought they deserved. The minister of war's cheerful direction to fill up the Zouave units and then create more as necessary offended the military professionalism of the officers on the ground.[23] It appeared to them as if France were exporting the social question to Algeria before the territory was fully pacified, and they complained about having to deal with these "French Bedouins" as if the real thing weren't enough of a problem.[24]

In the longer term, however, working-class Parisians in native garb proved an irresistible combination; it was as if Gavroche, Victor Hugo's archetypical Parisian *gamin,* had joined the Army of Africa. The native cunning of class and ethnic others merged to redefine the "African" soldier. The secret of the Zouaves, one officer wrote, was that "the Parisians spoke bad Arabic; the Bedouins and the Negros mangled their French, and everyone got along splendidly."[25] Observers, often to their delight, found it impossible to distinguish which of the bearded, sunburned, battle-hardened Zouaves were French and which were native. Colonial tales frequently feature officers newly arrived from France asking a Zouave what tribe he hails from and being surprised when the soldier identifies himself as a "beni-Mouffetard"—a resident ("son of" or *beni* in Arabic) of the Parisian Mouffetard street. "Beni-Mouffetard" soon became a common expression for a Parisian street urchin.[26] The Duke d'Aumale, one of Louis-Philippe's sons, allegedly had a similar experience: he asked his interpreter to inquire into the origin of a ferocious Zouave then holding the severed head of an enemy and was surprised when the Zouave answered in French that he was from the place de l'Estrapade in Paris.[27] Aumale drew the conclusion that the Zouaves' ethnic mixing of French and native was the key to their success. "Maintaining the individual intelligence characteristic of [Kabyle] irregular soldiers while retaining the verve and gaiety of true children of Paris," he wrote, the Zouaves "soon acquired all the reliability and precision of the most outstanding regiment."[28] The ethnic ambiguity of the Zouave, who might be either a scrappy Frenchman or a ferocious native warrior, was at the core of the later popularity of this mode of soldiering.

Given the improvisation at the origin of the Zouave battalions, it is not surprising that the ethnically mixed units were not an unmitigated success. Recruitment was difficult, although dedicated Zouave officers like Franciade Fleurus Duvivier, commander of the second battalion, believed that better results would follow greater effort.[29] In March 1832 the two Zouave battalions, each of which had enrolled just over 600 men, included only 314 native soldiers between them.[30] Desertion was a particularly serious problem, especially when deserters took their weapons with them back to their native communities. A report from December 1831 claimed that 800 natives, "Moors, Arabs, and even Kabyles," had joined the Zouaves only to desert with their uniforms and their guns.[31] Native Zouaves, like French conscripts, preferred to remain close to home, and they complained when their service took them far from their families and villages. Although native recruitment continued to grow in absolute numbers for several years, the percentage of native Zouaves declined from 56 percent in 1833 to 43 percent in 1836. When a third battalion of Zouaves was raised in Tlemcen in 1837, only 6 Arabs enlisted.[32]

Just over a year into their existence, the military command in Algeria considered eliminating the Zouaves completely and integrating remaining soldiers into the Foreign Legion, newly established in March 1831. The minister of war claimed that this move would bring the army into compliance with the law forbidding foreigners from serving in French military forces, although the legal status of the Foreign Legion was, in fact, just as dubious as that of the Zouaves, since both enlisted European foreigners, often men drawn to France in the wake of the July Revolution.[33] Integration into the legion would also have eliminated the situation in which officers commanded both French and foreign soldiers. Officers of the legion specialized in leading either natives or non-French Europeans, with no need to accommodate French soldiers' sense of what was due to them.

Already, however, the Zouaves had their defenders who maintained that the ethnically mixed unit played a crucial role in colonization—a Zouave idea had taken root. Duvivier reminded his superiors that the Zouaves were a fighting force habituated to the terrain and an instrument of "fusion of the various peoples destined to live in Africa." He acknowledged the desertions but denied that native troops were inherently unreliable. Zouaves deserted, he insisted, because of their justifiable discontent with French failure to equip them properly—uniforms and shoes were particularly slow in arriving. The Zouaves, like their officers, recognized that the Parisian volunteers were inferior soldiers, and the incorporation of this ragtag group further encouraged desertion. There was no question, Duvivier noted, that officering native troops was difficult: they were touchy and easily insulted so that officers had to adjudicate disputes constantly. He implied, however, that Zouave faults were also strengths and that the colonial military authorities needed their local knowledge, their endurance, and even their aggression and fierce sense of honor.[34] As commander of the Zouaves, he had created a battalion of roughly equal numbers of French and native soldiers whose complementary qualities suited them to the colonial project and who were, he insisted, "my eyes, my ears, and often my mouthpiece as well."[35] Zouaves had proved their worth in battle, he maintained, but the core of his defense was the ideological work they performed in creating a colonial society in which French leadership made the most of primitive native virtues.

Native recruitment fell off almost completely at the end of the decade, and by the early 1840s, the Zouaves were mostly Frenchmen in native dress. The remaining natives alongside Europeans who enlisted under fake Arab names helped maintain the exotic character of the unit. The Emir Abdelkader encouraged Zouaves to desert and join his guerilla war against French rule in the late 1830s.[36] As his success led French authorities to contemplate a long-term struggle in North Africa, the ethnically mixed Zouaves seemed to many a liability rather than an advantage. Looking for more reliable native troops, the army established new units exclusively for indigenous soldiers in 1841: an infantry regiment, the *tirailleurs algériens*, better known as the Turcos, and native cavalry, the Spahis. Discipline and surveillance of these troops was easier, and their organization was allegedly better suited to native needs: both Turcos and Spahis were allowed to live with their families during their service and to keep any livestock that they captured. The French imagined Spahi settlements as modern versions of Roman colonies—military and agricultural outposts that brought civilization to frontier regions. Turcos and Spahis both wore striking uniforms: the Turcos dressed very much like Zouaves, and the Spahis topped off their baggy trousers and cropped jacket with a dramatic white *burnoose*. They also acquired their own mythology, and stories circulated about their thrillingly barbaric practice of cutting off enemy ears.[37] The luster of the Spahis, in particular, attracted a good number of European volunteers, and that ethnic ambiguity gave the cavalry units an allure similar to the Zouaves'. Neither look enjoyed the international success of the Zouave, however.

Dressing the Zouave

French officers placed considerable faith in the ability of the Zouave uniform to fuse French and native soldiers into a functional—and dashing—unit. Zouave dress was a striking colonial fantasy to which the army command from the beginning gave considerable thought. The fabric was regular blue-and-red army issue, but the "Moorish" design set the Zouaves apart from other French soldiers. The most distinctive element was the *sarouel*—the baggy trousers available in wool or cotton canvas with a waist measurement of 2.4 meters that was still said to be narrower than those worn by natives. Like all French infantrymen, the Zouaves wore red trousers, but the baggy cut, cinched in below the knee, made the Zouaves immediately recognizable. They wore a short, open, collarless jacket, decorated with elaborate braiding.[38] A wool cap (*chéchia*) with a tassel was shaped like a fez, but it became a Zouave tradition to remove the leather stiffener and wear the soft cap precariously far back on the head.[39] On top of the *chéchia* was a green wool turban—over four meters long—that kept the head well covered and resonated with Islamic religious beliefs in ways that the French believed they could "take advantage

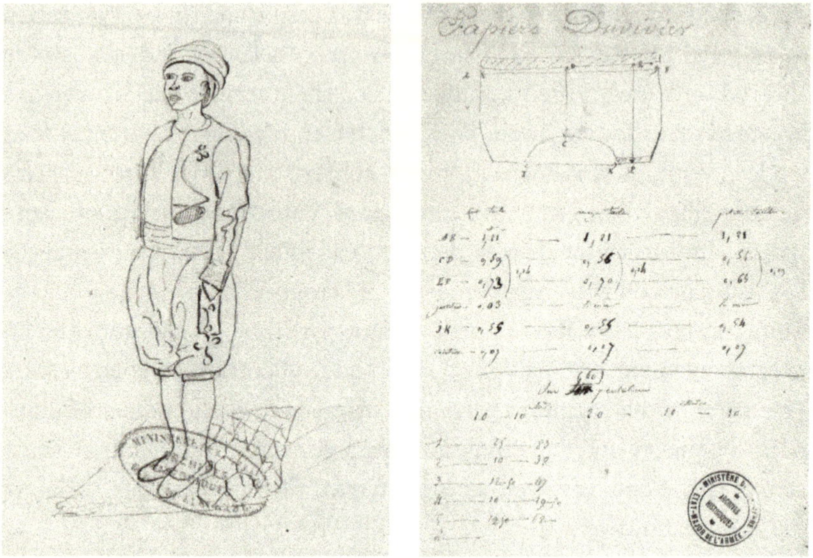

FIGS. 2A AND 2B. Sketch of the first Zouave uniform and pattern for Zouave trousers. "Description des vêtements et effets uniformes adoptés par le 2eme bataillon de zouaves," November 15, 1831. Copyright Service Historique de la Défense GR 1 H 10.

of."[40] At least one observer noted that green turbans had, in the old Regency of Algiers, denoted descendants of the Prophet, and thus, at least to French eyes, suggested a significant social promotion for rank-and-file Zouaves.[41] Around their waists Zouaves wrapped a four-meter-long woolen belt or sash that kept them warm to prevent dysentery and other diseases. French and native soldiers wore the same uniform except for the shoes. Frenchmen wore regular army issue, while natives, "because of the shape of their feet," wore a special design and, in the dry season, wore *babouches*, or slippers.[42]

Commentators on the Zouaves rarely failed to mention the practicality of the uniform. It was "unconstrained," "simple and loose" with "no collar and no straps to restrict movement."[43] The baggy trousers were equipped with a hole so that a soldier who forded a stream could empty the water from them, ensuring that they never became a liability. The gaiters, made of local goatskin, protected the calves from insect bites and from the brambles of the rough North African terrain. Zouaves carried a lighter backpack than most French soldiers, adding to their mobility. The wide turban and sash could keep a resourceful Zouave warm at night or patch his uniform in case of need. Duvivier asserted that, if it were up to him, the entire African army would adopt the sensible dress of the Zouave.[44] If, as observers regularly remarked, wars were won by warriors who accommodated themselves to the terrain, the Zouaves were France's key to control of North Africa.[45]

The striking look proclaimed that France's colonial project was not an exclusively one-way transmission of values and ideals: the Army of Africa would fuse manly virtues from both sides of the Mediterranean. French soldiers in North Africa would develop some native qualities as they came to terms with France's new colonial possessions. Frenchmen in native dress would enjoy greater autonomy as soldiers; they would be more mobile, and they would acquire some of the ferocity that characterized Kabyle warriors. Natives' knowledge of the terrain, once subjected to French military discipline, would make them excellent scouts, and nimble Zouave units would lead slower French infantrymen into combat. French and native soldiers, in their striking but uniform dress, would become fungible, equally dedicated to the African army. Except perhaps for their feet, there was no irreducible difference between them.

The Duke d'Aumale's account of his first sighting of Zouave soldiers captures some of the aesthetic allure that propelled their later success. The duke, who would later serve as governor-general of the colony, was only eighteen when he first arrived in North Africa in 1840, and he was eager to demonstrate his mettle by taking part in the pacification of France's newest colony. His heart beat faster, he recorded, when he first saw Zouaves' "sunburned faces" and their martial bearing in which "the seriousness of the battle-tested soldier mixed with a typically French gaiety." "Ils avaient un fameux chic!" he recorded later in his journal: they had such style! His eldest brother, the heir to the throne who had been with the army in Africa for most of the previous five years, shared his excitement: he squeezed his younger brother's arm and declared himself awash with joy.[46] The two young dukes no doubt agreed that these soldiers were attired in an eminently practical uniform, but the thrill they experienced watching Zouaves march had nothing to do with the sensibleness of their dress.

Foreign soldiers and exotic dress in the French army did not begin with the Zouaves; they had a substantial Old Regime and Napoleonic history. Mercenary soldiers serving French kings were common under the Old Regime, and they were the targets of revolutionary anger after 1789. The quintessential foreign unit was the Swiss Guard, whose function was to protect Louis XVI from all danger, including harm that might come from his own people. The guardsmen, easily identifiable in their red coats, were the object of popular hatred during the Revolution. In 1791, the new National Assembly decreed that no regiments would enjoy special status, uniforms, or disciplinary regimes within the French army, and six hundred Swiss Guard were massacred during and immediately after the seizure of the Tuileries Palace in August 1792.[47] The developing notion of the revolutionary nation in arms was incompatible with mercenary troops, and in the early 1790s, Frenchmen were disinclined to trust foreigners to protect their revolution.

As French armies crossed the nation's traditional frontiers and began creating an empire of sister republics and eventually satellite states, foreign soldiers quickly returned to French service. Especially under Napoleon's rule, France's army developed a tradition of non-French units. Foreign units composed of volunteers serving under their own flag and wearing nationally distinctive uniforms asserted revolutionary France's capacity to command the allegiance of men across Europe and beyond. The Irish Legion, for instance, raised in 1803, wore emerald green uniforms and carried a green standard emblazoned with a gold harp and the motto "Freedom of Conscience / Independence of Ireland."[48] Polish light cavalry wearing the distinctive *czapka* square hat joined Napoleon's Grande Armée in 1807. Napoleon's Egyptian campaign in 1798 led to the recruitment of several North African units: a light cavalry unit of Mamelukes and Coptic and Greek infantry units. The Coptic Legion wore a standard French infantry uniform distinguished only by its color, but the Greek Legion sported baggy trousers not unlike the Zouaves' along with a sash and a red skull cap. Typical of cavalry units, the Mamelukes' dress was particularly splashy. They complemented their Oriental turbans and sashes with Turkish weaponry: an enormous curved sword and a decorated dagger. Foreign troops, especially those with distinctive uniforms, were expensive, but under the empire as during the Old Regime they were worth the cost because they spared Frenchmen more dangerous or unpleasant duties. For Napoleon, they had the additional benefit of suggesting that the empire enjoyed the loyalty of other rulers' dissident subjects, like Irishmen or Poles. Foreign units and their uniforms were a vivid representation of empire and of Napoleon's ability to call on soldiers from a vast range of territories.[49]

The Mamelukes were particularly important predecessors of the Zouaves because of their North African origin, their reputed ferocity, and their visible presence on the Parisian scene during the empire, all quite similar to Zouaves later in the century. Orientalist fantasies attached themselves to the Mamelukes, whose apparently contradictory position in Ottoman society as an enslaved elite fascinated French observers. Mamelukes began their military careers as slave boys converted to Islam, but as privileged warriors they ruled over Egypt, with, Frenchmen believed, despotic cruelty. They were extraordinarily fierce and autonomous fighters, yet their unchecked bravery left them at the mercy of disciplined French infantrymen. When he sent an invading force across the Mediterranean, Bonaparte's proclamations clearly stated that the French made war on Mamelukes, not on the Egyptian people who would allegedly benefit from the restoration of their liberty.[50] Bonaparte nonetheless recruited the first Mamelukes during the Egyptian campaign, when in 1799 he assigned groups of Mamelukes who were willing to collaborate with his occupation to serve each of his generals. Many of these Mamelukes accompanied their officers back to France, and in 1801 they formed the core of a new Mameluke regiment. That regiment became part of Napoleon's Imperial Guard, and the emperor famously had a Mameluke bodyguard who slept outside his door every night.

The exotically uniformed Mamelukes—in fact an amalgam of Arabic-speaking North Africans, primarily but not exclusively Christians—

enjoyed a high-profile presence in the imperial capital. They were military booty in human form, fierce Orientals whose despotic instincts seemed barely kept in check by Napoleon's own, even greater, autocratic tendencies. Mamelukes appeared on stage and on canvas: painters especially loved them because, as Darcy Grimaldo Grigsby has observed, they were "so animate and individualized relative to the majority of the diminutive French soldiers, reduced in large part to the tedious repetition of red spots, white lines, and beige daubs."[51] As fierce, exotic warriors who pledged personal loyalty to Napoleon, Mamelukes represented imperial charisma and power, but their Parisian visibility concealed the fact that the Egyptian campaign had been a fiasco.

With the fall of the empire, Mamelukes paid the price for that association. During several days of rioting in Marseille in June 1815, angry crowds attacked any "Egyptians" they found in the city. Napoleon had just returned from exile on Elba for the Hundred Days, an effort to regain power that ended on the battlefield at Waterloo. The prospect of an imperial restoration led many citizens of Marseille to loot and burn the homes of North Africans whom they associated with Bonapartist militarism. Crowds murdered at least a dozen Egyptians and harassed lines of refugees leaving the city. The Marseille massacre marked the end of the Egyptian community's visible presence in the city, even though Arabic-speaking families remained and in some cases continued to draw pensions. Their numbers even grew with the addition of Arab Catholics who arrived in southern France as tensions with Greek Orthodox churches in North Africa rose. But they built their community around the use of Arabic at home and in private worship. External markers, like dress, that had made the "Egyptians" easy targets for mob violence in 1815, largely disappeared.[52]

Upon his accession to the throne in July 1830, Louis-Philippe officially restricted military service to French citizens, further distancing his army from the cosmopolitanism of the empire.[53] The overthrown Bourbon monarch Charles X, like his predecessor Louis XVI in 1789, had relied on an unpopular bodyguard of Swiss mercenaries, and closing military service to foreigners was another way that Louis-Philippe hoped to distinguish his monarchy from his predecessor's. The foreign uniforms that remained were longstanding features of the French army, like the dashing Hussars, whose tight trousers, heavily braided jackets, and large fur hats derived from romanticized Hungarian horsemen of the steppe. Hussars' distinctive slang, facial hair, and penchant for marauding anticipated the Zouaves, but they were officers, not enlisted men, and the cavalry had a long tradition of showy attire. Integrated into French and other European armies for over a century, Hussars had been naturalized and no longer struck observers as specifically Hungarian.

In the 1830s Zouave common soldiers had much less competition for the sartorial spotlight than would have been true for a previous generation. The men of the army that crossed the Mediterranean to invade Algeria in 1830 wore vivid red trousers, like all French soldiers, but otherwise, their uniforms were plainer and more uniform than those of previous decades. Compared to their counterparts of Napoleon's army, ordinary soldiers of the Restoration and then the July Monarchy dressed so as not to call attention to individuals' or units' exceptional qualities. Officers continued to wear well-tailored jackets vividly decorated with epaulettes and buttons; indeed, wearing a uniform was increasingly common at court, where it became an acceptable substitute for the lavish court dress of the Old Regime.[54] For the common soldier, however, the North African colonial project marked the beginning of a new stage of military dress that allowed ordinary infantrymen to take a starring role.

"African" Officers

The uniform on its own was not, of course, enough to transform a mixed group of North African natives and rowdy Parisians into an effective fighting force, and Clauzel recognized the importance of a strong officer corps from the beginning. The officers would, naturally, be French, and Clauzel emphasized their ideological commitment to the colonial project. He specified that they would not receive supplemental pay, because he wanted to recruit men who were more interested in promotion than in monetary bonuses.[55] Handling Zouaves would be a tricky business because officers needed to control their warrior instincts without diminishing their ferocity and to encourage their autonomy while simultaneously disciplining their individualism. Creating an "African" officer corps was from the beginning an important part of Clauzel's plan: these men would be the vanguard of France's mission to civilize North Africans.

Zouave officers dressed as Frenchmen: there would be no turbans or baggy trousers among the leadership of the battalion. They wore fitted trousers and tightly buttoned jackets with collars and epaulettes, like officers in other branches of the infantry. The sartorial difference between officers and men emphasized the Frenchness of the former and the Oriental difference of the latter. Unusually, the rank and file wore the more striking uniform. Officers enjoyed the services of talented tailors, and their outfits were hardly drab, but the famous Zouave "look" belonged to the enlisted men.[56]

Although they dressed differently, the reputations of Zouaves and their officers rose together, and Zouave service proved to be an excellent career move for many ambitious Frenchmen. As the major area of active operations for the French army, Algeria was a key part of the experience of French officers in the first half of the nineteenth century—it was the one place that promised regular battlefield promotions. For most of the century, service in the metropolitan army, whose job was to defend France proper, meant stultifying life in provincial garrison towns, with small-town sociability playing a larger role than the development of soldiering skills. Africa, in contrast, was where motivated officers found active service, and many were eager to take up Clauzel's challenge.[57]

From the beginning the Zouaves attracted a group of talented and determined young officers. For a generation of romantics, North Africa seemed like an attractive antidote to the failings of European society, and they were keen to test themselves against the challenge of a desert landscape. Men of aristocratic origin, especially, responded to the idea that native society was unapologetically elitist and that it recognized "natural" hierarchies that the Revolution had overturned in France. Officers influenced by the socialism of Henri de Saint-Simon saw Algeria as an ideal space for experiment: a new kind of modernity could develop from the importation of western technology into an organic society that had not been decimated by revolutionary individualism. Many officers appreciated Clauzel's characterization of military service as a civilizing mission, and they threw themselves into learning Arabic, mastering the details of the local social order, or excavating ancient archaeological sites. Algerian postings allowed them to fulfill paternalistic impulses as they investigated infrastructure or public health needs.[58]

The first generation of Zouave officers typified the career benefits of African service. Duvivier became a general in 1839 at age forty-five, Eugène Cavaignac in 1844 at age forty-two, and Léon Juchault de Lamoricière at only thirty-seven. All three were graduates of the prestigious École Polytechnique, and all left engineering units to join the Zouaves during the first years of the French occupation. All three learned Arabic and dedicated themselves to African service. Their careers blossomed with the expansion of France's North African empire, and they achieved political success and media celebrity as they climbed the promotion ladder.[59]

Léon de Lamoricière was the Frenchman most indelibly associated with the Zouaves as the officer with "especially African flair."[60] He cultivated the image of the model Zouave officer: a quintessential military professional with a streak of native wildness that made him an effective African officer. From an aristocratic, Breton family, he graduated fourth in his class from Polytechnique in 1824 and joined the corps of engineers. He was a member of the original French expeditionary force that invaded Algeria; he became a captain at age twenty-four, and he remained in Algeria with the French army for seventeen years. In Algeria, he saw both opportunity for quick advancement and a chance to enact the *noblesse oblige* of his forefathers, realizing the obligations of aristocracy that the Revolution in France had swept away.[61]

As a good Zouave, Lamoricière was attentive to the importance of dress. In an 1831 letter to his mother explaining that he had no immediate plans to return to France, he also noted that he was letting his beard grow— "that's the uniform."[62] Facial hair was a fashion statement that he shared with his men: their beards emphasized their elite status and their casual attitude toward military discipline.[63] The baggy trousers and the open jacket, however, Lamoricière left to his men. Their outfit resembled the

Mamelukes of the First Empire, he wrote, and was "a real mardi gras costume."[64] Lamoricière himself was unmistakably an officer: he wore carefully tailored tight trousers and buttoned himself into a high-collared coat with tails and epaulettes as befit his rank. He appreciated the Orientalist aesthetic, nonetheless. A military colleague, writing of his first encounter with Lamoricière, recalled that the twenty-nine-year-old officer was lounging in the doorway of the home of an Algiers Jew, sitting "Oriental" style on the ground, wearing a white *burnoose* over his uniform with a Zouave cap on his long, black hair.[65] On leave in Paris, Lamoricière visited artists' studios and posed for portraits that appeared in the press and in print shops. He liked to be represented with his dress denoting his success at crossing—and mastering—cultural boundaries: wearing the jacket of an officer but topped off with the soft Zouave *chéchia*, an indication of his loyalty to his "African" men, both French and native (fig. 3). These engravings reminded viewers of the well-known fact that Zouaves affectionately referred to Lamoricière as *"bou chéchia"* or the old man in the cap (*le père au bonnet*).

Lamoricière shared Clauzel's view that the Zouaves were natural soldiers: natives were "incomparable for their vigor, . . . their individual bravery, and their soldiering skills that come to them as naturally as hunting does to a poacher," Lamoricière wrote. They required French direction, however, to develop qualities like loyalty to a flag and the ability to move as a unit and face a line of fire without breaking.[66] "The close understanding between the men and their officers" was necessary to make native soldiers into good Zouaves. "Nowhere," Lamoricière asserted, "was discipline as strong" as among his Zouaves. They might retain a streak of independence "with regard to rules and regulations," but in battle where it really mattered, the Zouave obeyed his officers.[67]

According to his biographer, Lamoricière also appreciated the virtues of the Parisian volunteers who found themselves serving under him. Although he was no sympathizer with revolutions, Lamoricière thought that the volunteers had been badly treated. The July Monarchy, once it no longer needed revolutionaries, had shipped them off to North Africa with the promise of work in Algiers and then reneged on that promise by enlisting

FIG. 3. General Léon Juchault de Lamoricière. *L'Illustration* 1 (March 18, 1843): 37. Courtesy of Princeton University Libraries.

them in the army. Lamoricière sympathetically reported that they called themselves "slaves of liberty."[68] He saw potential in these disaffected Parisians, however. They were intelligent, and even though they were touchy about their rights and bristled at any insult, an officer who understood them could lead them effectively. Under Lamoricière's command, these Frenchmen acquired native qualities: they grew accustomed to the climate, and without depending on baggage trains or suffering from fatigue, they beat their enemy at his own game, denying him the advantage of his mastery of the terrain.[69]

Recognizing that administering a colony would require a different set of skills from those necessary to conquer it, Lamoricière learned Arabic and studied local history. He became "as Arab as a Frenchman can" because the Zouaves were "his work, his family, almost his property."[70] He was interested in all aspects of local life, and he studied questions such as the provision of medical care and the possibility of growing cotton. He organized Arabic lessons for promising Frenchmen under his command to encourage a fusion of French and native interests.[71] Alexis de Tocqueville, visiting Algeria in 1841, concluded that Lamoricière epitomized the colonial project: he was "the only real man in the colony." Lamoricière enjoyed his soldiers' "confidence and affection" while also "satisfying the civilian population," Tocqueville reported.[72]

In 1833, Lamoricière was appointed to head the first Arab Bureau, an institution that under his leadership would become key to military government in Algeria through the 1860s. The Arab Bureaux were military administrative units that served as a link between the army and local populations to provide intelligence and ensure the smooth working of colonial administration, from tax collection to legal judgments. The bureaux drew on the skills of "African" officers like Lamoricière; the staff spoke Arabic and spent long periods of service in North Africa. Like Lamoricière, who believed that colonial society needed native landowners, bureaux officers often sympathized with native society and invoked their authority to protect native land tenure against settler depredations. Consequently, European settlers in North Africa were increasingly hostile to the Arab Bureaux. Lamoricière's Zouave ideal of a fusion of French and indigenous qualities had little appeal to settlers, who considered bureau officers excessively "arabophile" in their policies.[73]

Lamoricière's interest in and even sympathy for native society did not prevent him from deploying horrific violence in the "pacification" of Algeria. We can estimate the number of French dead in the conquest of Algeria with reasonable accuracy—around seventy-five thousand in the first two decades—but the number of Algerian casualties probably exceeded a million, and historians now speak of genocidal violence in the establishment of French Algeria.[74] Zouave capacity for savagery—their ability to mobilize an alleged vice of native people to French ends—was always an important part of their appeal to French officers. Zouaves were ideal troops for the execution of raids (*razzia*) on native settlements, a strategy that was central to France's attempts to control the Algerian interior in the 1840s. Columns of soldiers attacked villages, burned homes, cut down orchards, and confiscated property, especially livestock, to destroy the economic foundations of native society. Highly mobile Zouaves, famed for their knowledge of local territory, were ideal *razzia* troops.

Zouaves also brought their allegedly native instinct for thievery with them to the *razzia*. Writers in the early colonial period repeated a story of a Zouave orderly warning his French officer not to leave valuables lying around because no native, himself included, could control his penchant for pilfering. The officer, charmed by his servant's "naiveté," followed the advice and went on to a successful colonial career with his orderly's loyal service.[75] Loot was the "motivating force" of a Zouave, so in a *razzia*, Zouaves were simply being themselves, ingeniously making do with what they could find and helping themselves to the unguarded property of others.[76]

Razzias weren't simply about theft, however; they involved beatings, murder, and sexual assault to terrorize communities and fracture the social bonds of native society. That kind of violence also came naturally to Zouaves. One of the Zouaves' earliest engagements was the first episode of French military violence directed against civilians in Algeria: after capturing the village of Blida in October 1830, French troops spent over six hours massacring its inhabitants. The killings in Blida were gratuitous: necessary neither to control the territory nor to defeat an enemy military force. Zouaves also participated in the most notorious instance of military brutality in Algeria: in 1845 French troops built fires at the mouths of the caves at Dahra to smoke out the fleeing villagers who had sought refuge there. A thousand people, including women and children, died.[77] Incidents such as these drew criticism in the French press and parliament, and Lamoricière famously wrote that his task in Algeria caused "some piece of himself to die each day."[78] His career, and those of his fellow African officers, however, suffered no ill effects.

A Zouave captain who later published a firsthand account of the Dahra episode justified the action against the "bourgeois sentimentality" of critics. He and his comrades were practical men, not the "savage beasts" that the liberal press made them out to be, he claimed, because they recognized that natives only understood violence: "there is no way to return such a race to sentiments of human decency," he wrote. His reference to "race" is tellingly ambiguous, however: what race did he claim the Zouaves were? Were they also natives who understood only violence or Frenchmen who understood mercy, but also knew when violence would achieve their ends? The distance between the native victim and the faux-native perpetrator was small, but significant. The "fanatical" natives who murdered French settlers and who would never surrender acted on the same impulses as the Zouave troops who hunted them down and murdered them in turn. The real gulf, the anonymous captain implied, was between the men who understood North Africa, on the one side, and their metropolitan critics who issued judgments "sitting in front of a nice fire with their feet in slippers."[79]

Assigning the violence of colonization to Zouaves provided a sort of alibi for the French: the brutality of Dahra derived from native soldiers' and their victims' lack of civilization as much as from the orders they carried out. The Zouaves performed what William Gallois describes as "mimetic violence"—violence that allegedly originated in an imitation of native society.[80] The French exorcised their fear of native violence by outdoing it, by exceeding the cruelty they attributed to Algerians. When Zouaves perpetrated that violence, the facsimile was all the more authentic. Moreover, Zouaves' cheerful good humor and blunt manners made their brutality seem to the French more like mischief than inhumanity.

The African officer and media celebrity Giuseppe Vantini, known as Yusuf, although a Spahi and not a Zouave, exemplified French fascination with violence performed by ethnically ambiguous actors. Vantini, born in 1808 on the island of Elba, had been captured as a boy by Barbary pirates and converted to Islam. He eventually escaped and offered his services as an interpreter to the French who had just arrived in Algeria. After brief service as Lieutenant Joseph, he adopted the name Yusuf and enjoyed a long career commanding native cavalry in all the major Algerian campaigns and later in the Crimea. On leave in Paris in his exotic garb, he was the toast of salon society, and portrait engravings accompanying tales of

his military prowess were widely available. In battle, his cruelty was famous, and the story of his gift to his commanding officer—a necklace of
enemy ears strung together—was widely known. Unconstrained by European scruples, Yusuf could fight the natives on their own terms, giving
France's civilizing mission a sharp edge by releasing some of its agents
from moral constraints.[81]

Other African, especially Zouave, officers brought their hybrid ways
of making war back to France. By 1848, when a new revolution in turn
overthrew Louis-Philippe and the Orléans dynasty, members of the first
generation of Zouave officers were mature leaders. Their colonial service paid off handsomely under the Second Republic, which replaced the
July Monarchy in February 1848. Eugène Cavaignac and Lamoricière both
served the republic as minister of war, and Duvivier became the military
commander of the city of Paris. They all participated in different ways in
the brutal repression of urban riots during the Parisian June Days of 1848,
during which Duvivier lost his life. Critics of the government's violence
attributed the brutality of the response to the generals' colonial experience, as men like Duvivier and Cavaignac applied "pacification" strategies
developed in Algeria to the situation in Paris. Louis Blanc, the socialist
head of the Second Republic's commission on labor, later reflected that
the French had not been content merely to "imitate Arab dress" but instead had imported the brutality of severed heads and hands to the world
of industrial capitalism and civil policing.[82] Others justified the massacre by drawing analogies between native Algerians and Parisian rioters,
both "uncivilized" people who responded only to violence. The widespread consensus that "African" methods of establishing order had come
to Paris, for better or worse, built on the ethnic cross-dressing of Zouave
service: disciplining unruly Parisians was a job for men who had become
"African."

As we read the barely concealed glee underlying accounts of severed
ears that circulated in French accounts of the new colony, as well as the
venom aimed at the insurgents of June 1848, it is difficult not to conclude
that Zouave dress licensed the French performance of savagery. These
swarthy, ethnically indeterminate soldiers and their officers exerted a fas-

cination on the French public that indicates that acts of violence whose ostensible purpose was to teach natives a lesson also spoke to a French audience. Zouaves accounted for the brutality of colonialism, setting it at a distance from French civilization while simultaneously justifying French participation in it. Tales of Zouave ruthlessness both exposed and disguised, celebrated and excused, a French capacity for cruelty.

Crossing the Mediterranean

Frenchmen and women were familiar with the Zouave stereotype in 1848 because the African soldiers' reputations had preceded them across the Mediterranean. Zouave fame reached Paris just as new forms of urban spectacle were making Paris into the capital of the nineteenth century.[83] Images of war proliferated in the albums, panoramas, museums, and stage performances of the era, and the Zouaves' distinctive uniform and ethnic ambiguity made them attractive subjects for artists interested in representing France's encounter with Algeria. The Zouaves' transplantation to Paris also demonstrated the irresistible attraction of their de-civilizing potential: Parisians loved the Zouave look that gave European men an opportunity to assume the characteristics of their primitive North African subjects. Within a decade of their formation, Paris, like Algeria, was a theater of Zouave action, and their prominence in the city's emerging culture of the spectacle emphasized that Zouave soldiering was a performance.

The 1837 seizure of the city of Constantine, which marked French determination to maintain and expand its North African possessions, drew Parisian attention to the African army and the Zouaves. The fall of the city, the site just a year earlier of a humiliating French defeat, was a vindication for the Army of Africa, and the cue for Zouaves' theatrical debut. Four theaters in July Monarchy Paris specialized in military spectacles, and they competed to turn actual events into theatrical fodder as quickly as possible, so their offerings had a strong ripped-from-the-headlines quality. The Cirque Olympique first presented a version of *The Taking of Constantine* in November 1837, just weeks after the real thing on October 13.[84] One reviewer complained that haste to satisfy viewers' taste for novelty produced uneven results: the audience could see red Zouave trousers beneath Mongol robes as performers quickly switched roles from the heroes of Constantine to the hordes of Genghis Khan.[85] Spectators did not seem unduly troubled, however, by the slippage between different types of exotic warriors, and *The Taking of Constantine* enjoyed a successful run. By the time it had exhausted its audience, the Cirque Olympique was ready to move on to *Mazagran*, the name of a town where a small French force held out against the much larger army of Abdelkader. The battle took place in February 1840; reports first appeared in a Paris newspaper on March 2, and it was on stage by mid-April.[86]

This popular enthusiasm for Zouaves was not simply a spontaneous twist of fashion. Many of the officers of France's new African army were attentive to representations of the colonial project and shaped its appearance in the metropole. The Duke d'Orléans, Louis-Philippe's heir, who served several tours of duty in North Africa, was an art collector with a taste for Orientalism who was particularly attentive to the imagery of French colonialism. The Salon of 1836 included a selection of paintings drawn from his own collection that were later reproduced as a lithographic album for sale. Orléans's sponsorship helped create a lively market for colonial imagery, and publishing houses soon released competing albums and illustrated histories of Algeria. These collections of images focused on the exoticism of the Algerian project: they represented massive encounters of French and native armies in vast, arid landscapes, portraits of ferocious native chiefs or, alternately, of African officers like Lamoricière or Yusuf who were simultaneously European and Oriental.[87] Readers who purchased these albums learned that France's role in North Africa made it the heir to great empires—from Carthage to Rome—that had ruled over the region. Lithographed Zouaves in these collections introduced French consumers to the Zouave persona: Auguste Raffet's Zouave has distinctly native features, of a piece with his turban and the long knife that swings from his belt (fig. 4). But he handles his rifle and bayonet with a confidence that proclaims him a well-trained French soldier. At the cheaper end of the market, purchasers could buy prints of Zouaves from the Epinal factory whose brightly colored figures celebrated

FIG. 4. Auguste Raffet, "Zouaves." Léon Galibert, *Historie de l'Algérie ancienne et moderne* (Paris, 1843). Courtesy of Tozzer Library, Harvard University.

France's new victories and linked them via a common pictorial vocabulary to earlier Napoleonic glory.[88]

Zouaves were also central characters in the paintings installed in the historical galleries of the palace of Versailles in 1837. Louis-Philippe had opened the Old Regime Bourbon palace as a museum to present the history of France to its citizens. The giant historical paintings that he commissioned for the museum aimed to reconcile competing political factions by presenting a coherent narrative of French military greatness. The galleries took visitors from the Crusades to the conquest of Algeria via the wars of Louis XIV and Napoleon: a sequence of victories intended to convince viewers that political differences among citizens and revolutionary regime changes mattered very little. The point of the massive canvases, as one art historian observes, was not so much the history of France as the *eternity* of France: the details of the battles, the soldiers, the uniforms, and the weapons run together, and the overall effect of the ensemble is uniformity.[89] Military victory was the "common, illustrious thread" that linked the galleries.[90]

This narrative of French martial glory culminated in a series of paintings in the African Rooms, galleries dedicated to France's conquest of North Africa. These galleries were an addition to the museum, which, at its opening, suffered from a sense that the glorious military past it represented was, definitively, in the past. Renovation of the African Rooms, which asserted a role for the July Monarchy in the parade of French military grandeur, began in 1837, months after the opening of the museum. The redecoration of the rooms involved military and African motifs, particularly in a series of friezes in a pastiche of ancient Egyptian style that represented Frenchmen as vectors of civilization, as for instance in a panel in which French officers drilled new Zouave recruits.[91] France's leading painters of battles, Horace Vernet and Hippolyte Bellangé, received commissions to immortalize the African deeds of Louis-Philippe's sons. The achievements of the heirs of the Orléans dynasty earned them both a place in the tradition of French military glory and recognition in the new postrevolutionary meritocracy.[92]

Horace Vernet, who produced the trio of paintings representing the taking of the city of Constantine, had enjoyed a long relationship with the Orléans family. Louis-Philippe funded the African Rooms personally so that he and Vernet could plan the decorative program without public input.[93] Historical accuracy and a sense of immersion in the North African field of battle were priorities for Vernet and his sponsor. The Orléans princes provided the painter with details of the battles so that the representation might be as authentic as possible. Vernet mobilized the techniques of the panorama, a new form of urban spectacle that sought to replace the experience of looking at a painting on a wall with that of standing in an environment created by a massive canvas that surrounded the viewer.[94] The scale of Vernet's images—the painting of the fall of Constantine (fig. 5) was roughly a five-meter square—enhanced its panoramic qualities and asserted the epic nature of the Algerian battle. Contributing

FIG. 5. Horace Vernet, *The Taking of Constantine* (1837).
Copyright RMN-Grand Palais / Art Resource, New York.

to their sense of being in the midst of the conflict, viewers might consult a guidebook that offered them a detailed, minute-by-minute account of the siege of Constantine that they were seeing on the wall, complete with extensive excerpts from newspaper coverage.[95]

In his depiction of the taking of Constantine, Vernet faced the dilemma of how to glorify the July Monarchy with a modern battle painting that strove for accuracy in its depiction of combat. The Orléans princes appeared in nine of the fourteen paintings produced for the African galleries, but although the Duke de Nemours had been involved in the battle for Constantine, he was not, in fact, present at the climax as French troops stormed the walls of the city. The general staff had judged the final assault too dangerous for the king's son and, indeed, General Charles-Marie de Damrémont died outside the walls of Constantine. Earlier battle painters might simply have inserted Nemours into the composition, but the reportorial aims of the gallery precluded that solution. Ultimately, viewers judged *The Taking of Constantine* the most accurate of the three paintings of the battle, in no small part because of Nemours's absence. Critics smelled propaganda in the paintings that included the duke, and, in contrast, they understood the focus on rank-and-file troops in *The Taking of Constantine* as a sign of authenticity. Like a panorama, the painting offers no single perspective from which the view of the spectator mimics that of the commander. The giant canvas does not resolve itself into a single, comprehensive account of battle that could be taken in by an individual gaze. For many critics, the dispersal of the action, such that it became impossible to comprehend the course of battle at a glance, captured an important truth about modern warfare.[96]

At the center of the painting, where one might expect to find the Duke de Nemours as hero of the affair, Vernet placed Lamoricière and his Zouaves. The commanding officer is a relatively small figure, surrounded by his men who throw themselves over the breach in the wall. The multitude of small details that offer the viewer paths into the panoramic painting involve ordinary French soldiers: infantrymen haul ladders into place; artillerymen peer into the breach that their cannons have created; and a drummer and two buglers stand to one side sounding the call to arms. The action swirls around Lamoricière, whose command over any individual soldier seems tenuous. The Zouaves, in particular, are ahead of Lamoricière; they have climbed the remains of the wall and turned toward the city. In their distinctive baggy trousers and turbans, they dash toward the right side of the canvas, even as Lamoricière waves his hat and urges men on to the left and over the wall. Initiative in battle, in this painting, belongs to the Zouaves rather than to their leader.

Vernet also paid attention to the Zouave as an individual character, not merely as a member of a unit in battle. In his 1847 study of *The Zouave at the Siege of Constantine* (fig. 6), Vernet returned to the walls of

FIG. 6. Engraving after Horace Vernet, *Zouave at the Siege of Constantine* (1847).
Authors' collection.

the North African city, but he focused on a single Zouave who stares out of the small canvas at the viewer. This Zouave is taking a break from the battle that, we can see, continues behind him. His pose is relaxed, his legs in their baggy trousers spread wide, and a brazier and a coffeepot at his feet suggest his ability to seize any moment of repose. The bloody bandage wrapped around the hand that rests between his legs alludes to the scars of battle, but Vernet leaves us in no doubt that he has inflicted more grievous wounds than he has suffered. Next to his right hip is the severed head of an enemy, and he holds a knife in his right hand, ready to butcher the rat he holds in his left. A pile of dead rats at his feet awaits a similar fate, on their way to be roasted over the fire. The bearded, swarthy soldier wears his costume unselfconsciously; it contributes to, rather than distracts from, the impression of barely disciplined ferocity.

Images like these percolated into Parisian culture, and the Zouave came to represent opportunity for individual initiative and glory as well as for liberation from the strictures of bourgeois society. Horace Vernet himself demonstrated the capacity of the Zouave uniform to turn national glory into private fantasy, as he wore it to at least one costume ball in 1840. "Ever since Africa," a critic for the *Gazette des Beaux-Arts* wrote in 1863, "he has been a Zouave. . . . He has the physiognomy, the beard, and the moustache."[97] The historical museum at Versailles and its African Galleries enjoyed public success, and their paintings were widely viewed and reproduced in lithographic albums and in the press. Vernet's *Taking of Constantine* first appeared with other paintings from the African Galleries in the Salon of 1839 before moving to the Constantine Room for the galleries' opening in 1842. Zouaves reappeared regularly at the Salon: one of the great successes of 1841 was Hippolyte Bellangé's *Taking of the Téniah de Mouzaïa*, which followed Vernet's lead in depicting battle as an unstoppable "hurricane of men" fully imbued with "French ardor and glory"—and the men in question were Zouaves and native Turcos.[98] Obituaries that followed the Duke d'Orléans's 1842 death in a traffic accident provided further occasion for Parisian audiences to familiarize themselves with North Africa and its Zouaves.[99]

By the early 1840s, the Zouave was a familiar character on the metropolitan scene, and the broad outlines of Zouave appeal were in place. His appearance in *Les Français peints par eux-mêmes*, the eight-volume compendium of French "types" subtitled "Moral Encyclopedia of the Nineteenth Century," confirms his arrival in the world of urban spectacle. Like the shop girl, the café owner, the gambler, the beggar, and the Parisian street urchin, the Zouave was a recognizable figure in the urban landscape, one whose "physiognomy" the volume promised to describe for eager readers. The Zouave featured in the final volume on provincial life, which opened with accounts of the inhabitants of France's regions—essays on Bretons and Alsatians, for instance—and then presented Jews and residents of France's North African, Antillean, and Indian Ocean colonies for Parisian readers.

The journalist Félix Morand, who wrote the section on "the French Algerian," found that the Zouave nearly defeated the method of the project. How could one describe *the* Zouave, he mused, when his nature was so heterogeneous? "Is he French or Oriental?" Morand asked before characterizing the Zouave as a "singular amalgamation resulting from the juxtaposition of completely different men, customs, ideas and beliefs."[100] The fusion of French and Oriental had produced fighting men who combined ferocity with cheeky good humor. The Zouave respected competence but lacked any automatic reverence for military hierarchy. Morand reported a story in which Zouave enthusiasm for murdering Arabs earned a rebuke from their officer, who warned his men with "brusque affection" that if they didn't calm down "next time, we won't take you with us." In their next engagement, the brave Zouaves saved that same officer from Arab marauders. As the officer reviewed his troops, he heard a voice from the ranks warn him, "if you keep it up, Sir, next time we won't take you with us."[101] This was the kind of soldier Frenchmen aspired to be: ruthless and efficient, respecting merit over rank, and insisting on democratic camaraderie with their leaders.

Even though most Zouaves by the 1840s weren't native, the idea of ethnic "fusion"—or, more accurately, playacting—remained central to his appeal. In the ranks of the Zouaves, Arab and Kabyle men might be civilized, and even more compellingly, French men might go native. In earlier generations, Morand claimed, a young man alienated from his family would go off and become a monk, but today "they go to Algeria and make themselves Arab, or as close to it as possible."[102] Despite the rhetoric of the civilizing mission, the romance of the Zouave lay in the de-civilizing possibilities of the role. It was a process that even worked for native Zouaves who, Morand assures us, soon abandoned religious prohibitions against alcohol and guzzled their wine rations as enthusiastically as any Frenchman.[103] Adopting French civilization didn't always imply polished manners. Bonhomie, bravery, and brutality constituted the common ground on which French and native Zouaves met. The early experience of the Zouaves, both in Algeria and in France, set the stage for the international celebrity they would enjoy by the middle of the nineteenth century. In Morand's assessment, they were "the finest soldiers in the world," a judgment that would echo from one theater of war to another over the following decades.[104]

2

THE SOLDIER OF MODERN LIFE

I n his 1860 book about the making of French Algeria, Ferdinand Hugonnet, an officer and former Arab Bureau chief, recounted a Zouave anecdote that captured the soldiers' initiative and disdain for petty regulation. A military inspector, Hugonnet wrote, questioned a Zouave junior officer about the unit's procedure for pitching camp. As the inspector demanded ever greater regulatory detail, the frustrated young man finally burst out in complaint about the pointlessness of the exercise. His men didn't pay this kind of meticulous attention to rules, and their negligence didn't matter because the Zouaves were "dedicated to Africa and would certainly never fight a war in Europe." Lamoricière, his commanding officer, agreed: "Us in Europe," he chuckled, "just imagine our baggy trousers."[1]

As Hugonnet and his readers knew very well, the Zouaves did serve successfully in Europe, and by 1860 the Zouave had become a well-known character, baggy trousers and all, not only on battlefields but in the nineteenth century's capital city, Paris. When the poet and critic Charles Baudelaire wrote in 1863 about "The Painter of Modern Life," he recognized soldiers like the Zouaves as performers of modernity who embraced its visual codes. Soldiers, like dandies and women, embraced "the *outward show of life.*" "[T]he military man has his beauty," Baudelaire wrote: "[a]ccustomed to surprises, [he] is with difficulty caught off his guard. The characteristic of his beauty will thus be a kind of martial nonchalance, a curious mixture of calmness and bravado." More specifically, he wrote that the Zouave projected "an exceptional quality of independence and . . . a livelier sense of personal responsibility."[2] Soldiers, Baudelaire noted, were accomplished performers, not only on the battlefield but also in daily life. They made themselves into spectacle, available to the gaze of the public. Audacity, imperturbability, ruthlessness, and good humor were already part of the Zouave persona, ready for the modern media of the nineteenth century—newspapers, lithographs, vaudeville theater, and photography—to catapult them to stardom.

Baudelaire's quintessential painter of modern life was Constantin Guys, a French artist employed by the *Illustrated London News* who achieved his greatest fame depicting events of the Crimean War. Baudelaire appreciated Guys's ability to capture fleeting moments and particular forms of beauty—often unconventional—that spoke to a specific era and audience. Guys's sketches from the Crimea, where he covered the Anglo-French war against the Russian Empire, catch soldiers in the military rituals of daily life, not the epic struggle of battle. Guys showed readers ordinary scenes of soldiers setting up camp, marching, drilling, transporting the wounded and, occasionally, burying the dead. According to Baudelaire, Guys's attention to "the ephemeral, the fugitive, the contingent, the half of art whose other half is the eternal and the immutable" made his work specifically modern.[3] It gave readers a sense of understanding the distant conflict intimately, from the inside out.

Like Guys, the Zouaves also came to prominence in the Crimea. Artists like Guys and reporters who wrote for newspapers and illustrated magazines seized on the Zouaves as protagonists of the conflict. From colorful but distant characters in a colonial adventure, Zouaves moved to the center of European popular culture. In the stories and images from the Black Sea that newspapers promoted, the Zouave emerged as a recognizable type, characterized by insouciance and inventiveness that belied his ferocity. Building on their fame in the press, Zouaves—some veterans and some professional actors—found a home in the theater, where their brand of cheeky good humor made them vaudeville stars in the 1850s and 1860s. In France, Zouaves enjoyed a close association with Emperor Napoleon III and the Bonapartist regime: as members of his Imperial Guard,

Zouaves were constantly in the presence of the emperor and present on the scene of urban spectacle that he created around him. They occupied a special role in the visual culture of the era, and both the last of the grand battle paintings and the first wartime photographs chose the Zouave as a favorite subject.

Zouave popularity in mid-nineteenth-century Europe depended on the soldiers' penchant for ethnic and gendered cross-dressing. By the time of the Crimean War, the Zouaves were nearly all Europeans, but they relished their Oriental dress and were delighted when observers mistook them for Arabs. Passing for native—and even, thanks to their green turbans, for devout Muslims who had completed a pilgrimage to Mecca—allowed them to infiltrate mosques where Europeans were not welcome, a subterfuge they reported gleefully. They also enjoyed the sexual ambiguity of their costumes. Both in their silhouette and in their attentiveness to decoration and display, Zouave uniforms carried a hint of femininity, which Zouaves embraced. That trace of the feminine made such a delightful contrast to the Zouaves' ferocity in battle and their blunt manners that it was something to welcome, not repudiate. The Zouave was always potentially someone else, out of place, in disguise, or in drag. Instead of an essential Zouave type, there was always instead another facet of the role.

Zouaves in the Theater of War

The Zouave road to international celebrity began with their first excursion out of North Africa: in 1854 the French armies that departed for the Crimean peninsula in the Black Sea included all three Zouave regiments. Historians often describe the Crimea as the first "media war," covered by the first war correspondents and photojournalists, and the Zouaves were stars of that media show.[4] Writing from the Crimea in 1855, the London *Times*'s "special correspondent" William Howard Russell praised the Zouaves as "probably the most perfect soldiers in the world." Russell specified that he evaluated them "with respect to all their military qualities and accomplishments, as well as to their dress and equipment, their powers of marching and endurance—everything, in short, that constitutes perfection in a soldier." The Zouaves, he concluded, were "picturesque and effective."[5] Russell's judgment was aesthetic as well as military. The baggy trousers and the dashing turban were an integral part of Zouave success, not an obstacle to it, he argued, and being picturesque was closely related to being effective.

The strategic goals of the French, British, Turkish, and Piedmontese allied forces in the Crimea were relatively obscure even at the time, and they disappeared easily amid the proliferation of war stories and pictures that featured in newspapers and, eventually, on stage and in galleries. The Crimean War pitted the Russian Empire against an alliance of France, Great Britain, and the Ottoman Empire in a conflict whose immediate cause was a quarrel over the protection of Christian minorities in the Ottoman-controlled Middle East. Intent on blocking Russian attempts to profit from Ottoman decline, Britain and France sent troops to the Balkans in 1853, and in 1854 these forces continued to the Black Sea. Their strategic goal was Sebastopol, Russia's main Black Sea naval base, on the Crimean peninsula. Taking the city proved more difficult than either French or British strategists expected, however, and the siege of Sebastopol lasted a full eleven months before the city fell to allied armies in September 1855.[6]

Although the war ended in allied victory over Russia, the Crimea was not a theater of glorious achievement, and it remains unfamiliar to all but serious military historians today. British memory associates the conflict primarily with disaster: the pointless charge of the light brigade against Russian artillery, immortalized by the poet Alfred Tennyson, for instance. Florence Nightingale, the other widely remembered Crimean figure, re-formed the wretched military hospital at Scutari that was more fatal to British soldiers than the Russians. In France, hardly anyone remembers the Crimea at all. Triumphant Frenchmen named a variety of Parisian landmarks after military victories, including the boulevard Sébastopol, which opened in 1855, and the Malakoff neighborhood, which originally featured a reproduction of a Russian tower seized by Zouaves. When Napoleon III's Second Empire collapsed in 1870, any desire to commemorate his war disappeared with it.[7]

Despite the distance, readers at home in France and England followed and commented on the Crimean War more extensively than any previous conflict. The telegraph delivered correspondents' stories with remarkable speed, so that reading the paper seemed like direct contact with the war. Constant coverage meant that reporters focused not only on grand encounters on the field of battle but also on small incidents of daily life rendered strange by their transposition to the theater of war. In publications like the *Illustrated London News* and *L'Illustration*, lithography gave readers the impression of an immediate comprehension of soldiers' everyday experience. Special correspondents like Russell enjoyed great freedom in their reporting, and their dispatches appeared alongside soldiers' letters submitted by their families. Lively debates about goals and strategy broke out in the letters-to-the-editor section of British papers, which allowed ordinary citizens to weigh in on the conduct of the war.[8] British reporters who were deeply critical of their government's management of the war often cited French military professionalism as a counter example—and they found the élan of the exotic Zouave warrior a telling contrast to failures of complacent British bureaucrats. The more heavily censored French press, in turn, happily reprinted British coverage.[9] French readers thus enjoyed a similar sense of immediacy along with a flattering impression of national competence.

Ulrich Keller argues that "[t]rying to probe beneath the picturesque surface" of the Crimean War is "an exercise in futility: Aesthetic factors enter the analysis at every point until one realizes that the spectacular visual appeal of Crimean warfare forms one of its *structural* characteristics."[10] What the Crimean War lacked in strategic lucidity and military achievement, it made up for in spectacle. William Howard Russell, in other words, was far from the only observer to see a close relationship between the picturesque and the effective, and Baudelaire's observations about the spectacular nature of modern life applied especially to the Crimea. Military men, newspaper reporters, nurses, even the tourists who visited the site of the conflict were aware of playing roles in and producing depictions of the war for the consuming public back at home.

In a conflict oriented around the production of striking images, Zouaves made ideal leading men. The basic outline of the Zouave character was already available: Arab ferocity combined with the insouciance of the Parisian street urchin. The exotic uniform was an effective, visually arresting shorthand for the Zouaves' blending of Orient and Occident, and the Black Sea, with its ethnic mix of Tartars and Armenians rubbing shoulders with Greeks and Jews, was a setting in which they seemed right at home. For the European reading public, the Zouave was an everyman hero. Zouaves were exceptional fighters, of course—the most perfect soldiers in the world—but they were also infantrymen, in units that any volunteer could join. They had flair and *esprit de corps,* but they made those virtues out of ordinary ingredients and were not an elite unit. Both during the long, dull months of siege and in the exciting, climactic moments of battle, the Zouave's charisma expanded and his fame grew.

Zouaves participated in all the major French engagements of the war. At the battle of the Alma, which immediately followed the September 1854 allied landing in the Crimea, Zouaves turned the Russian flank and opened the path to Sebastopol. In November of the same year, Zouaves were on the field at Inkerman when the Russian army attacked in an effort to disrupt the allied siege of Sebastopol. Inkerman, where visibility was so poor that officers were unable to see the field and give effective orders, was a victory for the French, and especially for French Zouaves, whose initiative was valuable under such conditions. The Russian forces did slow the allied advance, however, and forced French and British troops to spend a famously miserable winter in camp. Military activity resumed in the spring of 1855, and in August, French Zouaves along with Piedmontese and Turkish allies repulsed a Russian offensive at the Chernaya River. Zouaves were among the troops who, in September 1855, seized the Malakoff redoubt, ending the yearlong siege of Sebastopol and bringing the war to a successful conclusion.

Zouave showmanship began on the battlefield where, instead of relying on the close ranks of infantry lines, they maintained cohesion even as they flung themselves against obstacles and scrambled over or around them. Their fighting style depended on individual enterprise, a disdain for close formations, and an unconventional approach to battle. This technique updated traditional French martial pride in élan on the attack and overlapped with the innovative calisthenic training of the *chasseurs à pied*, a light infantry unit that developed in the metropolitan army in the 1830s and served alongside the Zouaves in Algeria.[11] At the battle of the Alma, for instance, the Zouaves crossed the river and scaled the bluffs on the opposite side to find a weak point in the Russian lines, which their colonel described as fighting "African style."[12] One regimental history recalled that Zouaves used small trees to vault themselves across the river until the saplings broke and became impromptu footbridges. Zouaves crawled on their bellies so that Russian shells sailed over their heads, then, having reached the opposite side, they quickly re-formed their ranks "with remarkable precision."[13] The Zouaves were able to penetrate the Russian line when they found a spot at the top of a steep slope left undefended because, allegedly, the Russian commander "regarded it as absolutely impassible even for goats."[14] Zouaves, however, made quick work of it, scrambling up the hill and digging their bayonets into the hillside to help them with the climb (fig. 7). Zouave "gymnastic powers" were so remarkable that one English captain asked a Zouave why he served in the army when his talents would earn him ten times as much in the circus. The Zouave, his sense of honor offended, replied that "the French soldier looks to something besides money" and refused in the future to display his skills before English officers.[15]

Although the Zouaves' real advantage was superior weaponry, journalists attributed the quality of their soldiering to African experience. Zouaves carried the latest Minié rifles against Russian forces armed with smooth-bore guns, but journalists found it more satisfying to dwell on the Zouaves' incorporation of the purported skills of Arab warriors. Zouaves were invulnerable to surprise, because they could put their ears to the ground and hear the enemy on the move from miles away, and they could shoot accurately while lying on their bellies. In short, Zouaves were unstoppable: neither enemy forces, difficult terrain, harsh conditions, nor fatigue halted a Zouave advance. "Zouaves have good teeth," one reporter remarked, and "when they're hungry, they gobble up fortifications, garrisons, cannons and flotillas."[16]

FIG. 7. "Zouave climbing the escarpment of the Alma," from Chantaume, *Expédition de Crimée: lettres d'un Zouave* (Paris: Firmin Didot frères, 1856). Courtesy of the Bibliothèque nationale de France.

The Zouave uniform generated considerable attention in the press, and the journalists' consensus was that the baggy trousers and colorful jackets were intrinsic to Zouave success. In their initial engagement, Russian troops mistook the Frenchmen in their exotic dress for Turks and assumed that they must be inferior soldiers—a misapprehension they soon regretted.[17] The Turks themselves allegedly appreciated their allies' Orientalist dress. According to a dispatch from Russell printed in the *Times* and then reprinted in France, nothing seemed more "effeminate" to

Turks than a British soldier "confined in a shell jacket, with closely shaven chin and lip, and cropped whiskers. He looks, in fact, like one of their dancing troops, and cuts a sorry figure beside a great Gaul in his blazing red pantaloons . . . beard *d'Afrique* and well-twisted moustache."[18] A few French officers, *L'Illustration* reported, tried out Zouave attire but went back to their buttoned-up jackets: "A pity," the paper reported, "because the Zouave dress is far more elegant, picturesque, and generally more attractive than the tunic, narrow trousers, and shako of our infantry."[19]

Much of the coverage focused on the practicality of Zouave dress. The collarless jacket attracted praise, especially during the initial summer of the war when, one French correspondent reported, British soldiers in their tight collars were dropping from heatstroke. An autopsy on one unfortunate Englishman revealed that he had died from a "ruptured aorta caused by his collar."[20] British commentators who agreed that their army had much to learn from the French cited the Zouave uniform as exemplary: "[t]he open collars of their coats allow free play to the lungs; the easy jacket, the loose trouser and the well-supported ancle [*sic*] constitute the *beau ideal* of a soldier's dress."[21] The Zouave jacket would "give room to the muscular development of a robust Englishman," one editorialist remarked, although he rejected the "useless voluminousness" of Zouave trousers.[22] Cotton Zouave underclothes, the *Illustrated London News* reported, were also very practical, and one might see Zouaves in camp "along the side of every stream . . . at all hours, scrubbing and rubbing away, with their arms up to their elbows in soapsuds."[23] The Frenchmen in their fanciful uniforms were cleaner, healthier, and more comfortable in battle than their British allies.

Clearly, however, the Zouave uniform did not attract widespread attention simply because it was practical—it was also alluring. The Zouave in his Oriental uniform was a ladies' man. The hint of gender ambiguity in his dress, with its bright colors, elaborate ornamentation, and full trousers did nothing to dampen his libertine reputation. As an article published in the *Figaro* in October 1855 suggested, a girl looking to taste "sweet love" should find a boyfriend among the "zou zous" even though, the author implied with a wink, she might find herself part of a harem. The curious lady should feel the bright, ornamented fabric of his jacket; indeed, she should slip her hand inside to touch his chest where she would find that his heart beat steadily in danger, but sometimes skipped a beat for love.[24] Zouaves on a sortie often returned with women in tow, and journalists congratulated them on their ability to locate women in areas the civilian population had evacuated.[25]

The luxuriant beards that Zouaves wore with their baggy trousers and sashes contributed to this sense of exotic—and potentially dangerous—masculinity. Zouave beards were also trendsetting. Facial hair gradually invaded the French army in the nineteenth century, beginning with officers and in the 1830s and 1840s moving into elite units.[26] Zouaves, however, wore their beards full and bushy rather than carefully trimmed and shaped: their beards alluded to their primitive nature rather than to their emulation of elites. In the Crimea, Zouave beards, like their uniforms, seemed to observers an intrinsic part of their success. The *Times* correspondent ridiculed the British generals to whom "the *imberbis* Apollo appears the *beau ideal* of a soldier" and concluded that a tidy beard looked much more military than the gashed cheeks and razor burn that efforts to shave in the field produced.[27] Again, the French press was happy to report that the British were adopting sensible French innovations, and starting in the camps of the Crimea, a "mustache movement" reshaped London fashion.[28] Facial hair was indispensable to the "cheeky scruffiness that marked the true Zouave," and the Crimean press coverage of Zouave beards and mustaches made them indispensable military accessories.[29]

Zouaves enjoyed an affinity with soldiers from Highland regiments, the most elaborately costumed members of the British army. As the long history of Franco-British enmity came to an end in the Crimean alliance, Zouave and Highlander were a natural pair: both from the primitive margins of the nation-state, and both instantly recognizable from their "national" or folkloric dress. Their elaborate—even fantastic—uniforms spoke to romantic fascination with "native" peoples at the edge of Europe. In both cases the uniform suggested a certain gender ambiguity: Scotsmen in skirts; Zouaves in trousers wide enough to be skirts. Their primitive ferocity, however, belied the possible effeminacy of their dress.

Zouaves and Highlanders themselves, being bluff, simple men, were largely oblivious to the geostrategic implications of their camaraderie but acutely aware of their shared passion for drink. When a reporter for the *Illustrated London News* offered the picturesque detail of "a Highlander and a Zouave . . . arm-in-arm, walking into wine shops" in Gallipoli, readers understood that such fraternization, though perhaps "trivial" in itself, represented a "vast revolution of national sentiment."[30] Several papers, both French and British, reported the story of the Zouave and Highlander who got drunk together and traded uniforms. "[W]hen the morning brought recollection," the *Times* recounted, the Highlander "must have been rather horrified to find himself in a fez cap, a blue jacket embroidered with red worsted, a bright blue sash round his waist, and enormous . . . scarlet pantaloons flapping about his legs." The fate of the Zouave, who woke up "in kilt and coatee, has not yet been satisfactorily ascertained."[31] At least one grog shop in Gallipoli advertised its wares with a sign featuring a Zouave and a Highlander shaking hands and clinking glasses.[32] When Napoleon III named General Aimable Pélissier Duke de Malakoff in 1856, the new peer's escutcheon expressed his pride in the allied victory and his affection for his men: it featured his blazon held up by a Zouave on one side and a Highlander on the other.[33]

Zouave affection for pets, like their friendship with Highlanders, was evidence of their intriguing primitiveness. They adopted the tradition of regimental dogs but insisted that their pets had to be useful: no cosseted lapdogs for Zouaves, who didn't feed any creature that wasn't doing its part for the unit.[34] One account of a Zouave dog notes that he became a beast of burden for his comrades. He wasn't a very big dog, though, so the Zouaves wanted to ensure that his load was never too heavy. When the unit marched in a Parisian victory parade, the little dog trotted down the boulevard wearing small pannier baskets labelled "Zouave treasury"—a reminder that Zouaves were jokers as well as animal lovers.[35]

The cat—not a traditional infantry mascot—was the animal most closely associated with the Zouaves. Carrying a cat into battle echoed some of the gender ambiguity of the Zouaves' ornamental uniform: cats, despite their feminine connotations, could be fierce warriors, just like men in baggy trousers. A story from the battle of the Alma featured a Zouave cat who saved his master by following him into battle, then licking his wound to stanch the blood until a doctor could arrive. That story circulated widely and continued in use in school textbooks into the twentieth century.[36] In "Le Chat du Zouave," a mock-heroic poem by Claude-Antoine Delétant, the eponymous feline hero shares many Zouave qualities, including a weakness for the opposite sex and ferocity in battle. By 1864 *Le Chat du Zouave*, which one reviewer described as "a Homeric farce," was the vaudeville on the opening night playbill of the new Petit Théâtre in Paris.[37] Writers defending the honor of cats in the years after the Crimea acknowledged that, although the regimental dog was a fixture in many military units, the Zouave cat was at least as faithful.[38] Newspaper illustrators represented the Zouave on the march with a cat perched on his rucksack, and a cat became the official emblem of the Third Zouaves. Zouaves could pull off the unlikely combination of cats and war, and it seemed fitting that the Zouave would choose an implicitly female animal as his best friend.

Although Zouaves were light infantry and theoretically carried little with them, they rarely lacked for anything because of their smarts and adaptability. Draner's Zouave (fig. 8), with a violin, a marionette, and a cooking pot strapped to his pack, is prepared to turn his hand to any trade.[39] Zouaves recognized that marksmanship and drill were necessary but not sufficient qualities for soldiering, and they were not too impressed with themselves to take on more humble tasks. A Zouave could pitch camp and forage under difficult circumstances, and he wasn't too proud to cook, sew, or clean. In multiple newspaper anecdotes, Zouaves briskly set up camp and get the coffee on the fire while British soldiers stand around arguing about the best location for tents. One Zouave who appeared in *L'Illustration* demonstrated his resourcefulness as he calmly ground his coffee beans in a mortar made of a Russian shell—a souvenir that grateful Zouaves later sent to a gentleman's club in France that had contributed funds to purchase home comforts for soldiers.[40] Zouave inventiveness turned everything to good account: in Zouave hands, a simple metal pin became a fishhook, and the entire unit soon enjoyed a fish fry fresh from

FIG. 8. Draner [Jules Renard], "Zouave of the Imperial Guard in Campaign Dress," from *Types militaires de 1863*. Note that the Zouave is lighting his pipe from the lit fuse of a grenade to the alarm of the officer behind him. Copyright Musée de l'Armée, Dist. RMN-Grand Palais / Art Resource, New York.

the Black Sea. Even in the wretched winter of 1854–55, the Zouave doctor Félix Maynard reported that Zouaves lived in cozy tents. He described one, known in the unit as the "bugler's boudoir," that had an improvised paved floor of flat stones, a wall-to-wall carpet foraged from a Russian home and cut to fit, and a fireplace with a makeshift chimney that drew efficiently. The tent was small, he reported, but large enough to fit a guest, and even the officers in the unit envied it.[41] The following summer, when hot weather produced nearly as much misery as the cold of the previous winter, Zouaves' African background served them well. They knew, for instance, how to locate water: finding a well that was nearly dry, they tied their turbans together to lower a man to its depths to return with a full bucket.[42]

Zouaves featured prominently in British accounts of the Crimea intended to criticize British quartermastering and management of the war effort. Presenting well-supplied French troops as a foil emphasized the failures of the British command; Maynard's account of the Zouave's snug boudoir, for instance, reappeared in the *Illustrated London News* just a few weeks after its initial publication.[43] "No Frenchman is frozen to death in the trenches, or appears on parade in tatters, or crushes green coffee between two stones, or gets a sheepskin coat served out to him in July, or is presented with a hatchet for the winter's wood-cutting—the edge of which, after an hour's use, becomes as round and blunt as the handle," according to another story in the *Illustrated London News*. Damningly, a journalist reported, Zouaves "have lately been teaching us how to sap and mine, how to storm fortifications, in fact, teaching British soldiers how to fight!"[44] William Howard Russell reported that "[t]he Zouaves are first rate foragers." When British officers' servants returned to camp empty-handed, Russell wrote, "lo! round the corner appears a red-breeched Zouave . . . a bottle of wine under his left arm, half a lamb under the other, and poultry, fish, and other luxuries dangling round him."[45] Although these articles intended to lay blame at the door of the British officer corps, when Zouaves were involved, the reporting suggested that French superiority derived as much from Zouaves' extraordinary abilities as from Britons' depressingly ordinary failures.

Foraging was a particular talent of the Zouave that gave him an advantage over his fellow Frenchmen as well as their British allies. Commentators pointed to the Zouave tradition of the *razzia* to explain Zouave encampments' abundant supplies: they returned from every excursion with loot. Zouaves commonly referred to themselves as "jackals" (*chacals*) and, as the lyrics of the "March of the First Zouaves" asserted, "the old jackal learned in Africa how to chase off famine . . . you always live off the enemy."[46] Zouaves inevitably returned to camp with livestock, carts, furniture, and, of course, women.[47] The British-Jamaican nurse Mary Seacole found their "complete and utter absence of conscientious scruples as to the rights of property" "amusing," because their "confounded trowsers" were capacious enough to "accommodate a well-grown baby or a pound of sausages equally well."[48] Although the Russians polluted wells along the road from the Alma to Sebastopol with chalk or manure, the Zouaves found well-stocked wine cellars and abundant vegetable gardens in abandoned homes and "enjoyed [themselves] as if they'd been on the Champs-Elysées . . . with no thought to the hardships of yesterday or tomorrow."[49] The illustrator Charles Vernier depicted Zouaves making themselves at home in an abandoned Russian dwelling in his engraving for the satirical Le Charivari (fig. 9). The British, in contrast, simply lacked the can-do spirit of the Zouave. They were too attached to home to be good soldiers and too set in their ways to be effective foragers, one French writer speculated: "A traveling gentleman takes with him his sheets . . . [and] an English soldier takes his umbrella and, if he could, he would take his wife."[50]

The Zouave would never take his wife into combat because he did not need her. Instead, faithful cantinières, uniformed women who worked as sutlers and who organized soldier canteens, accompanied Zouave units. Cantinières (also known as vivandières) were common in the French army dating back to the Napoleonic wars, and Napoleon III doubled their numbers during the Crimean War.[51] Zouave units were not unique in enjoying the services of cantinières, but the association between the two was particularly close, possibly because the women's uniform, with a short, full skirt worn over more fitted trousers, was similar in shape to the Zouaves' dress (fig. 11, below). Although cantinières' uniforms had no official status, their jackets generally mimicked those of their units, so that cantinières resembled fully fledged Zouave sidekicks. The women in uniform shared the Zouave reputation for ferocity, and several were decorated for bravery.[52] On one occasion, a dancing cantinière reportedly led Zouaves into the field at Inkerman.[53] Cantinières also enjoyed excellent publicity in the Crimea, particularly from British observers who appreciated their role in keeping soldiers well supplied. These uniformed women reached the peak of their popularity in the 1850s, appearing in lavish color albums

FIG. 9. Charles Vernier, "At Balaclava: What a pleasure to find a good piano, and especially good wine, when one is travelling." *Le Charivari*, November 14, 1854, later reprinted in Vernier's album *Nos Troupiers en Orient*. Courtesy of the Bibliothèque nationale de France.

as well as in cheaper prints mass-produced by the presses in Epinal. As Zouave novels appeared in the years after the Crimean War, the *cantinière* was the obvious heroine, although instead of military aggressiveness she more often displayed a brisk efficiency at ensuring that her men—both her husband and the other Zouaves in her care—were well supplied.[54]

Zouaves enjoyed especially good supplies of tobacco, and the Crimean War inaugurated a long relationship between the exotically dressed soldiers and smoking. A public subscription to provide comforts for the troops, which *L'Illustration* kicked off in late 1854, focused on tobacco. The illustrated paper offered an engraving of Zouaves smoking as a gift to subscribers. The anonymous artist who donated the original picture explained with the charming but self-incriminating honesty of a Zouave that, being both poor and a heavy smoker, he could not afford to donate either money or tobacco to the campaign. The watercolor of a pair of Zouaves savoring their pipes against a pile of sandbags as the battle rages in the background was his donation to the cause.[55] Tobacco was one of life's pleasures that a Zouave managed never to be without.

The fame of their well-supplied encampments made Zouaves in the Crimea sensitive to the charge that they were mere thieves. Zouave writers often sought to distinguish between what Zouave slang referred to as *chaparder*—harmless pilfering or enthusiastic foraging—and actual stealing.[56] It was true, a writer for the *Figaro* observed, that Zouaves didn't check for an owner's embroidered initials every time they came across a handkerchief on the battlefield. But no one was more trustworthy than a Zouave when it came to anything of real value. Indeed, Zouaves had guarded the most precious thing in the Crimea: Queen Victoria, when she visited the allied armies, had specifically asked for a Zouave escort, *Figaro* reported. A Zouave *chapardeur* had his own honor, and he wouldn't dream of taking more than *fristi,* which, the author explained, was slang for top-quality gourmet treats.[57] There were no *razzias* in the Crimea, Zouave writers maintained, even as they winked knowingly at incidents that risked infringing military law, alienating civilian populations, and undermining discipline. Colorful argot and lively tales took the sting out of Zouave theft and transformed it into another charming Zouave quirk.

Zouave Vaudeville

The Crimea's most important addition to the Zouave legend was theater, and the vaudeville stage reinforced the Zouave persona that the popular press had created. Vaudeville, in the nineteenth century, was a comical genre with musical numbers that recycled popular tunes with new lyrics. Stories featured contemporary characters whose efforts to deal with humorous situations structure the plot.[58] The Zouave type that newspaper readers were already familiar with made an ideal vaudeville character. As ordinary soldiers rather than aristocratic officers, Zouaves were well-suited to a low-brow genre like vaudeville. Because audiences knew what to expect of Zouaves before the curtain went up, they set plots in motion without requiring much in the way of characterization. In the theatrical guise of vaudeville, the Zouaves built on their Crimean victories to take Paris and London by storm.

Zouaves initiated their own vaudeville fame during the Crimean War in their camp at Inkerman, where they established a theater that captured the public imagination. They built a stage, hung a curtain that had originally been a tarpaulin draped over animal feed, lit the stage with candles reflected in the shiny surface of sardine cans, and enlivened the scene with paper lanterns. Zouave ingenuity found a new outlet in theatrical costumery and set design: wigs made from sheepskins, jewelry fabricated from scraps of tin, and all that extra fabric in the sash and turban could be pressed into service. Zouave talent for scavenging produced Russian ladies' dresses that decked out stage heroines. One British observer reported on a stage set that involved a potentially dangerous windmill crafted from bayonets and a Zouave turban.[59] Zouave talent, it turned out, was not limited to feats of military bravery.

We can construct a good image of the Zouave stage because reporters and memoirists never failed to comment on the Inkerman theater. Some customers—mostly officers—paid for seats, which were earthen ridges surrounding the stage. Money collected for tickets, which paying customers dropped into a cup held by a pretty *cantinière*, went to prisoner relief. Soldiers not in a position to make a contribution stood and watched from behind the rings of seats. Printed programs, sometimes reproduced in the press, announced the entertainments. Zouaves reprised favorites of the Parisian vaudeville stage in which gallant young men rescue pretty girls from a variety of predicaments, often involving foreigners with odd habits and funny accents.[60] Performances were remarkably varied—of necessity, journalists remarked, since the cast changed regularly with the fortunes of war. One memoirist recalled a single day in which "Russian bullets struck down the noble father, the lover, the comic relief and the ingénue."[61] Playbills invited spectators to "come armed, in case of attack."[62]

The Inkerman theater reflected the multinational spectacle of the Crimean War itself. Foreigners were a comedy staple of the texts Zouaves chose: sinister Germans appeared in the tale of *Pascal et Chambord*, while a Spanish dancing master chases the heroine who wears a mask to attend the *Bal du sauvage*.[63] It's likely, of course, that Zouaves rewrote some of these parts to address their favorite targets: their enemies and their allies in the Crimea. Mockery of the Russian foe was a perennial favorite as in one vignette in which a "Russian" general, addressing his troops, is suddenly struck with cramps and diarrhea and rushes off stage "clutching desperately at his nether garment!"[64] Englishmen were equally satisfactory butts of the joke, however. Zouaves reprised *Les Anglaises pour rire* (*The Make-Believe English Girls*), a success from the Parisian stage in 1814 during the allied occupation after the Napoleonic wars, that involves a pair of Frenchmen who dress up as English girls in order to circumvent their girlfriends' stern guardian.[65] Other performances involved an "English" soldier who knew only two French phrases: "Bono Franzis" and "Donnez-moi die Cognac, John-nee."[66]

Cross-dressing was the main source of laughs for Zouaves and their audiences. Zouaves played female roles not because there were no women available—remember the *cantinière* selling tickets—but because seeing gruff, bearded Zouaves in women's dress was part of the fun. The stage at Inkerman often presented plays that featured cross-dressing as part of the plot, such as *Les Anglaises pour rire,* but they were equally likely to perform comic romances that would not have involved drag until Zouaves decided to stage them. One Zouave allegedly died in a dress when a Russian sortie interrupted the performance and soldiers dashed out of the theater in costume.[67] This episode captured widespread attention and resonated in Zouave theater long after the battle. The notion of warriors in skirts—a look not so far removed from the Zouaves' usual voluminous trousers—titillated and amused audiences and became a staple of Zouave lore.

As the conflict in the Crimea wrapped up, the main theater of Zouave engagement shifted to western Europe, especially Paris and London, but the vaudeville theater remained a natural venue for Zouave performance. Zouaves had appeared on the Parisian stage beginning in the late 1830s, but the Crimean War made them into international headliners who could carry a plot and sell a production. The 1859 Italian Campaign, in which French troops supported the nationalist ambitions of Piedmontese forces and helped them drive the Austrians out of northern Italy, kept Zouaves in the headlines and on Parisian playbills.

Military spectacles, presented in large circus or hippodrome spaces, had become a staple of the Parisian entertainment scene in the 1830s and 1840s, so impresarios were ready to translate the Crimea into theatrical extravaganzas. *La Guerre d'Orient* premiered at the Théâtre impérial du Cirque in July 1854. The cast included a Zouave and a *cantinière* in leading roles, but the spectacle overwhelmed the plot: forty-three speaking roles, over two hundred extras, thirty stage-hands who managed twenty scene changes, horses, dancing girls performing an allegory of the allied nations, and the naval bombardment of Odessa, complete with a sinking ship and the landing of the French army.[68] To celebrate the end of the war, the Jardin d'Hiver in Paris opened *Zouaves, un tableau militaire,* with an all-woman cast that acted out an evening of historical spectacles that included Napoleon I at Austerlitz and the birth of the Prince Imperial.[69] Just over a year from the opening of the Inkerman theater in the Crimea, Zouave drag went both ways: Zouaves dressed as women were a proven crowd-pleaser, but women dressed as Zouaves turned out to have equal appeal.

British audiences also rushed to see the war, and, not surprisingly, Zouaves found a home in the pantomime, Britain's own cross-dressing theatrical tradition. Astley's Amphitheatre staged "The Battle of the Alma" just a month after the actual event in a spectacle so realistic that actors standing too near the mock cannon fire were seriously injured.[70] The 1855 Christmas pantomime at the Theatre Royal, Haymarket, featured Miss Mary Brown in the role of Columbine and "a grand military ballet of Zouaves and British Grenadiers" in which Miss Brown wore "the Costume of a Zouave." She reprised the dance and the costume in 1856 when she and a group of "military juveniles . . . march[ed] and countermarch[ed] in excellent style."[71] Louis Jullien, the maestro whose concerts began with him being shot out of a trapdoor, jeweled baton in hand, recognized the Zouaves as kindred spirits and organized a tour for them. Allegedly, the Zouave musicians he engaged direct from the Crimea played bugles that sounded only four notes whose "effect is such that on the field of battle, their shrill sounds have often struck terror into the hearts of the most daring enemies." More harmoniously, they performed a "Zouave Quadrille" arranged specially for them.[72] G. W. Reynolds, the prolific author of popular fiction that he marketed via his magazine *Reynolds' Miscellany*, knew a good plot line when he saw one, and he began churning out Zouave fiction immediately. In *Omar, a Tale of the War* (1856), the pompous English officer Sydney Hazelwood sneers at the Zouave sergeant who has saved his life but who remains, nonetheless, his racial and class inferior. In a plot twist that would have surprised no one familiar with the genre, the Zouave turns out to be a Polish woman—Hazelwood's estranged wife!—in disguise.[73]

Paris, however, was the site of Zouaves' greatest theatrical success, and vaudeville writers rushed Zouave-themed shows to the stage during the war. In the spring of 1855, just as the brutal winter that caused so many casualties was ending, the successful theatrical duo of Charles Dupeuty and Ernest Bourget mounted their new show, *Pilbox et Friquet, ou Zouave et Highlander*, in Paris. The writers had their fingers on the pulse of the news, and their script mobilized all the stereotypes that newspaper readers would have recognized. Beneath his Zouave turban, Friquet is a true "gamin de Paris," and Pilbox is a typical, genial Scotsman. Separated from their units behind enemy lines, they share biscuit and subscription tobacco and fall in love with the same *cantinière*. They spend the play trying to decide who gets to marry her, but at the denouement, we hear the familiar Zouave tune, "Marshal Bugeaud's Cap." The Zouaves have arrived to save them all, including the *cantinière* who declares her preference for a sailor, leaving Zouave and Highlander to console one another.[74]

Pilbox et Friquet opened a month before the first reports of the Zouave theater at Inkerman appeared in the press, and only five months later the theme of the Zouave play-within-a-play arrived in Paris. Just as the city of Sebastopol was falling to the allies, the Théâtre des Variétés opened *Le Théâtre des Zouaves* by another successful vaudeville team, Eugène Grangé and Eugène Cormon. In this fictional version of Inkerman, a troop of Zouaves prepares to put on a play. There are songs sung to popular tunes, Zouave slang, jokes about funny accents, and a thin plot. Two men vie for the lead role: one is a Zouave, a bluff, simple, brave man. The other is a Parisian showman who joined up—as an actor, not a Zouave, he specifies—when his fiancée left him at the altar back in France. The two are also competing for the heroine, a *cantinière* nicknamed Baïonette who turns out to be the actor's fiancée: she abandoned him to answer the call to arms, proving herself the braver soldier. The key point for our purposes is that the role both men want is that of the *jeune première,* the ingénue: they are competing *for* the girl and also *to be* the girl. Just at the moment when the Zouave and the Parisian actor have both donned skirts and wigs and are on the point of exchanging blows on stage, we hear Russian cannon fire. Our Zouave hitches up his skirts and grabs his weapon to respond while the actor hides in the prompter's cubbyhole. Naturally, the Zouave gets the girl, and the actor resolves to try his fortune on the American stage.[75]

Combat in Italy in 1859, in which Zouaves led France to victory, this time alongside the army of King Victor Emmanuel II of Piedmont, kept

FIG. 10. Eugène Cormon and Eugène Grangé, *Le Théâtre des Zouaves* (Paris: Michel Lévy frères, 1855). Courtesy of George A. Smathers Libraries, University of Florida.

Zouave theater in the public eye. As the Zouaves helped the Piedmontese expel Austrian troops from northern Italy, they continued their tradition of battlefront shows, producing satiric playbills announcing that Adelaide Ristori, the great Italian tragedienne, was regrettably unable to appear, and would be replaced by Jean Beauvallet, the Zouave bugler. The program promised entertainment such as a Zouave shaving without a mirror, and the evening closed with "the handsomest men of the battalion" performing a ballet.[76] The Italian Campaign was also a significant boost for the performing careers of Zouave veterans. A troupe calling itself the Inkerman Zouaves had begun appearing at the Théâtre des Variétés in 1856, but reviews were lackluster: the show was good enough, perhaps, for an army between battles, but not up to Parisian standards, one reviewer judged.[77] The renewed interest of the Italian Campaign propelled the Inkerman Zouaves to an international tour that began in London and continued on to multiple U.S. cities. Either the troupe upped its game or London reviewers were less critical than their Parisian counterparts: the *Illustrated London News* reported that the Zouaves were "real artists as well as soldiers, and act as skillfully as they fight."[78]

The Paris stage also welcomed back theatrical Zouaves in 1859. First off the mark was *Les Zouaves en Italie,* which opened May 28, 1859, about three weeks after France's declaration of war.[79] Eugène Grangé, who had written the successful *Théâtre des Zouaves* during the Crimean War, returned to the well with a gender-bending comedy in which an all-female cast played not only the Italian pupils of a girls' boarding school who overthrow the authority of their Austrian headmistress but also the Zouaves with whom the girls team up.[80] *La Voie sacrée ou les étapes de la gloire* (*The Sacred Way, or Paths to Glory*) at the Théâtre de la Porte Saint Martin featured Italian patriots, a dastardly Austrian and his unhappy Milanese wife, a French *cantinière* and, of course, a lighthearted Parisian Zouave to save the day.[81] The Folies dramatiques staged *En Italie* in which a troop of Zouaves appears on stage—whereupon "the whole theater burst out in cheers . . . women applauded, the actors sang impromptu couplets, and the crowd left yelling 'Long live the Emperor!'"[82] In *Les Jocrisses de l'Amour* (*Love's Fools*), the comic lead takes revenge on his girlfriend's

Zouave lover by stealing the unmistakable baggy trousers when he finds the couple *in flagrante delicto*.[83] Original musical theater took a little longer than vaudeville to reach the stage, but by the end of July, Jacques Offenbach opened *La Vivandière des Zouaves*. The heroine, Scipionne, whose name suggests her affinity for African Zouaves, is the granddaughter of a *vivandière* of Napoleon's army of the 1790s. The reviewer for *La France musicale,* recognizing the rushed nature of the effort, suggested that Offenbach had told his librettist to "put in a lot of *vivandières* and Zouaves" and hoped for the best.[84]

FIG. 11. Draner [Jules Renard], "The Zouave *Vivandère*," from *Types Militaires.*
Draner collaborated with Jacques Offenbach on costume designs.
Courtesy of the Bibliothèque nationale de France.

Zouaves at the *Fête Impériale*

Zouaves were major contributors to the pomp and glamor of France's Second Empire, the spectacular staging of Napoleon III's imperial power that historians refer to as the *"fête impériale."*[85] The First Empire of his uncle, Napoleon Bonaparte, had derived its legitimacy in part from success on the battlefield, and the Second Empire needed similar martial luster. Zouaves, as representatives of France's most important colony and the victors in France's most recent European war, asserted the empire's capacity for military victory. The empire required more than battlefield competence, however. Bonapartist legitimacy also relied on popular endorsement, expressed occasionally in the form of a plebiscite, but constantly on the mind of the emperor and his associates. The empire had to present itself to the people as a desirable form of government. To that end, Napoleon III also aimed for glamor, and the Zouaves, with their plebian charm, provided both. Their theatrical career from the battlefield to the theaters of Paris demonstrated their capacity to represent an updated version of Bonapartist imperial power: they combined brutal military muscle with urbane, modern sophistication.

The reconstruction of Paris under the leadership of the Baron Haussmann is the most famous example of Napoleon III's ambition, and Zouaves became a central element in the visual culture of the capital of the nineteenth century. Redesigned along grand boulevards that facilitated circulation and produced striking views of urban monuments, modern Paris was a stage for the theater of modern life.[86] Zouaves, with their consciousness of being characters in a spectacle, fit right in. In the Parisian world of urban *flânerie* where people were conscious of looking and of being looked at, we find Zouaves everywhere—and very much at home.

Giuseppe Castiglione's 1861 painting of the Salon Carré in the Louvre illustrates this intersection between Zouaves and urban entertainment (fig. 12). The Neapolitan-born painter who made a career in France mostly with genre scenes and portraits represents the Louvre as a site of genteel connoisseurship and sociability. Visitors to the museum gaze at paintings of all sizes, eras, and genres. An Ascension of the Virgin faces an el-

FIG. 12. Giuseppe Castiglione, *View of the Salon Carré in the Louvre.*
Musée du Louvre, copyright Erich Lessing / Art Resource, New York.

egant full-length portrait of a seventeenth-century gentleman. The view
stretches back into a string of galleries, and the grand decorative ceiling
draws the eye upward. Dwarfed by the salon, visitors stroll about. Art
students copy paintings, and tired visitors rest on the central sofa. In
the foreground, a pair of Zouaves, unmistakable in their wide red trousers, white gaiters and turbans, and blue cloaks admire the art. The lady
standing just past the Zouaves may also be contemplating the paintings,
but it seems more likely that she, like us, is looking at the Zouaves. They
are part of the spectacle at the Louvre, both producers and consumers
of urban life.

The figures at the Louvre were members of the Zouave regiment of
Napoleon III's Imperial Guard, a unit created in the midst of the Crimean
War. Napoleon I had established an Imperial Guard that served under

his personal command and included exotic and elaborately uniformed soldiers from conquered territories like Mamelukes and Polish lancers. His nephew similarly deployed Zouaves to represent French conquests in North Africa and the Crimea—France's two military victories since Waterloo—and Bonapartist rule. The Zouaves of the Guard promised future victories—a promise that the Italian Campaign realized, but that later engagements in Mexico and, especially, the Franco-Prussian War, disappointed.

The Zouaves of the Guard gave Parisians their first opportunity to see Zouaves in person, not just as characters in newspaper reports or actors on stage. Members of the Guard had to be taller than ordinary soldiers, which enhanced the effect of their dramatic uniforms.[87] They played a leading role in the parades of troops welcomed back from the Black Sea, events widely commemorated in engravings and verse celebrating, in the words of one poet, "France's heroes who had liberated Tartary and earned the recognition of the Muse of history."[88] The Zouave band regularly played at the Pré-Catlan, a fashionable promenade in the Bois de Boulogne, a park redesigned and inaugurated in 1854 as the pleasure garden of the new city, and a place where visitors might catch sight of the emperor himself, driving his own carriage along its lanes.[89] The inauguration of the new Longchamps racetrack in the park in 1857 involved a military review in which the stars of the show were, in the words of an American reporter, those "semi-Eastern troops, with turbaned head, flowing pantaloons, tight vests and milk white gaiters, performing their evolutions" that made "one [fancy] oneself transported to some strange Oriental shore."[90] The most famous Zouave in Paris today—the Zouave statue on the Alma Bridge—also dates from this post-Crimean period. Originally, a figure of a heroic French soldier stood against each of the pilings of the commemorative bridge: the Zouave, against which Parisians now measure the flooding of the Seine, is the only one who remains.[91]

The most famous Zouave of mid-nineteenth-century Paris was not the statue but a veteran of the Zouaves of the Guard. Henry Auguste Jacob, who had played the trombone in the Zouave band, earned his fame as a public healer in the 1860s.[92] He performed his first cure one day on parade: a little girl fell down and hurt herself in front of him, whereupon he picked her up, told her she was healed, and she skipped away. By 1867 the "fluidic power" of "the Zouave Jacob" attracted over a thousand people each day to the room in the rue de la Roquette, where he treated up to thirty patients at a time for a variety of ailments. Before he left the army in 1868, he wore his Zouave uniform, and afterward he appeared in a white *burnoose* with bare feet in sandals—a different kind of North African fantasy. He maintained all the brusqueness of a Zouave: he was famous for ordering crippled patients to stand and walk after his treatment, he used the informal "tu" with all of them, and he not infrequently swore. Although he was prosecuted several times, he kept his practice going until his death in 1913, in part because he did not charge for his services. Satisfied patients might leave tips, and he made a living by selling his lectures in brochure form and, especially, photographs of himself.[93]

The Italian Campaign cemented the privileged relationship that the Zouaves of the Guard enjoyed with the Bonaparte dynasty. Napoleon III personally led his forces into the field in a campaign that was brief and gratifyingly successful: allied French and Piedmontese armies quickly defeated Austrian forces at Montebello, Palestro, Magenta, and Solferino, allowing Victor Emmanuel to proclaim the existence of the Kingdom of Italy. The Italian king, like Napoleon III, was anxious to prove himself as a field commander, and he led troops into battle at Palestro where, according to many accounts, he foiled Zouaves' best efforts to keep him safe behind the lines. In recognition of his bravery, the Third Zouaves appointed him corporal of the regiment, a gesture that harkened back to the First Empire when soldiers referred to Napoleon I as "the little corporal." Victor Emmanuel's appreciation of the title led to the production of a marble statue of the king in Zouave uniform that is today in Milan's Museum of the Risorgimento.[94] The prominent role Zouaves played in the campaign suggested that both allied rulers—king and kingmaker—enjoyed the respect and the camaraderie of their most outstanding soldiers.

The Bonapartist dynasty particularly cultivated a relationship between the heir to the throne, the Prince Imperial, and the Zouaves of the Guard. Aware that Napoleon III would likely die before his son had reached maturity, the Bonapartes carefully managed the Prince Imperial's image—and that image frequently involved a Zouave costume, an example of which is now in the collection of the Chateau de Compiègne.[95] Even in early childhood, the Prince Imperial dressed in uniform and "drilled" troops.[96] In the 1867 Salon, Adolphe Yvon, best known for dramatic battlefield scenes, exhibited a charming image of the Prince Imperial surrounded by little boys (enfants de la troupe, or the sons of soldiers, sometimes orphans), all in uniform, with many little Zouaves among them.[97] The relationship between the Prince Imperial and his companions in the painting was both patronage and camaraderie, and it echoed accounts of Napoleon III and his Zouave guard. The painting also recalled newspaper accounts of birthday parties for the Prince Imperial at which the guests wore miniature uniforms: in 1863, when the Prince Imperial was seven, the son of a dead general attracted particular attention for wearing a Zouave uniform in honor of his father and the men he had commanded.[98] Popular prints of the boy prince with tough, bearded Zouaves suggested that the dynasty had a secure future. In France's Hope, by Jules David (fig. 13), for instance, a Zouave presents a petition to the Prince Imperial who assures him, "I'll give it to my father." Again, the young prince acts as both patron and comrade, this time to an adult Zouave whose loyalty to the dynasty is thus assured.

The Prince Imperial wasn't the only child wearing Zouave dress under the Second Empire. Among the many possible guises a Zouave might assume, he might be a little boy, as the many cartes de visite of child Zouaves attest. A cartoon by Cham mocks the fad: over a caption reading "The Chimney Sweep replaces the Zouave in Children's Fashion," an elegant couple strolls in the park behind their son, ludicrously dressed in rags, with a soot-darkened face.[99] Cham was wrong, of course: Zouave outfits for boys had considerable staying power and, while he might have seen a parallel between the two modes of dress, no parents wanted their boys to wear the clothes of actual chimney sweeps, who were the focus of much bourgeois charity. Like the contemporary sailor suit, Zouave dress became a signifier of childhood that referred simultaneously to the discipline of uniform and to the imaginative possibilities of play.[100] As with

FIG. 13. Jules David, "France's Hope: I'll give it to my father."
Courtesy of the Bibliothèque nationale de France.

many things Zouave, children's clothes weren't simply a French fashion. As far away as Hawai'i, we read of a children's party at the British Legation which Master James Robertson attended dressed as a "Highland Laddie" with Miss Florence Robertson in the costume of a "Young Zouave."[101] In Charles Wynne Nicholls's charming painting of a Victorian family at the seaside (fig. 14), the boy's Zouave costume and his sister's plaid wrap suggest that the hard-won Anglo-French harmony of Zouave and Highlander characterizes this family's life.

The military camp for the Imperial Guard installed at Châlons-en-Champagne in 1857 highlighted the intersection of military spectacle and urban entertainment that characterized Napoleon III's reign. The camp was a sort of "military universal Exposition": sharp drill, smart uniforms,

FIG. 14. Charles Wynne Nicholls, *A Victorian Family at the Seaside,* 1860s.
Copyright Wolverhampton Art Gallery.

and a printed program, all just a few hours by train from Paris, so that the
emperor and empress as well as ordinary visitors could watch the show.
Repeating his Italian performance, the emperor personally commanded
his guard on parade. A published program guided day-trippers around the
camp, which featured modern cast iron and glass buildings. Those who
couldn't make it to Châlons could follow the coverage in *Le Monde illustré*
or other Parisian papers. Châlons brought together all the key elements
of the empire in a spectacle for the general public.[102]

Zouaves were the stars of the garrison. Just as in the Crimea, their
section of the camp was the best organized and most comfortable: they
planted a garden to make it more agreeable and hung a sign in French and
Arabic directing visitors to the "Jackals' Camp." Even their dogs dressed
up in miniature Zouave costumes. The first rumors of the Zouave Jacob's
healing powers circulated at Châlons, and he received patients in his tent
until his commanding officers put a halt to his performance and he moved
it to a neighboring hotel. Tourists excited by the opportunity to enter the

Zouave camp could take the illusion home with them: the village outside the camp featured a shop selling Algerian items so that visitors might equip themselves with a caftan or a *burnoose*, finished off with a turban and North African slippers.[103] Visitors could imagine themselves in Algeria or in the Crimea, as they preferred, and assume the Zouaves' ethnically ambiguous identity.

The highlight of the camp was, inevitably, the theater: Zouaves staged an improvised "Arab fantasy" intended to transport viewers metaphorically to distant Africa. In the show-stopping number, Zouaves costumed as the women of Algeria, with hennaed fingers and toes, draped in veils and jewelry produced by the camp's tinsmith, did a pastiche of "Moorish" dance followed by a representation of a native wedding. The set even included a camel—"How did they manage that?" *Le Monde illustré* asked. There were fireworks on Sunday and sometimes a balloon ascent, with a gymnast doing tricks as he hung from the basket high above the crowd.[104] The presence of Zouaves established the link between the serious business of military training and the circus atmosphere of military showmanship—both came naturally to Zouaves.

Documenting the camp was an important affair, and the photographer Gustave Le Gray received the commission to record its activities, probably in the form of a souvenir album that the emperor could offer distinguished visitors and participants. Le Gray produced a series of rather stiff portraits of officers and a set of lively photographs of camp life, many of which feature Zouaves. All the photographs are horizontally oriented, with the people concentrated in the middle and the flat spaces and wide open sky of the drill fields at the top and the bottom. The tension between the photograph's claim to accuracy and the Zouave's fancy-dress approach to military service made—and make—these images compelling.[105]

Le Gray's photographs resonate with the image that the Zouave publicity machine had been generating since the start of the Crimean War, and they remind us that being looked at was an inextricable part of soldiering for the Zouaves of the Guard. Even intimate details of soldiers' toilette were subjects for performance: soldiers in their turbans and wide trousers watch as a barber performs a Zouave ritual, recreating the shorn head that contrasted with the luxuriant beard (fig. 15). They gamble, mill about their neatly arranged tents, or they prepare a meal. A soldier recounting a tale of some sort—a story of military valor or perhaps an especially lucrative foraging mission—seems as aware of the audience beyond the picture as he is of his immediate listeners.[106] We see in these images the crafty, ingenious Zouaves who pitch camp just like they take on the enemy: efficiently, and with a notable *joie de vivre*. Unsurprisingly, scenes of the Châlons camp were reproduced for stereoscopic viewing. Peering into the device, viewers could enter into the Zouaves' world, much as they had in their visits to the Jackals' camp with its theatrical performances and souvenir shops.[107]

FIG. 15. Gustave Le Gray, *The Zouave Barber,* from *Souvenirs du Camp de Châlons,* 1857. Courtesy of the Art Institute of Chicago.

Painting, Photography, and the Real Zouave

The advent of photography meant that the Crimea and other mid-nineteenth-century conflicts were venues for new claims about truth in visual representations of war. Ulrich Keller perceptively notes that discussions of the period focused on the ability of the media—newspapers as well as visual media—to represent the truth of war. Comparable interest in the capacity of the media to conceal wartime realities came later, but in the 1850s and 1860s, audiences assumed that the media they consumed were engaged in an effort to produce ever greater accuracy and truth.[108]

Spectators of the Crimean War recognized the potential for photography to transform the business of representing war, and historians regularly note that the first war photographers covered the conflict. Pictures in the illustrated press—some of which began as photographs and were then reproduced as lithographs—brought British and French consumers of news together via a common pictorial vocabulary. The work of a photographer like the Scotsman William Simpson, who went to the Crimea as a representative of the Colnaghi lithography firm, appeared in both illustrated newspapers and a luxury portfolio of wartime images, *The Campaign in the Crimea: An Historical Sketch* (published 1855–56). Panorama artist Jean-Charles Langlois consulted landscape photographs in his effort to produce an immersive experience that would transport the viewer from Paris to the *Siege of Sebastapol* and the *Battle of Solferino*.[109] To ensure the accuracy of his panorama, he traveled to the Crimea in the company of a photographer, Léon Eugène Méhédin, who, in addition to working on panoramas, produced an album of Italian war landscapes.[110] James Robertson's Crimean photographs of quiet, ravaged, post-battle landscapes, which he exhibited in London in 1855, similarly informed the experience of panorama viewers.[111] Photography became a regular part of the life of the soldier, and the Italian Campaign, which took place in a region well provided with studios, inaugurated the tradition of young men posing for a carte de visite before facing battle. Zouaves were both good photographic clients and good subjects for the battlefield scenes that photographers began producing for sale to a public anxious for authentic representations of war.[112]

As this staged image (fig. 16) of Zouave victory and its cost suggests, at mid-century most of the promise of photography for capturing the reality of war remained well in the future. The camera of the day required subjects to hold still for extended periods of time, which meant that an artist with a sketch pad or even an academic painter working on canvas could produce an image with greater spontaneity and consequently claim greater authenticity.[113] Not surprisingly, then, in the 1850s and 1860s paintings continued to shape popular impressions of war. Art historian Aude Nicolas has identified 140 paintings, including two panoramas, rep-

FIG. 16. Marie-Alexandre Alophe, *Group of Victorious Zouaves at Solferino.*
Courtesy of the Bibliothèque nationale de France.

resenting the Crimean conflict produced from 1855 to 1870.[114] Lithography made paintings, just like photographs, available to the readers of the illustrated press, so that this traditional genre had wide impact in the popular media.

Zouaves were useful to painters as they sought to respond to the challenge of photography by infusing battle scenes with movement in order to produce a sense of simultaneity and capture the confusion of battle. If the Zouaves visiting the Louvre in Castiglione's painting were exhibition regulars, they would have seen themselves everywhere. The presence of Zouaves set the narrative of battle in motion: viewers instantly knew that the initiative and daring of France's finest troops would determine the outcome of battle. The Zouave figures on the canvas were not merely cannon fodder or cogs in the machine of war. Even when represented as part of a formation, the Zouave brought personality to the image: his judgment and his actions, as much as those of his commanding officers, would lead to victory.

Battle paintings were a genre well suited to the goals of the *fête impériale,* and Napoleon III commissioned a set to add to the Versailles Historical Museum to commemorate his victories in the Crimea and Italy. Adolphe Yvon won the commission for the central canvas in the new Crimean Room: a massive (six by nine meters) representation of French troops seizing the Malakoff redoubt (fig. 17). The Malakoff was not the final act of the Crimean War, but it was an exclusively French victory, so it was an appealing climax to the emperor's Crimean installation.[115]

Yvon organized his depiction of the Malakoff to feature Zouaves—indeed, one critic described the painting as "the apotheosis" of the Zouave.[116] Zouaves initiated the attack, but by the time French troops reached the top of the fortifications and planted the tricolor—the moment Yvon chose to depict—soldiers from a variety of units would have been present. Yvon, however, shows only Zouaves, in their dashing, colorful dress, and Russians in dull, mud- and blood-stained uniforms. Yvon borrowed techniques from the panorama, and his canvas has multiple focal points, mostly featuring Zouaves: at the top of the redoubt, Zouave Corporal Libaut plants the flag, while a few yards away General Patrice de MacMahon

FIG. 17. Adolphe Yvon, *The Taking of the Malakoff*, 1857.
Copyright RMN–Grand Palais / Art Resource, New York.

gestures toward the retreating Russians.[117] The highest-ranking officer in the field that day, Marshal Pélissier, is nearly invisible, a tiny figure on a distant hillside to the right. As in a panorama, elements of the picture crowd to the front, drawing the spectator into the image: at the bottom right a dead Russian soldier nearly tumbles out of the picture plane, and in the center Colonel Collineau urges his Zouaves onward, toward the viewer.

The critic Théophile Gautier noted that capturing the Malakoff in paint was perhaps even more difficult than in real life, but Yvon had "fought like a real Zouave" to achieve his final result.[118] Gautier referred to the difficulty of reorienting a traditional artistic form toward modern experiences of combat, and he and Yvon both considered Zouaves suitable soldiers for the task. Gautier's comment also captures the mixed reception that the painting attracted at the 1857 Salon: writers shared his sense that battle painting was undergoing a dramatic transformation about which they had mixed feelings. The panoramic technique of distributing the viewer's attention across the canvas rather than concentrating it on a single point of denouement struck some viewers as incoherent: the battle ceased to be a legible narrative and became nothing more than an assembly of loosely connected episodes. Other viewers, however, found this a profoundly realistic way of representing modern warfare. The equal prominence of the general and the Zouave corporal shocked some viewers and thrilled others, convincing them that Yvon had captured the demo- cratic truth of war. Similarly, some viewers objected to the bloody corpses that appeared to spill out of the picture frame while others emphasized the truthfulness of the gore. Despite these debates, Yvon's work, as art historian Katie Hornstein notes, "enjoyed an afterlife as a graphic and photographic reproduction across a staggering array of emergent and es- tablished media."[119]

Horace Vernet, whose paintings for the Historical Museum had done so much to promote the Zouave in the 1830s and 1840s, was still a leader in the field, and he toured the Crimea in 1854 in order to produce accurate, as well as dramatic, images of French victory. His best-known images of the Crimea were also of the Malakoff, a subject that he painted in large and small formats, in both cases deploying Zouaves to represent the her- oism and the initiative of French soldiers. His first effort, a small canvas (forty by thirty-four centimeters) representing an explosion that blasts two Zouaves off their feet (fig. 18), shows the artist's efforts to push paint- ing to represent dynamic movement and sudden violence. The explo- sion in the middle ground propels a stone column toward one Zouave who staggers backward while the other Zouave falls forward, toward the viewer. The latter Zouave's upturned face seems to look directly at the spectator, and the rifle and the rock that the blast propels forward appear on the verge of leaving the canvas. The painting looks as if it should be viewed through 3D glasses, so determined is Vernet to create the impres- sion that the debris of the explosion might actually strike a spectator. Queen Victoria purchased the painting for Prince Albert for Christmas in 1857, but it circulated widely as a mezzotint published by Goupil earlier that year.[120]

Vernet's larger version of the Malakoff scene features a clearer narra- tive of French victory but a similar effort to pierce the picture plane and

FIG. 18. Horace Vernet, *Zouaves at the Malakoff*, 1856.
Royal Collection Trust / Copyright His Majesty King Charles III, 2023.

bring the image into the room with the audience (fig. 19). Vernet proposed this painting for the Versailles museum but lost the commission to his competitor and son-in-law Yvon; he sold the finished work to the hometown of the French general MacMahon. Unlike Yvon's panoramic, horizontally oriented image, Vernet organizes the Malakoff vertically around a central episode: the Zouave corporal Lihaut plants the tricolor on top of the redoubt, on which dead bodies, cannons, and other debris lay strewn. With his back to the viewer—an accurate touch, as the flag was a prearranged signal to the British forces in the rear—Lihaut is at the apex of the pyramid of dead and dying Zouaves that seems hardly contained within the picture plane. The other characters are officers: General MacMahon and the British liaison who will return to his superiors to report on the

FIG. 19. Horace Vernet, *The Taking of the Malakoff*, 1858.
Copyright Musée Rolin, Autun.

French victory. The painting assumes viewers' familiarity with the widely reported anecdote associated with the taking of the Malakoff: MacMahon, pointing at the ground where Lihaut plants the tricolor, tells the British officer to report that he has seized the redoubt and that the French flag will remain there.[121] MacMahon's line, "I'm here and I'm staying!" ("J'y suis et j'y reste!") became the motto of the Third Zouaves.

Yvon and Vernet's efforts at authenticity have a distinctly theatrical quality to them, and the centrality of Zouaves in the images enhances that impression of stagecraft. The Zouaves brought with them to the paintings their stereotyped personas and their baggage of vaudeville performance. Inauthenticity, then, was not just a problem with the medium of the battle painting—it attached itself specifically to the figure of the Zouave. It wasn't simply that military painting was a grand aristocratic tradition that seemed out of step with an increasingly democratic age or that it was losing out to more truthful modes of representation like photography. Rather, the Zouave was not capable of authenticity: he always came with theatrical trimmings and shared a knowing wink with his public.

Zouaves in contemporary photographs share that theatricality with their comrades in battle paintings. Photographed Zouaves of the era, especially those of the most famous photographer of the Crimean War, Roger Fenton, undermine photography's claims to immediacy and truth. Fenton delighted audiences and collectors with his firsthand images of the theater of war, and Queen Victoria and Napoleon III both purchased sets of his Crimean pictures. His photographs—especially his photographs of Zouaves—were records of performances, however. According to Ulrich Keller, in Fenton's hands, "photography emerged as a primary vehicle for the transport of the fictions which Victorian society needed to justify its wars no less than itself."[122] Zouaves conveying the message that military service was an opportunity for soldiers to demonstrate initiative, wit, and boldness were examples of these photographic fictions.

Fenton spent over a year in the Crimea, from February 1855 until June 1856, sponsored by the Manchester publisher Agnew and traveling with a letter of introduction from Prince Albert and thirty-six chests containing over seven hundred glass plates and various developing chemicals.[123] Like Gustave Le Gray, Fenton made a series of portraits of officers, most of which were formal and rather stilted. His staged photograph of the "Council of War" in which British, French, and Turkish commanders gather round a small table to plot their strategy was especially popular and was subsequently restaged on several occasions for paintings.[124] His photographs of common soldiers, however, became the backbone of his collection, and in them Zouaves jostle distinctively dressed Spahis, Tartars, Montenegrins, and Armenians in an Orientalist military spectacle.

FIG. 20. Roger Fenton, *Zouave and Spahi, Attendants of Maréchal Pélissier*, 1855. Courtesy of the Library of Congress.

Fenton's Zouaves captured a jaunty informality that presented the public with an attractive image of war and military service. Fenton appreciated the Zouaves as performers, as subjects who were genuine soldiers at the same time as they were characters available for the imagination. His photograph of a Zouave and a Spahi (fig. 20), for instance, suggests the Africans' reputation for both ferocity and playfulness. The pose of the two exotically garbed men is relaxed, lounging even, but they could leap into action at any moment. Their worn uniforms and the crumbling plaster behind them deliver the authenticity that photography promised— these are real soldiers, at the real front. Their ease in front of the camera, especially in contrast to the stiff pictures of their officers, suggests that they did not find it strange to be looked at and were prepared for the photographer's gaze. The image offered its viewers an insider's view of soldiering in distant lands.[125]

The authenticity of the Zouave, however, was never beyond question, and a "real" Zouave could be many things. Witness the multiple studio portraits Fenton took of himself dressed as a Zouave that he exhibited alongside his Crimean photographs. He probably took this self-portrait (fig. 21) in his London studio, but his Zouave performance is nonetheless

FIG. 21. Roger Fenton, self-portrait in Zouave dress, 1855.
Courtesy of the Getty Museum.

spot-on. The rough drape and the ragged furs that cover the floor and the seat suggest an improvised military camp on exotic shores. The full beard, the lounging pose, and the spread legs contrast with the erect rifle held between them and with his intense gaze. In a second studio costume study, Fenton similarly plays with the Zouave reputation for ferocious soldiering and an appreciation of the good things in life: he is at the ready either for a fight or for a drink. His rifle is cocked, but his pipe remains in his mouth. He could, with equal ease, throw himself into conflict or sink back into his fur-covered perch where his tankard awaits.[126]

Fenton promised authenticity, but his medium required static, carefully staged scenes, and his subject, Zouaves, offered a showman's awareness of his audience. His Zouaves demonstrate that the limitations on producing truth were not technological but rather intrinsic to the role of the Zouave as performer—that is, those limitations were bound up in the Zouave himself. In a sense, however, the staged performances that Fenton offered his audience were the genuine, authentic representation of the Crimean War. Representation and reality fused as performances, staged for the camera or for the theater audience, claimed to represent the truth of the war.

3

NATURALIZED IN THE NEW WORLD

ook at the Zouaves," urged Giuseppe Garibaldi in September 1859 as he exhorted fellow Italians to build on recent French assistance toward political unification of the peninsula. "In their simple, easy dress, they are the first soldiers in the world."[1] Invocation of the professional imperial army as the model for a homemade insurgency illustrated the elasticity of Zouaves as military exemplars. This pliancy helped to give new meaning to Garibaldi's recirculation of the familiar accolade, for the Zouave concept spread around the globe within the next decade in a wide variety of contexts. The Risorgimento spent much of the 1860s at war with a multinational army of Pontifical Zouaves that epitomized the broad appeal of Zouave soldiering. Great Britain introduced a Zouave uniform for its leading set of colonial troops, the West India Regiments. Polish nationalists rallied against Russia in the January Uprising of 1863 as the Zouaves of Death. A native military unit called the Zouave Guard organized in Hawai'i in time to participate in the 1864 funeral procession of King Kamehameha IV in a scarlet-and-blue uniform praised for its attractiveness and suitability for the Polynesian climate.[2]

The largest Zouave muster took place in the United States, where the number of northerners and southerners who enlisted as Zouaves during the Civil War exceeded the number of Zouaves in the French army. Americans never forgot the Zouave origin in the French conquest of Algeria, however, and transplantation of the military identity was an important aspect of the interchange between the two nations. Contrasting structures in the armed forces channeled this impulse in different directions. Zouaves stationed in North Africa or the Imperial Guard served in the French army, a highly centralized if geographically dispersed agency of the nation-state. Royal control of the army enabled Louis-Philippe and Napoleon III to associate the beloved Zouaves with the monarchy. In the United States, the Zouave movement grew outside the regular army, in local companies of state militia, and climaxed in the wartime recruitment of state-based units into the United States Volunteers and Confederate armies. Many Americans considered this grassroots independence a logical extension of the Zouave idea, though some military leaders tried to combine mass enthusiasm for Zouaves with the professional training characteristic of the French army.

In the United States as in France, popular culture shaped the Zouave image as a new kind of hero, but the relationship between military and commercial promotion of the image differed in the two countries. In France, public embrace of Zouaves supplemented government patronage and forged independent bonds between citizens and soldiers. In the United States, the emergence of *zouaverie* in popular culture preceded the enlistment of any Zouave soldiers. Paris fads spread quickly to New York and New Orleans, though Americans misunderstood some European context and modified the precedent to fit local circumstances. A force created for the subjugation of North Africa offered special resonance for an expansionist country defined by the racial politics of slavery and tempted by the prospect of further annexations in the Caribbean. Flirtation with gender conventions suggested fresh possibilities in a society that debated political feminism. The most influential American military organization to don Zouave uniforms won its fame for mixing martial drill and entertainment. Adaptation of the French original to the American environment offered a range of costumes and scripts at the outbreak of the Civil War.

Prelude to Popularity

American interest in Zouaves began in the mid-1850s. Although deeply engaged with North Africa in the era of the Barbary Wars, the United

States paid little attention to the colonization of Algeria a generation later. Hastily glancing at Horace Vernet's huge canvases at Versailles, rising young travel writer Bayard Taylor praised *The Taking of Constantine* for its "vivid look of reality" in the same year that Charles Baudelaire scorned Vernet's latest installment of the series at the Salon of 1846 as a mechanical, propagandistic mass of detail.[3] The contrast between the American tourist and the French critic signaled that institutional settings as well as national contexts shaped interpretations of the Zouave image. Art and music, journalism, and fashion elaborated and modified a Crimean fame refreshed by new military operations in Italy. Theater proved to be an especially influential medium. By the beginning of 1860, the varied representations of the Zouave produced a cultural figure primed for an American mobilization campaign.

The Crimean War acquainted Americans with the reputation of Zouaves. Newspapers relayed French and British accounts of the fierce and cunning troops from North Africa.[4] U.S. Army captain George B. McClellan, assigned to the Delafield Commission to observe the war and study leading European armies, reported in detail that the Zouaves "are what their appearance would indicate, the most reckless, self-reliant, and complete infantry that Europe can produce." The Zouave at his outpost was "the beau ideal of a soldier," and the marching Zouaves' movements were "the most light and graceful I have ever seen."[5] Americans read about the Zouave theater at Inkerman and the transfer of the emblematic friendship between Zouave and Highlander to the Paris stage.[6] William Edwin Johnston, wartime Paris correspondent for the *New-York Tribune* and from 1856 for the *New York Times*, adopted the pen name "Malakoff," a peak of Zouave glory. He and other postwar reporters noted the prominence of the Zouaves in the Imperial Guard and described the pleasures of Napoleon III and other day-trippers to the military camp at Châlons, where Zouaves were "ever foremost in getting up pastimes and have a wonderful facility for arranging masquerades."[7]

During the next few years, importations of the Zouave image explored its intersections with central themes of mid-century American culture, including inclinations toward bluster, anxieties about fraud, and ambitions for empire. Regular presentation of Grangé and Cormon's *Le Théâtre des Zouaves* on Broadway after the opening of the French Theatre in May 1858 was an unusually direct foreign-language transplantation.[8] Alfred Musard's high-profile series of promenade concerts was more typical in its plan to appeal to broad audiences. Musard featured his thunderous "Les Zouaves on The Malakoff: Grand Battle Quadrille," paired in some concerts with the "Marseillaise."[9] Expatriate painter Edward Harrison May stressed the same spread-eagle patriotism in his *A Zouave Telling the Story of the Taking of the Malakoff, in the Garden of Invalides*, a widely praised contribution to the National Academy of Design exhibition that opened during Musard's tour.[10] Many newspapers in the land of P. T. Barnum relayed an anecdote from the *Gazette des Tribunaux* about a Zouave trickster who duped an amateur naturalist into buying a previously unknown species of rat with a large trunk, which the old soldier had created by making a hole in the snout of one rat and inserting the amputated tail of another rat until it rooted.[11] The supreme Zouave confidence man in the United States was Henri Arnous de Riviere, who eloped with Mobile socialite Emily Blount after delivering a set of New York lectures on the Crimean War in full uniform. Kidnapping and bigamy suits, a duel, and de Riviere's supposed entanglement with filibusters in Nicaragua sustained press fascination with the scandal.[12] In the Wallack Theater's imperial captivity comedy *The Veteran; or France and Algeria*, which opened in January 1859 and ran for an impressive 102 nights, Zouaves embodied the brute force that ensured European dominance in North Africa. Typifying a recent tendency to incorporate sensational tableaux vivants in dramatic narratives, *The Veteran* highlighted Zouaves in the climactic two "pictures."[13]

The French military campaign in Italy in spring 1859 substantially expanded Zouaves' fame in the United States. The Franco-Piedmontese offensive touched American interests more closely than the Crimean effort of England and France to prevent Russian incursion on the Ottoman Empire. For Americans, the conflict advanced the epic struggle for Italian unification and measured the ambitions of Napoleon III, who risked but avoided intervention by Prussia and the German Confederation on behalf of Austria.[14]

Beyond these diplomatic considerations, the American press was much better prepared to cover the Italian Campaign than the Crimean War. Although the Atlantic cable completed in 1858 failed almost immediately, the project reflected a determination to build international connections. The title chosen for the *Atlantic Monthly* on its founding in 1857 illustrated the same eagerness, and the journal published a detailed history of Zouaves in August 1859.[15] American newspapers sought to duplicate the acclaim William Howard Russell's dispatches from the Crimea had brought to the London *Times*, making arrangements with correspondents in the more accessible Italian theater. *New York Times* founder Henry J. Raymond traveled personally to the seat of the war and achieved a memorable professional triumph by filing a report on the decisive battle of Solferino that reached the United States long before any competitors' accounts.[16] Especially important was the establishment of American versions of the illustrated magazines that had publicized the Zouaves in France and England during the Crimean War. *Harper's Weekly* launched in 1857. *Frank Leslie's Illustrated Newspaper*, founded two years earlier, settled into long-term stability after surviving the financial downturn of 1857–58.[17]

In reprinting French and British stories and adding original coverage, American newspapers highlighted Zouave zest for individual combat. William Edwin Johnston reported that the well-equipped Zouaves "do not care much about firing" and in the distribution of cartridges "showed all the prudery of a young girl to whom one offers a present." They preferred the head-on attacks for which they had trained with rigorous exercises in gymnastics and bayonet fencing. Poet W. H. Browne declared that "Naught could withstand the fierce assault / Of those Zouaves, like tigers leaping / O'er man and gun, with airy vault / And deep in gore their weapons steeping."[18]

The two-month war in Italy made "Zouave" a byword of American public life, with a variety of applications. William Lloyd Garrison called Whig orator Rufus Choate "a professional Zouave" because his speeches were "inflated, disjointed, flashy, sophomorical, . . . helter-skelter, and whatever characterizes the 'spread-eagle' school." The conservative *New York Herald* in turn argued, with a hint of racial mixing, that "abolition radicals of the school of Garrison, Phillips and Cheever may be fairly set down as the advanced guard, the scouts, the pioneers, the Zouaves and Turcos of the aggressive republican army." The *Louisville Democrat* complained that the principles of arch-southern politicians "fit as loosely as a Zouave's trousers, and are as easily put on or off." The comparisons could also be complimentary. The bravery of volunteer New York firefighters, the *Herald* cheered, "has never been surpassed, even, we may say, by the daring exploits of the Zouaves at Solferino."[19]

The war sparked a transatlantic vogue among young men for wearing fezzes, often marketed as "Zouave hats," and it revived in France and introduced to America a fashion for women's jackets modeled on the Zouave uniform. By February 1860 the French journal *Le Follet* declared Zouave jackets "the one requisite" for home wardrobes, though William Edwin Johnston thought the style was never as popular among Parisians as it became among foreigners. The casual waist-defining look, "the most coquettish of garments," certainly became a sensation in the United

FIG. 22. "La Mode—The Zouave Jacket," *Harper's Weekly* 4 (April 28, 1860).
Courtesy of the University of South Carolina Libraries.

States. Some designers even tried to adapt the trend to mourning cloaks, "as different from the common place cloak as the Zouave is from the regular soldier."[20] *Godey's Lady's Book* published fashion plates of Zouave jackets and supplied sewing and braiding patterns to readers. The magazine noted that young women particularly favored the pert adaptation of military style, an observation reminiscent of the newspaper accounts of a French gamine detected in Zouave uniform as she attempted to board a transport vessel at Marseille and join her lover in Italy.[21]

The racial as well as the gendered malleability of the Zouave gained new prominence in American theater. Bryant's Minstrels opened the most portentous stage presentation of Zouaves to follow the Italian Campaign in September 1859, a farce entitled "The Exiled Zouaves." French masquerade in North African dress offered blackface comedy an obvious target in current events. Only a few months earlier, Bryant's Minstrels had introduced another parody of exile, the walk-around "Dixie's Land," and the troupe sometimes performed the skit and the song in the same show, along with related pieces like "Plantation Scenes" and "African Polka." Within the next few years Zouaves in the North and South would claim "Dixie" as an anthem.[22]

The Zouave also continued to feed growing American tastes for spectacle. Louis Keller, the most ambitious tableaux impresario, mounted *The War in Italy* at Niblo's Garden before the end of June 1859. James Pilgrim's extravaganza *Garibaldi, or the Invasion of Sardinia* featured a vivid depiction of Zouaves in combat even though Zouaves did not participate in the southern sector of the Italian war.[23] James M. Nixon's Mammoth Circus conscripted the best-known branch of the French infantry into the entertainment cavalry, outfitting performers in Zouave costumes to execute "thrilling equestrian evolutions." P. T. Barnum did not fail to notice the expanding market. Monsieur La Pierre, advertised as a Zouave veteran who had lost a leg at the Malakoff, performed "a variety of astonishing gymnastic feats peculiar to that extraordinary military corps" as a prelude to evening theatrical productions at Barnum's American Museum.[24]

The productions that most fully measured American independence in imagining Zouaves combined the burlesque of minstrelsy with the orchestration of martial tableaux and acrobatics. *The Lady of the Lake*, written by Mortimer Thomson as a vehicle for comedian sisters Carry and Sara Nelson, opened at Niblo's Garden in June 1860. Carry took a breeches, or kilt, role as a knight obliged to save a fair maiden from "a low Highland ducal robber." Sara played the lady of the lake. When the brigand unleashed his ruffians, which the topical dialogue compared to the notorious Dead Rabbits gang, the spirit of the lake sent to the knight's aid a troop of forty female Zouaves, described in the stage directions as "Highland Amazons dressed in green plaid uniforms." The four beautiful ballet-dancing Gale Sisters led the kilted platoon through a set of marches and formations after dispatching the villains.[25] The mash-up recalled the theatrical pairing of Zouave and Highlander five years earlier in *Pilbox et Friquet* but with less concern for national types or character development and more enthusiasm for riotous visual display. During the same month, the husband-wife team of William J. and Malvina Pray Florence won audience applause by inserting a "Zouave March by the Amazons" into a travesty of Thomas Moore's Mughal romance *Lalla Rookh*.[26] Such extensive rehearsal prepared the role of the Zouave for one of the most memorable performances in the history of the United States.

Zouave Mania

The summer 1860 tour of Elmer Ellsworth and his United States Zouave Cadets (USZC) catapulted Zouaves to the center of the American martial imagination. Ellsworth came to focus on Zouaves through the concentration of his military ambitions on the militia. For a tailor's son from upstate New York without enough political connections for the West Point appointment he had coveted since childhood, the militia was the institution that offered an opportunity for military leadership. State militias, however, had been an object of American derision since the 1820s. Ordinary citizens resented the unequal burden of a needless public duty and recognized in large cities that militia suppression of urban disorder enforced class and ethnic hierarchy. Well-to-do citizens ridiculed the revelry of ineffectual musters and understood that the militia primarily tested the organizational and ceremonial talents of political aspirants.[27] Ellsworth aimed to demonstrate that voluntary militia service might be made popular. French Zouaves had won renown for flashy uniforms, individual prowess, camaraderie, and theatrical flair. To these traits Ellsworth proposed to add the ethical code of the emerging middle class. His phenomenal success presaged the election of his older friend Abraham Lincoln and linked the impending crisis to what observers called "Zouave mania."[28]

A widely noticed initiative in New Orleans in September 1859 illustrated the traditional foundations of the militia and the Zouave potential to tap new sources in popular culture. State legislator Henry Honoré St. Paul, dubbed "the Hotspur of the Senate" for advocating a reopening of the Atlantic slave trade, organized a unit labeled the *chasseurs à pied* to capitalize on excitement over the war in Italy and consolidate his political support. The distinction between the French *chasseurs* and their better-publicized Zouave comrades escaped most Americans, who described the shared devotion to athletic training as "the regular French Zouave drill."[29] Nativists looked skeptically on the soldiers' yellow-trimmed gray baggy trousers cinched at the knee. The *New Orleans Daily Crescent* conceded that "it is really very pretty and somewhat taking" but pointed out that "there is nothing of American nationality about it." Another newspaper pronounced the uniform "grotesque."[30] Local views of Zouaves brightened in April 1860, when the Varieties Theater production of John Brougham's travesty *Pocahontas* incorporated "the prettiest thing that anyone ever saw in the way of a stage parade," performed by fifteen young women under the command of actress Susan Denin. "They were in Zouave costume of the neatest make, finish and fit," raved the *Daily Crescent*, "and to the tune and chorus of 'Dixie's Land' they drilled and maneuvered with a dexterity and precision which some of our military companies would do well to study." The theatrical smash contributed to the southern popularization of "Dixie" and helped the Zouave militia receive favorable press notice at its next public appearance.[31]

Ellsworth more deliberately melded militia drill and show business. After he left home in early youth, he worked as a clerk at a dry-goods store in New York City and enjoyed exhibitions of the silk-stocking Seventh

Regiment.[32] He resettled in Chicago around the age of eighteen as clerk and later partner of Arthur F. Devereux, who was a year younger but came from a sufficiently privileged background to set up in business as a patent solicitor. The son of a Whig politician who had served as adjutant general of the Massachusetts Volunteer Militia, Devereux had blown through a West Point appointment in a blaze of alcohol-soaked conduct violations.[33] The friends were active in the Illinois militia, and after the partnership came to financial ruin shortly before the panic of 1857, Ellsworth started to find engagements as a drillmaster for nearby companies. He had doubtless read press coverage of the Crimean War closely. His interest in Zouaves deepened when he met fencing instructor Charles DeVilliers, with whose assistance Ellsworth became one of the preeminent swordsmen in Chicago. DeVilliers claimed to have served with the Zouaves, but French military records list no Zouave with that name; the Guadeloupe native's long criminal record suggests that the boast was fraudulent.[34] In April 1859, as France was preparing for the Italian Campaign, the fifteen remaining members of a Chicago militia company with which Ellsworth had a long association elected him captain to stave off disbanding for lack of interest. He accepted the position and resolved to make the unit a showcase. He started by renaming it the United States Zouave Cadets.[35]

Ellsworth attracted new members by offering a rewarding rigor. Subsisting on a diet of crackers and sleeping on the hard floors of law offices where he worked as a scrivener, the twenty-two-year-old commander set a Spartan example. His emulation of the French military contributed to the rise of the American cult of physical fitness, and the company spent hours in a Chicago gymnasium performing calisthenics and lifting weights. Ellsworth drilled his men relentlessly. He adapted William Hardee's standard U.S. Army drill book, a translation of the 1845 manual for French *chasseurs à pied,* to simplify and accelerate standard rifle-handling procedures.[36] He departed sharply from army precedent in his so-called Golden Resolutions, which prescribed expulsion from the company for any cadet who entered a saloon or a brothel or a billiard hall. Repudiation of the drinking, swearing, whoring, and gambling endemic in army life instituted the expectation of self-discipline that defined the mid-nineteenth-century bourgeoisie. Mutual commitment to this regimen and cultivation of the company armory as a recreational space strengthened the fraternal bonds of the young recruits, many of whom worked in clerical jobs that Ellsworth knew well. Their shared identity strengthened when the unit first wore Zouave uniforms in an exhibition drill in the armory in early August 1859. Around the same time Ellsworth redoubled efforts around a group goal, participation in the drill competition sponsored by the National Agricultural Society at its upcoming annual fair in Chicago.

A jury that included former U.S. Army captain George B. McClellan, now vice-president of the Illinois Central Railroad, awarded the USZC the first-place flag at the September fair, but the trophy meant little because the supposed national championship attracted only one other entrant, also from Chicago. Ellsworth, a colonel in the Illinois militia since his appointment to the unpaid position of paymaster general and assistant adjutant general, tried to leverage the local victory by daring any company in the regular army or a state militia to compete for the prize colors. When he renewed his unanswered challenge in the *New York Clipper*, the leading theatrical and sporting weekly, he observed that competitive drill "looks to something practically and permanently useful, as well as presently entertaining."[37] Ellsworth continued to blend exercise and spectacle as he planned to take the USZC on tour, nominally in search of rivals but focused on a series of well-publicized exhibitions. He printed and mailed seventeen hundred copies of his simplification of Hardee's manual of arms, to which Ellsworth added a program of movements for the cadets to execute in their drill. The routine borrowed extensively from the army manual of bayonet exercise that McClellan had translated from a French work. This section of the drill enabled Ellsworth to marshal his fencing experience and incorporate the dance-like rhythms of the art. The choreography also included a set of self-professedly "fancy movements" in which sections of the company marched in revolving circles or built human pyramids and chanted cheers.[38] Ellsworth devoted one-fourth of the book to the cadets' press clippings, prominently featuring the Golden Resolutions, and announced a tour that would proceed from the Great Lakes to the Erie Canal and down the Hudson River to New York City and

New England, circling back through Philadelphia, Baltimore, Washington, Cincinnati, and St. Louis.

From the July 4 launch of the tour, animated press praise heightened anticipation in the cities ahead. The cadets' wardrobe thrilled spectators. Of the four uniforms ranging from full dress to fatigue, the showstopper was the Zouave outfit featuring billowy scarlet pantaloons with a gold cord over a blue stripe, high gaiters and leggings, a blue vest with orange braid and moire facing, a darker blue jacket trimmed in red and orange, and a cap described as "the jauntiest little scarlet head-gear ever worn by a practical fighting man."[39] The brilliant outfit enhanced the visual effect as the cadets moved rapidly through "figures of crosses, double crosses, squares, triangles, like the dissolving figures of the kaleidoscope." They delighted audiences with novelty tricks like scaling walls by running up the inclined backs of stooping comrades. The eighteen-piece ensemble under the baton of Chicago bandleader A. J. Vaas added a festive complement to the company, which numbered about forty muskets. Sheet-music publisher Root & Cady brought out at least eleven editions of Vaas's "Zouave Cadets Quickstep," adorned in later versions by Edward Mendel's chromolithograph of Ellsworth standing in arms-folded pose alongside a cadet in the full Zouave glory of the rank and file (fig. 23). Exhibitions drew crowds estimated at five thousand in Detroit, twelve thousand in Rochester, and twenty thousand in Albany.[40]

The USZC's conquest of New York City was the stuff of legend. The cadets' fantastic uniforms created "a lively, spirited appearance, intermingled with a slight dash of the ferocious," amid an urban sea of broadcloth, and they enchanted crowds with synchronized cheers of "one, two, three, four, five, six, seven, Zouave, tig-aar!" An estimated crowd of ten thousand gathered in City Hall Park to watch a drill crafted to suggest the combat efficacy of the Zouave system.[41] The thirty-two men divided into small groups to minimize vulnerability and maximize individual latitude but sprang together for concerted action. Their athleticism and precision astonished veteran watchers of militia drills. Critics praised "an ease of motion, a dashing confidence, and an elasticity which we do not see in any of our own companies" and rated the process of stacking arms, in which

FIG. 23. A. J. Vaas, "Zouave Cadets Quickstep," Root & Cady (10th ed., 1860); Edward Mendel, lithographer. Courtesy of the Library of Congress.

Ellsworth took special pride, "the best thing in the military line we have ever seen."[42] Another exhibition the next day in Madison Square Park was equally successful.

The Zouave furor prompted broad reflection that metropolitan life had become "a continuous series of excitements." Following soon after the first visit of a Japanese diplomatic delegation to the United States, the cadets played their parts perfectly. They engaged in elaborate courtesies with units of the New York militia. Ellsworth presented a medal to Alexander Shaler, captain of the second company of the Seventh Regiment, for commanding the best-drilled unit the USZC encountered. They toured the immense *Great Eastern* steamship currently docked in the harbor, one of the technological wonders of the age. They had photographs taken and displayed at a Broadway gallery. They attended Joseph Jefferson's performance in *The Tycoon* at Laura Keene's Theatre and John Brougham's performance in *Pocahontas* at Niblo's Garden, at which the playwright and star improvised several quips about Zouaves.[43]

The coronation climaxed in an unprecedented exhibition at the Academy of Music. City leaders' requests for the engagement stressed that ladies could scarcely have attended the drills in outdoor parks.[44] The Academy of Music was the most prestigious venue in the country, with over four thousand seats. The USZC packed the hall at a standard ticket price of fifty cents. The polished floor and gaslights posed novel challenges, but Ellsworth and his company adapted easily. They performed the segment before intermission in blue dress uniform with white belts and the conclusion in full Zouave uniform. Ellsworth's choreography shifted tempo from rapid execution of the manual of arms through a flurry of loading and firing. They "evoked hilarity" with "a lively turn-down of the men, vulgarly designated the 'belly-movement.'" In another comic highlight, the thirty-nine cadets formed a circle in which each soldier's right hand rested on the shoulder of the soldier in front of him. The circle contracted until it suddenly came to a halt with the soldiers sitting in each other's laps. "Fixing bayonets quick as a flash," one reporter deadpanned, "they wheeled around and turned around and almost jumped Jim Crow." The show ended with a furious bayonet charge to the edge of the stage. The audience responded with "such applause as the great artists who have made the theater vibrate with their genius never received."[45]

A week later the cadets and the second company of the Seventh Regiment steamed up the Hudson River for a West Point exhibition that tested the American military establishment's attitude toward the Zouaves. Former secretary of war Jefferson Davis reviewed the drill, but the judge in the spotlight was tactics instructor William Hardee, currently the commandant of cadets. Hardee complimented the facility of the USZC but suggested that Ellsworth's departures from regulations in maneuvering his undersized company would become problematic in a larger body of men. This critique was more technical than common observations that

FIG. 24. "The Zouave Cadets of Chicago, Drilling in the Park in front
of City Hall, N.Y., July 14, 1860—Rallying by Companies to Repel Cavalry,"
Frank Leslie's Illustrated Newspaper 10 (July 28, 1860).
Courtesy of the American Antiquarian Society.

a small unit was always easier to manage and that Ellsworth's men were
exceptionally fit and thoroughly trained.[46] Hardee's skepticism about "the
utility of some of the fancy movements" was also more measured than
broad-brush grumbling that "the whole thing is a mere series of theatrical effects" worthy of "a troup[e] of dancing girls."[47] Drill performance
was central to military culture, and even Shaler's company of the Seventh
Regiment showed nervousness in taking the field after the USZC.[48]

West Point aspersions notwithstanding, the second half of the cadets'
tour remained a triumphant procession. In Boston they drew twenty
thousand to the Common and did two stage shows, for which scalped
tickets reportedly sold for ten dollars. In Philadelphia they performed
at the Academy of Music and before fifteen thousand spectators in Fair-

mount Park.[49] After reviewing an exhibition drill on the White House lawn, President James Buchanan congratulated the USZC for infusing a new military spirit into a nation whose insistence on a small regular army necessitated dependence on volunteer militia. By mid-August the cadets were back home in Chicago. The torchlight parade that greeted the company at the railroad station ended at the Wigwam, where the Republican Party had nominated Lincoln for the presidency three months earlier. Ellsworth soon disbanded the USZC, its mission accomplished. He took a job as a clerk and legal apprentice to Lincoln, whom he had come to know before the tour while in Springfield for his administrative duties with the Illinois militia. By October he was delivering campaign speeches.[50]

Ellsworth's transition from the USZC tour to the presidential race underscored the political tenor of his project. The reception of the cadets overlapped with the proliferation of Republican marching clubs called Wide Awakes after the May convention; several groups took the name "Zouave Wide Awakes," though Democratic marching clubs also claimed the Zouave label.[51] The USZC did not travel further south than the major border cities. A militia company in Columbus, Georgia, issued a spiteful challenge that Ellsworth chose to ignore.[52] The Golden Resolutions had partisan connotations. Admirers claimed that "the best class" of citizens embraced the company and praised Ellsworth for modeling "a manly and Republican character." Chicago mayor John Wentworth, himself a Republican moral crusader, declared that the USZC disproved "the old proverb, that 'a good soldier spoils the man.'"[53] The humor magazine *Vanity Fair* in turn scoffed at this sanitized definition of manhood and noted that many of the cadets were store clerks, an occupational group lampooned as "counter-jumpers" for their eagerness to serve women shoppers. A sarcastic exhortation to "'go in,' Counter-jumpers, like men!" situated the Zouaves' acrobatics in a feminized army of consumer capitalism.[54] The clash pointed toward the creative tension in Ellsworth's conception, which promised extraordinary individuality to the common soldier but demonstrated unprecedented group cohesion.

"The Zouave may now be regarded as naturalized in the New World," announced the *New York Times* after the performance at the Academy of

Music. A report possibly written by Henry Raymond, who had witnessed the Italian Campaign, stressed the differences between Ellsworth's self-disciplined cadets and the French Zouave, "a reckless, rollicking dog" who was "utterly regardless of right and wrong, dashing, drinking, swearing, carousing, fearless, able, with strong attachments and bitter hatreds." The contrast indicated that even the USZC could not monopolize the definition of a Zouave, "now a household word."[55] Ellsworth had developed his vision of the American soldier in dialogue with a French prototype that continued to command international acclaim. Both models flourished through close association with lively forms of popular culture. After the much-hyped Heenan-Sayers championship boxing match, the *New York Herald* mused that French Zouaves "are no more nor less than so many prize-fighters, each with the Legion of Honor as his belt in prospective."[56] Military institutions and the worlds of entertainment and sport would propose further resonance for the heightened prestige of Zouaves during the eight months between the end of the USZC tour and the outbreak of the Civil War.

The Uses of Momentum

The USZC tour sparked a debate over the incorporation of Zouaves into the American military. Admirers argued that Zouaves marked the end of armies recruited from an uneducated underclass and drilled into habitual obedience. French success proved that it was "no longer of so much importance that infantry should be solid, as that the men should be active, agile and acute—that they should act intelligently and bravely, singly, in pairs, in fours, and in tens." This shift fit American pride in self-reliance. Detractors retorted that Zouave flamboyance undercut collective discipline. The leading military newspaper labeled "humbug" the claim that Zouave jackets and trousers invested soldiers with a sense of freedom, insisting that uniformity should define military dress and battlefield usefulness should govern the design of drill exercises.[57] The debate took place not only in words but in the formation of militia units. Henry St. Paul's *chasseurs* in New Orleans and the USZC were among about a half-dozen companies founded or reorganized with Zouave identities between the April 1859 outbreak of the Italian war and the USZC tour.[58] More than seventy additional Zouave companies sprang up before the attack on Fort Sumter, of which two-thirds emerged in 1860.[59] Many followed directly in Ellsworth's path, but the trend extended to the San Francisco Zouaves in California and the Charleston Zouave Cadets in South Carolina. The popularity of the Zouave concept reshaped the discussion within military circles and entwined stage and martial Zouaves on the eve of the war.

The U.S. Army did not often feature directly in this conversation beyond repeated quotation of McClellan's report to the Delafield Commission. Newspaper editor Joseph C. Abbott, who served as adjutant general of the New Hampshire militia, suggested in July 1860 that the skills French Zouaves had developed in Algeria would translate well to American wars of settler colonialism in the West, "the kind of warfare which will be likely to occupy the United States for many years."[60] A contrary vein of comparison maintained that the army had already incorporated most military features of Zouaves. Hardee's manual, like the manual by Winfield Scott that it replaced, closely followed a French model, as did McClellan's translated bayonet guide. Delafield, now superintendent of West Point, was striving to catch up with the gymnastics innovations transforming armies across Europe.[61] The broad French influence conflated with the Zouave phenomenon in the rise of the *képi*, a soft cloth cap introduced in the French army shortly before the Crimean War and internationally popular afterward. The U.S. Army, a follower rather than a leader of fashion, adopted a forage cap with a similar look in 1858.[62] The kepi developed from a prototype worn in North Africa by French troops organizationally distinct from the Zouaves, who wore the *chéchia* with or without a turban, but the USZC and many later Zouave militia companies embraced the kepi.

Although Horace Greeley's influential *Daily Tribune* concluded that the lesson of the USZC was that the country should invest more in its militia than in "our unrepublican army," Ellsworth's post-tour initiatives aimed to coordinate the institutions.[63] Before leaving the USZC, he drafted an elaborate plan to expand it into a skeleton regiment that would prepare officers for active duty. After the success of Lincoln's campaign, Ellsworth concentrated first on Illinois legislation to restructure the state militia and later on efforts to establish a militia bureau in the federal War Department, which he hoped to direct. In all three undertakings, he proposed to compromise the sacred militia principle of elected officers by requiring rigorous examinations to certify competence, "thus removing the only barrier that has existed between the officers of the army and militia, and leading the way to a cordial co-operation and unity of feeling."[64] His failures revealed inexperience with the powerful interests involved in military administration, but his priorities reflected a shift in focus from the challenge of popularizing military service as the prospect of organizing large numbers of wartime volunteers became more foreseeable.

Frederick Townsend, the adjutant general of New York, was the military professional who most clearly developed a strategy to build on enthusiasm for the USZC. For almost four years he had supervised a force with more soldiers than the U.S. Army, though his volunteers of course served part-time. Unlike his counterparts in many states, Townsend was not a politician and would receive a field commission in the regular army early in the Civil War. The New York militia, rivaled in vigor only by Massachusetts, boasted a rate of participation ten times higher than that of Illinois. Townsend initially disparaged the "circus manœuvres" of the USZC, but he soon realized that Zouave fever might advance his longstanding plan to establish the militia as an effective reserve officer training corps in the event of full-scale mobilization. The opportunity to become a Zouave promised to "bring forward from civil life more of that great class of intelligent young men who have not yet been very much pervaded by military zeal," in large part because the Zouaves offered every soldier the flair, battlefield autonomy, and sense of community traditionally reserved to officers. Townsend agreed to become the commander of the new Albany Zouave Cadets, and as adjutant general he shepherded the unit into the New York militia as Company A of the Tenth Regiment. Like Ellsworth, he trained his soldiers exhaustively and arranged for the armory to become an agreeable recreational space. On his advice, the company later ordered uniforms from Paris that followed French army regulations, an emulation shared by other Zouave units that sought to mark themselves as more professional than the USZC. Townsend's goal was that everyone in the company should seek and receive an officer's commission in the event of a war; thirty-one of the sixty-six men on the roster at the beginning of 1861, as well as forty-three men who joined subsequently, did become Union officers during the Civil War.[65]

Townsend's Zouave turn appalled some of his military colleagues, but he hardly stood alone. The commanding general of the First Division endorsed his initiative. The Seventh Regiment, pride of the New York militia, hosted in Alexander Shaler's second company a bayonet class that practiced Zouave drill in Zouave trousers, and a corporal opened a regimental gymnasium billed as a "Zouave Manufactory."[66] Ellsworth's old friend Arthur Devereux, now back in Massachusetts in the captaincy his father had held a generation earlier, transformed the venerable Salem Light Infantry into a Zouave hothouse of future Union officers and drillmasters.[67] Evander M. Law, a graduate of the Citadel, formed a Zouave company at his Tuskegee Military Academy. Lew Wallace, the son of a West Point graduate, was an experienced militia officer and Mexican War veteran when he converted his Montgomery Guards in Crawfordsville, Indiana, into a Zouave company before the USZC tour. A public exhibition by the Guards in February 1860 inspired West Point graduate Francis A. Shoup to form a Zouave company in Indianapolis.[68]

A state legislator and son of a former Indiana governor, Wallace also illustrated the political and social uses of militia leadership, for which the Zouave craze presented opportunities. Newspaper editor James McQuade, heir to a local political machine and a whiskey fortune, guided his Utica Citizen Corps through adoption of a Zouave uniform amid his campaign for reelection to the New York legislature. As the source of McQuade's wealth suggested, many new Zouave companies did not adopt Ellsworth's code of conduct, though some stridently did. McQuade was also active in volunteer fire companies, like the militia an important site for performance of manhood and demonstration of leadership. In nearby Syracuse, cigar-maker Gustavus Sniper formed a Zouave company comprised largely of German immigrants and named the Munroe Cadets in honor of a state senator. Many of its members served in the same engine company. Such reinforcement of ethnic bonds was not necessarily inconsistent with high levels of military ambition. A faction among the French immigrants who comprised the Garde Lafayette regiment of the New York militia formed a flank company intended to match the distinction of the French Zouaves.[69]

Among the most significant of the independent Zouave companies to form during 1860 was the Fort Pitt Cadets, a group of about fifty African Americans in Pittsburgh captained by bricklayer Rufus Sibb Jones.[70] The initiative recognized that the rise of Zouaves added a new dimension to Black assertions of military competence given urgency by self-defense measures in response to the Fugitive Slave Act and protests against the Dred Scott decision that African Americans were ineligible for U.S. citizenship. The Weekly Anglo-African, founded in New York in 1859, observed during the Italian war that the American press had devoted much more attention to the Zouaves than the Turcos, "genuine blacks from Africa" who "have no superiors in the world or out of it." Turcos' prowess showed that military virtues were part of the African inheritance.[71] New Hampshire adjutant general Abbott, who would be elected to the U.S. Senate by an interracial Republican coalition in North Carolina during Reconstruction, considered it "quite remarkable that from a semi-civilized race in Africa came the pattern from which was formed the most serviceable corps in the finest army in Europe" but argued that French and American adaptations of the Zouave prototype "are both essentially the same as the African."[72]

Bryant's Minstrels also highlighted the racial implications of Zouave mania. The troupe first responded to the USZC tour with the burlesque "Chicago Zouave Cadets Drill," which scored "a palpable hit" in the judgment of the Clipper, but after a few weeks settled into a more permanent routine called "Polka à la Zouave." The skit built on the earlier repertory piece "African Polka," which had underscored the disruption of classical or romantic grace in the popularity of the animated folk dance and cast the minstrels' putative African identity as Bohemian, recently a fashionable term for counterculture rebels. The shift of the polka parody to a Zouave context extended these themes and emphasized that the faux-

African soldiers, like the comedians, performed in blackface. Recognizing the longstanding relationship between dance and military drill, the sketch indicated that the aristocratic regimentation that had prevailed in the age of the minuet and the dynamic progression of the waltz era were giving way to a less orderly grassroots movement. A reviewer admired the minstrels' "red peg-top pants, zoo-zoo jacket, and fatigue cap" and observed that "in such fine clothes we hardly expected such an *abandon*."[73]

The Bryant response to the USZC typified an eruption of satire. Hooley and Campbell's Minstrels mounted "The Great McSwattigan Zouave Drill." *Frank Leslie's Budget of Fun* printed a double-paged spread of cartoons (fig. 25).[74] Mortimer Thomson, under his pen name Philander Doesticks, wrote an oft-quoted apotheosis of the Zouave into the American canon of tall tales. "A fellow with a red bag having sleeves to it for a coat; with two red bags without sleeves to them for trowsers; . . . who

FIG. 25. "Zouave Fashions and Fancies: The Aerial Salutation. The proud Zouaves! Earth is not good enough for them to shake hands on!" *Frank Leslie's Budget of Fun*, September 1, 1860. Courtesy of the American Antiquarian Society.

can tie his legs in a double bow-knot around his neck without previously softening his shin bones in a steam bath . . . who can take a five-shooting revolver in each hand and knock spots out of the ten of diamonds at eighty paces, turning somersaults all the time and firing every shot in the air—that is a Zouave," explained Doesticks.[75] The foppish Ellsworth, who issued his commands with self-conscious panache, had invited this humor with a disarming wink. Even an admiring review acknowledged that the USZC drill was "somewhat ludicrous."[76]

The most influential Zouave satire was Laura Keene's burlesque extravaganza *The Seven Sisters*, which opened on Broadway in November 1860. The first woman in the country to manage a theater, the thirty-four-year-old Keene starred as Diavoline, a daughter of Pluto who traveled to earth and fell in love with a struggling playwright. With the aid of her sisters she secured production of his work by assembling "a feminine corps of Zouaves" that conducted a "Grand Zouave March and Drill." The production at one of the most artistically ambitious and socially respectable theaters in the nation took a decisive step toward what critics would soon call "the leg business." *The Seven Sisters* offered "seducing and fascinating legs," "shockingly low-necked dresses," and "good, tight-fitting clothes, with understandings of fascinating symmetry, and all the hands going into all sorts of positions before you." "Why, it beats the Zouave drill all hollow," concluded the *Clipper*. Another critic agreed that the women "knock Chicago [the USZC] out of sight."[77]

The centrality of Zouaves to *The Seven Sisters* reflected not merely their topicality but a resonance between the projects of Ellsworth and Keene. Like Bryant's Minstrels, whose hit, "Dixie," Diavoline sang at a climactic moment, the theatrical manager saw the USZC as fellow actors who donned costumes and played roles. Her version of the cross-dressed Zouave dance-drill that had percolated through previous stage productions applauded Ellsworth's transgression of military regulations. Playfully taking up his challenge to a competition, Keene poked fun at gender conventions epitomized by the military. Actresses wore revealing costumes in some numbers, but their Zouave uniforms resembled the feminist clothing promoted by Amelia Bloomer. A story about young

FIG. 26. Lotty Hough, Ione Burke, and Abby Leighton in *The Seven Sisters*, 1861. Courtesy of the Harvard Theatre Collection, Harvard University.

women's defiance of the patriarchal lord of the underworld, *The Seven Sisters* identified Zouaves as exemplars of a culture in which women might be both sexy and competent.[78]

The stage responses to the USZC that began before the company's tour reached Washington arrived at a logical culmination in December 1860 when James Nixon engaged the Inkerman Zouaves to make their American debut.[79] They had appeared at the Princess's Theatre in London during the summer, and favorable reviews drifted to the United States. One critic speculated that they had been professional comic actors before entering the French army.[80] New York reviewers agreed that the nine veterans were outstanding performers, but the shows drew poorly despite Nixon's intensive advertising. The disappointment measured a gap between French vaudeville and American theatrical styles. The Inkerman Zouaves performed farces in which they acted women's parts and sang popular songs like their anthem, "Le Rondeau des Zou Zous." The dramatization of the legendary mid-show attack at Inkerman included combat scenes, but the production was not primarily a spectacle. Crowds cheered most enthusiastically at the gala opening, in which the Zouaves of the Garde Lafayette joined in the martial pageantry.[81]

Beyond the stage, Zouaves personified several different sporting ideals. The Zouave, "who can climb a greased pole feet first, carrying a barrel of pork in his teeth," according to Doesticks, embodied animal perfection in muscular development. The French owner of a foal with an auspicious turf pedigree predictably named the horse "Zouave" during the Crimean War. The Zouave label also stood for state-of-the-art technique and exhilarating pleasure that made it appropriate for a racing schooner. The Brooklyn baseball club called the Zouaves shared in these connotations.[82] Thomas Wentworth Higginson, a leading philosopher of the new training regimens, argued more expansively that athletic excellence fostered "superior fineness of organization" encompassing mental as well as physical culture. "Any clown can learn the military manual exercise; but it needs brain-power to drill with the Zouaves," Higginson asserted in the *Atlantic Monthly*. Female ice-skaters in New York added a liberatory tone in favoring "a semi-Zouave costume, with a short skirt of a bright red, and pantalets of the same ruddy hue, fastened tightly around the ancle."[83]

As the crisis at Fort Sumter deepened, Americans in all regions prepared to face war as Zouaves. The New York Zouaves, a group that organized a few days after the USZC visit, began to sleep on boards in the Washington Square armory. The influential Hibernian Society in Charleston asked men to come in uniform to the Saint Patrick's Day ball and women "to appear in Zouave jackets, *à la militaire*." The sons of civic and commercial leaders in Cincinnati organized a Zouave company that performed an exhibition drill before a full house at Pike's Opera House and promoted an upcoming recital by the Zouave Operatic Concert Company in which men and women sang in full Zouave costume.[84]

It was in this atmosphere that the Inkerman Zouaves finally found in New Orleans the warm reception that had eluded them elsewhere. "There is something about the name of 'Zouave' that is highly pleasing to Southern ears in these 'piping times,'" remarked an editor after the troupe opened an engagement at the Academy of Music in March 1861. Louisiana's secession in late January had quickened military recruitment. Fire-eaters and cooperationists joined in planning Zouave companies.[85] Off the stage, the Inkerman ensemble offered instruction as combat veterans. After watching the Orleans Cadets drill under Charles Dreux, the Frenchmen borrowed their muskets and "showed the Cadets many things in the use of the gun and in military gymnastics that had never been dreamt of in their philosophy."[86] At the performances, audiences cheered a reenactment of the taking of the Malakoff with the help of local extras and enjoyed the Inkerman repertory of farces and songs. Zouave Leon drew praise as "the sprightly comedienne whom the ladies relish so well because they know she's a man, and whom the gentlemen admire because he can look and act so much like a woman."[87]

Appreciation of the Inkerman Zouaves did not merely take the form of applause. Enlistment accelerated substantially during their visit. Most notably, French immigrant Georges Auguste Gaston Coppens rapidly raised the first companies of a battalion outfitted in a dark blue Zouave jacket with gold trim, puffy red trousers, and a red fez.[88] At the beginning of April 1861, Coppens' Zouaves headed toward the irksome federal fort in Pensacola as the Inkerman Zouaves headed upriver for the next stop

FIG. 27. Coppens' Zouaves with *vivandière* (*left*), 1861.
Courtesy of the Library of Congress.

on their tour. The Crimean union of warfare and theater was launching a new spinoff.

The Togs of War

The call for Union troops after the fall of Fort Sumter established a recruitment context that soon produced more than 150 new Zouave units in addition to the deployment of companies organized in previous months. Lincoln's mobilization of seventy-five thousand state militia for three months was, in historian John D. Hicks's words, "an amiable legal fiction." Illinois, ordered to provide six regiments as the fourth-largest state, counted fewer than eight hundred uniformed militia in January 1861.[89] Existing companies did answer the April 15 summons, including the Camden Zouaves as Company G of the 4th New Jersey Infantry, the Canton Zouaves as Company F of the 4th Ohio Infantry, and the Johnston Zouave Cadets as Company K of the 3rd Pennsylvania Infantry. From the outset, however, military authorities sought to organize civilians without prewar military affiliations. On the day after Lincoln's proclamation, New York authorized the formation of regiments enlisted to serve for two years; the federal government invited three-year regiments on May 4. Especially in population centers where many men angled for a commission as colonel of a regiment or captain of a company, the decentralized process led to a competitive scramble for volunteers. Adoption of a Zouave identity often proved to be successful recruitment strategy, flexible enough to be applied in units with a variety of aspirations.

New York import merchant Abram Duryée, who had in 1859 stepped down from command of the Seventh Regiment after a decade as its colonel, illustrated the continued Zouave appeal among military perfectionists. Duryée immediately aimed to assemble a model regiment comprised of companies captained largely by fellow alumni of the Seventh, whose current officers had negotiated a special thirty-day stint in the militia call-up that would enable members to accept commissions in volunteer regiments. He chose as his lieutenant colonel Gouverneur Kemble Warren, a West Point salutatorian now back at the Academy as a mathematics professor after nine years in the prestigious engineering corps. With a clear plan of leadership, Duryée labeled his unit the Advance Guard Zouaves and soon attracted a rank and file, for which he arranged training from officers in the regular army. In Indiana, Lew Wallace again demonstrated that substantial military experience might mix with political ambitions. Appointed state adjutant general after the fall of Fort Sumter, he was in a position to handpick the companies he brought together in his Zouave regiment.

Zouave identity was an even more important recruiting tool for men without the military credentials of Duryée or Wallace. Rush C. Hawkins was a good example. He attended Alden Partridge's military academy in Norwich, Vermont, and served in the regular army as a teenager during the Mexican War but was afterward a New York lawyer without militia affiliation. A leading patron of Laura Keene's Theatre, he married into the wealthy Brown family of Providence. After the USZC tour he became a member and soon president of the New York Zouaves, an organization that developed from efforts within the Ninth Regiment of the New York militia to explore the possibility of creating a Zouave company. From this base, Hawkins persuaded New York governor Edwin D. Morgan to authorize him to raise a regiment, which Hawkins branded the First (Lightning) New York Zouaves.[90] New York merchant heir J. Lafayette Riker's organization of a Zouave regiment named for Fort Sumter commander Robert Anderson was a similar story. Twenty-two-year-old Waters W. McChesney, formerly a private in the USZC, put together a company called the National Zouaves and made it the nucleus for a regiment that took the same nickname.

Recruits did not always look for a Zouave unit to emphasize precision drill. An alternative expectation, more in line with anecdotes that had come to the United States from the French army, envisioned Zouaves as street brawlers. Former prizefighter William Wilson was, in the words of unsympathetic *Harper's Weekly*, "a doughty chief of the 'roughs'" who had "figured prominently in almost every mêlée of our turbulent city Democracy." He had earned a place in history by throwing the first chair from the gallery at William Charles Macready in the Astor Place Riot and later served a term as alderman for the predominantly Irish dockworkers on the southern tip of Manhattan. The mustering of Wilson's Zouaves before their training encampment on Staten Island featured much flourishing of Bowie knives and revolvers to punctuate loud vows of "Death to the Plug Uglies," the Baltimore gang that had attacked Massachusetts militia headed to Washington. The regiment closed the boisterous ceremony by singing "The Star-Spangled Banner" and "Dixie's Land."[91] Coppens's six-company battalion, said to have been filled out with recruits from New Orleans jails, was a Confederate counterpart. When the unit headed north from Pensacola, the officers unwisely sat together in the end car, which the soldiers uncoupled at a temporary stop and left behind as they rode to a spree in Montgomery. The incident was a worthy addition to French tales of Zouave tricksters.[92]

Another rowdy New Orleans unit, the Tiger Rifles, demonstrated that a company might maintain its Zouave character after incorporation into a larger unit. Companies organized as Zouaves before or after Fort Sumter often gave up their uniforms to adopt the dress of their regiment; some companies recruited with a Zouave name merged into a regiment before acquiring any distinctive gear. The Tiger Rifles, however, continued to wear their Zouave outfit after assignment to Roberdeau Wheat's First Special Battalion of Louisiana Volunteers. Supplied by a cotton planter and prominent racehorse breeder, the uniform featured white gaiters, roomy blue-and-white striped trousers, a red shirt, a red-trimmed blue or brown jacket, and a red fez with a long blue tassel. German-born office clerks recruited by Hesse-Cassel native Emil Duysing into the De Kalb regiment wore a Zouave uniform that differed from the Prussian style worn by other units of the immigrant regiment. Irish nationalist Thomas Francis Meagher organized a company drilled in Zouave tactics and dressed in a Zouave uniform with a bright green sash to reinforce the Sixty-Ninth Regiment of the New York militia, a participant in the April call-up that reenlisted after ninety days as the 69th New York Volunteer Infantry.[93]

As the Duysing and Meagher companies indicated, Zouave garb could support assertions of ethnic pride that ranged beyond the French origins of the look. A striking example was the American Zouaves, a Missouri regiment whose formation the War Department encouraged as a demonstration that Union loyalty in the state extended beyond German immigrants. Given a difficult recruitment challenge, the turn to a Zouave identity reflected its perceived appeal. The unit incorporated two Zouave companies that formed in Illinois but did not manage to affiliate with a regiment there and also recruited many Irish immigrants in St. Louis.

French-born volunteers did not propel the Zouave movement in the United States but were sufficiently numerous to accentuate the transatlantic theme. Joseph Gerard, a veteran of the African service who had founded the Pittsburgh Zouaves before the USZC tour, remained captain when the company joined the 7th Pennsylvania Infantry. Sculptor Edmond Baudin led the Philadelphia Zouaves into the 18th Pennsylvania Infantry. Severin Barthoult, a sergeant in Baudin's company, later recruited French immigrants as lieutenant in a three-year Zouave regiment, the 114th Pennsylvania. Felix Agnus, a French Zouave in the Italian War, enlisted in Duryée's Zouaves. Georges Auguste Gaston de Coppens's battalion included among its officers the French-born commander and his brother, Marie-Alfred de Coppens. Captain Fulgence de Bordenave had served with the French army in Algeria and the Crimea and spoke no English. Fellow captain Pierre Dominique Nemours Lauve, a fifth-generation native of New Orleans, illustrated the distinctive Gallic heritage of Louisiana. Coppens' Zouaves and the Governor's Guard militia battalion of Zouaves, which became the nucleus of a Louisiana infantry regiment, initially used French as their operational language.[94]

Of the nine Zouave regiments, approximately forty mobilized Zouave companies in non-Zouave regiments, and more than one hundred non-mobilized Zouave units to organize during the ninety days after Fort Sumter, the most closely watched was Ellsworth's undertaking.[95] In a thrilling inspiration, he announced on April 17 that he would raise a Zouave regiment comprised entirely of New York City firemen. The overwhelming response enabled Ellsworth to select his volunteers and led swiftly to the formation of an overflow regiment. Ellsworth chose as his lieutenant colonel thirty-two-year-old Noah Farnham, an elected foreman of a hook-and-ladder company who had served as assistant engineer in the fire department and first lieutenant in the second company of the Seventh Regiment. The captain of each company held a position in a fire company, and the first lieutenants were all USZC veterans. The adjutant was a recent West Point graduate. The Fire Zouaves' uniform, which combined influences of the USZC and the Seventh Regiment, featured a red shirt—the emblem of firemen—along with gray flannel jacket and trousers, both trimmed in red and blue, and a red kepi with a blue band.[96]

Ellsworth's logic was clear. As the *Herald* had observed after a city parade eight months earlier, volunteer firefighters "may be appropriately termed the Zouaves of civil life."[97] Like the French soldiers, American firemen were a social type, remarkable not only for their courage but for a working-class swagger expressed in their clothing and hairstyles. And like the Zouave, the firefighter's identity was inextricably bound to the theater. The firehouse and the theater were prime sites for production of class and gender in the city. The aura of the fire laddie had given rise to an urban folk hero, Mose the Bowery b'hoy, first portrayed by Francis S. Chanfrau at the Olympic Theatre in 1848. Unrefined but instinctively good-hearted, Mose was a sensation in a series of plays that Chanfrau took across the country in the 1850s. Theatrical fictions blended in complex ways with social realities. A skilled butcher, the character sustained the embattled ideals of artisan republicanism. His fondness for a good fight, summarized in Mose's worries that "if I don't have a muss soon, I'll spile," exaggerated firefighters' reputation for violence beyond its grounding in larrikin rumbles and gang connections, which intensified a political threat to volunteer firefighters also pressured by steam engines and insurance companies.[98] Ellsworth offered his recruits a chance for vindication. As in his effort to popularize the effete state militias, he proposed to upgrade the image of the rank-and-file American soldier, which the composition of the regular army had long associated with the urban underclass that filled Billy Wilson's regiment. Ellsworth reasoned that his fit, brave, aggressive, public-spirited firefighters made excellent military material, though the unruly b'hoys would require more nuanced discipline than the USZC counter-jumpers. His friends thought he was up to the task. Lincoln's shrewd assistant private secretary John Hay, who spent a good deal of time with his young contemporary, speculated after an inspection that "he must have run with this crowd some time in his varied career. He knows them and handles them so perfectly."[99]

Ellsworth knew that his men liked a show, and he put on an extravaganza for their April 29 departure from New York. The Fire Zouaves formed at their Canal Street headquarters at noon and received weapons, doubtless delighted to be armed with huge Bowie knives that could double as bayonets. They reassembled to watch the president of the fire department present them with a stand of colors and deliver a speech, gracefully answered by Ellsworth. They then received a grander national flag and regimental banner from Augusta Astor, a South Carolina belle who had married one of the wealthiest men in New York. The regiment marched twenty-four abreast up Broadway, preceded by a platoon of police, officers of the fire department, ten fire companies, and the Zouave drum corps, and followed by sixty-eight additional fire companies and the baggage wagon. They paused at the Astor House to receive an additional stand of colors from ladies at the posh hotel. By five o'clock they had boarded their steamship and heard a speech from Cassius M. Clay, a veteran of legendary knife fights as an antislavery politician in Kentucky.[100]

The Fire Zouaves and their escorts carried more than twenty banners in the parade, one of which was an American flag sent three days earlier by Laura Keene. *The Seven Sisters* continued to flourish, now fortified with patriotic tableaux nominally projected by "Uncle Sam's Magic Lantern." George Wilkes's sporting paper remarked in late April that "the war feeling has given zest to the evolutions of the pretty feminine Zouaves." Keene emphasized the kinship of stage and battle corps in a presentation letter that welcomed the Fire Zouaves to the national spotlight. "Brother Zouaves," saluted their sister Zouave: "I have the honor to present you a flag, which I am well assured you will carry in such a manner as to shed glory on our country and honor on the Zouaves."[101] Popular culture had combined with military institutions to create a role in which thousands of Zouave volunteers would venture their lives.

4

THE PRETTIEST AND BEST UNIFORM IN THE ARMY

*Z*ouaves are familiar straw men in American accounts of the Civil War. Leading historians have treated them as emblematic of an immature country at the outset of the conflict. Zouaves were "amateurs . . . in search of a war that would be all youth and flags and easy valor and rewarding cheers." Their colorful outfits were "ridiculous," even if the respected French army featured units that wore similar uniforms. Wartime pressures supposedly ended such gullibility. Zouaves were "not destined to be hardened by fire into the company of the elect." They serve as a narrative antithesis to the professionalization and emotional toughening that marked the Civil War transformation of the United States. The Zouaves' garish naiveté invites dismissal rather than the scrutiny devoted to the ideological models that unpretentious regular officers like U. S. Grant and William T. Sherman offered the postwar nation.[1]

This interpretation has tended to reduce the Zouave experience to the saga of the Fire Zouaves, the most widely publicized regiment on either side during the first months of the war. After their April 29 departure from New York, the Fire Zouaves advanced to Washington and bunked in the chamber of the House of Representatives in the U.S. Capitol. Their sojourn provided abundant newspaper copy, most dramatically when they applied their firefighting skills to a May 9 blaze at the Willard Hotel. Two weeks later, Ellsworth arranged for them to take part in the

opening Union expedition to occupy Alexandria on the day after the secession of Virginia. The twenty-four-year-old colonel began the operation
by personally removing a large Confederate flag flying from the roof of
a hotel, only to be shot and killed by the innkeeper on descending the
staircase. The first martyrdom of the war prompted national mourning
and demands for vengeance but also criticism of Ellsworth for recklessness.[2] Debate over the Fire Zouaves intensified after the first battle of
Bull Run, at which Ellsworth's successor, Noah Farnham, fell mortally
wounded. Several officers in the regular army, including the brigade and
division commanders, filed reports sharply critical of the regiment for
breaking and running under fire. Other witnesses maintained that much
of the unit regrouped quickly and fought tenaciously through the day.
Many commentators, most vigorously the *New York Times*, pounced on
the Fire Zouaves without considering the extent to which regular officers
had chosen an attractive scapegoat for the Union defeat. In turn the *New
York Tribune* pointed out that the rancor of the *Times* reflected eagerness
to instill discipline not only among volunteer soldiers but also within the
Bowery society represented by volunteer fire companies.[3]

As the story of the Fire Zouaves was more complex than a parable of
bravado and comeuppance, the significance of Zouaves in the Civil War
extended far beyond the 11th New York. Association of Zouaves exclusively with the early stages of the war is misleading, for they participated
in almost every crucial battle from Big Bethel to Five Forks. Zouave regiments were most prominent in the eastern theater, from the Peninsula
campaign to Antietam and Gettysburg and the Wilderness and beyond,
but the 11th Indiana and 8th Missouri fought with Grant from Fort Donel-
son to Vicksburg, the 76th Pennsylvania charged at Battery Wagner, and
the 17th New York Veteran Volunteers marched with Sherman to the sea
and through the Carolinas. The 155th Pennsylvania was one of the regiments that accepted the Confederate surrender at Appomattox.

Like the regular infantry, Zouaves comprised a small proportion of
the Union army but exercised a disproportionate influence as an ideal
type. The two groups were similar in size. The regular infantry accounted
for nineteen of the almost seventeen hundred federal infantry regiments

mustered across the four years of the war, and the Zouaves constituted about twenty-eight regiments.[4] It was not the Zouaves but the regulars who gradually disappeared under pressure. Unable to recruit replacements for their losses, the last bedraggled regular infantry units withdrew from the field in fall 1864. The Union army then included fifteen Zouave regiments, all of which served through the end of the war.[5]

Zouave persistence at home matched this endurance in the field. The simplest illustration was the wartime ubiquity of *The Seven Sisters*. Laura Keene's production was the show that best held audiences amid the Broadway downturn that followed Fort Sumter, and one wag proposed to "transfer Capt. [Abby] Leighton and the other officers of the company to our volunteer army at Washington."[6] The run ended in August 1861 after a record-setting 253 performances, but manager Frank Rivers began the road career of *The Seven Sisters* immediately afterward at the Howard Theatre in Boston. Keene brought her version to Baltimore in fall 1862, by which point the show was helping to popularize the Union recruiting song "Rally 'Round the Flag." Ben DeBar's production in St. Louis sparked controversy in July 1863 when the Confederate sympathizer tried to omit the song and accompanying parade of the national banner. John E. McDonough was the most relentless impresario. He staged *The Seven Sisters* in Washington in December 1861, with Susan Denin in command of the Zouave drill, after which McDonough toured various casts from Portland, Maine, south to Norfolk and west across the Mississippi River. President Lincoln joined his son Tad at a Washington performance at Grover's Theatre in March 1864. Three months later McDonough enjoyed a successful run with Effie Germon during the Philadelphia Sanitary Fair, and in November he was back in Washington at Ford's Theatre with a Zouave squad led by Charlotte Crabtree, billed as "the sauciest, most piquant, and vivacious star of the present period." McDonough returned the show to Broadway in late May 1865, a bookend to its premiere in the weeks after Lincoln's election.[7]

The continuous presence of Zouaves did not reflect mere inertia. Several of the most memorable units organized early in the war mustered out after two or three years. Half the regiments wearing Zouave uniforms in late 1864 had adopted them within the last two years. This group shared genealogical ties that showed the importance of Zouaves in the wartime construction of the Union army as a grand spectacle. Zouaves on stage also developed new acts. Erotic cross-dressing became more transgressive, and adaptations of military drill competed more directly with army exercises.

The extent to which the Zouave personified martial and theatrical performance made the figure a multivalent force. As scholars have recently pointed out, the war did not exclusively foster American realism and pragmatism; it also deepened the sensationalism and sentimentality that pervaded antebellum culture.[8] Individualists marked by their resistance to standard-issue uniforms, Zouaves became associated with both the zest for adventure and the immersion in pathos that characterized public images of rank-and-file soldiers. These attributes helped to make Zouave identity useful for women and African Americans. At the same time, preeminent wartime realist Winslow Homer highlighted Zouaves in paintings that juxtaposed the solidity of camaraderie against illusions of romance and depicted military service as an acceptance of random chance. Far from a superficial fad destined to be sloughed off by the logic of the war, Zouaves struck thoughtful observers as essential to the national drama.

Equal in All Respects to the Regulars and Better Drilled

Zouave identity in the Civil War encompassed several variable dimensions. Uniforms were the most obvious markers, but wartime conditions often interrupted the supply of distinctive clothing. Some groups retained a strong sense of Zouave character without wearing Zouave dress. Although the 19th Illinois had a dozen officers who toured with Ellsworth's US Zouave Cadets (USZC), including a regimental commander, only a few companies wore Zouave uniforms for a short time. The soldiers considered themselves Zouaves and operated a regimental newspaper called the *Zouave Gazette*. The 73rd New York, which originated as overflow in the recruitment of Ellsworth's regiment, embraced the nickname "Second Fire Zouaves" though the men wore dark blue *chasseur*-style button-up jackets that flared at the waist.[9] Uniforms varied considerably among units that wore Zouave designs. Regiments also differed in the extent to which they adopted other characteristics associated with the French Zouaves or the USZC. The most important common feature was excellence in drill technique. In this proficiency Zouave tendencies overlapped with the culture of the regular army, and career officers became key sponsors of Zouave units. Far more than the regulars, however, influential Zouave units personified the organization of Civil War armies into a regime of spectacle, administered in frequent troop reviews, and demonstrated the potential of the military as a platform of public performance.[10]

Zouaves institutionalized the unit autonomy in clothing that shaped the militia and carried into Union and Confederate armies at the outbreak of the war. Southern supply chains developed less fully, and a group like the Tiger Rifles in the First Louisiana Special Battalion had to rely on private sources and alternation with standard issue to keep their red-trimmed blue or brown Zouave jackets with baggy blue-and-white striped trousers and red fezzes wearable until the sixty-four survivors of the battalion were distributed among other Louisiana units after Roberdeau Wheat's death in the battle of Gaines' Mill.[11] In the North, in contrast, depots operated by the quartermaster general's office in New York and Philadelphia provided Zouave clothing until the end of the war.[12] Regiments made up a spectrum of flamboyance. At the gaudy pole were the 53rd New York, which imploded within six months of its organization in August 1861, and the more durable 114th Pennsylvania, for which founding colonel Charles Collis imported large quantities of French cloth later sewn by contractors under the supervision of the Schuylkill Arsenal. At the humbler end was the 8th Missouri, which wore standard-issue uniforms except for dark blue Zouave jackets with red trim along the edges, a large trefoil on each front panel, and complementary detail work on the cuffs.[13]

Regular officers recognized Zouave dress as a repudiation of army convention and sometimes bristled in response. Billy Wilson's 6th New York began the war in Florida, where two companies were detailed to Fort Jefferson in Key West. Garrison commander Lewis G. Arnold ordered the volunteers to burn their Zouave uniforms on arrival and replaced them with standard issue. John W. Phelps, an 1836 graduate of West Point who retired shortly before the war and quickly became a brigadier general in the volunteers, asked a gaily clad soldier at Ship Island, Mississippi, in 1862 to identify his outfit and was told that the private belonged to the Boston Fire Zouaves, a company in the 30th Massachusetts. Phelps sniffed that he "thought there was a circus here, and you were one of the clowns."[14]

Zouave fashion nevertheless did not lack for admirers. The formation of eight Union Zouave regiments and several enduring companies in late summer and fall 1861 to join the nine regiments organized during the first ninety days of the war indicated that Ellsworth's death and the controversy over the Fire Zouaves' performance at Bull Run had not shattered Zouave appeal.[15] When the 23rd Pennsylvania returned from ninety-days service and attracted few reenlistments for three years, David Birney reorganized the regiment around the Gymnast Zouaves, the leading Zouave company in Philadelphia. The unit raised fifteen companies dressed in Zouave uniforms from August 1861 until the clothing wore out after six months, which prompted lamentations for "the natty Zouave suit." The regiment remained known as Birney's Zouaves.[16] Other observers shared in appreciation for Zouave style. Quartermaster General Montgomery Meigs promised that one Zouave regiment's uniforms would be "the handsomest things in the army." Lew Wallace, a leading Zouave theorist, praised the attire of his 11th Indiana because "the effect was to magnify the men." After a visit to the 53rd New York, who aspired to emulate the French Imperial Guard in a costume featuring an ornately trimmed blue jacket, a sash of lighter blue, a yellow-trimmed vest, and a red fez, a newspaper correspondent opined that "it is a dress which gives the human figure a barbaric picturesqueness."[17]

Zouaves stressed the practicality of their wardrobe. They considered their garb "the best uniform for an active campaign" because the sash provided warmth and support, because the capacious trouser pockets were "almost equivalent to a second haversack," and especially because the whole ensemble was so comfortable. A soldier who joined the 9th New York in September 1862 and was obliged to transfer to a non-Zouave unit to complete his three-year commitment after Hawkins' Zouaves returned home in May 1863 complained that by comparison his new clothing was "stiff, clumsy, outlandish."[18]

Lurking behind such assessments was an awareness that Zouave dress offered an alternative to traditional enforcement of strict discipline on soldiers' bodies. When the Fire Zouaves' shoddy first uniforms began to fall apart six weeks after leaving New York, they received standard-issue replacements, including the uncomfortable leather neckstock. Arthur Alcock, a newspaper correspondent serving in the regiment, reported that the solution "does not please the boys, who like the loose, easy Zouave rig, and don't want to hold up their heads." Two weeks later the regiment gladly switched to a blue Zouave jacket, a red firefighter's shirt, and a red fez. Alcock deemed it "a very handsome uniform and one that becomes the boys amazingly." Across the many clothing variations in the separate Zouave regiments, a private in the 146th New York best summarized widespread satisfaction with the union of style and serviceability when he exclaimed that his outfit was "the prettiest and best uniform in the army."[19]

The debate over a potential impracticality of Zouave panache, the use of bright colors, underscored conceptualization of the uniform as a source of morale. Many observers expressed concern that red fezzes or red trousers made soldiers easier targets for enemy riflemen. George Wilkes, voice of the New York flash press, most fully refuted this argument. Pointing out that the British infantry wore red jackets, Wilkes noted that much of the aimed fire over any significant distance focused on officers and artillerymen. Moreover, he stressed, "more is gained to the army at large, by pleasing the fancy of the soldier, than is lost by the soldier in the extra risk it may subject him to." In the spirit of the Broadway gambling "sports" whom William Howard Russell called "the most over-dressed men I ever saw," Wilkes defended sartorial extravagance against the aesthetic restraint of the standard-issue U.S. Army uniform. The Zouaves, he wrote, were "gay, dashing, saucy, bold and confident." They drew strength from a popularity that "brings more soldiers to the [enlistment] roll than any other single invitation." Even if conspicuousness did cause additional casualties, "their fine clothes doubtless nurture that feeling of personal pride which is such a valuable element of courage."[20] Wilkes's logic focused on the battlefield but also applied to counterculture resistance to middle-class conformity in the city.

Beyond their uniforms, Civil War regiments incorporated several elements of the French Zouave image. Emil Duysing's company in the 41st New York showed familiarity with Zouave iconography when fifty of its members marched down Broadway to leave for the front with cats perched on their knapsacks.[21] Zoo-Zoos in many units wore their hair shorn closely in a cut designed to secure a snug fit for a fez.[22] Volunteers had little time for the physical training associated with French Zouaves, though a few units temporarily maintained a gymnasium.[23] Zouave regiments were not unique within the Union army in their enthusiasm for staging theatrical performances, but they were well represented among martial thespians and stood at the forefront in some cases. The 23rd Pennsylvania built a theater where the men put on nightly vaudeville shows while encamped in Bladensburg, Maryland, during winter 1861. The five-hundred-seat playhouse that the 9th New York adapted from Confederate barracks on Roanoke Island in summer 1862 became important to regimental identity and drew newspaper attention.[24]

The stage inclinations confirmed that Civil War *zouaverie*, like its Parisian counterpart, was an urban phenomenon. New York supplied more than half the Union Zouave regiments and together with Pennsylvania accounted for three-fourths. Additional groups came from Chicago, Cincinnati, Newark, and St. Louis. The most significant addition to the New Orleans–based Confederates was the company of South Carolina Zouave Volunteers recruited for Hampton's Legion in fall 1861 on the scaffolding of the Charleston Zouave Cadets.[25]

Emulation of the French was meaningful, but the USZC left an even more profound precedent in the exaltation of exhibition drill, which shined in the program of large-scale reviews developed by George B. McClellan and sustained throughout the war. These exercises were not the ordinary practice of the regular army. Dress parade was a hallowed daily ritual at every post and cultivated high standards of drill coordination and equipment maintenance, but many antebellum military installations housed only a single company. Public audiences were rare, as most of the army was scattered across the trans-Mississippi West. Paragon of professionalism Winfield Scott, "Old Fuss and Feathers," did not conduct elaborate troop reviews as commanding general in the Mexican-American War.[26] McClellan, who had witnessed massive military assemblies as a member of the Delafield Commission, launched an exhaustive series of reviews at the brigade and division levels as part of his effort to train and motivate the Army of the Potomac in fall 1861. He designed these events as spectacles that would "accustom the regiments to move together and see each other" so as to "infuse *esprit de corps* and mutual emulation." The climax of this initiative was a grand review at Bailey's Cross Roads on November 20 that brought together seven divisions or about seventy thousand soldiers. McClellan rode through the lines with the brigade and division commanders and staff officers and visiting dignitaries for an hour and a half, after which the army marched before the general-in-chief and the president for three hours. More than fifty bands provided constant music. Opened to the public, the extravaganza drew a crowd estimated at twenty to thirty thousand.[27]

Observers readily linked such performances to the European army reviews that reached a theatrical zenith in the Paris of Napoleon III. Color rather than line animated the French art of the military review, but McClellan domesticated the foreign example into step with Ellsworth's conception of Zouaves and antecedent inspiration in holiday militia demonstrations. The Army of the Potomac held brigade-level competitions in November 1861 to recognize the regiments that achieved the highest level of perfection in drill. The prize was a set of uniforms with accompanying gear that Quartermaster General Meigs had ordered from Paris. The uniforms were in the *chasseur* pattern, but winners widely understood them to be "real Zouave dress."[28]

Celebration of meticulous drill brought distinction to several regiments influenced by the USZC. The 11th Indiana maintained an extraordinary standard long after Lew Wallace left the regiment for higher ranks; passing through New York on a reenlistment furlough in March 1864, the unit put on an exhibition in City Hall Park sponsored by "friends who consider them the best-drilled regiment in the service."[29] Led by so many USZC alumni, the 19th Illinois also enjoyed a drill reputation as "second to none in the West."[30] The 44th New York, a select group recruited after Ellsworth's death and known as "Ellsworth's Avengers," similarly numbered several former USZC members among its officers, including the founding colonel, and became a highly regarded drill unit.[31] A soldier in the 9th New York, which originated in the New York response to the USZC, wrote in October 1862 that "a parade is a beautiful thing to look at, and ours attracts a multitude of gazes from the other regiments." The 10th New York, also rooted in Ellsworth's tour, quickly pushed out its former USZC founding colonel but remained sufficiently adept to win a corps-wide competition for extra furlough based on drill and appearance in early 1863.[32]

The regiment that most fully realized the Zouave potential in this regime was the 5th New York. Its flair for performance followed logically from its origins in the Seventh Regiment of the New York State Militia, but its chief choreographer was former West Point instructor Gouverneur K. Warren, who took control of the unit upon Abram Duryée's early elevation to brigade command. While the unit was stationed in Baltimore from late July 1861 through late March 1862, Warren paralleled McClellan's efforts in Virginia with his own course of intensive training and public exposition. When the 5th New York joined the Army of the Potomac for the Peninsula campaign, McClellan paired the regiment with the 10th New York in a brigade otherwise composed of regular infantry. Artillery officer Charles Wainwright recorded in his journal that Warren's volunteers were "equal in all respects to the regulars and better drilled." McClellan soon began to feature the well-publicized regiment, which included an officer who wrote for the *New York Times,* in grand reviews like the exercise held for the benefit of Spanish general Juan Prim in June 1862. The 5th New York remained a showcase troop until the expiration of its two-year enlistment in May 1863. Only a month before mustering out, the unit performed an exhibition in a review of 100,000 soldiers that General Joseph Hooker staged for Lincoln, who reportedly saluted the Zouaves as "the best-drilled regiment in the Army of the Potomac."[33]

The 5th New York was especially important because it became a seedbed for other Zouave regiments. After Warren sacrificed a shocking percentage of his men to save a battery at Second Bull Run, he sought and received McClellan's permission to organize a Zouave brigade in September 1862. When recruitment for the unit billed as the Second Duryée Regiment started slowly, Warren turned to two recently organized regiments commanded by West Point graduates. Colonel Patrick O'Rorke of the 140th New York had been Warren's favorite student at West Point, and Colonel Kenner Garrard of the 146th New York had graduated the year after Warren. Both groups imitated the drill culture of the 5th New York, commanded by Abram Duryée's distant cousin Hiram Duryea after Warren advanced to brigadier in an ascent that would eventually take him to corps commander. Garrard's men received their Zouave uniforms in June 1863, and O'Rorke's men received their set in January 1864 at the same time as the 155th Pennsylvania, another constituent of the brigade. One soldier wrote home that the first full-scale review of the Zouave Brigade was "the prettiest sight I have seen in the army" and "called beautiful by the large numbers of civilians who witnessed it."[34] Meanwhile several former officers of the discharged 5th New York recruited an organization that became the 5th New York Veteran Volunteers, which also joined the Zouave Brigade. The command received appropriate reinforcement in October 1864 when the unexpired enlistments in Ellsworth's Avengers were transferred to the 140th New York and the 146th New York. The Second Duryée Zouaves, the first step in Zouave expansion, mustered in as the 165th New York and began its service in New Orleans rather than with the Zouave Brigade in Virginia.[35]

Soldiers in the 5th New York and its progeny, like soldiers in the more immediate descendants of the USZC, learned orthodox preparations for battle. Warren trained the 5th New York in Hardee's tactics for light infantry and McClellan's bayonet exercise. Ellsworth's manual for the USZC reappeared in new editions, and James H. DeWitt, a USZC alumnus who served as major in the 72nd Pennsylvania, published a guide to Zouave tactics revised by John M. Gosline, commander of the 95th Pennsylvania. Zouave distinctiveness was largely a matter of emphasis within a standard range of options. For example, Hardee had outlined procedures for loading a rifle while the soldier was lying on his back, but Ellsworth had highlighted the common-sensical practice and associated it closely with Zouaves.[36]

The key to Zouave drill culture was a recognition that drill did not consist exclusively of preparation for battlefield situations. The hallmark drill of wartime Zouaves was McClellan's bayonet exercise. Bayonet skills instilled confidence and proved useful in combat even if edged weapons inflicted fewer than 0.4 percent of battlefield wounds. The 9th New York executed one of the most celebrated bayonet charges of the war in the battle of Roanoke Island in February 1862.[37] Zouave levels of bayonet dexterity and synchronization, however, mostly served to look impressive in reviews. A private in the 5th New York who saw that "the bayonet exercise is much like fencing" wrote to his mother that "it is a good exercise but I think that target practice would be more useful."[38] In harmony with their splashy uniforms, Zouaves' showmanship addressed audiences other than the enemy. Experienced commanders learned to incorporate the bayonet exercise into a dress parade.[39] A reputation for drill excellence fostered regimental pride and eagerness to maintain the esteem of other units and high-ranking commanders. The spotlight also created opportunities to represent the army to government officials and other civilians and translate the messiness of warfare into a flourish of armed precision.

Zouaves combined the disciplinary mechanism of the public spectacle with the varied management patterns of Civil War regiments. Lew Wallace argued that the relationship between officers and other ranks should

FIG. 28. Civil War bayonet drill of Duryée's Zouaves. *Harper's Weekly* 26 (April 22, 1882). Courtesy of the University of South Carolina Libraries.

be grounded in "the French *camaraderie*" rather than the British-style enforcement of subordination that characterized the U.S. Army. Rush Hawkins expressed similar sentiments but did not succeed in implementing them. The 155th Pennsylvania was a better example of *esprit de corps*. Founding colonel Edward Jay Allen, a railroad contractor, would "talk to privates just as if they were his equal in rank," and his successor Alfred Pearson, a Pittsburgh lawyer, capably boxed, sang, and pitched quoits with the enlisted men. The 5th New York was in contrast notorious for a rigid hierarchy that merged Warren's experience in the regular army and the shift from commercial to industrial labor relations signaled by the passage of leadership from the importer Duryée to the manufacturer Duryea. Future regimental historian Alfred Davenport recorded in July 1862 that "we all without exception hate our officers." Duryea's successor, Cleveland Winslow, continued the martinet style of command, which influenced his direction of drill performances as well as his imposition of punishments for rule infractions. Davenport considered him a "small brained dandy" and seethed that "he makes a fool of us trying to show off."[40]

Whether administered collegially or brusquely, the Zouave enactment of army pageantry illustrated the conjunction of display and surveillance. One practical feature of the distinctive uniforms was that they made it more difficult for a straggler to avoid detection of the unit to which he belonged. The 114th Pennsylvania exemplified the monitorial effects of Zouave prominence. The unit expanded from a bodyguard company for General Nathaniel Banks into a regiment in August 1862, shortly after Congress eliminated regimental bands, but Colonel Charles Collis arranged private funding for a fifteen-piece band that became the driving force of the unit after the battles of Fredericksburg, Chancellorsville, and Gettysburg. Because the regiment could supply excellent music and present a fine appearance, the 114th Pennsylvania served as headquarters guard for division commander David Birney from August 1863 to March 1864 and Army of the Potomac commander George Meade for the last year of the war. As in a troop review, the assignments brought the Zouaves into direct contact with high-ranking military brass and distinguished civilian visitors to the army. Such duties of representation encouraged high standards of martial pomp and drill precision.[41]

The Grand Review held in the nation's capital in May 1865 to celebrate Union victory marked the culmination of the review culture inaugurated in fall 1861. The 114th Pennsylvania marched at the head of the
reconfigured Zouave Brigade, followed by the 5th New York Veteran Volunteers, 140th New York, and 146th New York. Other Zouave regiments
participated elsewhere in the two-day parade along Pennsylvania Avenue.
Newspapers noted that the Zouaves "relieve[d] the general sameness of
uniforms" and "appeared to great advantage yesterday in all the hues of
the rainbow."[42] Perhaps the most remarkable military ceremony in American history, the Grand Review underscored the importance of spectacle in
the organization of Civil War armies, within which no element was more
spectacular than the Zouaves.

Zouave Stories

"They tell many good stories about the Zouaves," reported a correspondent for *New York Illustrated News* in September 1862. His example concerned a sentinel with an itchy trigger finger after Confederates killed several of his comrades on picket duty. The guard challenged a visitor, who
gave the countersign on demand. The Zouave conceded that the password
was correct but added that "I'm darn sorry, for I haven't shot a man these
two days." The variation on the firefighter Mose, spoiling for a "muss,"
suggests how much the American Zouave image still owed to the theatrical
milieu from which it emerged and how often accounts of Zouaves followed
familiar plotlines.[43] Beneath these generic patterns, the figure of the Zouave entered into wartime innovations in the relationship between genre
and narrative. Building on the precedent of the Crimean War, the Civil
War was a media phenomenon of astonishing proportions, experienced
by soldiers and civilians through transformations in the technology and
business structure of journalism that radiated across literature, the visual
arts, and popular music. The colorful Zouave offered an optimal protagonist in a crisis of national fragmentation that valorized the anecdote as a
historical record.[44] The stories told about Zouaves differed, but the most
flamboyant of volunteers personified the fusion of form and content and
thematized the place of the individual in the impersonal world of the war.

The dominant mode of storytelling in mid-nineteenth-century America was sentimental, and countless Zouave tales supported Mose's observation that the boys "may be a little rough outside, but they're all right here. (*Touches breast*)."[45] This heart tugging pulled several ways. Like his French vaudeville counterpart, the American Zouave was an incurable romantic. One newspaper declared in 1863 that "'Zouave' everywhere is but another name for courage and daring in war and love." Songs like "My Love He Is a Zou-Zu" acknowledged that this disposition did not necessarily guarantee fidelity ("a sweetheart can be found in each State, I am told, / By a young man, a Zou-Zu, only 19 years old"), but Zouaves nonetheless made delightful images for wartime Valentine's Day cards ("How my fond heart doats / On your trowser petticoats").[46]

New York litterateur Charles Dawson Shanly's poem "The Brier-Wood Pipe" was a popular depiction of the lovelorn Zouave published in *Vanity Fair* in July 1861 and widely anthologized after the war. Shanly's narrator was a Fire Zouave sitting down for a moonlight smoke after picket duty. Musing in the spirit of Mose ("I'm a rough, at best, bred up to the row and the riot; / But a softness comes over my heart, when all are asleep and quiet"), the Zouave slips into a reverie about the rich, beautiful woman who gave him a havelock at the regiment's departure from New York ("the lovely golden-haired lady ever in dreams I see"). He snaps to attention at the sound of reveille ("devils are we for battle—will there be angels there?") and kisses farewell to the pipe that brings him the sustaining fantasy of sexual fulfillment.[47]

Zouaves also tapped the vein of sentimentality centered on children. Zouave uniforms were popular costumes for children, and toy Zouave soldiers sold widely. Tad Lincoln owned a Zouave suit and a Zouave doll. *Harper's Weekly* published a Christmas story about a dolls' gala that featured a romance between the Parisian belle of the ball and an inexpensive but dazzling Zouave purchased at a benefit fair for soldiers.[48] Teddy Roosevelt's parents commissioned a photographic portrait of their four-year-old son wearing his open jacket, sash, and baggy trousers, and holding a fez with simulated turban. Thomas Nast highlighted this play kit in two paintings with which he tried to make the leap from sketch journalism

FIG. 29. Thomas Nast, *The Domestic Blockade,* 1862.
Courtesy of the Library of Congress.

to fine art. *The Little Zouave* (1862) and *The Domestic Blockade* (1862) situate the outfit in the bourgeois home, the social and economic environment that had shaped childhood in the nineteenth century. *Domestic Blockade* dramatizes the national significance of the Zouave-clad consumer by transposing the Civil War into a half-kidding but half-serious confrontation between well-to-do youth and an Irish immigrant domestic worker. Nast redoubled his Republican sympathies by circulating the picture in the middle-class media of the chromolithograph and carte de visite.[49]

Zouaves appeared often in the representations of suffering and death at the core of Civil War sentimentality. The first casualty to appear on the cover of *Harper's Weekly* was a Zouave in a Washington hospital. Mat-

FIG. 30. Matthew Brady, *The Wounded Zouave*, 1863.
Courtesy of the Library of Congress.

thew Brady produced an American version of Roger Fenton's staged photograph of a wounded Zouave during the Crimean War, which Thomas
Jones Barker had copied in the foreground of his *Allied Generals before
Sebastopol* (1859), a painting widely distributed in print versions. Brady's
composition recalled Harriet Beecher Stowe's best-selling melodrama
Uncle Tom's Cabin (1851) by highlighting the solicitude of a Black army
servant for a distressed soldier. Songs, poems, and stories recounted the
deaths of Zouaves.[50]

The most mawkish vehicle was the automaton *Dying Zouave*, which
debuted at the Museum of Anatomy in 1868. Apparently shot in the breast,
the moving wax figure opened and closed its eyes, wheezed, quivered, and
oozed out its lifeblood under the mournful gaze of a Sister of Charity. The
French-made apparatus wore a French uniform, but American promoters in the wake of the Civil War urged an immediate emotional connection to the scene. An advertisement called it "marvelous and touching,

all day." P. T. Barnum bought the automaton by 1870 and featured it the next year in his first great traveling circus. Charles Caleb Ward's painting *Coming Events Cast Their Shadows Before* (1871) recorded Barnum's poster for the *Dying Zouave* alongside a poster for Ann E. Leak, a woman born with no arms. Much more enticing than the nearby announcement of a YMCA lecture by temperance advocate John B. Gough, the circus placards captivate a family who fail to notice that their son is learning from Barnum the art of manipulation. The tear-jerking Zouave points toward the perceived vulnerability of sentimental society to confidence schemes, a major theme of mid-nineteenth-century culture.[51]

Maudlin narratives could challenge support for the war by highlighting its intimate costs and forcing comparison of loyalties to family and nation. "Song of the Volunteer's Wife" (1861), in which a Zouave's spouse learns of his death and slides with her children toward starvation, illustrated this potential.[52] Conversely, Zouaves were famously effusive patriots, as the evolution of *The Seven Sisters* indicated. Another prominent example was William S. Budworth's song "Zouave Johnny from Bull Run," which was popular enough to earn a place in Stephen Foster's montage of hit wartime lyrics, "The Song of All Songs." The ditty made a virtue from Fire Zouaves' boasts of their performance at Bull Run and provided a flag-waving rank-and-file endorsement of Union leadership from Scott and McClellan to Meade and Grant.[53]

If sentimental stories described the war as a period of individual sacrifice, sensational stories emphasized wartime opportunities for individual adventure. Picket duty was a frequent setting because it took place alone or in small groups. John Rogers's tabletop plaster sculpture of *The Picket Guard* (1861) featured a Zouave platoon in a composition that launched the domestic artist's profitable wartime career.[54] Like their French counterparts, Zouaves won fame for their unconventional escapades. A soldier from the 73rd New York contributed a letter to the *Sunday Mercury* in November 1862 that compared an upright corporal with "your real, harum-scarum, devil-may-care, out and out, New York born, Bowery-raised, dare-devil, Rebel-terror, fireman F.Z." who laughed at danger, murdered English grammar, and addressed the company officers by their Christian

names. "It is he who is the life of a bayonet-charge," the soldier concluded. The commander of the 54th Ohio called his regiment "as bloody
a set of preaching, praying, stealing, fighting riproaring zouaves as the
war turns out." Louisiana Zouaves remained legendary for hard drinking
and no-holds-barred fighting long after the units disintegrated under the
weight of heavy casualties.[55]

The Zouave fit squarely into the narrative role of the trickster, an antebellum staple of tall-tale humorous literature. A typical anecdote recalled
a Zouave sentinel who confiscated the horse of a Rebel who had taken
a loyalty oath, as the horse had not taken the oath. "Zouaves sly, shut
one eye / When they go to sleep," attested the song "The Zouave Boys."
Zouaves' reputation for self-parody animated spoofs of army life, including several question-and-answer sketches ("Q. What in your opinion, is
the most useful movement in the Zouave tactics? A. Running"). George
Arnold's letters to Vanity Fair in the character of McArone pointed out
that the fashionability of the Zouave, like that of the eighteenth-century
macaroni, thrived on caricature.[56] Robert Newell, writing as Orpheus C.
Kerr, also set several letters among the Zouaves. One report began with
Kerr "witnessing the most mournful sight that ever made a man feel as
though he had been peeling onions all the week," the slow death of a
roguish Fire Zouave named Shorty but ended with a postscript that "since
writing the above, I have learned that no such occurrence took place" and
that Shorty never enlisted in the Zouaves and was alive and well in New
York. Within the first few months of the war, the satirist questioned the
reliability of the eyewitness testimony that would exercise such influence
in the coming years.[57]

Some sensational anecdotes about the Fire Zouaves sought to discredit
them—like claims that the flags presented on Broadway had been found
in a trash can in Virginia, or that deserters from the regiment had traded
clothes with plantation slaves—and this pattern deepened after the New
York City draft riots of July 1863.[58] The army had disbanded the 11th New
York more than a year earlier after several reorganizations and a politi-
cized set of congressional hearings on Bull Run before the Joint Committee on the Conduct of the War.[59] The recruitment push that followed the
discharge of two-year regiments brought an effort to revitalize the 11th

New York, and the officer leading that project became one of the most notable victims of the riots, beaten to death and dragged naked through the streets. Recently returned members of the 5th New York and 9th New York were prominent in attempts to suppress the upheaval. Cleveland Winslow fired a howitzer repeatedly into a crowd and narrowly escaped when one of the former enlisted men in Duryea's Zouaves tried to shoot him with a Sharps rifle. The crisis led elites to conflate several sets of working and lower classes and identify them with the Fire Zouaves, whom one veteran of the urban scene called a "regiment of coves." Newspaper editor Henry Morford's novel *Days of Shoddy* (1863), written in the months after the riots, combined fiction with a detailed history of the Fire Zouaves through the battle of Bull Run. His view of the "miserable poltroonery" of the unit was shared by an anonymous novelist who declared that "the days when we thought the Five Points would fight, and that shysters could command, went out with Fire Zouaves and their kind."[60]

This judgment would persuade some later Civil War historians, but the most astute wartime witness to the possibilities opened by military mobilization saw different significance in Zouaves. Twenty-eight-year-old Winslow Homer's 1864 painting *The Brier-Wood Pipe* (fig. 31) presented a crisp rebuttal to Charles Dawson Shanly's poem of the same title. Homer's Zouaves do not wallow in a pipe dream about a beautiful woman with golden hair and jeweled hands and a white robe. Instead, one Zouave pauses between puffs while he intently watches a fellow Zouave complete the artisanal task of carving a pipe from the hard root seen in the lower left of the picture. Pleasant and durable brier pipes had only begun to win popularity in the 1850s.[61] The soldiers' sociability recalls the reputation for male friendship that French Zouaves earned through their relations with Highlanders, reinforced in the United States by several units since the USZC. By situating camaraderie not in shared danger or privation but in craftsmanship and the recreational art of smoking especially associated with Zouaves, Homer suggested that wartime fraternity offered a useful model for peacetime society.

Homer returned to the implications of army leisure in his most ambitious painting to date, the semi-monumental *Pitching Quoits* (fig. 32) from 1865. Quoits was an old Scottish game that had migrated to colonial Amer-

FIG. 31. Winslow Homer, *The Brier-Wood Pipe,* 1864.
Courtesy of the Cleveland Museum of Art.

ica but only blossomed into popularity in New York in the years before the war. The city had several clubs by 1860; the New York Club, founded by a volunteer firefighter active in local Democratic politics, counted seventy members. Matches often took place at taverns or billiard saloons that maintained quoits grounds. Players routinely competed for cash purses and prompted side wagers.[62]

Rather than casting proper quoits, or iron rings, Homer's Zouaves play "army fashion," in the words of art critic George Arnold, with horseshoes. The substitution was significant as more than a wartime improvisation. Pitching horseshoes was not yet a standard sport like quoits, but horseshoes had long served as a symbol of luck. In recording the transfer of tavern diversions to the military, Homer touched on the gambling rampant throughout the army and highlighted the element of chance. The stakes of wartime fortune were obvious. In April 1863 a caisson abruptly

FIG. 32. Winslow Homer, *Pitching Quoits*, 1865. Courtesy of the Harvard Art Museums / Fogg Museum, gift of Mr. and Mrs. Frederic Haines Curtiss.

exploded in an artillery camp near the 5th New York, whose uniforms Homer depicted, and burning fragments fell on Zouaves playing quoits. Alfred Davenport considered the incident "a curious illustration of the influence of war in making men thoughtless of life or death."[63] Soldiers learned to accept fortuity. Beyond this common military fate, Union soldiers represented a society increasingly propelled by capitalist organization of risk. Duryea's Zouaves was the favorite regiment in the Wall Street home of financial speculation. Like the camaraderie of *The Brier-Wood Pipe*, the competition of *Pitching Quoits* envisioned continuity from army pastimes to postwar America.[64]

Homer's genre paintings paralleled the works of Giuseppe Castiglione and Paul-Alexandre Protais in seeing meanings for Zouaves in everyday scenes rather than the climactic moments depicted by Horace Vernet and Adolphe Yvon.[65] Homer's emphasis on the soldiers' companionable stoicism differed from the viewpoints of Charles Dawson Shanly or Thomas Nast or Matthew Brady or P. T. Barnum or William S. Budworth or John Rogers or Robert Newell or Henry Morford, but each artist's strategy owed a debt to the newspaper and magazine squibs in which Zouaves featured so often. Whether described on the printed page or arrayed on canvas against drab camp backgrounds, Zouaves illustrated the vitality of color. If their presence in troop reviews enhanced grand public spectacles, Zouaves' popularity in anecdotal representations suggested that contemporary social life also staged informal spectacles for attentive observers.

An Ideal Amazon

During the war Zouaves flourished as a symbol of the instability of gender conventions grounded in military service. Stage productions of Zouave drill deepened as a counterpoint and sharpened as a challenge to the reputation Zouave regiments won in troop reviews. Zouave recruitment stimulated American importation of the French role of the *vivandière*, a woman with an established position in the army. Widely seen as women's clothing, the Zouave uniform offered a fluid identity to men who wore it and presented a logical disguise to women who sought front-line action. At the end of the war the invention of new variety routines refreshed the vitality of the Zouave as a cross-gender figure in theatrical performance, a proven site of inspiration for martial performance.

Many shows imitated and expanded on the female Zouave dance-drill that achieved such success in *The Seven Sisters*. At least five new productions with comparable show-stoppers appeared after the bombardment of Fort Sumter. The most substantial was *The Southern Refugee; or, False and True,* featured at the Canterbury Music Hall, the pacesetting example of the randy new venue known as the concert saloon. That pantomime appeared sporadically in New York and elsewhere around the country throughout the war, and the arrival of peace brought more gender-bending plays with large Zouave drills like W. B. Cavanaugh's *The Female Clerks of Washington* (1865) and George Edeson's *The Female Sharpshooters* (1869). The ensembles soon detached themselves from even the flimsiest of plot structures. The Female McClellan Zouaves were a stand-alone act at George L. Fox and James W. Lingard's New Bowery Theatre by late November 1861. Similar performances became common in variety shows across the country.[66]

The most widely traveled of the new drill companies was the Carter Zouave Troupe, which debuted in 1861 as the Seven Star Sisters but soon adopted the name of manager J. Heneage Carter. The cast eventually reached about twenty members who ranged in age from approximately seven years old into their early teens. The act toured the United States and the Caribbean relentlessly until Carter declared himself exhausted in 1868. Shows included singing, dancing, and wire-walking, but the undisputed centerpiece was the Zouave drill. The girls wore USZC uniforms and performed maneuvers outlined in Ellsworth's manual of arms. They were more plausible as a military homage than mature women who performed sassier knock-offs of *The Seven Sisters*, but the Carters' proud precision brought its own cheek. Advertisements quoted a veteran's testimony that "the Zouave drill is the finest I have ever seen, and during two years' service in the army I have never seen a squad or company of soldiers who could equal them in the rapidity and beauty of their 'stack arms.'" In the middle of the war Carter offered a thousand dollars to "any military men on the entire American continent" who could excel the troupe in stacking arms, but he found no takers for the wager.[67]

Women's stage appearances as Zouaves fused with more direct engagement in the war. Union spy Pauline Cushman, a professional actress, turned her 1863 performance as Plutella in a Louisville production of *The Seven Sisters* into a springboard for espionage by pretending to Confederate sympathies.[68] The relationship between Zouaves and *vivandières* demonstrated links between the playhouse and the battlefield. The heroic possibilities of army women circulated in Revolutionary legends of Molly Pitcher, but antebellum Americans knew the *vivandière* primarily as a theatrical role, especially through Donizetti's opera *The Daughter of the Regiment* (1840). The pairing of Zouaves and *cantinières* promoted by Charles Dupeuty and Ernest Bourget, Eugène Grangé and Eugène Cormon, and Jacques Offenbach transferred to the United States in the summer of 1861 with the opening of *America's Dream; or, the Rebellion of 1861* at the Winter Garden Theatre. Critics reported that Malvina Pray Florence, in the lead role of Yankee *vivandière* Jerusha Sparks, "exhibited a fine leg, &c., in a Zouave's dress which fitted very tightly behind." Sparks remained the dominant character when the play toured widely into mid-1862. Unlike her French predecessors, the Yankee *cantinière* was not merely an object of a soldier's affections. Playwright Robert Jones, who participated in writing *The Seven Sisters,* moved the female Zouave to the center of action, including the inevitable drill number. In at least some productions the actress who played Jerusha Sparks also played Elmer Ellsworth.[69]

Zouave regiments were the most conspicuous Civil War organizations to include *vivandières,* though they were not the only units with these volunteers. Louisianans were particularly enthusiastic about adoption of the French custom, and Coppens' Zouaves left for the front with three *vivandières.* Women also joined in the departure of Wheat's Battalion.[70] When David Birney converted the 23rd Pennsylvania to a Zouave regiment, he enlisted two *vivandières.* Virginia Hall, the well-educated twenty-two-year-old *vivandière* of the 72nd Pennsylvania, attracted a profile from a *New York Times* reporter who initially thought she was "a fine looking young boy, uniquely dressed" in an adaptation of the regimental uniform layered with a tunic skirt. Marie Tepe, often called Zouave Mary or French Mary, became one of the most famous *vivandières* of the war through her service with the 114th Pennsylvania. A native of Brest who emigrated around the age of fifteen, Tepe was one of the few Civil War *vivandières* to fulfill the commercial roles usually assumed in the United States by male sutlers, selling tobacco and whiskey. She also performed the nursing and housekeeping duties more common among American *vivandières* and reportedly came under fire thirteen times. Wounded at the battle of Fredericksburg, she received a medal for bravery from her division commander. True to Donizetti's model, Tepe married a soldier at the end of the war.[71]

Marie Tepe adopted a skirted variation on the outfit of Collis' Zouaves, but some *vivandières* chose Zouave clothing even though their regiments did not wear Zouave uniforms.[72] The leading Civil War novels about *vivandières* followed similar patterns. The protagonist of Justin Jones's *Virginia Graham, The Spy of the Grand Army* (1867) enlists as a cross-dressed drummer boy to protect her younger half-brother. When her commanding officer discovers her secret, he arranges for her to remain with the regiment as a *vivandière.* Obliged to devise an appropriate outfit, she fashions an ornately embroidered Zouave jacket. Now securely positioned in the army, she embarks on a dazzling espionage campaign, sometimes cross-dressed as a Confederate soldier. The heroine of *Dora Darling; or The Daughter of the Regiment* (1862) wears "Turkish trousers" under her short skirt.[73]

Americans associated *vivandières* with Zouaves not merely because both roles originated in France but because Zouave uniforms resembled women's clothing in the United States to a greater degree than in France. Women embraced Zouave jackets in France as a martial tribute like the popularity of the color magenta after the 1859 battle of Magenta, but Zouave jackets became a staple in the wardrobes of fashionable American ladies before soldiers adopted the look. Moreover, in the United States, billowy Zouave trousers evoked bloomers, the feminist reform dress that shared a grounding in Orientalist imagery and fascinated the country in the 1850s. A soldier in the 83rd Pennsylvania, which received French uniforms as prizes for drill proficiency, told a female cousin that "the pants looks as much like ladies bloomers as anything else."[74] Specialized athletic clothing expanded on the freedom of movement important to the bloomer concept and converged with the Zouave embodiment of fitness. Exercise evangelist Dio Lewis encouraged women to "provide themselves with the Zouave costume" in *The New Gymnastics* (1862), and Louisa May Alcott wrote a short story set in a gymnasium in which young women performed "Zouave movement." At the same time, resemblance to women's underwear shaped perceptions of the so-called "Zouave petticoat." When the 5th New York passed through Middleburg, Virginia, a young girl called to her mother, "Ma, come out and see, I declare, here is a whole Regiment of yankees dressed up in women's clothing."[75]

The extent to which this cross-dressing influenced soldiers' strategies of self-presentation is difficult to measure. It may have been a coincidence that Confederate adventurer Richard Thomas chose to masquerade as a French lady to board a passenger steamer and lead his Zouave company in seizing the ship in an attempt to capture a U.S. Navy sloop. Hawkins' Zouaves, with their strong theatrical culture, perhaps merely typified the sexual teasing of army units in giving Thomas Fisher, the regiment's leading performer of female roles, the nickname Kate Fisher, after the professional actress known for her song "The Zouave Boy." More distinctive was John A. H. Foster of the 155th Pennsylvania, who conducted a spicy correspondence with his wife that frequently looked ahead to their next conjugal meeting and used the names Davie and Betsy for their genitalia. After the regiment began to wear Zouave uniforms, Foster declared that "the pantaloons are the most comfortable things I ever had on," and he offered to send his set home so that his wife might make herself a petticoat from them. The figurative sharing of underwear was an erotic proposition for the couple.[76]

Unsurprisingly, the most direct reflection on Zouave gender ambiguity came from a woman, U.S. Sanitary Commission volunteer Katharine Prescott Wormeley. She served as a nurse on a hospital ship during the Peninsula campaign alongside Zouave soldiers detailed for similar duty. She initially thought that "for an American citizen to rig himself as an Arab is demoralizing," but a few weeks with the "kind, nimble, tender Zouaves" changed her view. She told her mother in June 1862 that "even their dress, which I once hated, seems to take them in some sort out of the usual manners and ways of men," a compliment accentuated by women nurses' frustrations with male surgeons and stewards. Wormeley reported that "they have none of the dull, obstinate ways of that sex,—they are unexceptionable human beings of no sex, with the virtues of both."[77]

The transformative clothing impressed many Americans as the appropriate outfit for women who sought to step beyond *vivandières*' audacity and pass as soldiers. Charles Wesley Alexander's *Pauline of the Potomac* (1862), with which the author launched a series of sensational narratives about the war as an opportunity to emancipate women from the confines of domestic life, illustrated the sartorial logic. The protagonist, whose first assignment upon entering the federal spy service is to intercept a rebel spy, shrewdly dresses herself as a Zouave. The gambit succeeds because she not only disguises her sex; she takes advantage of her opponent's inability to tell whether he is dealing with a Union or a Confederate soldier.[78]

A stage adaptation of *Pauline of the Potomac* opened in May 1864, but the fitness of Zouave uniforms for women warriors received livelier reinforcement from one of the smash hits of the war, Adah Isaacs Menken's

FIG. 33. Wesley Bradshaw, *Pauline of the Potomac,*
or General McClellan's Spy (Philadelphia: Barclay, 1862).
Courtesy of the American Antiquarian Society.

star turn in *Mazeppa*. A specialist in breeches roles who entered by way of
Cincinnati into New York sporting society, through which she was married briefly to boxer John C. Heenan and later to humorist Robert Newell,
the sultry actress took up the title role in adaptations of Byron's poem in
June 1861. She became legendary for her ostensibly nude performance of
the Tartar prince stripped of his clothing and lashed to his horse to ride
to his death on a steep cliff. Surviving the ordeal, Menken's version of
Mazeppa returned to do battle in a Zouave uniform. Performed for audiences across the country for the next several years by Menken and many

imitators in flesh-colored leotards, the drama of a woman acting the part of a prince who suffers symbolic castration but vindicates his manhood epitomized the shape-shifting potency of Zouave dress.[79]

Zouave units apparently did not include a disproportionate percentage of cross-dressed soldiers, though a military journal reported near the end of the war that "we now and then see persons of the softer sex in the fierce garb of the soldier, usually the gay uniform of the Zouaves, more convenient perhaps to them and more attractive from its bright colors."[80] Certainly some women shared the preference. Bridget Silk of Eastchester, New York, obtained a Zouave outfit "as a better disguise than ordinary male attire" in an attempt to enlist, but the obstacle of the medical examination prompted her to try instead to sign up, unsuccessfully, for the alternative adventure of a whaling voyage. Whatever the numbers in the field, the image of the female Zouave was sufficiently commonplace to sustain satire. When Congress debated the postwar expansion of the franchise in December 1866, some legislators maintained that "unless the ladies were prepared to serve in the militia—in the half petticoat, half pantaloons costume of the Zouave extremities, of course—they should not demand the right of suffrage."[81]

The female Zouave achieved a lasting public presence through the invention of a variety act called the Lightning Zouave Drill. Joseph H. Childers, who claimed to have been a USZC member, introduced the novelty routine that an early account in November 1863 described as "one of the most astonishing feats ever known—actually keeping time to music in the Manual of Arms with Musket." A year later, twenty-year-old Charles Austin picked up the rhythmic adaptation of the procedures for execution of standard rifle commands. Reviewers reported that the supposed Wisconsin veteran "handles the musket with ease, and turns and twists it around and about the various part of his body with amazing rapidity."[82] By summer 1865 he partnered with his new wife, Carrie Austin, who expanded the appeal of the act. Carrie outstripped her husband as an attraction and often performed solo, "going through all the evolutions of a real 'sojer man.'" Dressed in Zouave costume, she impressed audiences as "a lady of exceedingly attractive face and figure—an ideal Amazon."

She soon inspired imitators. The well-known dancer and pantomimist Marietta Ravel commissioned a full-scale play for herself in which she performed a Zouave drill in the guise of a French soldier. Women's skating pioneer Carrie Augusta Moore incorporated a Zouave drill in her ice show, and army veteran Kady Brownell worked up a routine. The Lightning Zouave Drill became such a standard female stage accomplishment that a preview of a rising performer noted that she "sings, dances, clogs, does a zouave drill, plays the banjo, and for one so young displays talents of a high order."[83]

The wife-and-husband drill team surpassed the powers of ordinary soldiers. After touring with the Hanlon Brothers' acrobatic show, the Austins earned a place in comedian George L. Fox's record-breaking 1868 pantomime *Humpty-Dumpty*. Reviewers hailed their routine and especially their pas-de-deux bayonet combat, "an act of thrilling interest, superb in the grace, facility and precision of accomplishment," enlivened by the danger nearly realized when Charles's bayonet grazed Carrie's forehead in rehearsal. Shortly after the Austins began this high-profile run, the Montgomery Light Guard of Boston, a company in the Ninth Regiment of the Massachusetts Volunteer Militia, visited New York to compete against a company of the Twelfth Regiment of the New York National Guard for what was advertised as the drill championship of the United States. Two members of the Montgomery Light Guard presented a drill at the Academy of Music intended to eclipse the Austins' performance at the Olympic Theatre, but the soldiers' effort was, in the judgment of the *Clipper*, "a very tame affair" in comparison with the Lightning Zouave Drill. The Austins' supremacy was particularly a victory for the female Zouave.[84]

The importance of Zouaves as symbols of gender instability reflected not merely the style of their clothing but a broader force of connotation that combined the uniform with Zouave characteristics elaborated in sentimental and sensational wartime anecdotes. Katharine Prescott Wormeley was pleased to find that Zouaves were tenderhearted. For other women, it was significant that Zouaves were independent-minded tricksters, eager to undertake perilous adventures. The reputation of Zouaves as stage performers was central to their representations of manhood and womanhood. Theater offered as much opportunity as any mid-nineteenth-century American medium for transgression of gender norms, and Carrie Austin built on many precedents in displaying what one listing called "her Zouavity."[85]

Zouaves on the Color Line

The Civil War provided a wide field for American elaboration of the racial ambivalences embedded in the imperial origins of the Zouave uniform as a European projection of African identity. In the United States as in French Algeria, cultural impersonation pointed toward more violent forms of exploitation and abuse. At the same time, white adoption of the nominally Black clothing suggested a cross-racial affinity and potential for partnership. European military strategists regarded Zouave dress as singularly appropriate for colonial people of color, a view that some white Americans sought to apply in the wartime recruitment of Black soldiers. Like counterparts elsewhere in the Black Atlantic world, African Americans recognized the prestige of Zouave uniforms as an endorsement of Black military prowess. By the peak of Reconstruction, the outfit was a prominent look of Black citizenship in the United States.

The war deepened the association between Zouaves and the quintessential racial mishmash of blackface minstrelsy.[86] Bryant's Minstrels staged a "Zouave Clog Reel" regularly in 1861–62, and other troupes developed their own acts. Joseph H. Childers introduced the Lightning Zouave Drill as a performer with Yankee Hill's Minstrels; Charles Austin developed his first routine while with Campbell's Minstrels. "My Love He Is a Zou-Zu" was a light revision of Dan Bryant's cross-dressed, blackface take on an old British ballad. W. S. Budworth carried his "Zouave Johnny" among several minstrel acts. Zouave units were prominent among army regiments that put on minstrel productions. Assigned to join the Union occupying force in New Orleans in December 1862, the 6th New York pushed the Original Christy Minstrels from the stage of the Varieties Theatre to present the show that the soldiers had honed on garrison duty in Fort Pickens. The 165th New York, which performed a minstrel act in New

Orleans a few months later, included among its number thirty-eight-year-old private and banjoist Tom Vaughn, one of the founding members of the famous Christy ensemble.[87]

Hawkins' Zouaves, whose members took pride in the extent to which the unit consisted of native-born volunteers of higher social and economic status than the average regiment, illustrated the link between racist mockery and physical cruelty. The Zouave Dramatic and Minstrel Club, managed by a corporal with Broadway experience, brought together many of the officers and men weekly during a long period of garrison duty on Roanoke Island in 1862. Burnt-cork burlesques were a standard feature of the repertory. Soldiers sought to fill out their wigs by urging local African Americans to cut their hair short in imitation of the Zouaves. Achieving little success, the soldiers resorted to kidnapping Roanoke Island inhabitants and carrying them to a squad room for forcible shearing. A year later, well-to-do volunteer Edward King Wightman observed that, "if there is any one thing the 9th Regiment agree in as a principle, it is that n——s were born to be abused." Black teamster George Stephens, later a soldier in the 54th Massachusetts, noted in January 1863 that Hawkins' Zouaves were "distinguished for their rowdyism and brutality to colored men" and that "more than one poor slave has met his death at the hands of this mob."[88] Other Zouave units drawn from aggressively Democratic constituencies showed similar tendencies. The 5th New York captured African Americans and tossed them in an outstretched blanket, a treatment the soldiers called "the Union drill." The 76th Pennsylvania tied African Americans' hands behind their backs and forced them to plunge their faces into a barrel of meal to find a coin.[89]

The rise of a more sympathetic reputation for Zouaves characteristically began with a newspaper anecdote. In late July 1861, as the numbers of escaped slaves seeking refuge across Union lines under the "contraband" policy increased dramatically, the *Chicago Tribune* printed a story about a former typographer for the newspaper who had followed Ellsworth to New York to enlist in the Fire Zouaves. According to the *Tribune*, the private was on picket duty on the road from Alexandria to Fairfax when a Virginia aristocrat approached in a carriage driven by a slave. The sentry demanded a pass, which the planter disdainfully sent the slave to present. The Zouave motioned the African American across the lines and informed the stunned white Virginian that the document authorized the bearer to pass but could not extend to another person. When the slave-holder tried to summon his driver back to the carriage, the guard pointed out that the pass did not permit travel in the direction of Alexandria. He sent the bondsman toward the Union camp and freedom.[90]

This trickster tale circulated in outlets that spanned the country and ranged in tone from the relentless *Liberator* to the irrepressible *Clipper*. The story launched its anthologized career in a popular collection of camp vignettes sold at railroad stations. *Douglass' Monthly* included it in an issue advocating stronger federal efforts to undermine slavery.[91] Thomas Hamilton, editor of the *Weekly Anglo-African*, joined the national craze for illustrated mailers by marketing a "Zouave and Slave Envelope." Often the only illustration in the weekly newspaper, the woodcut advertisement depicted a Zouave sentinel holding up his rifle to protect a fugitive from a grasping white southerner. Above the American flag floated a banner proclaiming "Slaves Contraband of War." Black abolitionists' celebration of the non-rendition policy, which leveraged an understanding of people as property, endorsed the alliance between African Americans and white Democratic urban workers against an overbearing foe and hinted at prospects for further cooperation. When the Fire Zouaves returned to New York in mid-August 1861 for an attempted reorganization, the soldiers reportedly smuggled into the city fourteen escaped slaves characterized as regimental servants.[92]

Winslow Homer repeatedly explored connections between Zouaves and African Americans. While visiting Fort Lyon, near Alexandria, in October 1861 he sketched a dancing soldier in a Zouave uniform. When the artist transferred the figure into a drawing for *Harper's Weekly,* he made the dancer a Black "contraband." Many of the spectators, including those most clearly illuminated by the bivouac fire, are Zouaves. The dancing Black cook in a later lithograph wears a tasseled fez. Homer situated Zouaves and African Americans similarly in relation to the animal world. Critics noted that his now-unlocated 1875 painting of a foraging party of Duryea's Zouaves, in which a soldier struggles with a calf, paralleled another Homer entry in two exhibitions, *Unruly Calf,* in which a young African American struggles with a calf.[93] The correspondence deepens the poignancy of Homer's major treatment of the relationship, the watercolor *Contraband* (1875). This work was part of a series of sympathetic paintings of Black children that the artist exhibited as white northerners weakened in their readiness to thwart the violent overthrow of Reconstruction. Homer looked back to the early phase of the war and the contraband policy that had created momentum toward emancipation and Union victory. The Zouave offers the youth his canteen, reciprocating the compassionate young Black man who offers a canteen to a wounded Zouave in Matthew Brady's wartime photograph. The veteran's gesture of camaraderie is much broader than the sentinel's defiance of the slaveholder in Ham-

FIG. 34. Winslow Homer, *Contraband,* 1875. Courtesy of the Arkell Museum at Canajoharie, New York; gift of Bartlett Arkell.

ilton's envelope. Emerging together from a stark black background, the childlike Zouave and the African American child look into each other's eyes and recognize a shared humanity.[94]

Enlistment of Black soldiers added further dimensions to the complex racial significance of Zouaves. Violent white supremacism spiraled from abuse of civilians to attacks on fellow Union volunteers. Billy Wilson's Zouaves drew national attention in spring 1863 for harassment of Louisiana Native Guard units contributing to the occupation of New Orleans. A Republican newspaper scoffed that "the sensibilities of these fastidious gentlemen—a set of promiscuous vagabonds, thieves, ruffians and shoulder-hitters, picked up in the stews of New York—are highly offended at the idea of a black man carrying a musket, and behaving himself decently!"[95] Even more serious was the aggression of the 165th New York against the 54th Massachusetts during the occupation of Charleston in the immediate aftermath of the war. After preying on local African Americans, the Zouaves instigated a series of street fights against the Black troops. Exasperated Union commander Quincy A. Gillmore removed the 165th New York to Battery Wagner on Morris Island, ironically the scene of the 54th Massachusetts's famous moment of glory, and ordered confiscation of the regimental flags and arms.[96]

The long debate over recruitment of African Americans brought the United States into a transatlantic discussion of Zouave dress as particularly appropriate for Black soldiers. Napoleon III approved the creation of the *tirailleurs sénégalais* in July 1857 in response to petitions from the French governor in Senegal; the soldiers would wear Zouave-like uniforms patterned on those of the *tirailleurs algériens*. Largely neglected in international press coverage of the Crimean War, the Turcos received more notice in the Italian Campaign, though certainly not parity with Zouaves. Even the *New York Herald*, rarely supportive of non-whites, reported that "the Turco is the concentrated essence of the Zouave." Most notably from an American perspective, the British army shifted its West India Regiments to Zouave uniforms after the Crimean War. Americans were keenly aware of these units. They were the most prominent colonial troops of the empire, dividing their time between garrisons across the Caribbean and garrisons in Sierra Leone and Gambia. American awareness of the West India Regiments intensified amid rumors of a pending British antislavery invasion of the Gulf Coast in the late 1850s. Reports of the new outfits circulated in American newspapers as well as London publications distributed in the United States.[97]

Early white advocates of African American recruitment into the Union army often shared a quasi-colonialist vision of Black Zouaves. In May 1861 a wealthy New Yorker offered to donate ten thousand dollars "to form a Zouave regiment, to be composed of colored men six feet high." Five months later, on the eve of the Port Royal expedition to low-country South Carolina, the *Evening Post* reported that "quantities of bright Zouave clothing have been taken along, with the intention of forming the negroes of the coast into Zouave regiments." Like the proposal for a regiment of tall African Americans, the endorsement of this plan imagined the Black Zouaves as barbaric force. Mobilization of former slaves in the Sea Islands would deflect insurrection and harness "the love of the negro for bright colors" illustrated by the West India Regiments.[98] Similar thinking informed David Hunter's choice of red pantaloons for the African Americans he recruited for active service in South Carolina in May 1862, by which point the 76th Pennsylvania created a strong Zouave presence at Hilton Head. An officer assisting the initiative predicted that "when they got their music going, and a few of the Zouaves dressed in uniform, all would enlist who were fit to serve." Over the next several months journalists routinely referred to the unit that would become the First Kansas Colored Infantry Regiment as the Kansas Zouaves d'Afrique. Army adjutant general Lorenzo Thomas, assigned to head Black military recruitment in the Mississippi River Valley, suggested to the secretary of war shortly before formal organization of the U.S. Colored Troops (USCT) in May 1863 that for these soldiers "a distinctive dress of less cost would be better— something a little more gay."[99]

African Americans applied different reasoning to reach the parallel conclusion that Black soldiers should be Zouaves. Pan-Africanist intellectual Martin Delany, later the highest-ranking Black officer in the Union army, most forcefully articulated the argument that "the origin and dress of the Zouaves d'Afrique were strictly *African*" and manifested Black military achievement. He reported that Haitian soldiers' technique of lying on their back to load weapons was "nothing but the original Zouave tactics introduced long years ago by native Africans among these people." Black egalitarian Alfred M. Green of Philadelphia similarly took pride in observing local African Americans practicing "the regular African Zouave drill, that would make the hearts of secession traitors, or prejudiced Yankees quake and tremble for fear." A correspondent of *Douglass' Monthly* pointed out that "France has some regiments of native Africans, who are incarnate devils on a field of battle" and proposed that the United States should similarly "advertise for the formation of an African Zouave regiment." Rufus Sibb Jones's Fort Pitt Cadets, who had been training steadily in Pittsburgh for two years, offered their service to the War Department in May 1862. Eighteen months later, Robert Hamilton announced in the *Weekly Anglo-African* that the 10th U.S. Colored Infantry was organizing in Norfolk as a Zouave outfit in blue jackets and trousers trimmed with red and a blue cap with a green tassel. "Their uniform is exceedingly becoming," reported Hamilton, "and make[s] them the finest-looking soldiers we ever saw."[100]

The War Department ultimately dressed the USCT in standard issue, a supply-chain convenience and for many African Americans a welcome certification of equal status, but the appeal of Black Zouaves did not disappear. A group of physicians argued to Secretary of War Edwin Stanton that the new recruits' "habits, physical natures, and the fact that many of them are to be used in the extreme South, demand an Oriental uniform, like that of the original Zouave d'Afrique" because such an outfit fit more loosely and ventilated more freely than a European uniform.[101] This emphasis on racial differences, especially in tropical environments, prompted the French army only a few months earlier to send a conscript Sudanese battalion to join the imperial forces in Mexico, where the Africans received uniforms based on the Turco pattern.[102] Thomas Wentworth Higginson, abolitionist author and commander of the pioneering 1st South Carolina (later the 33rd U.S. Colored Infantry), typified the activists determined to attack such stereotyping. He was alert to the resemblance between the Union base on the Sea Islands and the British garrisons in the West Indies, and he rejected the condescension he recognized in the red pantaloons Hunter had given the African Americans. When he wrote a widely published report on his troops after an early mission, however, he turned to a familiar standard of comparison. "There is a fiery energy about them beyond anything of which I have ever read, unless it be the French Zouaves," Higginson declared.[103] He was not content for Black soldiers to be colonial imitations, but he was proud for them to match the cross-dressed European prototype. Another USCT commander who maintained that "the negro is like the Turco" reasoned that "the Mulatto is like the Zouave" because he was "the type of an admirable soldier" who "unites in himself, physically speaking, the perfection of both races."[104]

The Zouave Black Atlantic continued to thrive as the Civil War came to a close. British journalist George Augustus Sala described Algeria, spitefully, in summer 1865 as an experiment in perfect racial equality where "the Zouave walks arm-in-arm with the Turco." The West India Regiments drew relatively little of the outrage prompted by the suppression of the Morant Bay rebellion in Jamaica, despite participation in the atrocities, and emerged as a symbol of Black fidelity to the rule of law. The units received a burst of favorable global publicity in 1867 when Samuel Hodge of the 4th West India Regiment became the first member of colonial forces to be presented with the Victoria Cross for his conspicuous valor in the capture of Tubabecolong on the Gambia River.[105] The most important new organization was the contingent of eleven Zouave companies formed by Bahian volunteers in 1865–66 to fight in the Brazilian war against Paraguay. Closely connected to Salvadoran street culture, the colorfully dressed Zuavos paraded in festivals before the outbreak of the war. Their principal commander, retired National Guard commander Joaquim Antônio da Silva Carvalhal, was a director of the annual Salvadoran independence day celebration as well as founding president of the society of veterans of the war of independence, and the Zuavos were a striking expression of popular Afro-Brazilian solidarity and autonomy, even to the point of maintaining distance from the army hierarchy.[106]

Within this transnational context, African Americans embraced the Zouave ideal in the postwar formation of militia units. The Hannibal Zouaves founded in Chicago in 1868, "uniformed like the renowned 'Turcos' of the French army," most directly asserted an African martial lineage. Other groups chose names that recalled the enlistment of Black troops in the Civil War. The Butler Zouaves, the most prominent militia company in the nation's capital, honored Benjamin Butler for his advocacy of African American service. The Lincoln Zouaves were their Baltimore counterpart, and the Douglass Zouaves aspired to a similar role in Pittsburgh. The Wagner Zouaves of Philadelphia took their name from the director of Camp William Penn, the suburban training facility for African American troops. Reconstructed cities in the former Confederacy with Black Zouave companies included Richmond, Memphis, Wilmington, Charleston, and Augusta.[107]

Zouave flamboyance served Black units well in the ceremonial appearances traditionally central to militia representation of the community. The conspicuous uniforms featured in annual processions for Independence Day or anniversaries of Emancipation or other civic occasions like the dedication of public buildings. The Butler Zouaves attracted considerable publicity for their high-profile role in the 1868 obsequies for Thaddeus Stevens.[108] The following spring, the Butler Zouaves and Lincoln Zouaves paraded in a select militia division at Grant's presidential inauguration. Militia volunteers gladly acknowledged the link between Black military service and suffrage, and the 1870 ratification of the Fifteenth Amendment became an important occasion for celebration and anniversary remembrance in many locations. Beyond their sartorial contributions to civic pageantry, Black units upheld the Zouave tradition of showmanship at exhibition drills and other events. In an 1871 visit to Stockton, the Sacramento Zouaves demonstrated "their proficiency in drilling at the tap of the drum" and sponsored a dance. The fine band of the Springfield Zouaves helped the African Americans stand out among the militia companies participating in the 1874 dedication of the monument at Lincoln's grave.[109]

In addition to their public enactment of Black citizenship, the Zouave units sought recognition in the organized militia. The Wagner Zouaves and the Douglass Zouaves joined the Pennsylvania National Guard in 1870, and the adjutant general of Washington mustered the Butler Zouaves into service the following year.[110] Neither the Lincoln Zouaves nor

FIG. 35. Metcalf & Clark, Baltimore, *The Result of the Fifteenth Amendment*, 1870.
Courtesy of the Library of Congress.

the Hannibal Zouaves achieved similar status, though the Hannibal Zouaves served in a temporary regiment after the Chicago fire of 1871. The
company made the most of its exclusion from the state militia by participating in political marches during the 1876 campaign.[111]

Shortly after the election, Captain Richard E. Moore and his men gave
up their Zouave name and uniforms. Only then did the rebranded Chicago
organization begin to make progress toward acceptance into the Illinois
National Guard.[112] Zouave identity had been a dynamic, flexible force in
the United States throughout the Civil War and for several years afterward. Zouaves epitomized the spectacle regime of discipline in wartime
armies. They served as colorful heroes in stories and pictures that appealed to audiences eager for the preservation of individuality amid the
vast mobilization. The gender and racial connotations of the Zouave uniform sustained a variety of approaches to central social fissures. By the
1870s, however, American Zouaves were facing powerful attack.

5

THE LIVERY OF ROME

Probably the strangest chapter in the story of the Zouave fad was the adoption of the uniform by men who volunteered to secure the territory of the pope against the army of the new, unified Italian state. At the same time as American Zouaves were performing on stage and facing civil war, ten thousand young men from twenty-five countries in Europe and the Americas traveled to Rome, where they put on the uniform to defend the temporal rule of Pope Pius IX.[1] They were devout Catholics who believed that the peaceful order of the world demanded a sovereign pope, but they also found the prospect of heroic action in exotic attire attractive. These pontifical soldiers forged a lasting connection between the Zouave costume and their brand of intransigent, anti-modern Roman Catholicism. They, too, claimed the title of "the finest soldiers in the world," although they had a different sense of what it meant: determination and fearlessness, certainly, but a Pontifical Zouave also anticipated suffering and welcomed martyrdom.[2]

The contrast between the pope's soldiers and the "jackals" of French North Africa or the Crimea was key to the Pontifical Zouaves' emergence as Christian icons. The public image of the Pontifical Zouave emphasized youth, gentleness, and general battle unreadiness. Death, rather than victory, was the purpose of Zouave service to the pope. These Zouaves would not scale walls, vault over streams, or battle their way to the enemy's lines like their French namesakes—rather, they would suffer and die martyrs' deaths. They eschewed wine, women, and song, at least of the vaudeville variety. The dissonance of the jaunty uniforms on the bodies of young men seeking to immolate themselves in the cause of the church was crucial to the Pontifical Zouaves' appeal. The Catholic Zouave with his distinctive silhouette was instantly recognizable—like a prayer-card image or a figure from a Bible story—as a symbol of extraordinary devotion to the church.

For all their differences, the Pontifical Zouaves and their counterparts in national armies shared a commitment to individualism: they would not be reduced to cogs in a military machine. Among Catholic Zouaves, the cult of the individual focused especially on death. Every casualty among the Pontifical Zouaves was a martyr for Christendom. Every death expiated the sins of secular society, so every Zouave soldier had the extraordinary capacity to redeem his fellow men. Some Zouaves exhibited such extraordinary Christian virtue that they were, in fact, saints, their supporters argued.

The Catholic Zouave survived the collapse of papal territorial sovereignty in 1870 when Rome fell to the forces of the Kingdom of Italy. Former Pontifical Zouaves did not, however, abandon the fight. Instead, they pursued their Christian combat in different theaters, bringing the cause of a supranational Christendom to their own nation-states. France, Spain, and Quebec became sites of Catholic Zouave engagement, and the determination of the original, Pontifical Zouaves in these countries attracted new recruits through the end of the nineteenth century and into the twentieth. The uniform thus continued to represent an a-national—even an anti-national—dedication to the cause of Catholic Christianity as young men who donned it asserted that their primary loyalty was to their faith.

Serving God in Rome

At the beginning of the nineteenth century, the pope was a temporal sovereign who ruled over much of central Italy and consequently an important obstacle to proponents of the Italian Risorgimento, the movement to create a unified Italian nation-state. The Second Italian War of Independence, which the French refer to as the Italian Campaign of 1859, put the Papal States in immediate danger. During this war, Piedmont and its king,

Victor Emmanuel II, with their French allies, succeeded in pushing out
Austrian forces and annexing most of northern Italy. In 1860, Giuseppe
Garibaldi and his band of a thousand red-shirted volunteers landed in
Sicily, then crossed the straits and took the city of Naples. By overthrow-
ing the Kingdom of the Two Sicilies that controlled the southern part of
the peninsula, Garibaldi radically altered the political situation in Italy.
Suddenly, an independent and unified peninsula was a real possibility. Responding to Garibaldi's challenge, Victor Emmanuel marched his troops
south into the Papal States. He met Garibaldi south of Rome, and in a
dramatic encounter, Garibaldi handed his southern conquests to the Piedmontese king.[3] The Papal States were then the last major impediment to
a unified Italy.

The pope's armed forces squared off against Victor Emmanuel's Piedmontese army at the battle of Castelfidardo in September 1860. Outnumbered by nearly four to one, the papal army suffered a decisive defeat.
Victory at Castelfidardo enabled Victor Emmanuel to annex the central
Italian provinces of Umbria and the Marches, uniting his northern conquests with the territories of the Two Sicilies. Defeat at Castelfidardo left
the papacy in possession of nothing more than Rome and its surrounding
territories, the rump of the former Papal States. This disastrous loss set
the tone for the volunteer recruitment campaign that would follow.

The success of his Italian Campaign left Napoleon III in an awkward
position, caught between his two Italian allies—Victor Emmanuel and
Pope Pius IX—who were themselves opponents. Napoleon had ended
French involvement in war against Austria in July 1859, negotiating an
armistice with the Austrian Empire without consulting his Piedmontese
ally. France received part of the province of Savoy and the city of Nice,
and Napoleon III, satisfied with Austria's defeat, was disinclined to pur-
sue the campaign further. Attentive to Catholic opinion in France, he had
supported papal rule in Rome with a small French armed force in the city
since 1849.[4] Backing the Piedmontese effort against the Austrian Empire
had not originally seemed to threaten France's Roman commitments, but
after Castelfidardo, papal Rome appeared very much at risk. At the behest
of his French ally, Victor Emmanuel held back from Rome, and he obliged

the impetuous Garibaldi to do the same. The situation by 1861, when Victor Emmanuel proclaimed the Kingdom of Italy, was clearly unstable and, in the eyes of Italian nationalists, untenable.

The threat to papal sovereignty in 1859–60 produced an influx of Catholic volunteers into the pope's army. Within the year, many of these volunteers were wearing Zouave uniforms and giving the Zouave a new, pious image. They came from a wide geographical area: the largest groups came from France and the Low Countries, and there were also significant numbers of volunteers from across the German states, the Slavic regions of the Austrian Empire, and Ireland. By the end of the 1860s, Pius IX's call reached across the Atlantic, and the diocese of Montreal organized a recruiting campaign that produced several hundred volunteers.[5]

This wave of international volunteers was intent on emphasizing their spiritual motivations and distinguishing themselves from mercenaries. Like the regular members of the pope's armed forces, most of whom came from the Swiss cantons, these volunteers received a wage and sometimes a recruiting bonus, but they were touchy about being described as mercenaries. Asserting that Rome was their spiritual homeland, they emphasized that they had an obligation to defend the Papal States that was comparable to or even greater than their obligation to defend their national homelands. Andreas Niedermayer, a German priest and historian, expressed this mix of national, spiritual, and cosmopolitan loyalties when he asserted that his fellow Catholics should "participate strongly in the greatest battle of our times, . . . give from our property what we can spare, and . . . provide a 'German Legion' for the glorious fighters for the Apostolic See."[6]

The motivations of individual volunteers varied widely of course, and not all were as devout as papal marketing asserted. The Irish contingent, for instance, included a group known as the "Kerry Boys" whose priest had encouraged them to enlist in order to spare his parish their rowdiness. Other Zouaves were drummed out of the ranks for behavior unbecoming a soldier of the pope. Maximin Giraud, who as a child had experienced a famous vision of the Virgin Mary at La Salette in France, was a coup for the Zouaves when he joined their ranks in 1865, but an equally great disappointment when he washed out six months later, court-martialed for drunkenness. Most famously, John Surratt, one of a small handful of U.S. volunteers, was on the run from the law, having been involved in the plot to assassinate Abraham Lincoln.[7] In general, however, the volunteers of the 1860s emphasized the purity of their motives and their belief that soldiering for the pope was a form of religious devotion.

The pope's new volunteers gave careful attention to their uniforms because they wanted to ensure that their special status as servants of Christ's kingdom on earth was immediately visible even to the casual observer. Mercenaries of the existing papal forces wore various uniforms, dressing as *chasseurs* and *bersaglieri,* among others. Irishmen expected to wear distinctive green and gold uniforms, similar to those of the Irish Legion in Napoleon I's army, but the promised outfits never materialized, leaving the volunteers disappointed with nondescript, secondhand, and dirty suits.[8] Zouave dress was an innovation in the papal army, and it succeeded in giving a special panache to the devout volunteers of the 1860s.

Zouave uniforms were not the only available plan, however: one of the first promoters of a volunteer force to defend the papacy advocated for crusader costume. The Frenchman Henri de Cathelineau was the grandson of the famous leader of the Royal and Catholic Army of nobles and peasants that fought in the Vendée against the forces of the French Revolution in the 1790s. He spent much of his youth in exile in the Iberian peninsula, fighting for the cause of throne and altar in Spain and Portugal—an "armed pilgrim of counter-revolution," as one recent historian describes him.[9] He found a calling worthy of his lineage in Rome, where he saw the rump Papal States as the final battlefield in the struggle against atheism and the forces of revolution. Thirty-two members of his family had died in the defense of the religion of their fathers, he announced, and as the oldest of his generation, he was stepping up to be next in line.[10] In 1860 he mobilized his impeccable counterrevolutionary and Catholic pedigree to encourage young men to join him in that apocalyptic combat.

Conjuring a romantic medievalism, Cathelineau promised the young men he signed up that they would be the "sons and heirs of the crusaders."[11] "The idea of a crusade is on everyone's mind," he wrote, offering his services to the papacy: "it will bring in a lot of people."[12] Cathelineau's evocation of the crusaders relied particularly on uniforms and other trappings of military life: he enticed recruits by assuring them that they would go to war in tunics with large crosses on them, like characters from Walter Scott's *Ivanhoe*. They would fight behind banners representing the Virgin and the upside down cross of St. Peter in silver on a blue field. Newspapers described the venture as a "new chivalric order," the "Knights of St. Peter," who would participate in an elaborate oath-taking ceremony before the pope.[13]

Cathelineau quickly succeeded in recruiting some sixty would-be crusaders. They were mostly from his native province of Brittany, a devoutly Catholic region where his invocation of a tradition of men in arms to defend the faith resonated well. Local newspapers reported on individual departures and praised the young Bretons who offered their lives in the defense of the papacy. One of these young men wrote back to his family, signing himself "Hyacinthe de Lanascol, crusader."[14] These idealistic Catholics were among the young men who fought, and, in many cases, including Lanascol, died on the battlefield of Castelfidardo.

Even before the disaster at Castelfidardo, however, Cathelineau's chivalric project had reached a dead end, because it conflicted with the plans of the pope's minister of war, the Belgian prelate Xavier de Mérode. Although Mérode wanted an international effort that would call Catholics to the defense of the papacy, he wanted soldiers, not romantic crusaders, to answer that appeal. Mérode mistrusted Napoleon III's commitment to the papacy, and he hoped to develop a pontifical army that would give the pope greater autonomy in international affairs. He did not, however, want to alienate the emperor by handing too much power to a man like Cathelineau, whose loyalty to France's deposed Bourbon monarchs was almost as great as his dedication to the pope. Mérode also suspected that Cathelineau was accepting deserters from existing pontifical units and consequently destabilizing the pope's forces.[15] An international volunteer movement that affirmed the willingness of Catholics around the world to bear arms in support of their Roman homeland would afford the pope some room to maneuver, but not if it alienated his allies and his own officers.

Mérode had identified the general to lead the expanded pontifical army he proposed: none other than Léon Juchault de Lamoricière, the Zouave hero of France's conquest of Algeria. Mérode had been a soldier prior to entering seminary, and his military career had taken him in the 1840s to North Africa, where he had served as an attaché to the French army, so he was familiar with Lamoricière's record. Since their time in Africa, Lamoricière had also found his way to the church. Catholic writers, drawing on a familiar trope, attributed his conversion to the influence of his devout wife. In 1847, the year that he led French forces in North Africa in the final defeat of Abdelkader, Lamoricière had married into an aristocratic family with connections to the Mérodes: Xavier de Mérode was a great-nephew of Lamoricière's mother-in-law.[16]

Lamoricière's route to Rome was indirect and surprising to many—ideologically speaking, he was far removed from Henri de Cathelineau. Although a loyal officer of the French king Louis-Philippe, Lamoricière rallied to the new republic when the July Monarchy collapsed in 1848. He served as minister of war in the provisional government of the republic and was among the most prominent of the "African" officers participating in the brutal repression of street protest in June 1848. His government service lasted until December 1848, when Louis-Napoleon Bonaparte, nephew of the Emperor Napoleon, won the first presidential election. Lamoricière refused to serve the so-called "Prince President" who in 1851 overthrew the republican constitution. The general was among those pre-emptively arrested during the coup d'état, and he was released on condition that he go into exile. His disaffection deepened a year later when Louis-Napoleon declared himself Emperor Napoleon III. In 1857, when Lamoricière was still in Belgian exile, his only son fell seriously ill, and the imperial government set unacceptable terms for his temporary return that, in the general's estimation, would have had him "cross the border on his knees." The child's death, without his father at his side, confirmed Lamoricière's scorn for Bonapartism as well as his turn toward the religion of his ancestors.[17] No longer either a soldier or a political figure and with a rediscovered Catholic faith filling the void, Lamoricière was primed for a new kind of military command.

Lamoricière brought his Zouave reputation—and the Zouave uniform—to Rome with him. He rejected Cathelineau's plan for an independent command as well as for distinctive crusader insignia—a look which, according to Louis-Antoine de Becdelièvre, one of the general's closest aides, "had various disadvantages, not least of which would be ridicule." Instead of fanciful costumes, Lamoricière, Becdelièvre, and Mérode believed, the papal army needed practical, modern uniforms, and Zouave dress fit the bill. The Zouave style reflected the way soldiers actually fought, Becdelièvre wrote: they unbuttoned their collars and tucked the bottom of their trousers into their boots for greater freedom of movement. Pius IX accepted the Zouave name as well as the characteristic dress, drawing the line only at the turban—"*troppo turco*," according to one report.[18] The pope's soldiers, then, adopted the French fantasy of North African tribal dress, but topped it off with a military kepi.

Breaking with the French military tradition, both officers and men wore the Zouave uniform. In the French army, officers wore fitted trousers and buttoned, collared jackets; the freedom of Zouave attire was for enlisted men only. The photograph of the Charette brothers (fig. 36) demonstrates the Pontifical Zouaves' studied indifference to rank. Like Cathelineau, the Charettes were descendants of a counterrevolutionary Breton family that had achieved fame defying the French republic in the 1790s. All four brothers served Pius IX: from the left, Louis, as a dragoon, and then Ferdinand, Athanase and Alain as Zouaves. Alain and Athanase were officers (second lieutenant and major), and Ferdinand enlisted as a private soldier, but all three wear the distinctive uniform. A final brother, Armand, joined the Zouaves after this photograph was taken.

In the epic combat that pitted Catholics against the forces of revolution, social distinctions were irrelevant, Zouaves asserted, although in fact great social gulfs separated their cohorts. The French were disproportionately noble, and one Piedmontese officer sneeringly remarked that his opponents' muster roll resembled the guest list for a ball at the court of Louis XIV.[19] Volunteers from Catholic minority communities of the Netherlands and Canada, in contrast, often came from quite humble backgrounds. Zouaves, especially aristocrats, were fascinated by their own

FIG. 36. The Charette brothers. Copyright Musée de l'armée, Dist.
RMN-Grand Palais / Art Resource, New York.

egalitarianism, asserting that Zouave service turned common men into a
"new nobility" that "rose from the ranks of the people."[20] Stories of young
men learning to darn their own socks were a staple of Zouave literature.
The officer who dressed like his men—and cared for his own uniform—
was a figure of Christian humility that appealed to the Zouave spirit.[21]

The irony of the pope's defenders wearing Muslim dress was lost on no
one, but this new variation on military cross-dressing proved irresistible.
To the spectacle of European men in "Arab" costume, the Pontifical Zouaves added the incongruity of devout Catholics in the dress of marauding,
barely disciplined "jackals." The Zouaves' cheeky stage reputation was

not incidental, since the pious young men serving the pope would never darken the door of a vaudeville theater or applaud the risqué jokes and drag performances of their stage counterparts. The pope's Zouaves were effective foils to their French namesakes whose well-established devil-may-care reputation enhanced the exceptional nature of these Christian soldiers. The Italian nationalist press might call them "pseudo-Zouaves," but that missed the point.[22] The Pontifical Zouaves were not fakes. Rather, they were creating a new variation of a highly elastic identity, and they did not need to imitate the ferocity of the Zouave original. What was authentic was not their soldiering but their faith.

The soldiers of the pope's army did not, however, reinvent the Zouave entirely. Alongside the rough soldiering, love of drink, and casual filching of supplies, another characteristic of the stereotypical French army Zouave was respect for religion. The Zouave as he emerged in the mass press of the Crimean War might regularly break the commandments, but he was not irreligious. On the contrary, he possessed the naive faith of a simple man. The popular figure of the "Trappist Zouave" was the most significant example of this instinctive religiosity. The story first appeared in the *Moniteur de l'armée*: a Zouave sergeant, serving in Kabylia and finding himself alone and severely wounded, promised the Virgin Mary that he would become a monk if he survived. Miraculously, he lived and made his way to the newly established Trappist monastery at Staouëli, whose abbot decided to test his resolve and his suitability for monastic life. Speaking to the assembled brothers, the abbot denounced the Zouave as a bad soldier and a coward. The falsely accused Zouave remained stoic, his head bowed in silent prayer, while the assembled Trappists considered his request. The next morning the abbot acknowledged the truth of the Zouave's bravery, praised his humility in the face of calumny, and welcomed him into the brotherhood. The story of this Trappist Zouave circulated through the French press in 1857, the year after the end of the Crimean War.[23]

Horace Vernet, who knew the pictorial value of a Zouave, ensured the celebrity of the Trappist Zouave in a painting for the 1857 Salon. Vernet depicted the Zouave enduring the abbot's test: he kneels and prays by a fresh grave, his striking uniform covered by a Trappist robe, and the scar

FIG. 37. Horace Vernet, *The Trappist Zouave*, 1857, photograph by Goupil. Authors' collection.

of his head wound clearly visible. Another Zouave, standing outside the enclosed churchyard, silently watches his comrade. The Emperor Napoleon III purchased Vernet's Trappist Zouave for his palace at Saint-Cloud. The painting was the subject of an early photographic reproduction (fig. 37) and was later engraved, so the image of the Trappist Zouave was widely available. A copy of Vernet's painting found its way to the monastery at Staouëli, where it was part of the itinerary for visiting tourists. Poems and popular songs followed, so the sustaining force of a simple Christian faith was an established part of the Zouave legend by the 1860s when Pontifical Zouaves joined the conflict in the Italian peninsula.[24]

With Lamoricière's recruitment to the papal cause, Catholic writers produced new accounts of French colonialism in North Africa that expanded on the alleged piety of France's Zouave soldiers. These accounts of Zouave Christianity and humanitarianism turned the actual Zouave record on its head: charity replaced the *razzia*, and Lamoricière's African Zouaves shared their bread with native women and children and returned to their barracks not with plunder strapped to their rucksacks, but leading Arab families whom they saved from death.[25] Vernet's *Première messe en Kabylie (First Mass in Kabylia)* from 1854 was another contribution to this sentimental vision of the re-Christianization of Algeria: Dom François Régis raises the Eucharist over an improvised altar on the site of what would become the Staouëli monastery while Zouaves kneel reverently in the foreground.[26] Catholic histories of French Algeria described France's colonial ambitions as an effort to restore North Africa to Christendom, and they cast the campaign against Abdelkader as holy war against the forces of Islam. Lamoricière's career, in this telling, pitted civilization against barbarism: he had combatted Islamic barbarians in North Africa, socialist barbarians in the streets of Paris in 1848, and, finally, atheist barbarians in Italy.[27] Commentators interested in the Roman Question whitewashed the brutal Zouave role in the French "pacification" of Algeria as well as the cheerful, amoral Zouave *chapardeurs* of the Crimea.

The Pontifical Zouaves maintained some of the insouciance of their French army namesakes: they were "the good Lord's devils," in the words of one song that was popular in their ranks.[28] Oscar de Poli, an early Zouave volunteer, reported that his companions were jokesters about everything except their commander, the pope, and their mothers, and they marched into battle cheerfully, with a light step.[29] Lamoricière, despite his conversion and his authentic piety, remained quick to anger, like a true Zouave. His officers chuckled knowingly when their commander on occasion deployed "the full African vocabulary, which the Roman atmosphere hadn't had time to purify fully."[30] The appearance of Pontifical Zouaves on sheet-music covers suggested their kinship with their Crimean brothers-in-arms. The Zouave who sings the "Departure of the Crusader" (fig. 38) on the deck of a ship as he hoists a papal flag into the sea breeze that takes him to Rome seems poised between martyrdom and stardom. The lyrics of the song are tragic, and his sweeping gesture might allude to the Crucifixion—but it would be equally at home in a musical number on the vaudeville stage.

FIG. 38. Countess René de Beaumont and Viscountess E. de la Besge, "The Crusader's Departure" (Paris: E. et A. Girod, n.d.). Authors' collection.

Although the performance style was not vaudevillian, Rome was none-theless a theater of sorts and the setting for many grand spectacles. The Zouaves, who wore a distinctive gray and red version of the Oriental cos-tume, quickly fit into the panorama of a city marked by grand religious processions featuring robes in fine fabrics, rich colors, and elaborate dec-oration. According to one Franco-Irish volunteer, the pope's troops kept up the Inkerman tradition, started a theater, and performed "fun and moral" vaudevilles that they ordered from Paris.[31] For Mardi Gras, Cana-dian Zouaves dressed as Indians wheeled a bark "canoe" along the Corso to the delight of the Roman audience, while other Zouaves adopted Italian traditions and rode a float dressed in Pierrot costumes.[32]

In spite of some kinship between French and Pontifical Zouaves, the differences were stark, mostly notably in the Pontifical Zouave's embrace of defeat and martyrdom on the battlefield. Castelfidardo set the tone for recruitment into the Zouaves: immediately after the battle, accounts of the deaths of papal soldiers, presented in hagiographical form, began to circulate. The most famous of these was the compilation by the French writer Anatole de Ségur, *Les Martyrs de Castelfidardo* (1863), that gathered accounts of the devout lives, final letters, and last words of soldiers who gave their lives for the pope. Families of dead Zouaves followed suit, publishing mournful tributes to their dead sons.[33]

These hagiographies emphasized the significance of every Zouave death, whether in battle or in hospital. The stories rang changes on similar narrative elements: evidence of youthful piety, enthusiasm for papal service, excruciating physical suffering, and an eager embrace of last rites. In spite of the repetition, these accounts asserted that Zouave deaths were not in vain and they were not anonymous. Even—especially—in defeat, they had served the pope's cause. Zouave soldiers who "acted without hope and died without glory" had nonetheless triumphed in God's grace.[34]

Victory in defeat and death was possible because the enemy the Zouaves faced was only secondarily the Piedmontese army or Garibaldi's soldiers. The real enemy was "revolution"—the forces of Satan mustered behind the secular state, atheism, and freedom of expression. "Revolution," according to this apocalyptic Catholic view, was not a particular event; it was neither 1789 nor 1848. It was, rather, a dark conjuncture of forces aimed at God and at God's order on earth. Having destroyed monarchies and disrupted Christian life in individual European countries, "revolution" was now preparing a fatal blow aimed at the successor to St. Peter and the rock upon which God built his church. Because this was no ordinary combat, ordinary paths to victory were no longer relevant.

Faced with such an enemy, individual soldiers and even entire armies were merely incidental players in the broader confrontation between good and evil, and only God could save the Papal States. Recognizing these stakes, the Pontifical Zouaves believed that defeat on the battlefield and their own deaths would ultimately result in victory for God's cause. Battle was an occasion for the pope's devout soldiers to suffer and to offer their pain to the Holy Father. The physical and emotional anguish of devout Catholics would expiate human sin, and the purpose of the pope's soldiers was to suffer without counting the cost in order to redeem the sinful world. Young men writing to their families from Rome frequently expressed this conviction that they were sacrificial lambs. Zouave biographies nearly always circle around to young men's desire to die and to make their lifeless bodies a rampart to defend the Vatican.[35] Dead bodies, the Zouaves believed, would be more effective than live ones in defending Christian social order.

Many biographies went out of their way to present their protagonists as gentle youths whom one would not ordinarily expect to find in any uniform, much less the costume of the rowdy Zouaves. Because the purpose of Zouave service was suffering and death, their efficacy as soldiers mattered little. These Zouaves were "virginal and modest" in appearance, often slight in stature.[36] We read of volunteers who were mere teenagers, who walked with crutches as children, or who suffered from chronic illnesses. Boys who died defending the pope "added the patina of Martyrdom to [their] baptismal Innocence."[37] The painting of the Villèle boys (fig. 39) in front of St. Peter's Basilica in Rome captures the impression of untested youth that Zouave hagiographies sought to convey. Louis de Villèle, the eldest, volunteered in 1860 shortly before his nineteenth birthday, and his brother Charles (on the right) joined a year later also at eighteen.[38] Not all Zouaves cultivated the boyish innocence of the Villèles: a collection of cartes de visite includes many Pontifical Zouaves whose beards would have fit right into a North African encampment.[39] For the most part, however, the Zouaves were young and certainly not battle-scarred. Seventy-five percent of French officers of the Pontifical Zouaves (and the majority of officers were French) were between sixteen and twenty-five when they signed up; they obviously brought limited command experience to their post.[40] Their contribution to the papal cause was a military version of the widow's mite.

Women and girls, too, could participate in the all-consuming defense of papal sovereignty as Zouaves, and despite their weakness, their contri-

FIG. 39. Jacques Pilliard, *Portrait of Three Pontifical Zouaves in front of St. Peter's Basilica*, 1863. Private collection.

butions, too, might be efficacious. Gendered cross-dressing among Christian Zouaves was different than on the vaudeville stage, but it was nonetheless present. Although no women actually wore the pontifical uniform, they regularly identified as Zouaves. Pupils in Catholic schools enrolled as "Zouaves in prayer" and declared their readiness to spill their blood for Pius IX. Their "enlistment papers" committed them to offer prayers and sacrifices for a specific period of service, and in some cases, girls signed in their own blood. Nuns, too, could be "Zouaves in prayer," and they often sent their papal nuncio detailed accounts of the hours of prayer and the acts of contrition and mortification that they contributed to the papal arsenal. Bernadette Soubirous, the visionary of Lourdes, wrote to Pius IX from her convent, noting that, "although unworthy," she was "Your Holiness's little Zouave."[41] Confidence in the power of expiatory suffering meant that an army of women like the bedridden Bernadette was, in fact, a force to be reckoned with. Their prayers and their anguish were effective weapons in the battle against revolution. The notion of cloistered women fulfilling the role of the Zouave had considerable staying power: as late as 1896, twenty-five years after the fall of papal Rome, Thérèse Martin, later Saint Thérèse of Lisieux, asserted that her desire to defend the church gave her the courage "of a crusader, a Pontifical Zouave."[42]

No one discounted these female Zouaves' contribution to the defense of Rome because ultimately it was not that different from that of their male counterparts. The most powerful Zouave soldiers were not generals like Lamoricière but enlisted men, and their power derived from their capacity for suffering, not from their ability to kill. Indeed, some Zouaves' extraordinary virtues suggested to their fellow Catholics that they were, in fact, saints and that their role as defenders of papal Rome continued after their death. Although nearly all Zouave stories drew on the tradition of hagiography, some explicitly claimed sainthood for their subjects.

The most famous Zouave soldier and putative saint was a Frenchman, Joseph-Louis Guérin, who died of wounds he sustained at Castelfidardo. His biographer, canon of the cathedral of the city of Nantes, where Guérin had been a seminarian, had relatively little to say about his subject's conduct in battle, noting only that no one went more gaily into combat. He paid close attention, however, to the devotional habits of Guérin's early life and, especially, to his final days of suffering in hospital. Despite intense pain, Guérin accepted death with resignation and begged God to forgive the Piedmontese who had wounded him. He received extreme unction and died with his eyes open, smiling in rapture.[43]

Guérin's Zouave uniform proved crucial to his case for sanctity. The priests who attended his death suspected that they might have witnessed the passing of a saint, and they arranged for the production of a death mask, the repatriation of the body enclosed in a triple coffin, and, of course, the biography. Confirming evidence soon appeared: six months

after his magnificent funeral in Nantes, Guérin, without identifying himself, appeared to a blind, paralyzed, and epileptic Italian girl whose doc-
tors had abandoned hope for her. When he asked what she prayed for,
she answered that she begged for sight. He told her to keep praying, then
returned the next night to tell her that her prayers had been answered.
As he directed, she stood up and saw clearly. She was able to identify
Guérin by his distinctive uniform: her mysterious visitor wore the same
dress as the Pontifical Zouaves she could now see walking through the
streets of her town. Shown a picture of Guérin, she identified him as her
mysterious visitor.[44]

The Zouave-saint was an irresistible figure for the apocalyptic moment
of the defense of Rome. Guérin's supporters in the diocese of Nantes
prepared a dossier to justify his canonization. Prayer cards of Guérin circulated widely, especially among Pontifical Zouaves themselves (fig. 40).
Thousands of visitors flocked to Guérin's tomb, where locals believed that
a lock of the Zouave's hair cured a young shepherdess. Pius IX was said to
keep a bust of this "holy Zouave" in his rooms.[45] Other families adopted
the template: letters from dead sons, snippets of their hair, scapularies
they had worn became not just objects of private remembrance but potential relics. The British Watts-Russell family, for instance, mourning their
seventeen-year-old son Julian, believed that he might be "the Guérin of
England." His body in its Zouave uniform lay "in graceful attitude, as if
he were asleep," and his "sweet smile" appeared "almost supernatural" as
they laid white roses and martyrs' palms around him. His grieving family
preserved his blood-stained uniform, arranged for the publication of his
biography, and welcomed pilgrims who wished to see for themselves the
body of a saint.[46]

Despite the extraordinary sacrifices of the Zouaves, the pope's army
went down in defeat in 1870. With the beginning of the Franco-Prussian
War, the Emperor Napoleon III withdrew French forces from Rome. Papal
rule could not survive without French protection, and the Zouaves' final
act was, once again, to shed their blood in defiance of the armies of the
Kingdom of Italy and the forces of revolution. The pope's army withdrew
to the walls of the city of Rome, but Pius IX determined that he would

FIG. 40. Joseph-Louis Guérin, ca. 1860. Courtesy of *Ouest France*.

not surrender the city without protest. The Pontifical Zouaves, massively outnumbered, led the resistance at the Porta Pia, the gate to the city, where Piedmontese bombardment breached the walls on September 20, 1870. Nineteen Zouaves died, and Pius IX retreated to his palace at the Vatican, where he remained a self-declared "prisoner" for the rest of his life.[47] Rome fell to the army of Victor Emmanuel and soon after became the capital of the kingdom of Italy.

Same War, Different Theaters

Defeat at the Porta Pia was not the end of the Pontifical Zouaves' story. Even as the pope's army disbanded and left Rome in the hands of its new

Italian masters, some Pontifical Zouaves continued their combat against irreligion and revolution in other theaters. Several thousand fought in the Franco-Prussian War: they hoped that the invasion of Protestant Germans would encourage Frenchmen and women to recognize the error of their ways and return to the Catholic Church. Others joined the army of the Spanish pretender, Carlos VII, and fought for the cause of monarchical legitimacy and Catholic Spain. Canadian Zouaves, roughly five hundred of whom had answered their bishop's call to serve in Rome, did not fight another war, but they returned home to combat nonetheless. The Association of Zouaves of Quebec continued to accept and drill new members until well into the second half of the twentieth century. The association organized several generations of young Catholic Quebecers in the struggle against secularization, communism, and Protestantism. Strikingly, in each of these cases, Zouaves kept their uniform. The baggy trousers and short, open jackets became symbols of Catholic alienation from the modern, secular world.

FRANCE AND THE SACRED HEART

In France, Henri de Cathelineau and Athanase de Charette negotiated the creation of a unit for returning Pontifical Zouaves known as the "Volunteers of the West." The provisional government, formed in September 1870 in the wake of the disastrous battle of Sedan and the abdication of Napoleon III, conceded a significant degree of autonomy to the Volunteers. Although the former soldiers of the pope mistrusted this Government of National Defense, composed primarily of parliamentarians who opposed the imperial government, they set their misgivings aside for the cause of the nation. They agreed to recruit from categories of men exempted from conscription by virtue of their age, their family situation, or their enrollment in a seminary. Most enlistments came from their home province of Brittany in western France—hence the Volunteers of the West.[48] They served with the French Army of the Loire and participated in its efforts to protect the city of Paris from Prussian forces.

Charette insisted that the Volunteers retain their distinctive Zouave dress. Disregarding the Zouave units of the regular French army, he asserted that the uniform was "the property of the whole Catholic world whose belief we represent; it is the livery of Rome, it is not ours to be disposed of at will and linked to the fortunes of an unstable government."[49] Fighting for God's cause might temporarily have taken the Zouaves to France, where Protestant Prussians threatened the eldest daughter of the Church, but they had to be ready to return to papal service, Charette insisted. For many Volunteers, the calamities of the war were a divine judgment on France, whose leader had abandoned the pope in his hour of need, and their own service was an effort to redeem French error. Their loyalties lay primarily with their church, not with the unstable provisional government that, Charette was confident, represented only earthly interests.

Most of the Volunteers were new recruits, not returning Pontifical Zouaves. Over five thousand men—three-quarters of the unit—signed up in the nine months between its formation in October 1870 and the end of the war, although nearly all the officers had served the pope in Italy. New enlistments came primarily from rural areas, and young men often enlisted in groups from a single school or, especially, seminary. They shared the Pontifical Zouaves' devout Catholicism: many of them went on to become priests after their service.[50] The press and even the French military hierarchy regularly referred to them as "Pontifical Zouaves," however, and neither Charette nor his men cared to correct the misapprehension. They believed that they were fighting the same war—for Christendom—against the same enemy: revolution. Only the theater of the conflict had changed.

The Volunteers adopted the Pontifical Zouaves' belief in expiatory sacrifice and their desire for self-immolation. The most significant moment in the Volunteers' war—and the central element of postwar myth-making—was the battle of Loigny, a bloody defeat that left two-thirds of the Volunteers who participated in it either dead or wounded. The Army of the Loire was attempting to break German lines south of Paris and to relieve the besieged city. At the village of Loigny, a small force composed largely of Volunteers charged German lines in December 1870. They expected support from other units that never arrived, and the result was disastrous. Like the Pontifical Zouaves before them, however, the Volunteers knew how to embrace defeat, and Loigny soon became a byword for expiatory sacrifice and for suffering that was more efficacious than victory.[51]

The Volunteers' flag with an emblem of the Sacred Heart of Christ was the centerpiece of their cult of sacrifice (fig. 41). Suspended from the top and shaped like a religious procession banner rather than a military standard, the flag was white silk, with Christ's heart in red velvet and, embroidered in gold, "Heart of Jesus, Save France." It solidified the association between the Zouaves' exotic dress and their Christian faith, affirming that their deaths would echo that of the crucified Christ and that their mingled blood would redeem France in defeat.

The Visitandine nuns who embroidered the banner interpreted it in prophetic terms that the Volunteers readily adopted. Sister Marguerite Marie Alacoque, whose seventeenth-century visions of the Sacred Heart in the convent at Paray le Monial were the origin of the modern cult, reported that Christ called on Louis XIV to build a chapel, consecrate France to his Sacred Heart, and place its image on the military standards of the kingdom. Two centuries later, and just a few years after Alacoque's beatification in 1864, French soldiers would finally march into battle beneath the Sacred Heart.[52] The Volunteers decided that a Pontifical Zouave who had served in Rome should have the honor of carrying it.[53] The appearance of the Sacred Heart on the battlefield, according to the commanding general Gaston de Sonis, was "electrifying."[54] Men launched themselves into combat crying out "Vive la France! Long live Pius IX!" The emblem of the Sacred Heart reinforced the link between the Volunteers and the pope's defenders, and it reached back to France's long counterrevolutionary, monarchist, and Catholic tradition. Charette's great uncle and Cathelineau's grandfather followed the banner of the Sacred Heart in the Royal and Catholic Army of the Vendée against the forces of the French Revolution, and decades later their descendants swore allegiance to the same cause at Loigny.

Gaston de Sonis became the most prominent figure of the battle of Loigny, and for decades afterward he incarnated the Volunteers' cause. Although Sonis, a career military officer, did not wear the Zouave uniform, he led the Volunteers into battle and shared their Catholic faith. Accounts of his command mobilized all Zouave stereotypes: gay bravery, egalitarianism, and the eager embrace of pain. As the outnumbered Volunteers advanced, one gallant officer cheerfully thanked Sonis for inviting him to such a charming party. In the aftermath of battle, with the field full of corpses wearing identical Zouave uniforms, Sonis observed that it was impossible to distinguish rank. One body that he had taken for a common soldier turned out to be the officer who had so politely thanked him just hours earlier. Sonis led the way in suffering: with his leg shattered by a bullet, he spent the night in the snow listening to the moans of the dying. One young, wounded Volunteer dragged himself over to his general and died with his head resting on Sonis's shoulder.[55]

Supernatural comfort sustained Sonis throughout the night on the battlefield as his experience of bitter defeat and physical agony made him a true representative of the Christian Zouave tradition. Never losing consciousness, he remained in communion with Our Lady of Lourdes, who soothed his pain. Sonis's sister, a Carmelite nun, woke suddenly that night with the conviction that the Sacred Heart of Christ was protecting her brother. Later, having recovered from the amputation of his leg, Sonis made a pilgrimage to Lourdes, where he left his Legion of Honor cross on the altar. Sonis's biographer, a prolific writer of hagiographies, extolled the extraordinary devotion of this man whose face, after his death, took on a "supernatural beauty" that caused those standing next to his bier to feel closer to heaven.[56]

Despite the disastrous battle of Loigny, the Volunteers of the West made a final, fictional appearance during the Paris Commune, an episode in which the city's left-wing government refused to surrender to the Prussians and declared its autonomy. Rumors of the Volunteers' participation in the repression of the Commune confirm the association between Zouave dress and reactionary Catholicism. In April 1871, four months after General Sonis and the remnants of the Volunteers lay in the field at Loigny, news circulated that "Pontifical Zouaves . . . Charette's Chouans, [and] Cathelineau's Vendéens" had attacked the people of Paris, *"shooting prisoners, slaughtering the wounded, and firing on dressing stations."* Robert Tombs has demonstrated that these reports were baseless, elements of a "Chouan myth" intended to generate support for valiant Parisians betrayed by their fellow Frenchmen.[57] Implicating the Volunteers of the West in the repression of the Paris Commune contributed to the Parisian sense that their struggle for municipal liberty was in fact an epic battle with the forces of counterrevolution. It also cemented the association between Zouave dress and Catholic reaction.

MOBILIZING VETERANS

A combination of military camaraderie and Catholic devotion undergirded the veteran organizing that Athanase de Charette, in particular, made his postwar calling. Over the course of the 1870s, as the Third Republic consolidated power, it became clear that there would be no restoration of a Bourbon, Catholic monarchy in France. Charette and his fellow Zouaves turned their attention to the task of keeping their brand of militant, legitimist Catholicism alive, and the Zouave uniform became an important symbol of this aim. Veterans wore it in public as a statement of their loyalty to the "prisoner of the Vatican" and the cause of Catholic Europe. Their sons might wear it as a school uniform, like the pupils of the Assumptionist order in Nîmes, who were training to be the next generation of soldiers in this fight.[58] Charette and his colleagues understood veteran organizing not as a peacetime activity, but as a different way of pursuing his military aims.

Veterans of the Volunteers / Pontifical Zouaves helped inspire the National Vow, a movement to atone for France's sins, foremost among which was the abandonment of Pius IX. Military defeat and the violence of the Paris Commune were, in Charette's view, further signs that God was punishing French atheism. The death of the archbishop of Paris, taken hostage and assassinated by supporters of the Commune, confirmed the Catholic Zouaves' conviction that France had become an apostate nation. The Vow bound those who took it in 1872 to fulfill the original demands of the Sacred Heart by building a church—the basilica of Sacré Coeur de Paris.[59] The Volunteers realized one element of Alacoque's vision by following the Sacred Heart into battle, and the National Vow would complete France's reconciliation with God by building the chapel

Christ had requested. Charette emphasized this continuity and promoted the National Vow in a widely publicized 1873 pilgrimage to Paray le Monial, where he laid the Zouave banner of Loigny on Sister Marguerite Marie's tomb. The gleaming white-domed church that looks down over the city of Paris from the Montmartre hill has, since its completion on the eve of World War I, been an assertion of the counterrevolutionary, Catholic vision of French history that Sonis, Charette, and their Zouaves fought for.[60]

The figure of a Zouave occupies a key position in the decorative program of the basilica, a fitting tribute to the Zouave role in its conception and implementation. The visitor walks through a dark nave, which opens on to an apse with a domed ceiling covered in a sparkling mosaic. At the center, Christ, his arms outstretched, reveals his heart, in gold on his chest, to the worshiper. Two registers of figures extend on either side of him: above are saints in heaven, and below are the church's defenders on earth. At Christ's left among the earthly are the men responsible for the construction of the basilica including, prominently, Gaston de Sonis wielding his sword and Athanase de Charette in Zouave uniform, carrying the Loigny banner of the Sacred Heart (fig. 41). The Sacré Coeur mosaic permanently identified the Zouave uniform with intransigent Catholicism: the Zouave sword remains ready to defend the pope and Christian France at all times.

Veteran organizations were another arena in which to promote the Zouave as a symbol of Catholic devotion. In 1871 the League of Saint Sebastian assembled former Pontifical Zouaves from Britain and Ireland who vowed to "joyfully return to the Capital of Christendom . . . once again to range ourselves under the standard of the Cross, and if need be die in its defense."[61] Identification with Saint Sebastian, the first Christian martyr, typified the Zouave embrace of suffering and death: the choice of a patron saint reminded members that their willingness to take up arms and return to Rome was less belligerent than sacrificial. In the same year, Canadian Zouaves established the Allet Union, named after their Swiss commanding officer. In addition to holding themselves ready to return to Rome, they organized aid for poor members and campaigned for a mon-

FIG. 41. Olivier Mersen, mosaic, Sacré Coeur, Paris, with Sonis and Charrette (*right*). Courtesy of Basilique Sacré Coeur de Montmartre. Photograph by Sophie Lloyd.

ument to the bishop of Montreal, Ignace Bourget, who had called Canadians to volunteer.[62] In the 1870s local associations of former Pontifical Zouaves also emerged in the Low Countries, where members frequently wore their Zouave uniforms to march in religious processions.[63]

Charette's prestige as a Zouave officer and an active defender of papal interests ensured that he enjoyed considerable influence over Zouave associations outside of France. When the Association of Former Zouaves and Pontifical Volunteers in Brabant (Belgium) wrote formal statutes in 1894, they included a letter of approval from Charette. Taking their cue from the French National Vow, the Belgian Zouaves mobilized to raise a subscription for their own national basilica of the Sacred Heart, begun in 1905 on the Koekelberg plateau overlooking the city of Brussels. Canadian Zouaves similarly sought Charette's approbation in the 1880s before reorganizing the Allet Union as the Association of Quebec Zouaves and admitting members' sons. Charette traveled extensively, maintaining connections to Zouave groups: in 1882, Canadian Zouaves in the town of Saint-Hyacinthe even changed the date of their celebrations of the feast of Saint John the Baptist, patron saint of French Canada, to coincide with Charette's visit.[64]

Charette's centrality to the Zouave movement was on full view when, in 1885, he invited all former Pontifical Zouaves to a twenty-fifth anniversary celebration of the formation of the unit at his home at La Basse Motte, in Brittany. Hundreds of ex-Zouaves from all over western Europe and as far away as Canada converged on his rural estate some fifteen kilometers outside of Saint-Malo and attracted considerable media attention. Charette collected newspaper stories published across France and from as far away as Valparaiso, Chile, in a souvenir book, *Les Noces d'argent du régiment des Zouaves pontificaux, 1860–1885* (*The Silver Anniversary of the Regiment of Pontifical Zouaves*). The event itself was a celebration of the sacrifices that Zouaves had made as young men and the Christian fraternity that endured into their mature years. At an outdoor altar draped in the papal colors of yellow and white, Charette himself served at mass, wiping away tears as the priest, also a former Pontifical Zouave, elevated the host before the assembled veterans and their families. Fifteen-year-old Guillaume de Bouillé, who presented the Volunteers' Sacred Heart flag, was the son and grandson of men who had both died carrying it at Loigny. The sight of this boy, kneeling beneath the flag stained with the blood of his ancestors, was the emotional highlight of the day, which closed with a banquet for over a thousand guests. In Zouave fashion, aristocrats dined with common folk and cheerful toasts to Zouave gaiety followed mournful testimony of Zouave suffering.[65]

Charette imagined himself at the center of an international network of Catholic men linked to one another by these enduring bonds of devotion and sacrifice. At the banquet at La Basse Motte, he read telegrams testifying to the solidarity among Zouaves around the Catholic world. He attended similar anniversary gatherings in the Low Countries later that year. In 1892 he established a Confraternity of the Sacred Heart at La Basse Motte with a governing board whose members represented different national associations. Any ex-Pontifical Zouave could join, have his name inscribed on the wall of the memorial chapel, and benefit from indulgences and the prayers of other confraternity members.[66] *L'Avant-Garde*, the magazine for Pontifical Zouave veterans that appeared from 1892 to 1932, opened its pages to comrades across France and beyond to publish accounts of veteran banquets, memoirs of Zouave service, obituaries, classified ads, and Catholic news items of general interest. German ex-Zouaves, for instance, who lived in a Prussian-dominated German Empire with an overtly anti-Catholic policy that made Zouave organizing unlikely, used the pages of *L'Avant-Garde* to keep up with old comrades and to remember their youthful service.[67]

SPAIN AND THE CARLIST WAR

Not all former Zouaves were content to trade their Roman and Franco-Prussian military experience for reunions and fundraising: a small cohort of ex-Pontificals made their way to Spain to fight in the Third Carlist War. Convinced that Spain was the new theater in the ongoing combat against atheism and revolution, these Zouaves enlisted in the cause of the Catholic Pretender, Carlos VII. The 1868 overthrow of Queen Isabel II and the subsequent selection of Amadeo, Duke of Savoy and son of the Italian king Victor Emmanuel II, as king revived Carlism, a movement that supported the male line of Spanish Borbón descent. Amadeo's 1873 abdication and the proclamation of a republic amidst civil turmoil gave Carlist forces the opportunity to seize large sections of Navarre and the Basque province. The seventy thousand troops of the Carlist army were enough to hold large sections of the north, but never sufficient to take the city of Bilbao. Carlists hoped that the republic would collapse into chaos and open the door to restoration of Carlos VII. In fact, however, a coalition of politicians and generals negotiated the ascension of Isabel II's son, Alfonso XII, in 1874. His promise to rule as a good Catholic, a loyal Spaniard, and a liberal constitutionalist signaled the end of Spanish Carlism.[68]

The Zouaves who joined the cause served under Alfonso de Borbón, Carlos's brother and their own brother-in-arms, who had joined the Pontifical Zouaves in 1868 at the age of eighteen. Don Alfonso signed up as a common soldier and allegedly peeled his fair share of potatoes before accepting an officer's commission as an act of obedience to the pope. In 1870 he participated in the last stand at the Porta Pia, where he wielded a sword that had belonged to his grandfather Carlos V and his great-uncle Carlos VI.[69] Three years later, in support of his brother's bid for the Spanish throne, he put his command experience to the test by forming a Zouave unit. Of the twelve Spaniards who had served under him in Italy, nine joined the new Carlist Zouaves, which also attracted several dozen international volunteers, most of whom had passed through the Pontifical Zouaves, the Volunteers of the West, or both.[70] Charette had a finger in this pie as well: in 1872 he offered Don Alfonso the muster roll of Volunteers of the West.[71]

Spaniards were of course aware of the international fame of the Zouave, and not only in its Catholic version. Many Zouaves in the French army were Spanish, part of the wave of Mediterranean immigration to France's colony in North Africa. Spanish coverage of the Crimean War reminded readers that some of the fearsome Zouave fighters who "launched themselves like tigers, erupting in high-pitched, frightening screams," were emigrants to Algeria, chased out of Spain by "our civil discord."[72] The international Zouave craze had barely reached Spain in the 1870s, however: Madrid had only one militia group in 1869, the short-lived Zouaves of Liberty, composed mostly of railway workers with liberal political views. The field was largely clear for Don Alfonso's Carlist Zouaves to promote the association between Zouave dress and intransigent Catholic devotion.[73]

Don Alfonso's battalion wore the Zouave uniform in the same colors as their pontifical counterparts—indeed, because the Carlists never established successful supply lines, some of them wore the same uniforms that had already seen service in Rome several years previously. Alfonso recommended that his old comrades from Roman days bring their uniforms with them, and one American journalist remarked on the shabby clothes "riddled and torn by bullets" that had, remarkably, spared their wearers.[74] The large red beret that replaced the kepi differentiated the Spanish Zouaves from their papal predecessors.

The Carlist uniform, even more than its Roman antecedent, emphasized the Catholic piety of the soldiers who wore it. Every man pinned the emblem of the Sacred Heart of Christ on his chest, and even chaplains wore Zouave dress along with an incongruous clerical collar. The Spanish Zouaves marched behind a banner inspired by the flag of the Volunteers of the West that featured the Sacred Heart of Christ flanked by the arms of Pius IX and Spain. Carmelite nuns, working to Alfonso's own design, embroidered it, and, like the Loigny banner, it became an important element in the Zouave mythology, making its final appearance in 1936 on Don Alfonso's coffin in his Austrian exile.[75]

María de las Nieves de Braganza y Borbón, Don Alfonso's wife, was perhaps the most famous of the Carlist Zouaves, and her example is a reminder that women, too, could be Catholic Zouaves. The couple married in 1871, shortly after Alfonso's Roman service ended, and in their wedding photograph he wears his Zouave uniform. Doña Blanca, as she was known, remained with her husband at the front throughout the Carlist War where she, too, donned the beret and the short jacket alongside a riding skirt that might easily pass for Zouave trousers. Like a true Zouave, she never pulled rank: though she was the daughter of the king of Portugal, she unhesitatingly did her husband's laundry at the front. Photographs from the campaign depicted her as her husband's military partner: both wearing Zouave dress with the Carlist beret, they examine a map, and her riding crop echoes his sword (fig. 42). A dramatic painting of the battle of Alpens shows Doña Blanca at the center, riding sidesaddle on a white horse with the banner of the Sacred Heart (and her husband) behind her.[76]

These images of the intrepid Zouave princess crystallized opposing views of the Carlist movement. The royal couple's liberal and anticlerical opponents condemned her as a "circus Amazon" and an "Attila in skirts" whose "manly spirit" called into question the virility of her husband and their followers. Catholic supporters, however, praised "la generala" and compared her to Isabel of Castile, heroine of the Spanish Reconquista. According to this view, her Catholic faith guided her understanding of when

FIG. 42. Alfonso de Borbón and María de las Nieves, from María de las Nieves de Braganza y Borbón, *Mis memorias sobre nuestra campaña en Cataluña en 1872 y 1873 y en el centro en 1874* (1938). Courtesy of the Bibliothèque nationale de France.

to violate social conventions in order to protect God's order on earth. This debate over how to interpret Doña Blanca's Zouave appearance continued to divide Spaniards into the 1930s when María de las Nieves published her memoirs of the Carlist movement in an effort to maintain the relevance of the Borbón line in the era of the Spanish Civil War.[77]

CATHOLIC ZOUAVES' LAST STAND: QUEBEC

The phenomenon of Pontifical Zouaves lived longest in French Canada, where men continued to wear Zouave dress to assert their loyalty to their church a full century after the fall of Rome. Canada sent five hundred Zouave soldiers to Rome, including a contingent of just over one hundred who arrived after the fall of the Porta Pia. Recruitment began in earnest in 1867 after two early Canadian volunteers, Hugh Murray and Alfred LaRoque, were injured defending the pope at the battle of Mentana. The bishop of Montreal, Ignace Bourget, encouraged young French Canadians to follow Murray and LaRoque and form a battalion of Zouaves "to show the world ... that the name of the immortal Pius IX is blessed in the cold countries of the north."[78] Leading citizens established Catholic Committees to raise funds: they encouraged everyone from business magnates to small children to donate money and prayers.[79]

Bourget was a committed ultramontane, and he believed that the fate of Canada's Francophone Catholics depended on that of the pope. Strengthening the Catholic faith of the population seemed imperative after the British North America Act of 1840 (also known as the Act of Union) had abolished the largely Francophone parliament of Lower Canada. Anglophone Protestants dominated the newly formed Province of Canada. Bourget was under no illusion that a few hundred Canadian Zouaves would make much difference to the outcome of the Risorgimento, but he did believe that they could stiffen the resolve of Catholic Canadians and inoculate them against the missionary efforts of Francophone Swiss Protestants who were proselytizing in the area. The movement to recruit and equip young men for the pope's cause mobilized ordinary believers in ways that sermons, pastoral letters, and parochial fundraising had failed to do. Enlistments came from all over French Canada, and recruits, many of whom were from modest social origins, purchased their passage and equipment with the financial support of their parishes.[80] According to the Canadian Zouaves' chaplain, "the wounds of the Holy Father had become the wounds of the nation."[81]

Although the Canadian Zouaves saw little fighting in Italy, they returned home to heroes' welcomes and enjoyed great prestige in French Canadian society. Canadian veterans of the pope's army fulfilled all of Mgr Bourget's expectations, reminding generations of French Canadians of their obligations to the Catholic Church. Returning Zouaves were central to the creation of a French-Canadian identity in the decades after the fall of Rome.

Schemes to colonize the Quebec wilderness with Catholic Francophones focused on ex-Zouaves: the Société Générale de Colonisation de

Montréal paid Zouave veterans five dollars per month for two years and equipped colonists with oxen and other communal resources. Relatively few Zouaves actually settled at Piopolis, whose name indicates the organizers' desire to create "the pope's own parish" in faithful Quebec. Nonetheless, the idea that hearty former Zouaves would tame the back country during the day and spin tales of their Roman glory days at night, all the while discouraging their fellow French Canadians from emigrating to the United States, was powerfully attractive.[82]

Ex-Zouaves were not particularly interested in civilizing the Canadian wilderness, but they were keen to maintain their collective identity in urban Quebec. Their sons enrolled in Quebecois schools where they served in militia companies dressed as Zouaves until 1879, when the federal government forbade Canadian pupils wearing the uniform of a foreign army.[83] In the 1880s veterans expanded membership of their association to include those sons, and by 1900 the Association of Zouaves of Quebec (AZQ) admitted any young man of good character who wished to perpetuate the memory of "the crusaders of the nineteenth century." Forty-three companies, almost all in the province of Quebec, kept the Zouave tradition alive. Until the 1980s, Zouaves in Quebec drilled, marched in processions, went on pilgrimages, appeared at funerals, and eventually organized sporting leagues, amateur theatricals, picnics, ping-pong, and bingo.[84]

The Zouave uniform was central to the success of the AZQ, and it appeared on the streets of Canadian cities long after it had disappeared into European museum collections. A French missionary of the Sacred Heart posted to Quebec wrote in 1906 of his astonishment at encountering an armed Zouave in full pontifical dress on the tram, where "no one else seemed surprised" at his anachronistic presence.[85] Quebec veterans of Pius IX's army treated their uniforms as relics, and that status rubbed off onto early twentieth-century versions that nuns sewed for the AZQ members. Association statutes meticulously detailed the signs of respect due to the uniform: members should not dishonor it through poor conduct, and they should return it upon departure from the unit. In the early years of the association, members were often buried in their

Zouave dress. In 1910, the AZQ trademarked the uniform in order to limit its circulation in Quebec society. When, in 1961, a comical TV character wore the Zouave uniform, the AZQ complained to Radio-Canada, which promptly re-costumed the character and apologized. When the association modernized its uniform in 1964, there were protests within its ranks as the new version with its straight-leg trousers lacked the sentimental and devotional connection to the papacy.[86]

The AZQ was a cornerstone of what scholars describe as the "French Canadian church-nation": Catholicism gave French Canadians political and historical consciousness, and groups like the Zouaves established the traditions and ceremonies of Quebecois nationalism.[87] Ironically, the uniform of a mid-nineteenth-century international military force became a symbol of nationalist pride in the twentieth. Canadian men in Zouave dress represented devout Catholicism, anti-communism, and unyielding attachment to province and language. Their association and its uniform, proudly worn in public and passed down through generations, demonstrated their determination to maintain the traditions of a besieged religious and linguistic minority. AZQ membership peaked in the 1950s just before the Quiet Revolution secularized Quebecois society and gave young people new educational and entertainment options. Vatican II broke with the Catholic Church's most intransigent positions and encouraged Catholic enclaves like Quebec to open up to modern political and social life. In the 1970s the AZQ moved away from military exercises, recognizing that young people in an era of making love, not war, found pretend soldiering off-putting. The Quebec Zouaves' final public appearance announced their persistent loyalties, however: eighty-four members in uniform welcomed Pope John Paul II to Quebec in 1984.[88]

Quebecers were the last to abandon the mobilizing power of Catholic *zouaverie*, but it diminished slowly in Europe as well. In 1957, *Pro Petri Sede*, the magazine of Belgian and Dutch Zouave veterans founded in 1922, wrote that, as members reflected on their thirty-five-year history, they concluded that "the Zouave epic" had come to an end in 1929 with the signing of the Lateran Treaty that resolved the standoff between the papacy and the Italian government by creating Vatican City. Decades—

and a world war—having passed since that treaty, it was time to bury the hatchet and, instead of continuing to "parade in the streets in the romantic uniforms of the pontifical Zouaves," readers should "put them in a museum, next to the uniforms and the red shirts of Victor Emmanuel."[89] The fancy dress of the Zouaves would rest peacefully next to the fancy dress of their opponents, the two causes, church and nation, having, in the long run, proven not so incompatible after all.

That juxtaposition of ideologically opposed but materially similar uniforms had been central to the success of Catholic Zouaves from the beginning. The fervent religious devotion and yearning for martyrdom of the Catholic Zouave had taken shape against the foil of the hard-drinking, womanizing, battle-scarred "jackal" of North Africa. Their outfits differed only in details of color schemes, braid patterns, and the turban. In both cases the uniform proclaimed the individuality of the man who wore it. In the same years that Catholics were mobilizing around the loss of Rome and their Zouaves' defeat, their French counterparts were similarly consolidating their legend and re-inventing themselves as republican soldiers. The coarse, fierce Zouave of the Army of Africa never effaced his devout, fragile double of the papal army, however.

6

SOUNDING THE RETREAT

The Zouave retreat from international stardom was uneven, and Zouaves on opposite sides of the Atlantic took different paths to obsolescence. The fad ended relatively quickly in the Americas, with the uniform relegated to a performance costume outside Quebec. In France, however, Zouaves retained their high profile throughout the last decades of the nineteenth century, and their role as empire-builders accelerated under the Third Republic, a regime that was as committed to colonial expansion as its predecessor. The transformation of warfare that took place in the Great War unseated the Zouave from his role in the French popular imagination. Decolonization finished him off, with all regiments disbanded in 1962 when Algeria achieved independence.

The year 1870 was a key moment in this bifurcation of Zouave history. France's defeat that year in the Franco-Prussian War led to the fall of the Second Empire and of Napoleon III, who had often associated his rule with Zouave troops. Papal Rome collapsed in the same year when French troops withdrew from their garrison, leaving the outnumbered papal forces to face the army of the Kingdom of Italy on their own. Many Pontifical Zouaves returned home while others went on to fight for related causes: the union of throne and altar in France and Spain and francophone Catholicism in Canada. In the United States, military authorities sharpened their critique of flamboyant volunteers by blaming French defeat in the Franco-Prussian war on its Zouave warriors. That diagnosis of the French loss was largely limited to the United States, however; the

French assessment of the war, conducted by the leadership of the newly installed Third Republic, did not lay blame with Zouaves. With the events of 1870, the Zouave moment was clearly coming to an end, the international fad had run its course, and the Zouave look retreated to its origins in France and the French empire.

Zouaves of the Republic

In its homeland the Zouave look had never been just a passing trend, and Zouaves continued to occupy their central role in the Army of Africa and in broader French culture. Zouave dress symbolized a defiant patriotism, which is why the soloist Jules-Célestien Devoyod wore it in the opening days of the Franco-Prussian War at the Paris Opéra to sing Charles Gounod's jingoistic new song "To the Frontier" in a rousing performance that one reviewer described as "very martial, *very authentic.*"[1] Despite the collapse of the empire a month later, the capacity of Zouave dress to evoke nationalist sentiment persisted. Although the French engaged in extensive soul-searching following the 1870 defeat, Zouaves emerged from the process unscathed and observers continued to invoke the clichéd judgment that Zouaves were the finest soldiers in the world.

Remarkably, given the close association between the Zouaves of the Imperial Guard and Napoleon III, no commentators found particular fault with their military performance, in part because the broader trend was for critics to hold common soldiers blameless. Military reforms focused on creating a citizen army via expanded conscription, regional recruitment, and a deliberate utilization of the peacetime army as a school of citizenship, none of which was incompatible with *zouaverie*. Other assessments called for thoroughgoing transformation of the educational system on the oft-cited grounds that the true victor in the war was the Prussian schoolmaster. Although the Prussian army and Prussian society often served as a model for French reforms, no one suggested abolishing the distinctively French Zouave units.[2]

The Imperial Guard, including its Zouave members, was of course disbanded. After their defeat at Metz, the Zouaves of the Guard cut their regimental flag into pieces that they distributed among the officers and men of the unit before returning to Algeria. They immediately reconstituted as the Fourth Zouave Regiment, however, joining the historic three regiments that had served in the Crimea. In 1891 officers of the Fourth established a commission to recover the fragments of the flag, and the unit's 1897 regimental history proudly asserted that the Fourth Zouaves were the heirs of the Imperial Guard.[3] This very brief hiccup in the history of the emperor's Zouaves indicates that the Third Republic readily assimilated the military culture of its imperial predecessor.

The Zouaves rebounded quickly from their association with Bonapartism because the Third Republic shared the previous regime's ambitions for overseas expansion, and the Army of Africa was the institution capable of delivering colonial conquests. The new republic's first colonial challenge—the Kabyle uprising of 1871—occurred in Algeria, and Zouave regiments returned to home to meet it. The Franco-Prussian War encouraged Kabyle leaders to confront colonial rule because much of the African army had crossed the Mediterranean to defend France, leaving only forty thousand French troops in North Africa. Native landowners also knew that the collapse of the Second Empire would augment the power of settlers in the colony. Napoleon III had conceived of Algeria as an "Arab Kingdom" that he ruled in the interests of its native people, which in practice meant concentrating power in the hands of the army and the Arab Bureaux. Bureaux officers, who often spent their entire careers in Algeria, learned local languages, and sympathized with indigenous people and their claims to land, frustrated settlers. Colonists looked to civilian administrators to back their claims to the colony's resources, and their staunch republicanism reflected their dislike of Arab Kingdom policies. The installation of the Third Republic signaled to natives and colonists alike that the balance of power in the colony was about to shift decisively toward settler interests.[4]

The recently defeated Zouaves thus found themselves in reconstituted units fighting on their home territory whose French-imposed place names recalled their earlier victories. One of the first colonial villages to fall to insurgents was Palestro (now Lakhdaria), founded in 1868 and named after the site of Zouave victory in Italy. A new battle of Alma took place in the spring of 1871 as insurgents encircled and burned the town of that name (now Boudouaou) in April.[5] After the repression of the insurrection, the Zouave presence in the landscape expanded as settlers established new footholds like the village of Lamoricière (today Ouled Mimoun), founded in 1869 with a European population that trebled in the next five years as capitalist agriculture came to the region.[6]

With Algeria secured for the new French republic, the Zouaves went on to play key roles in all of the major colonial ventures of the fin de siècle. All four Zouave regiments participated in the invading force that established a French protectorate over Tunisia in 1881. The First, Second, and Third Zouaves took part in France's campaigns in Indochina in the late 1880s, and the Second, Third, and Fourth served in China in 1900–1901 as France joined an allied response to the Boxer Rebellion's challenge to Western colonialism. Back in North Africa, all four Zouave regiments fought in Morocco between 1907 and 1914.[7]

A growing phalanx of soldiers in African-derived dress joined the Zouaves in their imperial campaigns during the Third Republic. The strategy of deploying native soldiers in exotic uniforms remained central to the pursuit of empire into the first decade of the twentieth century. When Napoleon III created the *tirailleurs sénégalais* in 1857, their costume resembled that of the Zouaves and the *tirailleurs algériens* or Turcos: baggy trousers, open collarless jacket, and the *chéchia*. The Spahi uniform for native cavalry also enjoyed considerable prestige outside North Africa: the French army included Black African and Indochinese Spahis. Units of Moroccan *goumiers,* clad in a striped knee-length robe (*djellaba*) and bearing an elaborate, curved dagger, joined the French army in 1908.[8]

Zouaves' imperial exploits ensured that they persisted as popular symbols of military valor and ingenuity in the visual culture of the metropole. Paper soldiers, ready to be cut out, pasted to cardboard, and mobilized into armies for childhood games, remained popular, as did their more expensive metal versions. By the turn of the century, Zouaves rivaled zebras in children's ABC books that increasingly focused on simple, graphic illustration. The Zouave Jacob's faith-healing business continued until his death in 1913, and he survived several legal challenges at the fin de siècle.[9]

FIG. 43. Jean de Brunhoff, *ABC de Babar* (Paris: Editions du jardin des modes, 1934). Courtesy of the Bibliothèque nationale de France.

The Zouave's career as a consumer brand took off under the Republic. The Zouave had demonstrated early marketing potential: even before the Crimean War, we find him, for instance, advertising a "Zouave mixture," which promised to cover gray hair in the moustaches and sideburns of middle-aged men.[10] At the end of the century, Zouave marketing accelerated, with the Zouave serving, for instance, as logo for the aperitif Amer Picon, which was made in Marseille but originally developed in Algeria as an antimalarial tonic, and the Dijon-produced Absinthe Mugnier.[11] The Crimean Zouave became the main advertising icon of the cigarette-rolling-paper company Braunstein frères, which began selling flat booklets of papers in 1879. According to their publicity, a resourceful Zouave invented the cigarette when a stray bullet snapped his clay pipe at Sebastapol. Unperturbed by the close call, he ripped off a bit of paper from his bag of gunpowder, rolled his tobacco up in it and enjoyed his smoke. The company's "Zig Zag" brand refers both to the Zouave and to the layout of the interleaved papers dispensed one at a time, introduced in the 1890s.[12] France's most infamous racialized brand—Banania, a powdered drink made of cocoa and banana flour—featured Zouave dress although not a Zouave: its brand ambassador was a grinning, pidgin-speaking *tirailleur sénégalais* in a *chéchia*.[13]

Zouaves held the foreground as military painting of the Third Republic continued the turn away from heroic battles and toward smaller-scale genre scenes and realistic depictions of soldiers' experience that had begun during the Crimean War.[14] The Zouave was a figure of anecdote—his presence convinces the viewer that there is something interesting going on behind the painting, a true story, probably involving reckless bravery and *joie de vivre*. A painting like Alphonse de Neuville's enormously popular *Les Dernières Cartouches* (The Last Cartridges) from 1873 makes no effort to render the battlefield legible or to locate the scene in the larger course of the war (fig. 44). We see only a corner of the action, a group of French soldiers taking cover in a house that has come under attack. Several are grievously wounded, but they prepare their resistance nonetheless. A Turco stands at the window, ready to fire but husbanding the last, precious cartridges, and his dark skin stands out against the pale blue wallpaper. We don't know how he found himself there with men from other units (and in fact there were no Turcos present in this engagement), but we can imagine stories of how a colonial soldier might behave in such a predicament and speculate about how he might extricate himself. Thanks to the narrative drive of the painting, *Les Dernières Cartouches* was the inspiration for three early films, two of which (by Georges Méliès in 1897 and Pathé in 1899) replace Neuville's Black Turco with a European soldier in Zouave dress.[15]

The Zouave energy invested in theater in the 1850s and 1860s redirected itself toward fiction at the fin de siècle. The most famous example is Alphonse Daudet's "Le Mauvais Zouave" (The Bad Zouave), a short story in which an old Alsatian joins the Zouaves to finish the service commitment of his faithless son.[16] More important than the "bad Zouave"

FIG. 44. Alphonse de Neuville, *The Last Cartridges*, 1873.
Copyright RMN–Grand Palais / Art Resource, New York.

son in this story is his fifty-five-year-old father, who, at the recruitment depot at Sidi-bel-Abbès, exemplifies all of the Zouave's best qualities. In Daudet's story as in so many other tales, anyone can be a Zouave, because patriotism and toughness are not limited to the young.

The Zouave affinity for anecdote made him an excellent character for writers of pulp fiction, who often included a Zouave story or two in their output.[17] As with painting, the fictional Zouave set stories moving in an economical fashion, sparing authors the trouble of extended character development. When a French translation of the English novelist Ouida's 1867 hit *Under Two Flags* appeared in 1888, the new title, *Cigarette, cantinière des zouaves*, directed the reader's attention to the vivacious *cantinière* rather than the unjustly dishonored English aristocrat who enlists in the French army under a *nom de guerre*. The English original doesn't specify what kind of soldiers Cigarette served, but the French translator, extrapolating from the observation that she could "swear, if need be, like a Zouave," assigned her to the regiment.[18] The popular interest in all things Zouave especially fueled the career of the prolific writer Louis Noir.

A Zouave veteran of the Crimea and the Mexican expedition under the Second Empire, Noir recycled his military experience in a series of tales with Zouave heroes in the last decades of the nineteenth century. Noir wrote military memoir, North African travelogue, and adventure fiction—over 250 titles in all. His formula in each genre relied on his way with a human interest story and eye for the telling detail, and the Zouave was an endless reservoir for both.[19]

The career of the nationalist politician and one-time Zouave Paul Déroulède demonstrates how fully republicanized the Zouave became within the first decades of the Third Republic. Déroulède built a right-wing movement dedicated to national revenge (*revanche*) for France's 1870 defeat. Famously, he opposed colonial expansion because he believed that it distracted his fellow citizens from seeking vengeance against Germany. Déroulède ruptured the traditional links between monarchy, Catholicism, and conservative politics as well as the assumption that republicanism was a revolutionary ideology. His politics were conservative, republican, and secular. The army, which would necessarily be the tool of national revenge, was central to his ideology, and the popular appeal of Zouaves helped to propel his movement forward.[20]

An aspiring poet in his mid-twenties, Déroulède fought in the Franco-Prussian War as a Zouave. He started the war as an officer in the *Garde mobile*, a reserve unit of minimally trained and equipped citizens that he found unsatisfying. Eager for action, he quit to join the Third Zouaves as a simple soldier alongside his younger brother. Seventeen-year-old André was wounded in the disastrous battle of Sedan, where both young men were taken prisoner. After seeing to his brother's safety, Paul escaped, returned to France, joined the Turcos, and won the Legion of Honor for his role in the battle of Montbéliard.[21] His military experience fueled a postwar career as France's "poet of revenge," and he found literary success in 1872 with the publication of the best-selling *Chants du soldat* (Songs of a Soldier). The collection refers repeatedly to both Zouaves and Turcos, drawing on classic stereotypes of the cheerful boldness of the Army of Africa—these "children of the golden sun" who were "lively dancers of a deadly dance."[22]

In 1882, Déroulède founded the Ligue des patriotes to promote the cause of French national renewal and revenge, and his campaign cultivated both literary and artistic images of Zouave soldiers. Déroulède's own poems were a launching pad: "Le Clairon" (The Bugler), about a dying Zouave who continues to play for his comrades, was a hit for the popular singer Mademoiselle Amiati, who was known to wrap herself in the tricolor on the music hall stage.[23] Edouard Détaille and Alphonse de Neuville, the most prominent military artists of the era, were both members of the organizing committee of the league, and their work, alongside that of many of their colleagues, regularly appeared in the journal of the movement, *Le Drapeau* (The Flag). The magazine was generously illustrated, with the front cover always featuring a striking sketch of a military figure, and further drawings accompanying the stories of army life, histories of great battles, and the activities of patriotic sporting clubs. The visual appeal of Zouaves ensured that they featured prominently.[24] *Le Drapeau* promoted Paul Déroulède alongside his revanchist ideology: Ernest-Jean Delahaye's painting of Déroulède leading his Turcos into the city of Montbéliard, first shown in the Salon of 1899, appeared on a double-page spread that same year. The magazine sold prints of the image, as well as a biography of Déroulède, for five centimes each.[25] In 1907 Edouard Détaille paid tribute to his friend with a canvas that returned to the scene of his political coming of age: Paul and André Déroulède at Sedan. Paul, defiant in a colorful Zouave uniform with his rifle slung across his back, supports his wounded brother as the battle rages behind them. An engraved version appeared in an obituary for the poet in the pages of *Les Annales politiques et littéraires* in February 1914, months before the outbreak of the war that Déroulède had promoted so energetically (fig. 45).[26]

Déroulède's embrace of the Zouave and the Turco was ironic, given his strong anti-colonialism, and it indicates the extent to which republican Frenchmen saw Algeria as an integral part of France, not a colony at all, since its integration into the nation as three departments in 1848. Déroulède served in units of the African army, but he in no way saw himself in the service of empire—he was defending France from its Prussian enemy, not expanding its rule over foreign peoples. Images like Détaille's paint-

FIG. 45. Edouard Détaille, Paul and André Déroulède at Sedan,
Les Annales politiques et littéraires, no. 1598 (February 8, 1914).
Courtesy of the Bibliothèque nationale de France.

ing of the Déroulède brothers on the field at Sedan located the Zouave firmly in the metropole: they are blood brothers defending one another and their fellow citizens, not Frenchmen on a civilizing mission abroad. Although the Zouave look retained its exotic flair, it had become a uniform for France's sons who possessed neither colonial experience nor imperial ambition.

Déroulede's right-wing nationalism did not monopolize the possibilities of *zouaverie*, of course. Zouaves were so ubiquitous as to remain available for a variety of purposes, and they might appear on the left or the right of the political spectrum. Zouave service was an important expression of citizenship for Algerian Jews, recently enfranchised by the Third Republic in the Crémieux Decree of 1870. By 1914, as many as a quarter of the soldiers in some Zouave regiments were Jewish, although numbers were lower among officers.[27] In the ranks of metaphorical Zouaves, we find Emile Zola, creator of the naturalist "experimental novel" that shocked bourgeois taste in the late nineteenth century, who, art critic Jacques de Biez asserted, "sees everything as a zouave." Zola was in his element in (literary) battle, where he deployed his prose like a Zouave with a rifle: instead of firing from a distance, "he uses its bayonet without mercy, turning it round and round in the stomach of his victims with the persistence of an African."[28] The characterization evoked the ferocity and the agility of the African soldier, imperfectly concealed, the critic argued, beneath the writer's unassuming dark suit.

Similarly, the visual field of *zouaverie* extended well beyond the military paintings of the Third Republic. Vincent van Gogh, for instance, found Zouaves fascinating for largely apolitical reasons: he saw them as personalities formed by interesting assemblies of shapes and colors, not as representatives of a republican order. In June 1888, during his stay in the southern French city of Arles, van Gogh undertook portraiture for the first time. He produced two paintings and several sketches of a Zouave from the local garrison whom he described as "a boy with a small face, a bull neck, and the eye of a tiger."[29] With limited funds, van Gogh had difficulty finding subjects, and it seems likely that the Zouave, unsurprised at being singled out by a painter's gaze, would have been willing to pose in exchange for a modest sum.[30] The "horribly harsh" colors of the soldier's gaudy uniform attracted van Gogh, who reported to his brother that he would "like to be working on vulgar, even loud portraits like this." Van Gogh's paintings nod to the inescapable Zouave of republican France's popular culture: the bold colors and graphic quality of the paintings echo the paper soldiers and ABC books of the era. The kinship between van Gogh's Zouaves and the cheerful, big-hearted figures of popular imagination, however, was superficial. The Zouaves of Arles, as van Gogh repeatedly described them, were "ugly," the seedy regulars at the brothels that van Gogh also frequented.[31] Two Zouaves, in fact, had recently been murdered following a fight in a brothel, and van Gogh, who attended the inquiry into the crime, "took advantage of the opportunity" to visit the

FIG. 46. Vincent van Gogh, *The Zouave,* 1888.
Courtesy of Van Gogh Museum, Amsterdam (Vincent van Gogh Foundation).

brothel in question.[32] His Zouave's slouching posture, thick body, and sickly complexion all suggest the louche underworld of prostitutes, venereal disease, and bar brawls.

The ubiquitous Zouave was a desirable identity to claim after 1870, and although Zouaves quickly became the Republic's soldiers, republican Zouaves never monopolized the public's attention. *Zouaverie* remained politically labile at the end of the nineteenth century. A lot depended on context: the Zouave could equally be a republican empire builder or an intransigent Catholic who would never accept the republic. Déroulède's Zouave performance was secular, but also increasingly anti-parliamentarian, even protofascist. Zouaves were symbols of French patriotism, but deracinated Zouaves also performed among the "rough riders of the world" in Buffalo Bill's Wild West show that toured France in 1905.[33] Zouave celebrity established under the empire continued to expand in republican France, with barely a hiccup in 1870.

The Decline of the American Zouave

In contrast, the devastating French defeat in the Franco-Prussian War sharpened an attack on American Zouaves that began at the end of the Civil War. With the disbanding of the U.S. Volunteers, militia units became the institutional base for Zouaves as Elmer Ellsworth had projected in 1860. The new structural dynamics of the militia differed sharply, however, from the antebellum situation. The U.S. Zouave Cadets aimed to reinvigorate a moribund community tradition. The postwar lobbyists who founded the National Guard Association in 1878 instead sought, with eventual success, to cultivate close ties with the disdainful regular army at the cost of weakening relationships with local communities. Public spectacles and attraction of recruits became less important than legislative funding for encampment sites, armories, and shooting ranges. The transformation of priorities led to the expulsion of Zouaves from the American military establishment by the 1890s despite their continued grassroots popularity. Zouaves remained prominent in commercial entertainment for another generation, but they ceased to offer a satirical counterpoint to the rigidity of military organization. As stage Zouaves moved from burlesques and minstrel shows to the corporate domain of the railroad circus and vaudeville circuit, their flamboyant nonconformity faded into a social regimentation increasingly modeled by marching bands and chorus lines. Zouaves became an object rather than a vehicle for parody.

The acknowledged Civil War achievements of Zouaves proved to be more of an obstacle to their incorporation in the militia than any battlefield failures. The 5th New York, 9th New York, and 10th New York each provided the nucleus for a high-profile postwar regiment of the New York State National Guard. The combat veterans delighted crowds but irked militia insiders with their irreverent attitude toward unnecessary discipline. "Many of them consider that they are conferring a great favor upon their officers in allowing themselves to be drilled at all," grumbled the military correspondent for the *New York Times*.[34] Veterans' associations emerged as alternatives to the social organizations that ex-soldiers first sought in militia units. Former Zouaves gathered in these groups to celebrate their wartime contributions for decades. The oft-maligned Fire Zouaves, for example, established Noah Farnham Post No. 458 of the Grand Army of the Republic (GAR), headed by former regimental commander Charles McKnight Loeser.[35] The 155th Pennsylvania illustrated lasting pride in Zouave identity in 1889 by topping the regimental monument at Gettysburg battlefield with a statue of a soldier in a Zouave outfit even though the unit did not receive Zouave uniforms until six months after its participation in the struggle for Little Round Top.

Beyond the complications of integrating veterans into militia units, National Guard leaders and their allies opposed Zouave uniforms as antithetical to the goal of imitating the regular army. Even as the Zouave organizations formed in late 1865, some commentators urged "substitution of the United States Army blue regulation dress for the present light and fancy dress of many regiments of our National Guard." The *New York Times* initially saluted "the bright and dashing Zouave dress" that the 5th New York "wore with such distinction" in the war but soon criticized the famous ensemble as "slip-slop." The *Army and Navy Journal* came to regard the collarless, unbuttoned jacket and fez with turban as "slouchy."[36] J. Henry Liebenau, former adjutant of the Seventh Regiment acting as assistant inspector general of the New York State National Guard, published a tirade in his 1868 report on the regiment organized around the former 10th New York. "I do not think it possible, in our National Guard, at least (if anywhere), to inculcate the principles of steadiness, discipline or drill into a body of men uniformed in the careless, untidy and loose uniform of a zouave," Liebenau argued. "The very dress itself is demoralizing, and should at once and forever be abandoned by our State troops." In his comments on the former 5th New York, he repeated that "the zouave uniform is in no manner conducive to good order, military discipline or effectiveness in drill."[37] The militia incarnation of the 10th New York dissolved shortly afterward. The successors to Duryée's Zouaves and Hawkins' Zouaves both gave up their Zouave uniforms before disbanding within a few years.

Militia reformers' scorn for Zouave uniforms converged with wider erosion in the influence of Zouave élan. Emory Upton's revision of the infantry drill manual, adopted by the War Department in 1867, absorbed key Zouave and chasseur principles by accelerating the speed of movements and stressing individual initiative and responsibility in skirmishing. Upton also expanded the operational importance of four-man subunits derived from French models. Lew Wallace, who had proposed a rival tactics manual that the army rejected, argued for further incorporation of Zouave methods, but adherence to Upton's manual became a rallying point for insistence on standardization of militia practices. The overall primacy of drill declined with the surge of attention to marksmanship evidenced by the founding of the National Rifle Association in 1871. Parades and exhibitions gave way to target practice as a focal point for militia.[38]

Upton shrewdly packaged his system as a wholly American distillation of lessons learned in Civil War battles.[39] The posture typified a triumphant nationalism that undercut the transatlantic Zouave movement. When the army convened a board in 1862 to consider new uniforms, the panel showed considerable interest in adoption of a chasseur-style infantry outfit before dissolving without modification of the status quo. The postwar process that eventually yielded new regulations in 1872 featured more resistance to imitation of foreign uniforms and more celebration of American tradition.[40] More generally, postwar Zouaves did not benefit from the embattled reputations of influential Civil War sponsors, including George B. McClellan and Gouverneur K. Warren. William T. Sherman, a consistent critic of Zouaves, set the tone for the regular army with which postwar militia reformers aimed to align.

This context framed American commentators' emphasis on Zouaves' responsibility for national collapse in the Franco-Prussian War. Particularly influential was *New York Herald* correspondent Januarius MacGahan, cousin of official American observer Philip Sheridan, a guest of Prussia who derided the forces of Napoleon III. MacGahan called the Zouaves "a sort of cancer sore in the ranks" and reported that "their regimental demeanor does not frighten the matter-of-fact Germans, nor does their gymnastic agility save them from the shattering balls of the needle gun." A newspaper analysis from West Point, perhaps written by leading faculty member Dennis Hart Mahan, blamed the Zouaves for fostering "over-confidence, contempt of his enemy, and too great individual license in the soldier." Sherman, emphasizing that colorful conspicuousness brought battlefield vulnerability, similarly argued that "the French Zouaves, in their picturesque but unserviceable uniforms, were mowed down as badly at Sedan as their New York prototypes were at Bull Run."[41]

In spite of such criticism, Zouaves remained popular in the United States. About 150 Zouave units achieved official affiliation with state militias after the Civil War, and many informal companies organized as political marching clubs and recreational outlets. Pennsylvania, which lagged behind the militia reform movement, accounted for more than forty of the recognized units, but pace-setting New York yielded more than twenty. Examples could be found from Massachusetts to California. Illinois organized eight new militia companies in 1872, of which four were Zouave.[42] Merritt P. Batchelor, who had toured with Ellsworth in 1860, discovered the density of the postwar field when he set out in 1871 to replicate the U.S. Zouave Cadets' success with the Heath Zouaves of Pittsburgh. Where the USZC's drill challenge had met only amazement, the Heath Zouaves encountered their equals in the Cincinnati Zouave Battalion on the first stop of the tour, which proceeded no further.[43]

The San Francisco Cadets, commanded by Charles E. S. MacDonald, illustrated the persistent allure of Zouaves. MacDonald, a Scottish emigrant said to have served in the Austrian army, made a fortune in liquor and real estate in San Francisco and Sydney. He captained the Ellsworth Rifles of the California militia before the 1863 organization of the cadets. After the war the Zouave company remained a unit of the state force but developed into an exhibition troupe that combined McClellan's bayonet exercise with the teachings of Danish American fencing impresario Thomas H. Monstery. The cadets' showstopper was a drill performed blindfolded, which placed the wealthy young soldiers at the mechanistic extreme in the Zouave duality of individual empowerment and group coordination. A performance at the Seventh Regiment armory in New York in 1873 drew two thousand spectators and frequent applause, though the *Army and Navy Journal* sniffed that "the nature of the movements places them beyond strict military criticism, no regard being paid to the Tactics as prescribed for the use of the Army and militia, and their utility is very questionable."[44] MacDonald later turned to drilling a group of Native Americans whom he presented in quasi-Zouave uniforms at the Olympic Theater in New York in 1876 to demonstrate that the United States might develop an aboriginal force comparable to the Turcos. The exhibitions moved to London after the battle of Little Bighorn undercut American receptivity, but MacDonald's well-publicized proposal to the secretary of the interior indicated the ongoing association of Zouaves with imperial assimilation.[45]

Instead of expanding to new populations, Zouave uniforms gradually disappeared from state militias. When Pennsylvania finally joined the reform movement in 1878, the legislature required soldiers to wear the common uniform of the Pennsylvania National Guard.[46] Two years later Frederick Townsend, antebellum sponsor of the Albany Zouave Cadets, returned to the office of adjutant general in New York and launched a campaign to enforce a standard uniform. The Albany Zouave Cadets had stopped wearing Zouave outfits in 1870. Townsend's first target was the Fourteenth Brooklyn, which adopted a *chasseur*-style uniform after the USZC tour and wore it during the Civil War as the 84th New York. The inspector general condemned the regiment in 1882 for "a most objectionable and slouchy fatigue dress in the shape of a Zouave blouse," and soon afterward the unit switched to state service attire.[47] The national trend was firmly established when Illinois mandated a variation on the regular army uniform in 1884.[48] Among the last holdouts were the Veteran Zouaves of Elizabeth, New Jersey. Formed in 1867 by newspaper publisher and politico J. Madison Drake, the company consisted of veterans but not generally wartime Zouaves, and adoption of the Zouave name, dress, and drill testified to the postwar appeal of the identity. Governor George B. McClellan arranged admission of the unit to the New Jersey National Guard in 1878. The company made constant public appearances and plausibly claimed to be the most widely traveled militia unit in the country. In 1893, however, the state militia expelled the Veteran Zouaves for failure to wear standard uniforms.[49]

Drill competitions were important sites for mediation between public enjoyment of Zouaves and their increasingly tenuous status in the military establishment. An extension of Union rewards for well-drilled regiments, competitions within and between militia units became common immediately after the Civil War and expanded into large-scale interstate contests in the early 1880s. From the outset, Zouave companies competed in a separate category from ordinary infantry. Zouave drills delighted spectators, and promoters offered substantial cash prizes for winners though not the top premiums reserved for performance of standard tactics. The military press regarded these encampments as useful only for underdeveloped state militias that needed to stimulate enthusiasm and recruits. For a more mature National Guard, "the scope of these drills is so limited that superexcellence hardly repays the pains taken to acquire it" and distracted from more important goals. Zouaves may have impressed "nursery maids and children," but their unconventional drill was merely "monkey business."[50]

The well-funded, widely publicized contests fostered the rise of drill companies independent of any state militia. Thomas J. Ford's company of Chicago Zouaves dropped out of the Illinois National Guard in 1882 to focus on exhibitions. Missouri, a hotbed of crack teams, illustrated the more gradual divorce that took place in some other states. The Bain Zouaves of St. Louis, a National Guard company and leading contender in early encampments, merged in the mid-1880s into the Busch Zouaves, a proprietary advertising initiative of brewing magnate Adolph Busch. Drillmaster T. Rosser Roemer was twenty-one years old when he founded the group in 1883, near the age Ellsworth had been when he took charge of the USZC. The Busch Zouaves won many contests and marched in Grover Cleveland's first inaugural parade. The Hale Zouaves of Kansas City also joined the state militia, but in 1892 the Missouri National Guard spurned an application from the Walsh Zouaves. Although some competitions pleased militia enthusiasts by limiting competition to state forces, many promoters were unwilling to follow suit. National Guard officials instead enforced separation. A revealing brouhaha took place after the Neeley Zouaves of Memphis, a company in the Tennessee National Guard, won the 1895 interstate prize in a victory over the Chicago Zouaves, the Busch Zouaves, the Hale Zouaves, and the Walsh Zouaves. The state militia promptly disbanded the unit and court-martialed its commander for taking the troops out of the state without permission. The Neeley Zouaves continued to compete as a privately chartered corporation.[51]

Military repudiation of Zouaves redefined their position in the world of entertainment. When the Lightning Zouave Drill emerged as a variety act during and after the Civil War, an important part of the routine was the theatrical appropriation of the standard manual of arms. The prominence of veterans as performers reinforced the overlap between the field and the stage. One of the best-known Zouave drillists was John E. Burk, who had enlisted in the 4th New York as an eighteen-year-old drummer boy. After the war he secured an appointment as armorer and drum-major for the militia regiment organized around Duryée's Zouaves. He made his debut in 1868 at the soirée of the regimental Drum Corps Association and soon advanced to professional appearances in which he "handled a musket with a celerity only suggestive of lightning and a skill suggestive of a veteran Zouave."[52] Will C. Burton, who performed in a husband-and-wife team with Minnie Rainforth that flourished until their marriage dissolved, had served in the 19th Illinois, a Zouave regiment officered by many alumni of the USZC. More than a half-dozen other Zouave drillists advertised themselves as holding military rank. George F. Waters added an homage to the prototypical Zouave by performing under the name Lieutenant George Ellsworth. Sergeant William H. L. Hamilton named his son Elmer Ellsworth Hamilton.[53]

The Lightning Zouave Drill gradually waned as soldiers complained that "prizes are offered by citizens for superiority in manipulation of the piece—seldom for execution with it."[54] A few latecomers enjoyed long careers, but by 1889 an advertisement scoffed at "old time Zouave drills."[55] Frank Kissell best personified the transformation of the Lightning Zouave Drill. Born in 1865, he could not claim veteran status to reinforce his assertions of authenticity when he came on the scene in the late 1880s. He also lacked the ironic accompaniment of a female partner. The negative reviews he drew while touring with Haverly's Mastodon Minstrels in 1892 prompted J. H. Haverly to recommend his dismissal. Kissell responded by reversing the spelling of his last name to reinvent himself as Hadj Lessik, self-proclaimed "Arab gun spinner." Moroccan immigrant Hadj Tahar had been performing in the United States as a "champion Arab gun-spinner" for several years, incorporating the act in the "Whirlwinds of the Desert" acrobatic show.[56] Kissell's metamorphosis recalled the Zouave tradition of imperial cross-dressing, though now the asserted claim was imitation of exotic fantasy rather than arrogation of native strength.

The last major phase of Zouave performance in the United States was the shift of exhibition drill from encampment competitions to circuses and vaudeville. The Aurora Zouaves were the key transitional group. Founded in 1887 by thirty-four-year-old machinist George Albert Hurd, the company never affiliated with the Illinois National Guard. It took third place at the interstate contest held in Kansas City in 1890 and first place in Indianapolis the following year. After another half-dozen years on the competitive circuit, the Aurora Zouaves joined Buffalo Bill's Wild West for the New York seasons in 1897–98, shortly after James A. Bailey assumed management of the show and began to refashion it from a pageant toward a circus. Interstate drill contests collapsed with the Spanish-American War, and the Aurora Zouaves performed for the next several years with Buffalo Bill's Wild West, the Barnum & Bailey Circus, and the Forepaugh & Sells Circus.[57]

The Aurora Zouaves' success prompted imitators. Harry C. Devlin, whose father served as quartermaster general of the Michigan militia and opened a business college in Jackson, reorganized the school's cadet corps as the Devlin Zouaves in 1895 after watching the Aurora Zouaves in competition. Eight years later the company followed its model in touring with Buffalo Bill's Wild West. Thirty-eight-year-old glass dealer Frank Keller formed a group of young men in Streator, Illinois, about sixty miles from Aurora, into a Zouave ensemble that debuted at a state GAR encampment a week after the Aurora Zouaves' first appearance with Buffalo Bill at Madison Square Garden. The Streator Zouaves completed a brief apprenticeship in county fairs and soon won fame on the vaudeville circuit. After a long international tour, Keller quit and created Captain Keller's Zouave

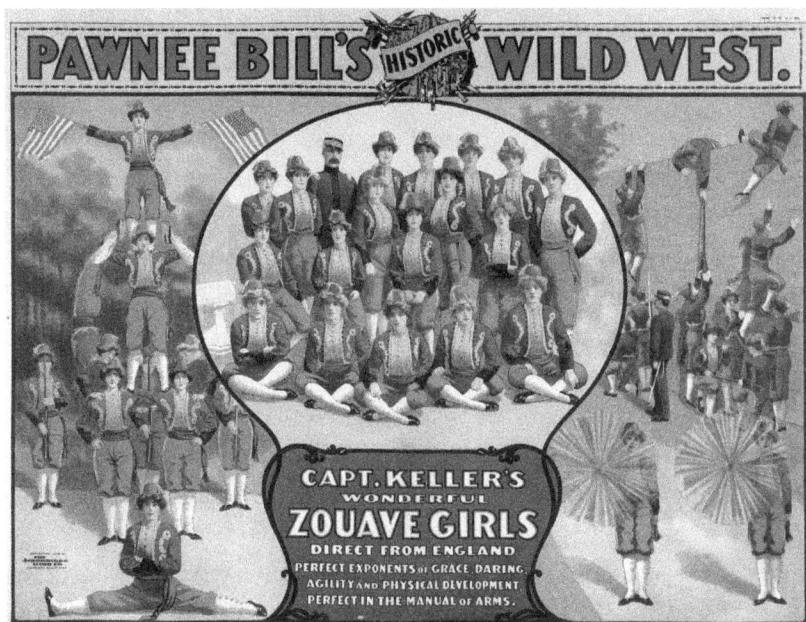

FIG. 47. Strobridge Lithographing Company, *Pawnee Bill's Historic Wild West: Captain Keller's Zouave Girls*, 1906. Courtesy of the John and Mable Ringling Museum of Art Tibbals Collection. Gift of Howard and Janice Tibbals.

Girls, who joined Pawnee Bill's Wild West in 1906. The Pekin Zouaves of Illinois and the Hoosier Zouaves of Indiana were also prominent vaudeville troupes in the early twentieth century. Wallace M. Ewing's Zouave Band, which appeared regularly at fairs and circuses, built on an increased tendency since the late 1880s to dress bands in Zouave uniforms. The thirty-five musicians in the ensemble included sixteen young men who doubled as a drill team.[58]

This generation brought a different approach to maneuvers that had been part of the Zouave repertory since the days of the USZC. Ellsworth's unit had mixed acrobatic and comical stunts with tactical formations in a performance designed to skewer the stolidity of prevalent military thinking. The latest Zouave routines did not bear specifically upon any military practice, although they resonated with the army homage that suffused Buffalo Bill's Wild West and the broader surge of American jingoism in the era of the Spanish-American War. An 1899 review of the Streator Zouaves noted that "serious soldiering has had much consideration of late, and so in twelve minutes of these exercises what impresses observers is more the evidence of patient training and exact discipline than the suggestion that any of these are real fighters' tricks." The indispensable climax of each circus and vaudeville act was the scaling of a wooden wall set up on stage. Ellsworth's men had surmounted lower walls by walking over the inclined backs of fellow Zouaves, a humorous nod toward the renowned agility of French Zouaves. Their descendants treated the challenge as a sport in which the team worked together to hoist up the first soldiers and haul up the rest. Advertisements and newspaper reports kept tally of the results. In July 1898, seventeen Streator Zouaves scaled an eighteen-foot wall in one minute and five seconds. By October 1901 the company claimed to be able to go over a twenty-foot wall in twenty seconds. Les Belles Zouaves, a group of sixteen women performing the next year at the Dewey Theater named for the naval hero of Manila Bay, topped a twenty-foot-high simulated fort in twenty-two seconds.[59]

The cross-marching, rifle-spinning, pyramid-building Zouaves of the early twentieth century presented America's first half-time show, pointing the way toward the brass sections and baton twirlers that would appear on football fields in the next few years. This aesthetic drew on the zest for spectacle that had long inflected American visions of Zouaves. The conflation of militarism, sport, and entertainment differed from its predecessors, however, in its disregard for the irony fundamental to Zouave identity since the Crimean War. Circus bandmaster Karl L. King's rousing "Gallant Zouaves" (1916), dedicated to Harry C. Devlin's troupe in the Sells-Floto Circus, celebrated the industrial force and predictability of the ensemble. Such a self-propelled performance did not provide the medium for satire that animated the Zouave routines of Dan Bryant, Laura Keene, or Charles and Carrie Austin. After the Great War, pianist and composer Mana-Zucca undercut the pretensions of the pseudo-soldiers in "The Zouaves' Drill" (1924), a musical pun on the meanings of scale in which the insistent momentum of ascending two-note motifs dissolves into descending glissandos suggestive of slapstick rather than a heroic escalade.

The most thoughtful parody of vaudeville Zouaves was Buster Keaton's two-reel comedy *The Playhouse* (1921). The twenty-six-year-old Keaton grew up in a vaudeville family, and his film examines the stage tradition and its relationship to motion pictures. The opening reel centers on a blackface minstrel show in which Keaton plays all the comedians, musicians, and audience members, a cinematic tour-de-force revealed to be the dream of a stagehand napping on the job. The theme of entertainment as illusion continues into the vaudeville show that begins after the stagehand's awakening. Zouave drill fits into this program as not merely a canonical routine but a socially significant charade. After a Zouave company abruptly quits, the stagehand hires a group of ditch-diggers who put on the act, including the inevitable wall-scaling, with many pratfalls. In the front row of the audience, two stereotypically one-armed Civil War veterans join together to applaud vigorously. The ex-soldiers typify the logic of self-projection in admiring the martial pantomime of Zouaves who are not actual warriors or even actual vaudevillians. The vignette suggests Lost Generation wariness of militarism personified by Civil War pensioners. *The Playhouse* warns that movies constitute the most powerful of all illusory machines, though Keaton's happy-marriage ending preserves faith in a reality waiting to be seized from the hall of mirrors.

The pathetic artificiality of the Zouave defined the last major American appearance of the figure in Margaret Mitchell's *Gone with the Wind* (1936). The fictional relationship of Scarlett O'Hara and Rhett Butler explores the imaginative transgression of gender and racial boundaries central to the Civil War sensation of Zouave outfits, but the novel depicts the costume as a caricature of the role reversals that deepen sexual psychology. Dimwitted Stuart Tarleton announces this theme in the opening scene of the book when he objects to joining a Zouave troop because "I'd feel like a sissy in those baggy red pants. They look like ladies' red flannel drawers to me." One of Mitchell's foils to the manly Rhett Butler is the emasculated René Picard, husband of Scarlett's rival Maybelle Merriwether. First seen in the blue-and-white baggy trousers of the Louisiana Tiger Rifles, Picard goes on after the war to drive a pie wagon from which he sells his mother-in-law's baked goods to occupying Yankee troops. He eventually becomes

FIG. 48. Alberto Morin as René Picard and Mary Anderson as Maybelle Merriwether
in publicity still for film adaptation of *Gone with the Wind,* 1939.
Courtesy of the Margaret Herrick Library.

a pillar of bourgeois Atlanta but remains as he first appeared, "a grinning
little monkey of a man." The Zouave is a mere entertainer. Mitchell, who
shared contemporary fascination with the works of Sigmund Freud and
the sexology of Havelock Ellis, was alienated from such superficiality by
her premise that insight characteristically took the form of penetration
to an inner authenticity.[60]

Although bemused by boyish versions of martial vainglory and determined to recognize women's struggles, Mitchell endorsed an understanding of soldiering as a social institution that revealed a true version of
personal character, an idea that had become commonplace in the United
States since the 1890s. That view differed sharply from the thinking of
thousands of volunteers who went to the Civil War in Zouave outfits.

They expected to play a role, for which they chose a costume that drew its connotations from theaters no less than battlefields. The consolidation of mass culture celebrated by the film adaptation of *Gone with the Wind* (1939) obscured the sophistication of the Civil War generation the movie depicted. By the time cinema and television contributed to a renewal of interest in the relations between media images and social realities, including the cross-pollination of Hollywood and military performance, the Zouave precedent lay buried beneath decades of circus and vaudeville acts disconnected from combat. A reorganization of the Devlin Zouaves in the early 1920s, sponsored by an American Legion post in Jackson, Michigan, survived long enough to appear on the *Ed Sullivan Show* and march in the inaugural parade for John F. Kennedy. The quaint exhibitions reinforced the distance between war zone and playhouse, realms that Zouaves had originally integrated.

French Zouaves in the Great War

The mockery that Americans attached to Zouaves in the early twentieth century had no parallel in France, where Zouaves still stood for quintessentially French valor and initiative, served up with élan and good humor. French Zouaves were jokesters, as always, but not the butt of the joke. When the literary critic André Billy praised the novelist Colette in 1921 for her "frank pride in being a Frenchwoman and the daughter of a Zouave," there was no irony in the statement; Billy was asserting that Zouaves and their daughters were as important during the Great War as they had ever been. Colette's wartime journalism—a series of human-interest essays published in *Le Matin* describing life in villages on the front line and on the Parisian home front—had been essentially patriotic. Leaving behind the universalist and humanitarian qualms that so often characterized women's writing, Billy asserted, Colette had proven herself worthy of her Zouave father.[61]

Billy's confident claim belied the fact that by 1921 many French men and women had concluded that twentieth-century warfare had rendered the Zouave irrelevant. Zouaves were not targets of mockery, but they no longer inspired the enthusiasm that Billy was trying to evoke. Zouave individualism proved ill-suited to the First World War, which marked the end of the Zouave's long prominence as a symbol of French military valor. The Great War was the first conflict in which the individual was not the basic unit of combat: artillery shells caused the vast majority of casualties rather than bullets from weapons fired by individual soldiers.[62] Qualities like those associated with Zouaves—bravery, gaiety, initiative—no longer seemed relevant to battle. Although Zouaves began the war in 1914 wearing their traditional uniform, they soon abandoned it for a look that made them less visible as a distinctive unit within the French army and, as individuals, to German gunners. Collective suffering and anonymous death were the new hallmarks of twentieth-century soldiering.

Colette herself invoked the memory of her father, Captain Jules Colette, in order to link the Zouave heroes of the Crimea and Italy to the French soldiers of the trenches. Captain Colette, his daughter asserted, was "a Zouave, a real Zouave, like so many Zouaves from 1859 to 1915." He lost his leg in the Italian Campaign at Melegnano, a wound that he described to Napoleon III, who was visiting the ranks, as "a scratch." The emperor, impressed by this cheerful stoicism, asked what he could do for the young officer, who replied that he had plenty of medals, but that he could use a crutch, which the emperor, of course, provided.[63] Decades later, his daughter invited suffering soldiers on France's Western Front to identify with the cheerful insouciance of this earlier generation of Zouaves. Colette writes of meeting a young amputee who is eager to hear about her father: how much, exactly, of his leg had been cut off? Captain Colette learned to walk again, and even run, didn't he? And his wife, Colette's mother—she was a pretty girl, wasn't she?[64] Colette, whose own scandalous, cross-dressing, exhibitionist, theatrical past suggested that she was something of a Zouave herself, was the ideal vehicle for promoting the idea that *zouaverie* would carry France's soldiers through this new war.[65] The Zouave's daughter offered the broken young men of the Western Front the promise of a future: they would recover, walk again, meet girls, and father children.

Zouaves themselves did their best to live up to their reputation. They regularly reminded themselves that the siege of Sebastapol had involved trenches and mud—it was a war for moles, just like the Western Front.[66] The Third Zouaves welcomed the arrival of Italian allies by naming King Victor Emmanuel III to his grandfather's rank of corporal on the anniversary of the battle of Palestro.[67] There were more opportunities for professional entertainment in France than there had been in the Crimea, including the chance for Zouaves to see themselves on film.[68] Nonetheless, the Zouaves revived their theatrical tradition. In the vaudeville revue *Au clair de la . . . dune* (By the light of the dune) a journalist visits a trench where a Zouave and a German prisoner sing of their love for the same object—the largest sand dune in the sector, who, herself, sings of her preference for Zouaves. *C'est à schlitter partout* (*schlittage* was the system of makeshift planks that created pathways in the mud of trenches, and the joke of the title is untranslatable) and *Jamais deux sans trois* (Things come in threes) followed this initial success. The revues recycled jokes about Zouave prowess, praised Zouave ingenuity in responding to the rigors—and boredom—of trench life, and offered opportunities for drag performance, including a line of dancing "Zouave Girls" (in English in the original). References to the Crimea accompanied jokes about camouflage and complaints that gas masks required Zouaves to shave their famous beards.[69] The Zouaves were well represented in the world of trench journalism: *La Chéchia*, written by the same team that produced Zouave revues, began appearing in the summer of 1915, and *Le Zouzou* followed a year later. The newssheets offered prizes (guess the date of the end of the war!), parodies (of Déroulède's "Le Clairon"), and announcements of Zouave festivities.[70] As a reminder that Zouaves weren't just any soldiers, their paper included an "Algériana" column, humorous tales of African life, and plenty of Zouave slang. As in the 1850s, the stage Zouave passed easily from the front lines to the Parisian stage: wartime reviews performed in Paris and other cities returned to the Zouave as an inexhaustible source of cheerful plots.[71]

In November 1914, toward the end of the "race to the sea" in which each side tried to outflank the other, one Zouave enjoyed a star turn as an exemplar of gallant heroism. German troops who had taken the Zouave prisoner advanced using him as a human shield, and French officers ordered their men to hold their fire. The Zouave in question yelled back

FIG. 49. O'Galop (Marius Rossillon),"Heroic words: Shoot anyway, boys!" Courtesy of the Bibliothèque nationale de France.

at his comrades, "For God's sake, shoot anyway; they're Huns!" and died in the resultant friendly fire. This act of bravery, implying that individual courage could make a difference in the course of the war, caught the popular imagination. Songs, postcards, toy soldiers, and even tabletop bronze sculptures commemorated the Zouave's heroism.[72] A variety of images reproduced the panache of his gesture: he shouts with his head thrown back, his chest pushed forward to meet the bullets.

When René Clozier, a Zouave who had been part of the editorial team of *La Chéchia* and its revues, published his memoirs in 1931, he returned to the story of the heroic Zouave, but on a bitter and disillusioned note. Assigned to investigate the incident for the production of a postcard, Clozier's narrator discovers that it dissolves into conflicting accounts. There was one Zouave hostage or there were three. It was foggy and hard to see or it was a perfectly clear day. The Germans walked along the road or they strode through the fields, and they passed houses on either the right or the left. Maybe it was actually the *Germans* who yelled, "Don't shoot, we're Zouaves." One witness affirms that taking the Lord's name in vain—*nom de Dieu*, the hostage shouts—was an officer's invention, "so it would sound more Zouave."[73] Clozier's memoirs suggest the exhaustion of the Zouave type in the Great War: the postcard, of course, exists, but we can't be confident that it represents anything more than wishful thinking and propaganda.

Despite the efforts of Colette and a variety of publicists to recapture the Zouave's gallant spirit, many observers shared Clozier's sense that the Zouave's run as a symbol of French military manliness was over. Zouaves themselves recognized that trench warfare was not their element. The Second Zouaves' souvenir history of the war—tellingly describing itself as a *Reliquary*—acknowledged that soldiers were "ill prepared for this nagging, drawn-out conflict." The brave Zouaves persisted with their bayonet charges, which ultimately produced nothing but "bloody testimony" of the futility of "the mystical belief in offensive war."[74] Soldiers who suffered patiently were not as appealing as Zouaves who vaulted over obstacles and scaled cliffs, but abnegation and endurance came to define the war experience on the Western Front.

Ultimately, the *poilu* displaced the Zouave as the quintessential Great War type. The nickname combined affection with bitterness over the scale of the slaughter. It referred to the soldier's hairiness (*poil* is "hair"), and it gestured toward the wretched conditions in the trenches, where cleanliness, to say nothing of a close shave, was nearly impossible. It also alluded to the soldier's virility: he was the kind of guy with "hair down there" (*du poil au bon endroit*), as the saying went.[75] The *poilu* appeared in songs, postcards, novels, and in the titles of trench newspapers. The revues that were popular both at the front and among civilians often featured *poilus*. "*Poilu*" was a single label that described a wide variety of Frenchmen: Parisians and provincials, bourgeois and workers, Catholics and freethinkers, conscript and career soldiers all found themselves in the trenches, often nearly unrecognizable beneath their scruffy beards and the mud of northeastern France.

Were colonial soldiers like the Zouaves *poilus*? Zouave soldiers sometimes referred to themselves that way: both *La Chéchia* and *Le Zouzou* addressed their readers as *poilus*. After the war, however, when they wrote regimental histories that detailed wartime activities and commemorated those who had died in the service, they never described a Zouave as a *poilu*.[76] Historians tend to use "*poilu*" to refer to soldiers from the metropole, and Emmanuelle Cronier, describing the origins of the term, specifically notes that it excluded colonial troops.[77] There were, however, native *poilus*—native, that is, to some place other than metropolitan France—such as the Senegalese infantryman who appeared on a postcard in a series called "Les Poilus."[78] In general, the differences that the term *poilu* effaced derived from the society and the politics of the metropole, not the empire. The *poilu* was a Frenchman defending his home, not a colonial who would return to a distant land of his own.

Half a million "native" troops served in France during the Great War, however, even if mythology of the *poilu* tends to efface their role. The colonial military units that originated in a desire to spare Frenchmen the cost of garrisoning an empire were central to defending the homeland less than a century later. Their soldiers paid in full the so-called "blood tax," although for many of them who were colonial subjects rather than French citizens, the right to vote did not compensate the obligation of military service. Instead, their sacrifices paid for alleged benefits of assimilation and civilization. As Richard Fogarty has observed, "military necessity led the French to consider using colonial subjects as soldiers," but a commitment to the notion of a republican civilizing mission "allowed them to do so without a sense of guilt or hypocrisy."[79]

Zouaves played an important role in reorganizing the Army of Africa to meet the challenges of defending the metropolitan homeland instead of extending the frontiers of the empire. Accelerated recruitment of colonial subjects increased the need for officers who "understood" natives—both literally and figuratively. Stunningly high mortality rates among junior officers in the early months of the war also spurred demand for men who could move into officer ranks. To the leadership of the African army, Zouaves looked like officer material: they were white men with military experience and language skills who could be quickly trained to replace the fallen. Some observers suggested that the overt racism of Algerian settler society made Zouaves particularly *unfit* for command of native troops and led to abuse that might discourage colonial recruitment. Decades of myth-making around Zouave initiative and élan, however, carried the day and convinced the military hierarchy that Zouaves were an effective link between the *poilu,* his homeland, and colonial soldiers.[80]

Although the *poilu* shared some qualities with the Zouave, he was a very different character who exemplified different approaches to war. The *poilu* displaced the Zouave by assuming some of his characteristics: insouciance in the face of danger, a way with the ladies, and a tendency to grumble about orders all came to be associated with the *poilu.* Unlike the Zouave's cheerfulness, the *poilu*'s gaiety was bitter and tinged with despair, however. Zouave jokes had been broad and uncomplicated; in contrast, *poilu* humor was dark and rancorous. Most important, though, was the fact that the Zouave's embrace of the impetuous bayonet charge and his ability to demonstrate individual initiative found no place in narratives of World War I. Zouave élan was useless in the trenches where modern warfare had completed its work of turning men into cogs of a machine.

The abandonment of the instantly recognizable baggy trousers, open jacket, and *chéchia* for soldiers on active duty contributed significantly to the eclipse of the Zouave. Following the heavy losses of the first months of the war, the French command reconsidered uniforms in the winter of 1914–15. The red trousers of all infantry units, not just the wide-legged Zouave *sarouel,* seemed less dashing now that they made easy targets. The open Zouave jacket offered inadequate protection against the cold and rain of northeastern France. Zouaves started the war with their distinctive silhouette and bright colors, but they ended it in the same drab overcoats as the rest of the army.

The British army had already moved toward increasingly plain uniforms at the turn of the century. The West India Regiments, which had adopted Zouave dress in the late 1850s, modified it substantially for combat in West Africa in the last decades of the century and then abandoned it for an all-khaki look.[81] Zouave costume remained the regiment's dress uniform, although over the course of the twentieth century it was increasingly associated with performance and tourist spectacle. Today, military bands in Jamaica and Barbados wear Zouave uniforms to perform on public holidays and in military reviews. Khaki, of course, was originally a colonial costume: the British Indian Army adopted it on the northwest frontier near Lahore, and the word derives from the Urdu word referring to the color of dirt. The Corps of Guides, fondly called "mudlarks," wore khaki outfits with a red sash in the late 1840s, and the rest of the British army in India had adopted khaki by 1885.[82] All British forces in the Boer War of 1900 wore field-service khaki, and the army considered it a proprietary marker of British identity. British authorities shot a local man dressed in khaki for impersonating a British soldier, and many Boers flatly rejected an official effort to dress them in khaki on the grounds that it was the color of the enemy.[83]

Some French commentators had recommended similar reforms in military—especially Zouave—dress before the Great War. Beginning in 1901, Zouave bicyclists wore narrower trousers with sixty-eight centimeters less material around their waist, a money-saving innovation that was extended to other Zouaves in following years.[84] A 1910 article in the *Journal des sciences militaires* went so far as to claim that the Zouave uniform "defied French common sense." The entire army needed reform, the writer asserted: officers should dress like their men and not rely on epaulettes and braid as the source of their authority. The advent of smokeless gunpowder in the 1880s meant that visibility on the battlefield was no longer as crucial for unit cohesion and led some military leaders to consider exchanging the red trousers of the French infantry for a neutral color.[85] This proposal did not go over well in all quarters: a former minister of war protested, "Red trousers *are* France!" (*Le pantalon rouge, c'est la France!*).[86] Other commentators continued to insist on the advantages of a loose fit for enterprising soldiers like the Zouaves. On the eve of war in 1914, the view that the distinctive Zouave uniform reinforced esprit de corps while remaining practical prevailed, and Zouaves crossed the Mediterranean to defend France wearing their traditional garb.

With the redesigned uniform distributed in 1915, the distinctive Zouave silhouette disappeared and men in the trenches looked largely alike, regimental distinctions being reduced to details of insignia. The defining feature of the new *poilu* silhouette was the Adrian helmet, an innovation that demonstrates that aesthetic considerations persisted even as the French army designed a more functional uniform. None of the standard army issue forms of headgear, including the Zouave *chéchia*, offered any protection, and head wounds, especially from shrapnel, were common as the conflict settled into the trench lines that characterized the Western Front. The French were the first to develop a protective helmet, known as the *casque Adrian* after Intendant-General Louis-Auguste Adrian, who designed it. Adrian drew his design in part from the popular images of military artist Edouard Détaille. The aesthetic quality of the helmet—its "charming harmony," "simplicity," and "martial lines"—contributed to its success.[87] One American observer noted that the helmet "was attractive in its lines and it added martial distinction to its wearer—which proved, in the opinion of many officers, a more important argument for its use than its ballistic value."[88] Uniform improvements in the Great War may have taken steps toward utility, but they never abandoned aesthetic principles of seduction.

Zouaves sometimes mourned the loss of their distinctive dress, but their complaints were muted because the identity that the outfit had represented was diminished as well. In one trench revue from 1916, Zouaves mockingly sang about "a good steel helmet / that gives you a warlike look / and sometimes a migraine, too"—and they regretted that "there wasn't much left of the Zouave outfit, and the helmet finished it off!"[89] Industrialized warfare, however, more than a helmet, was what really finished off *zouaverie*. Zouave jokes were no longer in the service of military efficiency as they had been in Africa and the Crimea. Rather, humor—of a dark, bitter variety—was the only available insulation from the efficiency of modern warfare. The protection it offered *poilus* was ultimately a source of pathos rather than pride.

Decolonization and Disappearance

Although their uniform only appeared on parade, Zouaves survived the Great War, and new Zouave regiments formed during and after the conflict. Zouaves fought in the Second World War and in Indochina and Algeria to maintain France's colonial possessions. Decolonization—specifically, Algerian independence—finally did the Zouaves in, not modern warfare. All of France's Zouave units were disbanded in 1962, the year of Algerian independence.

Without French Algeria, there could be no Zouaves. Despite Zouaves' international travels and the layers of meaning and local color that the outfit had acquired over the course of the nineteenth century, they never really escaped their point of departure. Zouaves remained the soldiers of the *razzia;* they were the men who lit fires at the mouths of caves to asphyxiate women and children. Zouave regiments were key institutions of *pied noir* society—that is, they were strongholds of the white settlers in Algeria who were the most intransigent opponents of French retreat from its colony. Echoing *pied noir* anger, dissident elements of the French army spearheaded violent opposition to Algerian independence, notably through the terrorism of the OAS (Organisation de l'armée secrète, or Secret Army Organization).[90] In the 1960s as at the moment of their origin, Zouaves were inseparable from imperial conquest and colonial rule.

Zouaves might have suffered an eclipse after the Great War in the popular culture of the metropole, but in Algeria they were ever present in the form of monuments and statues recalling the conquest. The most significant Zouave monument—to Lamoricière and the Zouaves—went up in Constantine in 1908 on the site where the Zouaves launched their attack on the city in 1837. Lamoricière, wearing his trademark *chéchia* and brandishing his sword, leads the charge toward the breach of the city walls. On the pedestal are a Zouave bugler, sounding the charge, a female nude representing "civilization," and the mass of Zouaves following their commander into Constantine.[91] The towns of Koléa, Saida, Saint-Eugène, Tiaret, Philippeville, and Candle all erected Zouave monuments in the first decades of the twentieth century.[92] The 1930 centenary commemorations of French rule focused on the army: the torch relay from the military monument in the center of Algiers to the newly inaugurated stele at the original landing site of the French army at Sidi Ferruch reenacted the invasion.[93] Even if Zouaves no longer stood in for the French soldier in the metropole, in Algeria they continued to represent French military power.

Some units and lore of the Army of Africa survived decolonization in modified form and relocated to the metropole. The Foreign Legion is currently the repository of much of the romance and legend that previously attached to Zouaves.[94] The traditions of Spahis and Turcos continue, albeit in attenuated form. The First Spahi Regiment today wears the distinctive navy-and-white hooded *burnoose* of their colonial ancestors for ceremonial occasions. Their immediate predecessor, the Premier régiment de marche des spahis marocains, was created during the Second World War and was one of only eighteen military units named a "Compagnon de la Libération," an award for distinguished service in the cause of a free France. Regimental lore has it that these Spahis survived because General de Gaulle, hero of Free France and president of the Republic in 1962 when the Algerian War ended, refused to dissolve any unit bearing that title.[95] Members of the First Regiment of *tirailleurs* consider themselves the heirs of the Turcos. Their insignia includes the motto "Always first" in Arabic script as well as a swallow with crossed bones in its beak—a reference to the Turcos' nickname of the Great War, the "swallows of death" (*hirondelles de la mort*).[96] On parade, the regiment's band wears Zouave-style trousers, jacket, and *chéchia* and plays traditional North African instruments.[97]

Zouaves, with their unbreakable link to settler society, have not persisted in the same fashion. There was a brief effort to revive Zouave traditions in the French army in 1982, when the Ninth Regiment of Zouaves was reactivated at a commando training center in Givet in the Ardennes. Commandos, both as soldiers trained to show initiative and troops often engaged in protecting French interests in Africa, seemed fitting heirs to Zouave tradition. They received the flag of the Ninth Zouaves that recorded the unit's participation in the battles of the Yser and Verdun, among others, and on parade they wore the red Zouave *chéchia*. They trained in techniques that their Zouave predecessors would have recognized—scaling obstacles, notably—as well as urban warfare, rescue from battle zones, and use of explosives. They stopped using the name "Zouaves" in 1999 but retained the flag and the traditions of the old regiment until 2006. Since that time, French Zouaves have found their home exclusively in veterans' associations and museums.[98]

Although the path to folkloric status was longer for the Zouave uniform in France than in the United States, the destination was, ultimately, the same. Cartes de visite preserve hundreds of Zouaves, primarily French and American, but other nationalities as well. Some of them were soldiers, and some of them were performers, and it can be difficult to tell the difference between the two without a sharp eye for the uniform details of braiding, caps, and insignia. By the twentieth century, close attention to what the specialists call uniformology wasn't always enough to make the distinction between military performance and spectacle. The military bands of the West Indies in their Zouave dress perform in both theaters, and Canadian Zouaves only gradually acknowledged that their uniform would never, in fact, see battle in defense of the pope. It is not surprising that Zouave uniforms in the French army were parade dress for several decades before their final disappearance.

Zouave outfits that appear in museum cases, old cartes de visite, and other ephemera are the traces of a nineteenth-century mode of warfare that claimed to give individual men and women scope for expression and even self-aggrandizement. Vital to that opportunity for distinction was a cheery trivialization of violence that in the twentieth century has come to seem obscene. *Zouaverie* deployed humor and charm to make the brutality of war and colonialism more palatable, but world wars and decolonization have mostly taken the shine off of Zouave cultural arrogance and arrogation. Several generations of searching inquiry into imperialism's myriad forms have made us rightfully skeptical of its most deceptive manifestations, like the genial, clever Zouave. When we encounter hints of the recrudescence of *zouaverie,* that scholarship should give us the tools to respond and to ask what the vivid costume of the Zouave actually conceals.

ENCORES

I t is in the nature of fashion to revisit its archive and recycle its ideas, and Zouave dress is as subject to that process as any other fad. Although Zouaves have receded from public consciousness since their heyday in the 1860s, they nonetheless make occasional comebacks that remind us that Zouave qualities—verve, daring, and individual distinction—remain desirable and that imperial conquest—*zouaverie*'s backdrop—continues to appeal. In the first decades of the twentieth century, the French *couturier* Paul Poiret updated the Zouave look in women's fashion from the 1860s, this time focusing not on the jacket but on the trousers. His "pantalon-Zouave" was a *sarouel,* draped in luxurious silks and worn with orientalist accessories, including caftans and turbans.[1] Half a century later, in 1976, Yves Saint Laurent, the Algerian-born designer, sent Zouave trousers down his Paris runway. The *New York Times* noted that the show was "replete with high drama as well as comic relief," in good Zouave style.[2] These Zouave reappearances played on the theme of nostalgia, a sentiment implicit in the "folkloric" elements of the Saint Laurent show that the *Times* reporter identified. Not quite fifteen years after the collapse of French Algeria, nostalgia for the colonial life was finding its way into key institutions of French culture.

Zouave encores commonly express a desire to recover or achieve insight into bygone mindsets. Zouaves occasionally revisit the themes of their mid-nineteenth-century popularity, and recent ventures in performance, the visual arts, and public life recall the Zouave moment of the

1860s. The desire common in that era to cross the boundaries of gender and ethnic identities has not vanished, and, as in earlier times, it continues to have effects that run the gamut from illuminating to toxic. U.S. Civil War reenactors have devised elaborate schemes designed to achieve unmediated access to history. Their colorful uniforms, at odds with a self-evident modern logic of survival typified by camouflage, are a vehicle for time travel, for experiencing the past as it allegedly was. Italian artist Paolo Ventura embraces an enigmatic past as a springboard for creative fantasy. His spectral Roman Zouave calls attention to the gulf between an event and its shadow. Finally, returning to Paris, the site of Zouaves' initial success, a far-right group calling themselves the "Zouaves Paris" has reduced the historic complexity of its eponyms to a destructive core of hatred and violence. These varied theaters of engagement demonstrate the lasting resonance of the Zouave moment.

Reenactment

Shortly after the last embers of Zouave fancy drill faded away in the United States in the 1960s, Zouaves emerged as a prominent element in a new genre of pseudo-military performance, Civil War reenacting. The ancestry of late-twentieth-century reenacting included veterans' reprises of campfire storytelling, staging of sham battles, and costumed interpretations at outdoor museums, but this new version of Civil War reenacting stood apart for its bold claims to provide direct experience of the past. The practice attracted many participants and prompted a wide range of commentators to regard it as characteristic of the era.[3] Impersonation of Zouaves illustrated the nostalgic impulses of reenactment, though the promise of an immediate relationship to history ironically highlighted the most thoroughly mediated soldiers of the Civil War.

Zouaves presented a solid foundation for a pastime centered on simulation of material culture. Terry Daley's formation of a group committed to resurrection of the 5th New York in 1971 was a seminal event in shaping ideals of the endeavor. The distinctive uniforms created period flair and opened a field of bodily experience in wearing unfamiliar clothing. A later reenactor observed that donning the sash and turban required exceptionally close cooperation in dressing and reported that "when one pulls up the baggy red wool pantaloons, with the deeply drooping crotch, there is an immediate feeling of freedom down under"—an experience that opened paths of empathy to the nineteenth century.[4]

Daley's troop was a building block for larger organizations such as the National Regiment, but the principal unit for hobbyists remained the company, among which Zouaves were well represented. Companies of Duryée's Zouaves headquartered in New York, southern California, and northern California followed the influential Daley group based in the mid-Atlantic region, where the regiment had been active during the war. The 11th Indiana, the 8th Missouri, the 140th New York, the 165th New York, the 17th New York Veteran Volunteers, the 72nd Pennsylvania, the 76th Pennsylvania, the 114th Pennsylvania, the 155th Pennsylvania, and the Salem Light Infantry inspired imitators. Several groups that chose a non-Zouave unit as their "primary impression" developed a Zouave "second impression" to be ready to accommodate demand. A company in Oregon made the Louisiana Tiger Rifles its main offering and the 5th New York a Union back-up. The 62nd New York, which ranked among the less visible Zouave units during the war, nonetheless sparked two companies in Australia and another in Germany.[5]

Brian Pohanka, who joined Daley's company at the age of twenty-three in 1978 and remained active until his death in 2005, charted the reverberations of the Zouave initiative. Scion of an automobile-dealing dynasty, Pohanka became fascinated with Zouaves through a youthful visit to the Musée de l'Armée in Paris after immersion in the Civil War centennial. His career as an editor for Time-Life Books enabled him to conduct and foster research on Zouaves and positioned him to serve as historical consultant for high-profile Hollywood films like *Glory* (1989) and *Gettysburg* (1993) and the television documentary series *Civil War Journal* (1993–95), all of which relied heavily on reenactors. He became a leading advocate of Civil War battlefield preservation, linked to reenactment through ideals of sensory experience. For Pohanka, the 5th New York was an optimal model because it was a famously well-drilled unit, in which each soldier translated the tactics manual to muscle memory.

His cinematic work notwithstanding, Pohanka did not identify these exercises as showmanship. Like verisimilitude in accouterments, military discipline was a physical path to authenticity and particularly the hard realities of fighting effectively and dying bravely. Pohanka's posthumously published book about the 5th New York aimed to describe the feel of marches, encampments, and battles with little attention to the social and cultural significance of the regiment. He declared his satisfaction with the truth he had achieved through reenacting by identifying himself on his tombstone as "Capt. 5th N.Y. Vol. Inf. / Duryée's Zouaves."[6]

Daley's and Pohanka's leadership reflected a yearning to repossess the past. As thoughtful commentators observed, "reenacting at its root is a subspecies of nostalgia" reinforced by opposite tendencies.[7] Dissatisfaction with the superficial materialism and social fragmentation of contemporary life prompted admiration for supposedly settled values of an earlier age. The genius of reenacting was to seek a solution by looking backward but pressing forward to more intense forms of artificiality and atomization. An Australian reenactor of the Anderson Zouaves pointed out that reenactors preferred reproductions to relics because Civil War artifacts inevitably betrayed the passage of time; genuineness was anachronistic in the reenactor's vision of authenticity.[8] For all the promotion of camaraderie within the subculture, the valorization of corporeal and affective experience as the essence of "living history" isolated the individual as arbiter of the meaning of the past and rejected the collective processes of professional scholarship. Civil War reenacting was an especially effective vehicle of nostalgia for the baby boomers who defined the pastime because the struggle over nationhood served as an elegy for the disintegration of the mass culture that flourished in their youth. Reenactors elevated the clothing fad to the symbol of an era, so that Zouave uniforms encapsulated the 1860s just as poodle skirts and bell bottoms exemplified their decades a century later.

Reenacting was a spirited and sometimes poignantly conflicted practice, but its creed of authenticity obscured a deeper kinship with the Zouaves so often impersonated. Reenactors never understood Zouaves as constructions of playhouses as well as battlefields. Although a twenty-first-century reenactor specialized in portrayals of Elmer Ellsworth and

Civil War sesquicentennial anniversary ceremonies included restaging of the martyr's funeral, the overlap between the U.S. Zouave Cadets and burlesque dance-drills did not fit the program.[9] Consistent with their compression of history into a personal experience, reenactors readily embraced the familiar narrative of the Civil War as a period of national maturation. Zouave pretenders merely insisted that crack regiments like the 5th New York had participated in that growth. This longing for stability did not appreciate the extent to which historical Zouaves saturated in their nineteenth-century media environment enacted roles in their costumes and sustained their performances into the inscrutability of death.

From Memory to Fantasy

Italian artist Paolo Ventura's candidly postmodern renewal of the Zouave tradition in the visual arts was less ambivalent than Civil War reenactors' participation in the Zouave theater tradition. Born in Milan in 1968, Ventura grew up in a talented family dominated by his father, a well-known illustrator of children's books. Ventura worked for most of the 1990s as a fashion photographer before launching a more individual and imaginative practice. He won an international reputation with the publication of *War Souvenir* (2005), a book for which he built and photographed elaborate dioramas of figurines in cardboard settings conjured by his grandmother's memories of Italy during World War II. He followed similar procedures until expansion of his studio space enabled him to enlarge his set constructions and insert himself as an actor in the scenes he photographed. When the Rome Photography Festival and the Museo d'Arte Contemporanea (MACRO) commissioned him to develop a project about the city, Ventura produced *Lo Zuavo Scomparso* (*The Zouave Who Disappeared*), published as a volume in 2012. The series of pictures identified the papal Zouave as a source of insight into the workings of personal and public remembrance and the uses of artistic precedent.

Lo Zuavo Scomparso presents the story of a Zouave—Ventura himself, photographed in costume—who comes to Rome to visit the city and mysteriously vanishes on the tenth day.[10] Ventura's vision of the Eternal

City is an austere invention that evokes the mid-twentieth-century urban carnival through modernist architecture, the deterioration of older buildings, a cinema, and a street-fair shooting gallery. The anachronistic Zouave creates a fanciful mash-up. For an overview of Ventura's career, novelist and critic Francine Prose chose as her epigraph Italo Calvino's praise for poetry that manages "to fashion a dream without resorting to escapism" and recognizes "the force of reality which bursts forth into fantasy."[11] Ventura announces his magical realism by portraying himself in one photograph as an illusionist in black tails with a top hat in one hand and a large rabbit in the other. He balances manipulation of the shared past and appeal to an inner realm. Focus on the Zouave recalls childhood immersion in a world of tin soldiers and "let's pretend" military dress fabricated at a high standard in Ventura's household.

War is for Ventura a crucial form through which the subconscious mixes private experience with history and cultural representations. His *Death and Resurrection* (2015–18) and *Ex-Voto* (2017) reflected on the centennial anniversary of the Great War, including the conflation of life and death on the Western Front and the corrosive effects of time's passage on family memories of the lost. Ventura has indicated that he often begins his compositions with an aesthetic attraction to the color and shape of an object, such as the Zouave uniform, and that he responds to the "choreographic aspect" of the military. He ties these visual motifs to an interest in war as a constitutive social experience and a psychological metaphor. Like a clown's costume, a soldier's uniform erases individuality but exposes fundamental patterns of thought. Ventura has stated that because of his efforts to forge personal identity in struggles with his overbearing father and the complexities of life as an identical twin, "I identify myself a great deal in the figure of the soldier."[12]

Lo Zuavo Scomparso explores the archetypal potential of the papal Zouave. Ventura's soldier wears the brightly colored outfit of a French Zouave rather than the more subdued gray of the Pontificals, but the narrative situates him in Roman history. Ventura gently dramatizes the conflict between the Catholic Church and the Italian nation-state. The second image of the sequence, a view from a townhouse terrace, juxtaposes the dim dome of Saint Peter's under overcast skies in the background and a sunlit Italian tricolor waving in the foreground. Contrary to the mocking promise of the shooting gallery that "you win every time," the papal Zouave personifies a historic defeat. His erasure, however, is formative. Swallowed up by the city, he epitomizes a capital defined by sack, decline, occupation, and poverty no less than imperial glory. He is last seen sitting in interior darkness next to the open door of an upper-story terrace on February 14, anniversary of the martyrdom of Saint Valentine in third-century Rome. The palimpsest combining the feast of liturgical veneration and the commercial celebration of romance forms a backdrop for Ventura's wistful warrior.

Ventura's attention to the papal Zouave typifies his engagement with art history. His cityscapes recall the Roman paintings of Antonio

FIG. 50. Paolo Ventura, from *Lo Zuavo Scomparso* (2012). Copyright the artist, courtesy of the artist and Edwynn Houk Gallery, New York.

Donghi and the Roman films of Federico Fellini. In one picture a black-clad worker carrying a ladder walks along a cobblestone street toward the doorway of a Legnano bicycle shop, echoing Vittorio De Sica's *Bicycle Thieves* (1948). Although Ventura's work has involved many media, eventually including construction of opera sets, his commitment to photography remains foundational. The problems of shooting war run through several projects. In a collaboration with the Central Institute for Catalog and Documentation he sought to bridge a gap between popular understanding of the Risorgimento and the American Civil War by manufacturing images of Risorgimento casualties in the style of Matthew Brady and Alexander Gardner.[13] *Lo Zuavo Scomparso* revisits another photographic legacy of the Zouave heyday, the custom of soldiers posing for commercial portraits. Ventura's Zouave stands before a painted backdrop of a basilica dome and a Roman pine tree, like the many soldiers of the 1860s who staged theatrical cartes de visite before risking death. Because Ventura plays the role of the Zouave, moreover, the photograph is an homage to Roger Fenton's self-portraits as a Zouave during the Crimean War. The artist locates a forerunner supporting his conviction that photography "was reborn richer, freer, more intelligent" through late-twentieth-century abandonment of longstanding claims to depict reality.[14] In his characteristic medium of representation as well as his lost battle for sovereignty, the Zouave illustrates the creative stimulus of affectionate remembrance.

Fantasies of Violence: Paris's New Zouaves

Zouaves made a recent reappearance in Paris, where a small group of violent, hard-right activists christened itself "Zouaves Paris" (ZVP) in 2017. They specialized in street fights in which bands of young men attacked unsuspecting enemies. Some of these assaults were in the context of large gatherings: Zouaves set upon members of SOS Racisme, identified by the T-shirts they wore to protest a political rally for the right-wing presidential candidate Eric Zemmour in December 2021. The incident led to the arrest of the Zouaves' leader, Marc de Caqueray-Valmenier, who was identified in video footage, and to the dissolution of the ZVP in January 2022.[15]

On other occasions, the ZVP has attacked individuals: customers sitting at the Saint-Sauveur in Ménilmontant, a bar favored by local anti-fascists, for instance. On another occasion in a Paris Métro station, the ZVP beat up a man wearing a T-shirt with the slogan "Justice for Adama," a reference to the 2016 death in police custody of Adama Traoré, a Black Frenchman.[16]

The Zouaves of today do not wear red trousers or, certainly, turbans. Black T-shirts, bulging biceps, and ski masks are more their style. Their deployment of the "Zouave" label, however, is significant. It is irreverent and provocative, "a bit of a joke" according to journalists for the left-wing streetpress.com.[17] It evokes the French saying "faire le zouave," which since the late nineteenth century has referred to misbehavior, often of the childish variety: "fais pas le zouave" (stop acting like a Zouave) is a parent's chastisement of a naughty child. The ZVP's wordplay obfuscates relationships within the ecosystem of far-right organizations, where groups form alliances, dissolve under police pressure, and reorganize. Other, similar, groups include "Guignol Squad" in Lyon, the "Zoulous Nice," and "Alliance Scandale" in Toulouse, apparently apolitical names that playfully challenge authorities to a game of whack-a-mole as they identify and dissolve each of these cells in turn. The Zouave title also resonates with the American "Proud Boys," whose name suggests that they are "funny dudes, not Nazis" and that the Left can't take a joke.[18] Proud Boys and Zouaves both play on the contrast between childhood and violent mobilization while also suggesting that boys will be boys.

Although the ZVP was small—a few dozen members—they were adept at branding, and the "Zouave" name gave them an instantly recognizable swagger. The French far right is profoundly fragmented and often extremely local, and the ZVP was a tiny group operating in a region, Paris, that has not recently been a good recruiting ground.[19] Attraction to a fascist style united members: the symbolism of Celtic crosses, Nazi salutes, combative cartoon rats, and above all street-fighting stood in for their "nonexistent" "ideological foundation."[20] In this absence of a common political program, ZVP branding was key. They were, unsurprisingly, at home on social media. They filmed their hit-and-run attacks and regularly posted their exploits on Telegram, the channel favored by France's far right.

Many strands of French right-wing tradition converged temporarily in the ZVP. Racist, anti-immigrant sentiment was the most obvious, and the Zouaves' choice of name suggested a nostalgia for France's colonial era as well as a desire for an allegedly lost ethno-national community. Traditional Catholicism played a role: Marc de Caqueray-Valmenier is the son of an aristocratic, Catholic family and was briefly a member of the Action française, a monarchist group that has been active in one form or another since the turn of the twentieth century.[21] The ZVP was also well connected to the contemporary world of urban youth consumerism. Their methods and some of their members emerged from football hooliganism; during the 2018 World Cup in Paris, Zouaves attacked supporters of the Algerian national team, and they also participated in organized "free fights" with rival hooligan and neo-Nazi groups.[22]

Fragmentation on the far right is, according to Nicolas Lebourg, a consequence of the contradictions of "being fascist in a postmodern . . . era."[23] Lebourg's analysis suggests that these latter-day Zouaves are nostalgic for an earlier era of ideological confrontation as well as the last days of French empire. They regret the passing of a clear class-based politics, rigid gender roles, and the racialized colonial order. They look back wistfully to the 1970s when a large, nationally unified, intellectually ambitious, anti-Marxist student Right (usually associated with Groupe Union Défense, or GUD) confronted a similarly coherent student Left. In the absence of such a clearly delineated field of combat, neofascists like the ZVP seem like rebels without a cause. Their fascist forebears had a project, but these Zouave heirs aren't planning a revolution. In lieu of a program, they have the virtual world of social media followers and "likes."[24]

* * *

The nostalgia of twenty-first-century Zouaves misses a central element of their predecessors' appeal: enthusiasm for the rapidly unfolding present. The Zouave moment of the 1850s and 1860s was not retrospective. Organized to represent a new empire, the soldiers of modern life came to epitomize the verve of mid-nineteenth-century Paris, the cutting edge of fashion and art and entertainment. The freshness of the trend helped it spread around the world. Recycling of the past inevitably lacks the buoyancy of the original Zouave spirit.

Even if recent Zouaves lack the forward-looking orientation of their precursors, they capture many of the elements that propelled the Zouave fad to international prominence. Above all, Zouave dress was a vehicle for individual fantasy. The uniform empowered individuals to play a dramatic role. The first Zouave soldiers found it both practical and exciting to assume the clothing of their adversary as they asserted French capacity to absorb native military qualities in the process of colonial conquest. These imperial agents invented a character that developed radically through the Crimean War and Italian Campaign, with the theatrical properties of the uniform underscored on stages at the front lines and at home. Ready for international export, the Zouave transformed in various ways upon arrival in the British West Indies or Poland or Brazil or the United States or the Papal States. The American entertainment industry and the American military intersected in the production of especially robust variations on the French version. The pontifical army further showcased the pliancy of the Zouave by fostering a multinational Catholic model. The pleasures of assuming an alternative identity depicted in Paolo Ventura's photographs were fundamental to Zouave popularity.

The adaptability of the Zouave template resulted from gender as well as racial cross-dressing. Zouave dress was an outlet for male desire for self-expression through clothing in an era dominated by the black business suit: an assertion that men might wish for more latitude than the discreet pattern of a tie or the width of a lapel to express themselves. Civil War reenactors understand the appeal of the uniform as well as nineteenth-century recruits did. Plenty of Zouave soldiers, going a step further, used their Zouave service to explore drag performance. Women, too, could be Zouaves, and elements of the uniform found their way equally to fashionable bourgeois women and to risqué dancing girls. In a sense, the Zouave was its own, potentially bigendered identity. Women Zouaves weren't manly any more than Zouave soldiers were effeminate. Rather than crossing from male to female or vice versa, they crossed into

Zouave territory and enjoyed the pleasures of an expanded range of expressive possibilities.

The Zouave was and remains a charming figure. His exploits are funny, and he is a delightful scamp. His—and her—cheerful cross-dressing and rejection of essentialism appeal to our contemporary sensibilities. As we chuckle over the Zouave's exploits, however, we must remember that he originated as an instrument of colonialism, even of genocide. Beguiling soldiers have often played unspeakable roles in military theaters.

ACKNOWLEDGMENTS

Camaraderie features prominently in all Zouave tales, including the writing of this book. More than solo authors, life partners who write a book together need the clear-eyed, external perspective and backing of friends and colleagues. Our Zouave project emerged out of a circle of supportive colleagues, generous friends, and loving family, and it is a pleasure to be able to thank them here.

We have been fortunate to present early versions of this work in a variety of venues. We are particularly grateful to Christina de Bellaigue and David Hopkin, who welcomed us to their seminar in Oxford; to Jeff Burson for an invitation to speak to the European Section of the Southern Historical Association; to Alex Mikaberidze, Christine Haynes, and Mike Leggiere, who organized a keynote address for the Consortium on the Revolutionary Era; and to Val Littlefield, who included us in the Beaufort symposium on the First South Carolina Regiment. We have also taken our Zouave drill to meetings of the American Historical Association, the Society for French Historical Studies, the Organization of American Historians, the Society for Civil War Historians, and the American Culture Association / Popular Culture Association, where audience members and fellow panelists sharpened our presentation.

For guidance, references, and good counsel we are indebted to Mary Elizabeth Brown, Hollis Clayson, Martin Conway, Bruno Dumons, Mark Everist, André Fleche, Robert Gildea, Ferdinand Göhde, Charles Kimball, Kelly Mezurek, Michał Rastaszański, Jennifer Sessions, Martin Simpson,

Madeline Steiner, Mike Vorenberg, and Jeffrey Zvengrowski. Ava Gartman, at the beginning of a promising career as a fashion historian, provided valuable research assistance.

Ken Perkins, David Hopkin, Joe Peterson, Sarah Gardner, and Aaron Sheehan-Dean generously read portions of the manuscript. We are extraordinarily lucky to count such fine historians as Lesley Gordon and Steve Harp among our old friends, and their insightful comments on the manuscript have enriched it immensely.

The University of South Carolina, where between us we approach a half-century of service, has generously supported this project, and we are grateful to our colleagues in the History Department and the College of Arts and Sciences. The Office of the Provost funded archival research, and sabbatical leave advanced the manuscript toward completion.

Bringing this project to publication, we have been fortunate to work with Rand Dotson and the staff at LSU Press. Colleagues around the world have helped us locate the illustrations for this book: Michèle Boissin Pierrot (Musées de Vienne); Myriam Doriath, Laetitia Espanol (Musée Villèle, Réunion); Joyce Faust (Art Resource); Clare Marlow (Wolverhampton Art Gallery); and Aude Nicolas.

Because we share a life as well as a research project, this manuscript has taken up residence at our dining table as well as at our desks. We are fortunate to have many friends who have continued to visit even as our home became something of a Zouave encampment: Kara Brown, Saskia Coenen Snyder, Tom Lekan, John Lane, Allison Marsh, Rebecca Stern, and Doyle Stevick have maintained their cheerful demeanor under a double dose of *zouaverie*, all the while providing insight and support.

Both our families have cheered us and our Zouaves on. Veronica Brown helped us keep matters in perspective by growing up, taking on graduate school, a career, and New York City while we fussed with Zouaves. The award for extraordinary achievement in costume design goes, uncontested, to Gerard Brown. Our parents, especially, deserve heartfelt thanks. Long ago when the project was just a vague idea, Kay Harrison read accounts of the Inkerman Zouaves on microfilm reels of the New Orleans *Time Picayune*. Doug Harrison's regular requests for progress reports keep us on task. Lou Brown will not see the Zouaves between hard covers, but he and Helen Brown lived a partnership that continues to inspire us. All four of them remind us that the Zouaves are in service to the marriage and not the other way round, and we dedicate the book to them, with love and thanks.

NOTES

Abbreviations

ANJ	*Army and Navy Journal*
BnF	Bibliothèque nationale de France
CDT	*Chicago Daily Tribune*
HW	*Harper's Weekly*
ILN	*Illustrated London News*
NYC	*New York Clipper*
NYDTr	*New-York Daily Tribune*
NYEP	*New York Evening Post*
NYH	*New York Herald*
NYT	*New York Times*
OR	*Official Records of the Union and Confederate Armies*
PP	*Philadelphia Press*
SHD	Service historique de la Défense

Introduction: The Zouave Moment

1. Jean-Marie Bérot, *La Presse* (Paris: La Presse artistique, n.d. [ca. 1868]); Bérot, *Le Siècle* (Paris: La Presse artistique, 1865).

2. Many thanks to Jérôme Discours for information about Louis Joseph Badout.

3. The scholarship since Edward W. Said, *Orientalism* (New York: Pantheon Books, 1978), has been vast. For exemplary works in fields pertinent to Zouaves, see, for example, Jill Beaulieu and Mary Roberts, *Orientalism's Interlocutors: Painting, Architecture, Photography* (Durham: Duke University Press, 2002); Charlotte Jirousek and Sara Catterall, *Ottoman Dress and Design in the West: A Visual History of Cultural Exchange* (Bloomington: Indiana

University Press, 2019); Patrick Porter, *Military Orientalism: Eastern War through Western Eyes* (New York: Columbia University Press, 2009).

4. For suggestive parallels, see Graeme Dawson, "The Blond Bedouin: Lawrence of Arabia, Imperial Adventure, and the Imagining of English-British Masculinity," in *Manful Assertions: Masculinities in Britain Since 1800*, ed. Michael Roper and John Tosh (London: Routledge, 1991).

5. Michel Mégnin, *La Photo-carte en Algérie au XIXe siècle* (Paris: Non lieu, 2000); David Prochaska, "The Archive of *Algérie Imaginaire*," *History and Anthropology* 4, no. 2 (1990): 373–420; Beatrice Ivey, "Virtual Returns: Colonial Postcards Online and Digital 'Nostalgérie' among the Former European Settlers of Algeria," *Humanities and Social Science Communications* 9, no. 112 (2022), doi.org/10.1057/s41599-022-01134-3.

6. Jennifer Pitts, *A Turn to Empire: The Rise of Imperial Liberalism in Britain and France* (Princeton, NJ: Princeton University Press, 2006).

7. Much of the scholarship on Orientalism focuses on a false dichotomy between Orientalism's collectively repressive and individually liberating potential: for example, John M. MacKenzie, *Orientalism: History, Theory, and the Arts* (Manchester, UK: Manchester University Press, 1995).

8. J. Hopkins, "Sur la guerre aux Etats-Unis," *Le Moniteur des armées*, May 26, 1861.

9. See recently Peter Brooks, *Henry James Goes to Paris* (Princeton, NJ: Princeton University Press, 2007); Leanne M. Zalewski, "The Golden Age of French Academic Painting in America, 1867–1893," PhD diss., City University of New York, 2009; Edward Berenson, *The Statue of Liberty: A Transatlantic Story* (New Haven, CT: Yale University Press, 2012); Yasmin Sabina Khan, *Enlightening the World: The Creation of the Statue of Liberty* (Ithaca, NY: Cornell University Press, 2010); Francesca Lidia Viano, *Sentinel: The Unlikely Origins of the Statue of Liberty* (Cambridge, MA: Harvard University Press, 2018); Sarah Vowell, *Lafayette in the Somewhat United States* (New York: Riverhead Books, 2015); Laurent Zecchini, *Lafayette: Héraut de la liberté* (Paris: Fayard, 2019); Michael Andrew Bonura, "French Thought and the American Military Mind: A History of French Influence on the American Way of Warfare from 1814 through 1941," PhD diss., Florida State University, 2008.

10. For a historical account that suggests that *furia francese* retains a hold on the French military imagination, see Fabrice Clée, "*Furia francese*: Representations, Limits, and Reality Checks, Or Why the French Armed Forces Kept a Bayonet on the HK416," *Brennus 4.0. Lettre d'information du centre de doctrine et d'enseignement du commandement*, June 2019, www.penseemiliterre.fr/ressources/30118/51/1gbfuriafrancese.pdf.

11. Paddy Griffith, *Military Thought in the French Army, 1815–51* (Manchester, UK: Manchester University Press, 1989); Ian C. Hope, *A Scientific Way of War: Antebellum Military Science, West Point, and the Origins of American Military Thought* (Lincoln: University of Nebraska Press, 2015).

12. Gilles Aubagnac, "Le Camouflage et la grande guerre: du corps exhibé au corps masqué," *Corps* 12 (2014): 91–101; Danielle Delouche, "Cubisme et camouflage," *Guerres*

mondiales et conflits contemporains 171 (1993): 123–37; Stéphane Audoin-Rouzeau, "Massacres: Le corps et la guerre," in *Histoire du corps,* vol. 3: *Les mutations du regard. Le XXe siècle,* ed. Jean-Jacques Courtine (Paris: Seuil, 2006), 281–320.

13. Odile Roynette, "L'uniforme militaire au XIXe siècle: une fabrique du masculin," *Clio: femmes, genre, histoire* 36 (2012): 109–28.

14. Aubagnac, "Le Camouflage et la grande guerre."

15. David Bell, *The First Total War: Napoleon's Europe and the Birth of Warfare as We Know It* (New York: Houghton Mifflin, 2007).

16. Thomas Doherty, *Projections of War: Hollywood, American Culture, and World War II* (rev. ed., New York: Columbia University Press, 1999).

17. Jerry Wasserman, "Transcultural Cross-Dressing: Zouave Performance from the Crimea to Michael Jackson," *alt-theatre* 3, no. 3 (2011): 10–17.

18. Chloe Chapin, "Masculine Renunciation or Rejection of the Feminine?: Revisiting J. C. Flügel's *Psychology of Clothes,*" *Fashion Theory* 26, no. 7 (2022): 983–1008.

19. David Kuchta, *The Three-Piece Suit and Modern Masculinity: England, 1550–1850* (Berkeley: University of California Press, 2002), extends the chronology of this renunciation to the seventeenth century and usefully complicates the claim that "bourgeois" identity was formed in opposition to "aristocratic" modes of dress.

20. James Laver, *British Military Uniforms* (London: Penguin, 1948), 22–24. Paul Fussell, *Uniforms: Why We Are What We Wear* (Boston: Houghton Mifflin Co., 2002), 11–15, 186–89, and Jennifer Craik, *Uniforms Exposed: From Conformity to Transgression* (Oxford, UK: Berg, 2005), rehash Laver's theory and more generally illustrate the difficulty of developing a comprehensive synthesis of uniforms that addresses many different types of dress.

21. Thomas S. Abler, *Hinterland Warriors and Military Dress: European Empires and Exotic Uniforms* (Oxford, UK: Berg, 1999), 8, unpersuasively applies the same schematization to both khaki and Zouave dress.

22. Jeanne Teboul, "Combattre et parader: Des masculinités militaires plurielles," *Terrains et travaux* 2, no. 27 (2015): 99–115.

23. Walter Benjamin, "Paris, the Capital of the Nineteenth Century," in *Walter Benjamin: Selected Writings,* ed. Michael W. Jennings et al. (Cambridge, MA: Harvard University Press, 1996–2003), vol. 3: 32–49; John Bierman, *Napoleon III and His Carnival Empire* (New York: St. Martin's, 1988); Matthew Truesdell, *Spectacular Politics: Louis-Napoleon Bonaparte and the Fête Impériale, 1849–1870* (New York: Oxford University Press, 1997).

1. Projections of Empire

1. Jo Burr Margadant, "Gender, Vice, and the Political Imaginary in Postrevolutionary France: Reinterpreting the Failure of the July Monarchy, 1830–1848," *American Historical Review* 104, no. 5 (1999): 1461–96.

2. C.-A. Julien, *Histoire de l'Algérie contemporaine,* vol. 1: *La Conquête et les débuts de la*

colonisation (1827–1871) (Paris: Presses universitaires de France, 1964), chap. 2; Jennifer E. Sessions, *By Sword and Plow: France and the Conquest of Algeria* (Ithaca, NY: Cornell University Press, 2011).

3. Paul Azan, *Les Armées françaises d'outre-mer. Conquête et pacification de l'Algérie* (Paris: Villain et Bar, 1931), 20–25, 30.

4. Bertrand Clauzel, *Observations du général Clauzel sur quelques actes de son commandement à Alger* (Paris: Henri Dupuy, 1831), 6.

5. Anthony Clayton, *France, Soldiers, and Africa* (London: Brassey's Defense Publishers, 1988), 6–10.

6. Clauzel, *Observations,* 58–59.

7. Clauzel, *Observations,* 58–59; Gillian Weiss, *Captives and Corsairs: France and Slavery in the Early Modern Mediterranean* (Stanford, CA: Stanford University Press, 2011); David Todd, "A French Imperial Meridian, 1814–1870," *Past and Present* 210, no. 1 (2011): 155–86, 169–70. Sessions, *By Sword and Plow,* 177–83.

8. Clauzel, *Observations,* 35.

9. Peter Burroughs, "An Unreformed Army? 1815–1868" in *The Oxford History of the British Army,* ed. David G. Chandler and Ian Beckett, 166–86 (New York, 1994); Stephen P. Cohen, *The Indian Army, Its Contribution to the Development of a Nation* (Berkeley: University of California Press, 1971).

10. [François-Alexandre Desprez], *Journal d'un officier de l'armée d'Afrique* (Paris, 1831), 85.

11. Clauzel to the Minister of War, September 8, 1830. SHD 1 H 4 dossier 5.

12. *Encyclopédie du dix-neuvième siècle: répertoire universel des sciences, des lettres et des arts* (1836–53), s.v. "Kabyle," vol. 14: 800.

13. Patricia M. E. Lorcin, *Imperial Identities: Stereotyping, Prejudice, and Race in Colonial Algeria* (New York: I. B. Tauris, 1999).

14. Pascal Duprat, "Une guerre insensée. Expédition contre les Kabyles ou Berbers d'Algérie," *Revue indépendante* 19 (1845), qtd. by Lorcin, *Imperial Identities,* 31. See also Emile Keller, *Le Général de la Moricière. Sa vie militaire, politique, et religieuse* (2 vols., Paris: J. Dumaine, 1874), vol. 1: 135, 196–97.

15. Henri d'Orléans, Duke d'Aumale, *Les Zouaves et les chasseurs à pied* (2nd ed., Paris, 1855), 15. Aumale's essay originally appeared over the signature "V. de Mars" in the *Revue des Deux Mondes,* March 15 and April 1, 1855.

16. Anselme Guy, *Mission du Commandant du génie Guy à Tunis* (Paris: Henri Dupuy, 1831), 7.

17. Minister of War to Berthezène, April 25, 1831, SHD 1 H 7 dossier 3 sous dossier 2.

18. *Alger, ou considérations sur l'état actuel de cette régence* (Paris: Delaunay, 1833), 33–34.

19. Minister of War to Clauzel, December 31, 1830. SHD 1 H 5 dossier 6 sous dossier 2, and March 11, 1831, SHD 1 H 7 dossier 3 sous dossier 2.

20. Minister of War to Clauzel, March 6, April 7, 1831. SHD 1 H 7 dossier 3 sous dossier 2.

21. Clauzel, qtd. by Douglas Porch, *The French Foreign Legion: A Complete History of the Legendary Fighting Force* (New York: Harper Collins, 1991), 13. See also *Explications du Maréchal Clauzel* (Paris: Ambroise Dupont, 1837).

22. Ministry of War to Berthezène, April 30, 1831, SHD 1 H 7 dossier 3 sous dossier 2. "Corps des Zouaves, 1er bataillon, Contrôle nominatif des réfugiés espagnols incorporés le 19 juin 1831," July 1831, SHD 1 H 8 dossier 2.

23. Minister of War to Berthezène, April 7, 1831. SHD 1 H 7 dossier 3 sous dossier 2.

24. General Berthezène, qtd. by Julien, *Histoire de l'Algérie* 1: 85. On emigration as a means of resolving the social question more generally, see Sessions, *By Sword and Plow*, 264–70.

25. [Captain] François-Basile Peyronny, *Considérations politiques sur la colonie d'Alger* (Paris: Dentu, 1836), 191.

26. See for example Jean-Joseph Gustave Cler, *Souvenirs d'un officier du 2e de zouaves* (Paris: Michel Lévy, frerès, 1859), 4. Alfred Delvau, *Dictionnaire de la langue verte: argots parisiens comparés* (2nd ed., Paris, 1866), iii, 29.

27. "Album," *Petit Courrier des dames: modes de Paris*, January 20, 1836.

28. Orléans, *Les Zouaves et les chasseurs à pied*, 28.

29. See for example Duvivier to Minister of War, November 1, 1831, SHD 1 H 10 dossier 3, recommending recruiting in Tunis and providing better transport for recruits.

30. "Analyse sur la réorganisation des bataillons Zouaves" March 1832, SHD 1 H 12 dossier 1, and "Situation de la Division d'Alger au 1er Mai 1832" in SHD 1 H 13 dossier 1. Henri Dutailly, "Les premiers zouaves," *Revue historique des armées* 132 (1978): 43–52.

31. General Boyer, qtd. in a file on the proposed reorganization of the Zouaves, May 15, 1832, in SHD 1 H 13 dossier 1.

32. Dutailly, "Les premier zouaves," 46.

33. Ministry of War, Duke de Dalmatie, to General Duke de Rovigo, December 31, 1831, SHD 1 H 10 dossier 3. Porch, *The French Foreign Legion*, 3–5.

34. Duvivier, "Notice sur le 2e Batt. des Zouaves et sur l'organisation à donner à ce corps," February 6 and July 15, 1832. SHD 1 H 15 dossier 2.

35. Duvivier to the Governor, December 18 [corrected to 28], 1834. SHD 1 H 29 dossier 3.

36. Voivol to M le maréchal, October 31, 1833. SHD 1 H 22 dossier 1. Dutailly, "Les premiers zouaves," 46.

37. Robert Huré, *L'Armée d'Afrique: 1830–1962* (Paris: Charles-Lavauzelle, 1977); Raymond Noulens, *Les Spahis, cavaliers de l'armée d'Afrique* (Paris: Musée de l'armée, 1997), 28; Clayton, *France, Soldiers, and Africa*, 244–80; Razik Menidjel, *Les Tirailleurs algériens* (Paris: Publibook, 2007). Spahi settlements: Xavier Yacone, "La colonisation militaire par les smalas de spahis en Algérie," *Revue historique* 242 (1969): 347–94. Spahi lore: Charles Marcotte de Quivières, *Deux ans en Afrique* (Paris, 1855), 66; Florian Pharaon, *Spahis, turcos et goumiers* (Paris: Challamel ainé, 1864), 165–67.

38. Clayton, *France, Soldiers, and Africa*, 200, notes that the practice of using sleeve braiding to indicate rank began with the Zouaves and spread to other units.

39. Jean-Louis Lacarde, *Zouaves et tirailleurs: les régiments de marche et les régiments mixtes (1914–1918)* (3 vols., Les Jonquerets de Livet: Edition des Argonautes, 2000), vol. 2: 547.

40. Duvivier, "Description des vêtements et effets uniformes adoptés par le 2eme bataillon de zouaves," November 15, 1831, in SHD 1 H 10 dossier 2.

41. Claude Antoine Rozet, *Relation de la guerre d'Afrique pendant les années 1830 et 1831* (2 vols., Paris: Firmin Didot frères, 1832), vol. 2: 22–23.

42. Duvivier, "Description des vêtements."

43. Peyronny, *Considérations politiques*, 190; L.B. [Léon Blondel], *Aperçu sur la situation politique, commerciale et industrielle des possessions françaises dans le nord de l'Afrique, au commencement de 1836* (Paris: Imprimerie royale, 1836), 38–39.

44. Duvivier, *La Solution de la question de l'Algérie* (Paris: Gaultier-Laguionie, 1841), 166–69.

45. L.B., *Aperçu sur la situation politique*, 38–39; Duvivier, *La Solution*, 167–71.

46. "Je nage dans la joie": Henri d'Orléans, duc d'Aumale, *Correspondance du duc d'Aumale et de Cuvillier-Fleury* (4 vols., Paris: Plon-Nourrit, 1910–14), vol. 2: xvii.

47. J. Bodin, *Les Suisses au service de la France* (Paris: Albin Michel, 1988).

48. Stephen McGarry, *Irish Brigades Abroad: From the Wild Geese to the Napoleonic Wars* (Dublin: History Press Ireland, 2013), chap. 15. The Irish Legion was the only foreign unit to receive an imperial eagle (194).

49. Robert Solé, *Bonaparte à la conquête de l'Egypte* (Paris: Seuil, 2006), 72–73, 136; Eugène Fieffé, *Histoire des troupes étrangères au service de la France depuis leur origine jusqu'à nos jours* (2 vols., Paris: Dumaine, 1854); John Elting, *Swords Around the Throne: Napoleon's Grande Armée* (New York: Free Press, 1988); Guy Dempsey, *Napoleon's Mercenaries: Foreign Units in the French Army under the Consulate and Empire, 1799–1814* (London: Frontline Books, 2016), lists foreign units and includes details about uniforms.

50. Juan Cole, *Napoleon's Egypt: Invading the Middle East* (New York: St. Martin's Press, 2007), 11–12, 53–54; Ian Coller, *Arab France: Islam and the Making of Modern Europe* (Berkeley: University of California Press, 2010), 58–60.

51. Darcy Grimaldo Grigsby, *Mamelukes in Paris: Fashionable Tropes of Failed Napoleonic Conquest* (Berkeley: University of California Press, 1996), 11.

52. Coller, *Arab France*, chap. 5.

53. Porch, *The French Foreign Legion*, 3–5.

54. Philip Mansel, "Monarchy, Uniform and the Rise of the Frac, 1760–1830," *Past and Present* 96 (August 1982): 103–32.

55. Clauzel, *Observations*, 36–38.

56. Keller, *Le Général de la Moricière* 1: 75; Alison Matthews David, "Decorated Men: Fashioning the French Soldier, 1852–1914," *Fashion Theory* 7, no. 1 (2003): 3–37.

57. Clayton, *France, Soldiers, and Africa*, 9–11.

58. Clayton, *France, Soldiers, and Africa*, 6–10. Antoine Picon, "L'Orient saint-simonien: Un imaginaire géographique, anthropologique et technique," in *Enquêtes en Méditerranée:*

les expéditions françaises d'Egypte, de Morée, et d'Algérie, ed. Marie-Noëlle Bourguet, Daniel Nordman, Vassilis Panayotopoulos, 227–38 (Athens: Institut de Recherches néohelléniques, 1999); Osama W. Abi-Mershed, *Apostles of Modernity: Saint-Simonians and the Civilizing Mission in Algeria* (Stanford, CA: Stanford University Press, 2010).

59. Colonel Pamart, "Les Polytechniciens de l'Armée d'Afrique," *Revue historique de l'armée* 2 (1954): 19–25.

60. Ferdinand Hugonnet, *Français et Arabes en Algérie* (Paris: Ferd. Sartirous, 1860), 146.

61. Keller, *Le Général de la Moricière;* Edmund Burke, "The Terror and Religion: Brittany and Algeria," in *Colonialism and the Modern World,* ed. Gregory Blue, Martin Bunton, and Ralph Crozier, 40–50 (New York: Routledge, 2015); Griffith, *Military Thought in the French Army, 1815–1851,* 39.

62. Qtd. in Keller, *Le Général de la Moricière* 1: 55.

63. Gil Mihaely, "Pilosité et virilité entre le Premier Empire et la Première Guerre mondiale," *Napoleonica* 30, no. 3 (2017): 132–54.

64. Qtd. in Keller, *Le Général de la Moricière* 1: 55–56.

65. Général du Bail, *Mes souvenirs, 1820–1851* 1: 15, qtd. by Nicolas Schaub, *Représenter l'Algérie. Images et conquête au XIXe siècle* (Paris: CTHS INHA, 2015), 104.

66. Keller, *Le Général de la Moricière* 1: 64–65.

67. Qtd. in Keller, *Le Général de la Moricière* 1: 74.

68. Qtd. in Keller, *Le Général de la Moricière* 1: 57.

69. Keller, *Le Général de la Moricière* 1: 60, 64–65.

70. "Bulletin," *La Revue de Paris* 47 (1837): 196–203, 199.

71. Keller, *Le Général de la Moricière* 1: 117–18.

72. "Le seul homme du pays," Tocqueville to Louis de Kergorlay, May 23, 1841, in Alexis de Tocqueville, *Œuvres complètes,* vol. 13: *Correspondance d'Alexis de Tocqueville et de Louis de Kergorlay* (2 vols., Paris: Gallimard, 1977), 87. On Tocqueville's views on Algeria, see Olivier Le Cour Grandmaison, *Coloniser, exterminer: Sur la guerre et l'état colonial* (Paris: Fayard, 2005), 100; and Pitts, *A Turn to Empire,* chap. 7.

73. Kenneth J. Perkins, *Qaids, Captains and Colons: French Military Administration in the Colonial Maghrib, 1844–1934* (New York: Africana Publishing Co., 1981), chap. 2; Jacques Frémeaux, *Les Bureaux arabes dans l'Algérie de la conquête* (Paris: Denoël, 1993).

74. Jennifer E. Sessions, "Colonizing Revolutionary Politics: Algeria and the French Revolution of 1848," *French Politics, Culture, and Society* 33, no. 1 (2015): 75–100; Le Cour Grandmaison, *Coloniser, exterminer,* 138–52; William Gallois, *A History of Violence in the Early Algerian Colony* (New York: Palgrave Macmillan, 2013); Benjamin Claude Brower, *A Desert Named Peace: The Violence of France's Empire in the Algerian Sahara, 1844–1902* (New York: Columbia University Press, 2009).

75. The story appears, for example, in Claude Antoine Rozet, *Voyage dans la régence d'Alger, ou description du pays occupé par l'armée française en Afrique* (3 vols., Paris: Arthus Bertrand, 1833), vol. 2: 117, and Adolphe de Fontaine de Resbecq, *Alger et les côtes d'Afrique* (Paris: Gaume Frères, 1837), 54–55.

76. Charles Sédillot, *Campagne de Constantine de 1837* (Paris: Crochard et Cie., 1838), 46–47.

77. Brower, *A Desert Named Peace,* 16–17, 22.

78. Lamoricière to Gustave d'Eichtal, October 25, 1839, qtd. by Picon, "L'Orient saint-simonien," 238.

79. A. B. [Capt. Blanc], *Les Grottes du Dahara, Récit historique par un ancien capitaine de Zouaves* (Paris: M. Blot, 1864), 10, 7.

80. Gallois, *History of Violence,* 81–82. See also Le Cour Grandmaison, *Coloniser, exterminer,* 150–52, for a careful account of the novelty of French repressive violence.

81. Jean-Pierre Bois, "Le Général Yusuf, 1808–1866. L'aventure au service de la France," *Bulletin de la Société archéologique et historique de Nantes et de Loire-Atlantique* 133 (1998): 249–61.

82. Louis Blanc, *Histoire de dix ans* (Paris, 1842–44), vol. 5: 168–69; Sessions, "Colonizing Revolutionary Politics"; Le Cour Grandmaison, *Coloniser, exterminer,* 308–34.

83. Sun-Young Park, *Ideals of the Body: Architecture, Urbanism and Hygiene in Postrevolutionary Paris* (Pittsburgh: University of Pittsburgh Press, 2018), is a recent approach to the subject that is attentive to both Oriental motifs and the military athleticism associated with Zouaves.

84. Hélène Puiseux, *Les Figures de guerre. Représentations et sensibilités, 1839–1996* (Paris: Gallimard, 1997), 44.

85. *Figaro,* December 23, 1837.

86. Puiseux, *Les Figures de guerre,* 44; Charles Dejob, "La défense de Mazagran dans la littérature et les arts du dessin," *Revue d'histoire littéraire de la France* 19, no. 2 (1912): 318–40. Dejob notes at least six theaters across France performing accounts of Mazagran (329).

87. Examples include: *Croquis d'après nature faits pendant l'expédition de Mascara* (Paris, 1837); Adrien Berbrugger, *Algérie historique, pittoresque et monumentale* (Paris, 1843); Auguste Raffet, *La Retraite de Constantine* (Paris, 1837), and *La Prise de Constantine* (Paris, 1837). Schaub, *Représenter l'Algérie,* 147, 152–53, 280–89.

88. Schaub, *Représenter l'Algérie,* 280–89; David Hopkin, *Soldier and Peasant in French Popular Culture, 1766–1870* (Woodbridge, UK: Boydell Press, 2003).

89. Puiseux, *Les Figures de la guerre,* 34.

90. Katie Hornstein, *Picturing War in France, 1792–1856* (New Haven, CT: Yale University Press, 2017), 87.

91. Aurélie Cottais, "Les salles d'Afrique: construction et décor sous la monarchie de Juillet (1830–1848)," *Bulletin du Centre de recherche du château de Versailles* (2010), journals.openedition.org/crcv/10498.

92. Sessions, *By Sword and Plow,* 85–89.

93. Jennifer E. Sessions, "Ambiguous Glory: The Algerian Conquest and the Politics of Colonial Commemoration in Post-Revolutionary France," *Outre-mers, Revue d'histoire* 350–51 (2006): 91–102, 100–101.

94. Hornstein, *Picturing War in France*, 115–16; John Zarobell, "Jean-Charles Langlois's Panorama of Algiers (1833) and the Prospective Colonial Landscape," *Art History* 26, no. 5 (2003): 638–68.

95. Charles Gavard, *Galéries historiques du palais de Versailles* (Paris: Imprimerie royale, 1840), 265–71.

96. Hornstein, *Picturing War in France*, chap. 3; Sessions, *By Sword and Plow*, 111–12.

97. Léon Lagrange, "Artistes contemporains: Horace Vernet," *Gazette des Beaux-Arts* 15, no. 5 (November 1863): 464; Daniel Harkett and Katie Hornstein, "Introduction" in *Horace Vernet and the Thresholds of Nineteenth-Century Visual Culture*, ed. Daniel Harkett and Katie Hornstein (Hanover, NH: Dartmouth College Press, 2017), 1–22, 13.

98. "Salon de 1841," in *La France littéraire*, nouv. ser., vol. 5 (1841): 41; see also "Salon de 1841," *Les Coulisses: petit journal des théâtres, de la littérature, et de la bourse*, May 2, 1841.

99. In addition to newspaper coverage, see, for example, *Notice biographique et nécrologie du Prince royal duc d'Orléans* (Paris, 1842); Louis Bovin, *Souvenirs de la vie du duc d'Orléans prince royal* (Paris, 1842).

100. Félix Morand, "L'Algérien français—Le Zouave, le Spahi, le Zéphyr," in *Les Français peints par eux-mêmes, encyclopédie morale du dix-neuvième siècle* (Paris, 1840–42), vol. 3: *Province*, 267–83, 270–71.

101. Morand, "L'Algérien français," 270.

102. Morand, "L'Algérien français," 276.

103. Morand, "L'Algérien français," 271.

104. Morand, "L'Algérien français," 270.

2. The Soldier of Modern Life

1. Hugonnet, *Français et arabes en Algérie*, 37–38.

2. Charles Baudelaire, *The Painter of Modern Life and Other Essays*, trans. Jonathan Mayne, 2nd ed. (London: Phaidon, 1964), 24–25 (emphasis in the original).

3. Baudelaire, *The Painter of Modern Life*, 12; Karen W. Smith, *Constantin Guys: Crimean War Drawings, 1854–1856* (Cleveland: Cleveland Museum of Art, 1978).

4. Philip Knightley, *The First Casualty: The War Correspondent as Hero and Myth-Maker from the Crimea to Iraq* (3d ed., Baltimore: Johns Hopkins University Press, [1975] 2004), 1–17.

5. William Howard Russell, "The British Army in the Crimea," *Times* (London), November 7, 1855, 10.

6. Orlando Figes, *Crimea: The Last Crusade* (New York: Metropolitan Books, 2011); Alain Gouttmann, *La Guerre de Crimée, 1853–1856. La première guerre moderne*, 2nd ed. (Paris: Tempus, 2006).

7. Sima Godfrey, "La Guerre de Crimée n'aura pas lieu," *French Cultural Studies* 27, no. 1 (2016): 3–19.

8. Stefanie Markovits, "Rushing into Print: 'Participatory Journalism' During the Crimean War," *Victorian Studies* 50, no. 4 (2008): 559–86.

9. Anthony Dawson, "The French Army and British Army Crimean War Reforms," *19: Interdisciplinary Studies in the Long Nineteenth Century* 20 (2015), doi.org/10.16995/ntn.707.

10. Ulrich Keller, *The Ultimate Spectacle: A Visual History of the Crimean War* (Amsterdam: Gordon and Breach Publishers, 2001), 4. See also Stefanie Markovits, *The Crimean War in the British Imagination* (New York: Cambridge University Press, 2009).

11. John A. Lynn, *The Bayonets of the Republic: Motivation and Tactics in the Army of Revolutionary France, 1791–94* (Urbana: University of Illinois Press, 1984), 185–93; Griffith, *Military Thought in the French Army*, 61, 78–79, 107–9, 119–21.

12. Cler, *Souvenirs d'un officier du 2e zouaves*, 139; see also his comments on "a soldiers' battle" in which officers leave their men to their own initiative, 144, and Louis Noir, *Guerres de mon temps: Campagne de Crimée* (Paris: 1869), 64, who distinguished English and Russian soldiers, who maintained their formations, from their French counterparts who relied on élan.

13. Simon Godchot, *Le 1er régiment de zouaves, 1852–1895* (2 vols., Paris: Librairie centrale des beaux-arts, 1896–98), vol. 1: 53–54.

14. "The French Scaling the Heights," *ILN*, October 14, 1854.

15. "The Source of French Bravery," *ILN*, May 19, 1855.

16. *Figaro*, October 15, 1854.

17. Amédée de Damas, *Souvenirs religieux et militaires de la Crimée* (Paris: Jacques Lecoffre, 1857), 33. Also reported in the *Times (London)*: "From various sources," October 12, 1854, and the *Journal des débats politiques et littéraires*, October 21, 1854.

18. "The British Expedition," *Times (London)*, May 10, 1854; *Journal des débats*, May 12, 1854; *Le Constitutionnel*, October 21, 1854.

19. Frédéric Lacroix, "Les Zouaves," *L'Illustration*, November 4, 1854, 306.

20. *Journal des débats*, June 24, 1854.

21. *Times (London)*, May 23, 1854.

22. N.C.C., "Military uniforms," *Times (London)*, June 8, 1854.

23. "A Good Example to Our Men," *ILN*, February 24, 1855.

24. Léo Lespès, "Les Zouaves," *Figaro*, October 14, 1855.

25. *Journal des débats*, October 3, 1854.

26. Mihaely, "Pilosité et virilité."

27. *Times (London)*, April 19, 1854.

28. *Journal des débats*, June 24, 1854; British soldiers were permitted to wear facial hair beginning in 1854: Susan Walton, "From Squalid Impropriety to Manly Respectability: The Revival of Beards, Moustaches and Martial Values in the 1850s in England," *Nineteenth-Century Contexts* 30, no. 3 (2008): 229–45.

29. Godchot, *Le 1er régiment*, 65.

30. "Foreign and Colonial News," *ILN*, May 13, 1854, and "The Allied Forces at Gallipoli," *ILN*, September 30, 1854.

31.*Times* (*London*), May 23, 1854. Also reported in *ILN*, May 27, 1854, and *Journal des débats*, May 22, 1854.

32. *Journal des débats*, June 14, 1854.

33. Henri de la Perrière, *Des Tenants, supports et soutiens dans l'art héraldique* (Rome, 1910), 61; and *L'Illustration*, January 17, 1857, 44. Zouave and Highlander also appeared together in battle paintings of the Crimea, discussed below. See, for example, the renditions of the battle of the Alma by Eugène Lami and Horace Vernet, discussed in Aude Nicolas, "Les rapports franco-britanniques à travers la peinture militaire représentant la guerre de Crimée," *Revue historique des armées* 264 (2011): 19-31.

34. Godchot, *Le 1er régiment*, 67. See also the carte de visite of the dog Magenta, the terror of the Austrian enemy during the Italian Campaign, whose photo was reproduced in both *Le Monde illustré* and *L'Illustration*: Louis Delpérier, *La Garde Impériale de Napoleon III* (Nantes: Editions du Canonnier, 2000), 94.

35. *Le Constitutionnel*, August 18, 1859.

36. *Revue britannique. Recueil international* 25 (1855): 114; and Damas, *Souvenirs religieux et militaires*, 90-92. The story appears as a lesson for children in *L'Education catholique, revue de l'enseignement chrétien* 12, no. 6 (1891): 82-83, and was still being reprinted in the 1920s: *Les Jeunes: Organe officiel de la Fédération gymnastique et sportive des patronages de France*, December 21, 1924.

37. Claude-Antoine Delétant, "Le Chat du zouave," in *Fables et contes en vers* (La Rochelle: J. Deslandes, 1857), 253-70. "Petit théâtre," *Le Tintamarre*, January 29, 1865; "Chronique," *La Comédie*, December 4, 1864.

38. See, for example, Jean Gay, *Les chats. Extraits de pièces rares et curieuses en vers et en prose* (Paris, 1866).

39. Godchot, *Le 1er régiment*, 65-66.

40. See Henri Durand-Brager's sketch in *L'Illustration*, February 19, 1855, and "A Zouave testimonial of Gratitude," *ILN*, January 26, 1856.

41. Félix Maynard, *Souvenirs d'un Zouave devant Sébastopol* (2 vols., Paris: Librairie nouvelle, 1855), vol. 2: 15-19. Maynard's hero, a Zouave bugler, sets up cozy accommodations on several different occasions in the book, starting with a horse box that he uses as a cabin onboard ship (vol. 1: 16-17).

42. Cler, *Souvenirs d'un officier*, 151.

43. "Zouaves Making Themselves Comfortable," *ILN*, January 12, 1856. See also Eustace Clare Grenville Murray, *Pictures from the Battle Fields, by "the Roving Englishman"* (London: G. Routledge and Co., 1856), esp. chap. 23 on "The Zouave."

44. "Letters from the Camp at Sebastapol," *ILN*, November 17, 1855. Dawson, "The French Army."

45. "The War: The British Expedition," *Times* (*London*), April 28, 1854.

46. "La Marche du 1er Zouaves": "Le vieux chacal pour chasser la famine / A des moyens qu'en Afrique il apprit / Les maraudeurs fournissent les cuisines / On vit toujours au frais de l'ennemi."

47. *Journal des débats,* October 3, 1854.

48. Mary Seacole, *Wonderful Adventures of Mrs. Seacole in Many Lands* (1857; New York: Oxford University Press, 1988), 105, 117.

49. Damas, *Souvenirs religieux et militaires,* 34–35. See also Cler's account of celebrations around a foraged piano: *Souvenirs d'un officier,* 134–35.

50. *Journal des débats,* June 24, 1854.

51. Thomas Cardoza, *Intrepid Women: Cantinières and Vivandières of the French Army* (Bloomington: Indiana University Press, 2010), chap. 5; Gil Mihaely, "L'effacement de la cantinière ou la virilisation de l'armée française au XIXe siècle," *Revue d'histoire du XIXe siècle* 30 (2005): 1–19.

52. Cardoza, *Intrepid Women,* 154; Cler, *Souvenirs d'un officier,* 91–92, 125; Lacarde, *Zouaves et tirailleurs* 2: 551. Delpérier, *La Garde Impériale,* 96, reproduces a carte de visite of the *cantinière* Mme Teyssère.

53. W. Baring Pemberton, *Battles of the Crimean War* (London: B. T. Batsford, 1962), 155; see also A. W. Kinglake, *The Invasion of the Crimea: Its Origin, and an Account of Its Progress down to the Death of Lord Raglan* (9 vols., 1863–87; London: William Blackwood and Sons, 1901), vol. 9: 107–8.

54. See, for example, Gustave Graux, *Le Roman d'un Zouave, scènes de la vie militaire* (Paris: L. Tintelin, 1864). See also Pierre Zaccone, *Les Zouaves* (Paris: A. de Vresse, 1859); and Félix Yvert, *Les Zouaves* (Paris: Garnier frères, 1855).

55. The engraving titled "Great, subscription tobacco!" appeared in *L'Illustration,* January 2, 1855. See also *L'Illustration,* December 23, 1854, and January 15, 22, 1855; and the brochure signed by "a woman who doesn't smoke": *Appel à la bienfaisance publique* (Paris, 1854).

56. According to Lorédan Larchey, *Les Excentricités de la langue française en 1860,* the word *chaparder* derives from *"chat-pard"* or a wild cat. The Project for American and French Research on the Treasury of the French Language (ARTFL) database indicates that usage of the word climbed steeply between 1850 and 1900, then fell equally sharply.

57. "Les Zouaves," *Figaro,* October 14, 1855.

58. Until 1864 spoken-word theater was limited by law to venues like the Comédie Française. At mid-century, vaudeville was the most popular theatrical genre in Paris, with over two hundred new productions mounted every year: Dominique Leroy, *Histoire des arts et spectacles en France* (Paris: L'Harmattan, 1990), 139–49; and Henri Gidel, *Le Vaudeville* (Paris: Presses universitaires de France, 1986).

59. Windmill: "La comédie des zouaves" in *Revue britannique ou choix d'articles traduits des meilleurs écrits périodiques de la Grande Bretagne* (Paris, 1854), 496; "Récréation au camp," *L'Illustration,* May 26, 1855, 325–26. See playbills in *ILN,* August 18, 1855; Godchot, *Le 1er régiment,* plate between 68–69; *L'Illustration,* June 9, 1855, 368.

60. See Alexandre Protais's sketch, "The stage during a production of *The Make-Believe English Girls,*" in *L'Illustration,* May 26, 1855. Jules Clartie, "Le théâtre au camp," *Revue d'art dramatique et musical* 20 (1905), 24, lists titles of vaudevilles performed at Inkerman.

61. Paul de Molènes, *Les Commentaires d'un soldat. Premiers jours de la guerre de Crimée. L'Hiver devant Sébastopol. Derniers jours de la guerre de Crimée. La Guerre d'Italie* (Paris: Michel Lévy frères, 1860), 180. *ILN*, August 18, 1855.

62. Clartie, "Le théâtre au camp," 23–24.

63. Anicet Bourgeois and Edouard Brisebarre, *Pascal et Chambord, comédie en deux actes* (Paris: Ve Dondey-Dupré, 1839); Cogniard frères and Achille Bourdois, *Le Bal du sauvage* (Paris: Michel Lévy frères, [1854]).

64. Cler, *Souvenirs d'un officier*, 124. The English translation is from Cler, *Reminiscences of an Officer of Zouaves* (New York: Appleton and Co., 1860), 152.

65. The popularity of the play in the Crimea led to a Parisian revival: "Spectacles du 26 Août," *Le Constitutionnel*, August 26, 1856.

66. Sewrin and Dumersan, *Les Anglaises pour rire* (Paris: Mme Masson, 1815); "The Siege of Sebastopol from our Special Correspondent," *Times (London)*, May 24, 1855.

67. [Jean-François Jules] Herbé, *Français et Russes en Crimée. Lettres d'un officier français à sa famille pendant la campagne d'Orient* (Paris: Calmann Lévy, 1892), 54.

68. Albert and Lustière, *La Guerre d'Orient, drame militaire en trois actes et vingt tableaux* (Paris, 1854); reviewed in "Théâtre impérial du Cirque," *Le Nouvelliste: quotidien politique, littéraire, industriel et commercial*, July 13, 1854.

69. *Le Nouvelliste*, August 23, 1856.

70. Victoria and Albert Museum, "The Story of Circus," www.vam.ac.uk/content/articles/t/the-first-circus/; J. S. Bratton, "Theater of War: The Crimea on the London Stage, 1854–5," in *Performance and Politics in Popular Drama*, ed. David Bradby, Louis James, and Bernard Sharratt (New York: Cambridge University Press, 1980), 119–38. No Zouaves appeared in the spectacle at Astley's, which specialized in equestrian performance. Real-life Zouave veterans guided visitors around a giant model of the siege of Sebastopol at the Surrey Zoological Gardens in the summer of 1855, during the siege itself. "Surrey Zoological Gardens," *ILN*, June 2, 1855. *Figaro*, November 25, 1855, was unimpressed by the 25-franc weekly salary the gardens were offering: authentic Zouaves, the newspaper believed, could command more.

71. *The Butterfly's Ball and the Grasshopper's Feast, or Harlequin and the Genius of Spring. A New Comic Christmas Pantomime Founded on Roscoe's Popular Poem* (London: W. S. Johnson, 1855), 16 premiered at the Theater Royal, Haymarket, December 26, 1855. "The Christmas Pantomime," *ILN*, January 12, 1856.

72. On Jullien's performance style, see Alan Walker, *Franz Liszt, the Weimar Years, 1848–1861* (Ithaca, NY: Cornell University Press, 1989), 273. For the Zouave tour: *ILN*, May 17, 1856, and "Arrival of the Africa," *NYH*, May 29, 1856.

73. Ellen Rosenman, "Beyond the Nation: Penny Fiction, the Crimean War, and Political Belonging," *Victorian Literature and Culture* 46, no. 1 (2018): 95–124.

74. Charles Dupeuty and E. Bourget, *Pilbox et Friquet ou Zouave et Highlander* (Paris: Librairie théâtrale, 1855), premiered April 6, 1855; "Chronique de Paris," *L'Illustration*, April 14, 1855.

75. Eugène Grangé and Eugène Cormon, *Le Théâtre des Zouaves* (Paris: Michel Lévy frères, 1855), premiered September 1, 1855. See also Alphonse Arnault, *Les Zouaves* (Paris: Michel Lévy, 1856), in which a dashing Zouave lieutenant wins the love of a Russian woman while his soldiers' battlefield theater provides comic relief. Stage Zouaves also appeared on their home turf: Loizillon, *Les Zouaves en Crimée. Vaudeville en un acte* (Constantine: Abadie, 1854), premiered in Algeria. The Russian enemy turns out in fact to be an oppressed Pole, and the Zouave saves a maid from marriage to a brutal Cossack.

76. Charles Adam, *La Guerre d'Italie: Histoire complète des opérations militaires dans la péninsule* (Paris: N. J. Philippart, 1859), 257.

77. *La Sylphide: journal de modes, de littérature, de théâtres et de musique*, August 30, 1856. Another Zouave veteran was performing at the same time in Marseille: his promotional literature promised that raucous audiences could not intimidate a man accustomed to cannon fire. *L'Argus et le ver-vert réunis*, October 14, 1855.

78. "The Theaters," *ILN*, July 28, 1860.

79. *Journal des débats*, May 28, 1859. Other Italian Campaign plays: *Sur la frontière* opened Aux Délassements, *La Question d'Italie* at the Variétés, *Sur le Po* at the Palais Royal. Albert Monnier, "Théâtres," *Le Journal amusant*, May 28, 1859.

80. Eugène Grangé and Lambert-Thiboust, *Tant va l'autruche à l'eau* (Paris: Michel Lévy frères, 1859), premiered May 31, 1859. The script describes a Turco, but press coverage makes it clear that the role went to a Zouave: Charles Monselet, "Théâtres," *Le Monde illustré*, June 4, 1859.

81. "Courrier de Paris," *L'Illustration*, July 9, 1859.

82. "Théâtres," *Le Constitutionnel*, May 23, 1859.

83. Théodore Barrière and Lambert-Thiboust, *Les Jocrisses de l'amour* (Paris: Librairie nouvelle, 1865).

84. A. Aldini, "Bouffes Parisiens. Les Vivandières de la Grande Armée," *La France musicale*, July 10, 1859. See also A. Dureau, "Bouffes Parisiens," *Le Ménestral: journal de musique*, July 10, 1859.

85. Truesdell, *Spectacular Politics*.

86. The literature on the renovation of Paris is enormous. See especially David H. Pinckney, *Napoleon III and the Rebuilding of Paris* (Princeton, NJ: Princeton University Press, 1958); David Harvey, *Paris, Capital of Modernity* (New York: Routledge, 2005); and, most recently, Christophe Charle, *Paris, 'capitales' des XIXe siècles* (Paris: Seuil, 2021).

87. David, "Decorated Men," 24.

88. Léon Bezout, *Vers adressés à Sa Majesté impériale Napoléon III: le retour de Crimée des régiments de la ligne et de la Garde impériale* (Paris: E. Brière, 1856).

89. Richard S. Hopkins, *Planning the Greenspaces of Nineteenth-Century Paris* (Baton Rouge: Louisiana State University Press, 2015). See also the Zouave drummer in James Tissot's painting *Beating the Retreat in the Tuileries* (1867).

90. "Our Paris Correspondent," *NYH* April 22, 1857.

91. The bridge opened in 1858. The other figures, which have since been removed, were a *chasseur à pied*, a grenadier, and an artilleryman.

92. J.-J. Lefrère and P. Berche, "Le Zouave Jacob ou la thaumaturgie par le magnétisme," *Annales Médico-psychologiques, revue psychiatrique* 169, no. 9 (2011): 571–77; Auguste Hardy, *Les miracles de la rue de la Roquette. Histoire merveilleuse du zouave guérisseur* (Paris: Ch. Schiller, 1867).

93. Henry Jacob, *L'Hygiène naturelle par le Zouave Jacob ou l'art de conserver sa santé et de se guérir soi-même* (Paris, 1868). The BnF has several photographs of Jacob with throngs of patients and admirers: see, for example, gallica.bnf.fr/ark:/12148/btv1b53111269d.item and gallica.bnf.fr/ark:/12148/btv1b53111270s.

94. Antonio Zobi, *Cronaca degli avvenimenti d'Italia nel 1859* (Florence: Grazzini, Giannini e C., 1859), vol. 1: 484; and Alfred Delvau, *Le Petit Caporal des zouaves* (Paris: Lécrivain et Toubon, 1859). On the Italian Campaign, see Frederick C. Schneid, *The Second War of Italian Unification, 1859–1861* (Oxford, UK: Osprey, 2012). Reporters recounted ever more elaborate tales of Zouave bravery and insouciance: Auguste Humbert, *Victoires et conquêtes des armées alliées, deuxième partie, Campagne d'Italie* (Paris: Savin et compagnie, 1859), 193–94; Francis Wey, "Le Zouave," *Argus méridional: journal littéraire et artistique*, July 10, 1859.

95. "Costume de zouave du Prince impérial," art.rmngp.fr/en/library/artworks/costume -de-zouave-du-prince-imperial.

96. Augustin Filon, *Memoirs of the Prince Imperial (1856–1879) from the French of Augustin Filon* (London: W. Heinemann, 1913), 9–10, 12.

97. For more on Adolphe Yvon, *Le Prince impérial offrant une collation aux enfants de troupe*, see Julia Thoma, *The Final Spectacle: Military Painting under the Second Empire* (Berlin: De Gruyter, 2019), 270n215.

98. *Le Petit Journal*, March 17, 1863.

99. "Le costume de zouave remplacé par celui de ramoneur," www.parismuseescollections.paris.fr/en/node/721671#infos-principales.

100. Clare Rose, "What Was Uniform about the Fin-de-Siècle Sailor Suit?" *Journal of Design History* 24, no. 2 (2011): 105–24.

101. *Pacific Commercial Advertiser* (Honolulu), April 2, 1864.

102. Eugenia Janis, *The Photography of Gustave Le Gray* (Chicago: University of Chicago Press, 1987), 86; Sylvie Aubenas, "Boulevard des Capucines: The Glory of the Empire," in *Gustave Le Gray, 1820–1884*, ed. Gordon Baldwin (Los Angeles: J. Paul Getty Museum, 2002), 131–36; Chris Pearson, *Mobilizing Nature: The Environmental History of War and Militarization in Modern France* (Manchester: Manchester University Press, 2012), 16–37. Charles Bousquet, *La Garde impériale au camp de Châlons* (Paris: Blot, 1858), is the souvenir program of the event.

103. *Le Monde illustré*, September 26, 1857 (garden), and October 3, 1857 (shop and sign); Pearson, *Mobilizing Nature*, 18 (dogs); Lefrère and Berche, "Le Zouave Jacob."

104. *Le Monde illustré*, October 3, 1857.

105. Janis, *The Photography of Gustave le Gray*, chap. 6; *Une Visite au camp de Châlons sous le Second Empire* (Paris: Musée de l'Armée, 1996).

106. Le Gray, *Zouave Storyteller*, is in the collections of the Art Institute of Chicago, www.artic.edu/artworks/144431/zouave-storyteller-le-recit.

107. Janis, *The Photography of Gustave le Gray*, 161n14.

108. Keller, *The Ultimate Spectacle*, 75–76. See also Hornstein, *Picturing War in France*, chap. 4.

109. The panoramas do not survive, but photographs and Langlois's sketches do: *Jean-Charles Langlois, 1789–1970: Le Spectacle de l'histoire* (Paris: Somogy, 2005), 147–84.

110. Frédéric Gerber, Christien Nicaise, and François Robichon, *Un Aventurier du Second Empire, Léon Méhédin, 1828–1905* (Rouen: Bibliothèque municipale, 1992), 13–18. Méhédin's album, *Campagne d'Italie en 1859*, is in the BnF.

111. Luke Gartlan, "James Robertson and Felice Beato in the Crimea: Recent Findings," *History of Photography* 29, no. 1 (2005): 72–80.

112. Zouaves often asked to be photographed with *bersaglieri*, Piedmontese light infantry troops whose elaborate plumed hats made them an effective substitute for Highlanders: *La Lumière, revue de la photographie*, June 11, 1859.

113. Ulrich Keller, "Photography, History, (Dis)belief," *Visual Resources: An International Journal of Documentation* 26, no. 2 (2010): 95–111.

114. Nicolas, "Les rapports franco-britanniques," 20.

115. Thoma, *The Final Spectacle*, 84–88, 147–50, 188–202. The Crimean Room was disassembled in the early twentieth century.

116. Arsène Alexandre, *Histoire de la peinture militaire en France* (Paris, 1889), 274, qtd. by Thoma, *The Final Spectacle*, 183.

117. Gartlan, "James Robertson and Felice Beato," 72–80.

118. Qtd. by Thoma, *The Final Spectacle*, 170.

119. Hornstein, *Picturing War in France*, 157.

120. "*Zouaves at the Malakoff* signed and dated 1856," www.rct.uk/collection/406470/zouaves-at-the-malakoff.

121. Nicolas, "Les rapports franco-britanniques."

122. Keller, *The Ultimate Spectacle*, 126. See also Helen Groth, "Technological Mediations and the Public Sphere: Roger Fenton's Crimea Exhibition and 'The Charge of the Light Brigade,'" *Victorian Literature and Culture* 30, no. 2 (2002): 553–70.

123. On Fenton's time in the Crimea, see Keller, *The Ultimate Spectacle*, 120–57; Nicole Garnier-Pelle, *Roger Fenton et la guerre de Crimée (1855). Aux origines du reportage de guerre* (Dijon: Faton Eds, 2021); and Gordon Baldwin, *Roger Fenton: Pasha and Bayadère* (Los Angeles: J. Paul Getty Museum, 1996); and the catalog for the exhibit *Crimée, 1854–1856, premiers reportages de guerre* (Paris: Musée de l'Armée, 1994).

124. Keller, "Photography, History," 100. See the print in the collection of the Metropolitan Museum of Art: www.metmuseum.org/art/collection/search/269654.

125. Baldwin, *Roger Fenton*, 76–78.
126. *Zouave, 2nd Division*, www.metmuseum.org/art/collection/search/676536.

3. Naturalized in the New World

1. "General Garibaldi at Home," *NYH*, November 10, 1859, 4.
2. "Funeral of the Late King," *Pacific Commercial Advertiser*, February 4, 1864; W. D. Cribbs, "Campaign Dress of the West India Regiments," *Journal of the Society for Army Historical Research* 70 (Autumn 1992): 174–88. The Polish "Zouaves of Death" were the project of French expatriate François de Rochebrun, a veteran of the Crimea who ran a fencing studio in Krakow in the early 1860s. They wore a black uniform with, in place of the traditional braiding, a large white cross on the front. In addition to contemporary coverage in the French and British press, see Kamil Kartasinski, "Zuawi smierci w swietle wybranych pamietnikow powstanczich" (The Zouaves of Death as portrayed in the memoirs of the January Uprising), in *Powstanie styczniowe: motywy, walka, dziedzictwo*, ed. Antoni Maziarz (Warsaw: Wydawnictwo DiG, 2014), 113–28; Andrea F. Bohlman, "Orienting the Martial: Polish Legion Songs on the Map," in *Hearing the Crimean War: Wartime Sound and the Unmaking of Sense*, ed. Gavin Williams (New York: Oxford University Press, 2019), 105–28.
3. J. Bayard Taylor, *Views Afoot; or, Europe Seen with Knapsack and Staff* (New York: Wiley and Putnam, 1846), 372; David Kelley, ed., *Baudelaire: Salon de 1846* (London: Oxford University Press, 1975), 161–62. Timothy Marr, *The Cultural Roots of American Islamicism* (Chapel Hill: University of North Carolina Press, 2006), situates the importation of Zouaves in a gendered image of worldly liberty typified by Taylor's accounts of the East in the mid-1850s. Timothy Roberts, "The Role of French Algeria in American Expansion in the Early Republic," *Journal of the Western Society for French History* 43 (2015): 153–64, discusses the limited early response to the conquest. Philip Kearny, *Service with the French Troops in Africa* (New York, 1844), 22, touched briefly on "the far-famed Zouaves."
4. "Intelligence from the Seat of War," *NYH*, March 6, 1854; "The Zouaves: Their Origin, Organization and Characteristics," *NYEP*, January 13, 1855; *NYT*, February 6, 1855.
5. *Report of the Secretary of War, Communicating the Report of Captain George B. McClellan, One of the Officers Sent to the Seat of War in Europe, in 1855 and 1856*, Senate, Special Session, Ex. Doc. 1 (Washington, DC: A. G. P. Nicholson, 1857), 43.
6. "Trade in Turkey," *NYT*, June 29, 1854; "Dramatic and Musical Matters," *NYH*, January 15, 1855; "Dramatic and Musical Matters," *NYH*, May 7, 1855; "Affairs in France," *NYDTr*, June 29, 1855.
7. "William Edwin Johnston," *New England Historical and Genealogical Society Register* 40 (October 1886): 413–14; "Our Paris Correspondence," *NYH*, January 20, 1856; "Our Paris Correspondence," *NYH*, April 22, 1857; "The Camp of Chalons," *NYT*, October 9, 1857; "Foreign News," *HW* 1 (October 17, 1857): 663; "Life in Paris," *National Era*, October 22, 1857 (quotation).

8. "Dramatic and Musical Affairs," *NYH*, July 18, 1858; James Oliver Morgan, "French Comic Opera in New York, 1855–1890," PhD diss., University of Illinois, 1959, 34.

9. Bethany S. Goldberg, "Bernard Ullman and the Business of Orchestras in Mid-Nineteenth-Century New York," in *American Orchestras in the Nineteenth Century*, ed. John Spitzer (Chicago: University of Chicago Press, 2012), 225–46; Vera Brodsky Lawrence, *Strong on Music: The New York Music Scene in the Days of George Templeton Strong*, vol. 3: *Repercussions, 1857–1862* (Chicago: University of Chicago Press, 1999), 120–25.

10. *NYDTr*, May 4, 1858; "The Lounger," *HW* 2 (May 15, 1858): 306–7; "Sketchings," *The Crayon* 5 (June 1858): 178.

11. "Rats with Trunks," *HW* 1 (February 7, 1857): 87; "Foreign Correspondence of the Era," *National Era*, February 26, 1857; "A French Rat Story," *Wheeling Daily Intelligencer*, March 2, 1857; "The Rat-Elephant," *NYC*, March 14, 1857; James Cook, *The Arts of Deception: Playing with Fraud in the Age of Barnum* (Cambridge, MA: Harvard University Press, 2001).

12. "The Lecture Season," *NYH*, April 6, 1857; "Personal Intelligence," *NYH*, June 19, 1858; "The De Rivière Romance," *NYH*, July 10, 1858; "Mike Walsh and De Riviere," *NYT*, July 26, 1858; *NYDTr*, August 14, 1858.

13. J. Lester Wallack, *The Veteran; or, France and Algeria* (New York: Samuel French, 1859); T. Allston Brown, *A History of the New York Stage: From the First Performance in 1732 to 1901* (3 vols., New York: Dodd, Mead and Co., 1903), vol. 1: 499; "Amusements," *NYT*, January 8, 1859; Jack W. McCullough, *Living Pictures on the New York Stage* (Ann Arbor, MI: UMI Research Press, 1981), 49–64.

14. Paola Gemme, *Domesticating Foreign Struggles: The Italian Risorgimento and Antebellum American Identity* (Athens: University of Georgia Press, 2005); Howard Rosario Marraro, *American Opinion on the Unification of Italy, 1846–1861* (New York: Columbia University Press, 1932), 225–57.

15. [H. S. Post], "The Zouaves," *Atlantic Monthly* 4 (August 1859): 221–30.

16. Augustus Maverick, *Henry J. Raymond and the New York Press for Thirty Years* (Hartford: A. S. Hale and Co., 1870), 238–41.

17. "Zouaves Leaving Versailles by Torch-light for the Seat of War," *HW* 3 (June 4, 1859): 356; "The War in Europe," *HW* 3 (June 11, 1859): 377–78; "The Battle of Montebello—The Zouaves Charging through the Streets," *HW* 3 (June 25, 1859): 408; "The Charge of the Zouaves at Palestro," *HW* 3 (July 9, 1859): 444; "A Zouave Charge at Solferino," *HW* 3 (July 23, 1859): 476; "A Zouave in Luck," *HW* 3 (August 20, 1859): 535; "Foreign News," *HW* 3 (September 10, 1859): 583. *New York Illustrated News* began publication in November 1859.

18. Malakoff, "Our Paris Correspondence," *NYT*, June 23, 1859; "A Charge of the Zouaves," in "The Poetry of the War," *NYH*, July 24, 1859. "The Zouaves," *NYH*, May 28, 1859, and "The Zouaves," *NYH*, July 11, 1859, are especially useful translations of Parisian overviews.

19. *National Era*, August 4, 1859 (Choate); "Political Intelligence," *NYH*, September 12, 1859 (southern); "Triennial Parade of the Fire Department," *NYH*, October 18, 1859; "The John Brown Meeting at the Cooper Institute," *NYH*, December 16, 1859 (abolitionists).

20. "Something New," advertisement, *Richmond Daily Dispatch*, October 24, 1859 (Zouave hat); "The Fall Fashions," *NYH*, September 23, 1859 (mourning cloaks); "Fashions for February," *NYH*, February 18, 1860 (requisite, translated from *Le Follet*); Mrs. Pullan, "Ladies' Department," *NY Leader*, May 5, 1860 (coquettish); Malakoff, "From Paris," *NYT*, November 29, 1860. "Fashions for January," *NYH*, January 18, 1859, and "Fashions," *Godey's Lady's Book and Magazine* 58 (January 1859): 94, indicate that the style was waning in France and little known in the United States before the Italian war.

21. "Personal," *NYDTr*, May 24, 1859; "Incidents of the War," *NYH*, June 16, 1859; "Fashions," *Godey's Lady's Book and Magazine* 59 (December 1859): 487, 567; "The Zouave Jacket," *Godey's Lady's Book and Magazine* 60 (April 1860): 295.

22. "Bryant's Minstrels," *NYH*, September 5, 11, 1859; Robert C. Toll, *Blacking Up: The Minstrel Show in Nineteenth-Century America* (New York: Oxford University Press, 1977), 56–57.

23. "Niblo's," *NY Leader*, June 25, 1859; "New Bowery Theater," *NYH*, September 24, 1859.

24. "Nixon's Mammoth Circus," *NYH*, October 10, 1859; "Barnum's American Museum," *NYT*, April 10, 1860.

25. "Niblo's Garden," *NYDTr*, June 19, 1860; Mortimer Thomson, *The Lady of the Lake: A Travestie in One Act* (New York: Samuel French, 1860), 2, 28–30.

26. "Wallack's Theater," *NYDTr*, June 26, 1860. Zouaves do not appear in William Brough, *Lalla Rookh; or, the Princess, the Peri, and the Troubadour* (London: Thomas Hailes Lacy, 1858).

27. Mark Pitcavage, "An Equitable Burden: The Decline of the State Militias, 1783–1858," PhD diss., Ohio State University, 1995, is the best overview.

28. "The Zouave Mania," *NYEP*, August 20, 1860; "The Zouave Mania," *NYH*, August 25, 1860.

29. "Local Intelligence," *New Orleans Daily Crescent*, September 5, 1859; James Paisley Hendrix Jr., "The Efforts to Revive the African Slave Trade in Louisiana," *Louisiana History* 10 (Spring 1969): 99–100. For national attention see "Personal," *NYDTr*, September 9, 1859; "*Domestic Intelligence*," *HW* 3 (September 17, 1859): 598–99; "New Orleans Correspondence," *NYH*, November 10, 1859; "Mustered In," *NYC*, November 19, 1859, all of which call the company a Zouave unit.

30. "Local Intelligence," *New Orleans Daily Crescent*, November 4, 1859; "Special Correspondence of the Democrat," *Pointe Coupee Democrat*, January 28, 1860.

31. "Amusements Last Evening," *New Orleans Daily Crescent*, April 10, 1860 (quotation); "Varieties," *New Orleans Daily Crescent*, April 21, 1860; "The Inauguration of the Statue of Clay," *The Register* [Monroe, LA], April 26, 1860. "The History of the Tune 'Dixie,'" *NYC*, January 27, 1872, reports that this production took place in April 1861, an error picked up in some scholarship. On the southern career of "Dixie," see Coleman Hutchison, *Apples and Ashes: Literature, Nationalism, and the Confederate States of America* (Athens: University of Georgia Press, 2012), chap. 4.

32. Adam Goodheart, *1861: The Civil War Awakening* (New York: Alfred A. Knopf, 2011); Lesley J. Gordon, "'Novices in Warfare': Elmer E. Ellsworth and Militia Reform on the Eve

of the Civil War," *Journal of the Civil War Era* 11 (June 2021): 194–223; and Meg Groeling, *First Fallen: The Life of Colonel Elmer Ellsworth, the North's First Civil War Hero* (El Dorado Hills, CA: Savas Beatie, 2021), offer recent profiles of Ellsworth. Charles A. Ingraham, *Elmer E. Ellsworth and the Zouaves of '61* (Chicago: University of Chicago Press, 1925), and Ruth Painter Randall, *Colonel Elmer Ellsworth: A Biography of Lincoln's Friend and the First Hero of the Civil War* (Boston: Little, Brown and Co., 1960), remain valuable for details highlighted here. We have spelled out the designations of militia regiments and used numerals for U.S. Volunteer regiments to clarify the distinction between those organizations. For example, the longtime commander of the Seventh Regiment organized the 5th New York after the attack on Fort Sumter.

33. Robert E. Lee to George H. Devereux, December 22, 1853, rpt. in *RR: America's Autograph Auction*, catalog no. 373 (July 13, 2011): 115.

34. "A Man of Accomplishments Turns Rascal," *NYH*, July 31, 1866; Thomas P. Lowry, *Tarnished Eagles: The Courts-Martial of Fifty Union Colonels and Lieutenant Colonels* (Mechanicsburg, PA: Stackpole Books, 1997), 136–40. DeVilliers, who arrived in New York in June 1850, may also have been the perpetrator discussed in "Court of General Sessions," *NYH*, February 21, 1852. He evidently did return to Europe during the Crimean War. "Personal Intelligence," *NYH*, April 20, 1854.

35. Randall, *Colonel Elmer Ellsworth*, 37, traces his connection with the National Guard Cadets to November 1856.

36. E. E. Ellsworth, *Manual of Arms for Light Infantry, Adapted to the Rifled Musket, with, or without, the Priming Attachment, Arranged for the U.S. Zouave Cadets, Governor's Guard of Illinois*, [1860]; Brent Nosworthy, *The Bloody Crucible of Courage: Fighting Methods and Combat Experience of the Civil War* (New York: Carroll & Graf, 2003), 79–80.

37. "National Fair Record," *Chicago Daily Times*, September 2, 1859 (jury); "Double Drilled Colors," *Chicago Press and Tribune*, September 27, 1859 (original challenge); "Challenge Drill Still Open," *NYC*, December 3, 1859 (quotation).

38. Randall, *Colonel Elmer Ellsworth*, 173; Ellsworth, *Manual of Arms*, 103; George B. McClellan, *Manual of Bayonet Exercise: Prepared for the Use of the Army of the United States* (Philadelphia: Lippincott, Grambo, and Co., 1852).

39. Ellsworth, *Manual of Arms*, app. 24; "The Zouaves in New York," *NYH*, July 15, 1860.

40. Ingraham, *Elmer E. Ellsworth*, 34 (kaleidoscope), 70, 74, 80 (crowds); "The Chicago Zouaves," *NYT*, July 9, 1860 (band); Alison Hinderliter, "Zouave Cadets Quickstep, Dedicated to the U.S. Zouave Cadets, Governor's Guard of Illinois," in *Chicago by the Book: Publications That Shaped the City and Its Image* (Chicago: University of Chicago Press, 2018), 18–19.

41. "The Zouaves in New York," *NYH*, July 15, 1860. The USZC adopted the tiger as an emblem because it appeared on the prize flag.

42. "The Zouave Cadets of Chicago," *Frank Leslie's Illustrated Newspaper* 10 (July 28, 1860): 152–54.

43. "The Military Furore," *NYT*, July 16, 1860; "The Chicago Zouaves," *NYT*, July 17, 1860; "Attractions of the Metropolis," *NYH*, July 17, 1860 (excitements); "Maj. Gen. Alexander Shaler," *NY Leader*, May 4, 1867.

44. "The Zouaves," *NYDTr*, July 18, 1860.

45. "The Zouaves: Their Drill at the Academy of Music," *NYT*, July 20, 1860; "The Zouaves," *NYDTr*, July 20, 1860. The reporter assumed readers' familiarity with Thomas D. Rice's blackface anthem "Jump Jim Crow" (1828), which featured the chorus "Weel about and turn about and do jis so / Eb'ry time I weel about I jump Jim Crow."

46. "The Chicago Zouaves," *NYH*, July 27, 1860; "The Zouaves at West Point," *NYT*, July 27, 1860. "The Chicago Zouave Cadets," *NYH*, August 4, 1860, elaborated a similar criticism.

47. "The Zouaves," Macon *Weekly Georgia Telegraph*, August 10, 1860.

48. "The Zouaves at West Point," *NYT*, July 27, 1860.

49. "The Gallant Zouaves," *NYDTr*, July 27, 1860; "Military Matters," *NY Leader*, July 28, 1860; "The Zouaves at Philadelphia," *NYDTr*, July 31, 1860; "General Summary," *NYC*, August 11, 1860.

50. Randall, *Colonel Elmer Ellsworth*, 198.

51. Jon Grinspan, "'Young Men for War': The Wide Awakes and Lincoln's 1860 Presidential Campaign," *Journal of American History* 96 (September 2009): 357–78; "The Presidential Campaign," *NYT*, October 1, 1860; "Miscellaneous Political Items," *NYH*, October 8, 1860; Daniel J. Miller, *American Zouaves, 1859–1959: An Illustrated History* (Jefferson, NC: McFarland Publishing Co., 2020), 195, 198, 202.

52. "To the Editor of the Herald," *NYH*, July 20, 1860; "The Chicago Zouaves and the Columbus Guards," *NYDTr*, August 4, 1860.

53. Ingraham, *Elmer E. Ellsworth*, 66 (best class), 110 (Wentworth); "Col. Ellsworth, of the United States Chicago Zouaves" *Frank Leslie's Illustrated Newspaper* 10 (August 11, 1860): 188.

54. "Discovery for Counter-Jumpers," *Vanity Fair* 2 (August 18, 1860): 96; Brian Luskey, *On the Make: Clerks and the Quest for Capital in Nineteenth-Century America* (New York: New York University Press, 2010).

55. "The Zouaves on the Stage," *NYT*, July 20, 1860 (naturalized); "The Zouaves: Their Drill at the Academy of Music," *NYT*, July 20, 1860. See also Personne (Edward G. P. Wilkins), "Something Good from Peoria," *NY Leader*, July 21, 1860.

56. "The London Times on the Great Fight," *NYH*, May 2, 1860.

57. "The Chicago Zouaves—the Most Serviceable Military Drill," *NYT*, July 17, 1860 (no longer); "Uniforms—What Are Good and What Are Bad," *Military Gazette* 3 (August 1, 1860): 225–26; "The Zouave Drill—What Books to Use," *Military Gazette* 3 (August 1, 1860): 226; "The Dress—Does It Make the Soldier?" *Military Gazette* 3 (August 1, 1860): 229 (humbug).

58. Miller, *American Zouaves*, 88, 194, 390–91, firmly documents companies in Philadelphia; Pittsburgh; and Crawfordsville, Indiana; and a fleeting initiative in Paterson, New

272 NOTES TO PAGES 109–110

Jersey. A few of the companies listed in note 59, below, may also have formed before July 1861. "Our Richmond Correspondence," *NYH*, October 30, 1859, appears to have been incorrect in reporting the formation of a Zouave company in Richmond after John Brown's raid on Harpers Ferry.

59. Miller, *American Zouaves*, lists *Alabama:* Alabama Zouaves, Eufaula Zouaves; *California:* San Francisco Zouaves; *District of Columbia:* National Rifles, Washington Zouaves; *Georgia:* Thomasville Zouaves; *Illinois:* Chicago Zouaves Cos. A–B, Ellsworth Zouaves Co. F, Rockford Zouaves, Springfield Zouave Cadets, Zouaves (Piper City); *Indiana:* Fort Harrison Guard (Terre Haute), Independent Zouaves (Indianapolis), Logansport Zouave Guards, National Zouaves (New Albany), Zouave Cadets (Indianapolis), Zouave Guards (Indianapolis); *Iowa:* Burlington Zouaves, Mount Pleasant Zouaves; *Kansas:* Union Guards (Leavenworth); *Kentucky:* Marion Rifles (Louisville); *Louisiana:* Avegno Zouaves (New Orleans), Coppens' Zouaves (New Orleans), Crescent Rifles (New Orleans); *Maine:* Bethel Zouaves; *Maryland:* Law Greys (Baltimore), Maryland Guard Battalion (Baltimore); *Massachusetts:* Salem Light Infantry; *Michigan:* Adrian Guards, Coldwater Zouaves, Detroit Zouave Cadets; *Minnesota:* St. Anthony Zouaves; *Mississippi:* Lauderdale Zouaves; *New Jersey:* Camden Fire Zouaves, Communipaw Zouaves; *New York:* Albany Zouave Cadets, Brooklyn Zouaves, Cleveland Zouaves, Clinton Zouaves, Davis Light Guards (Syracuse), Federal Guard (NYC), Fire Zouave Militia (Troy), Garde Lafayette (NYC), Hawley Guard (Syracuse), Munroe Cadets (Syracuse), National Zouaves (Brooklyn), National Zouaves (NYC), New York Zouaves (NYC), Rochester Light Guard, Seneca Falls Zouave Cadets, Syracuse Citizens' Corps, Syracuse Zouaves, Utica Citizens Corps, Utica Seymour Artillery, Utica Zouave Cadets (military eligibles), Washington Continentals (Utica); *Ohio:* Buckeye Zouaves, Canton Zouaves, Cincinnati Zouave Cadets, Cleveland Zouave Cadets, Cleveland Zouave Light Guard, Cowles Tiger Zouaves (Bedford), Dayton Zouaves, Springfield Zouave Cadets; *Pennsylvania:* Fort Pitt Cadets (Pittsburgh); Freeport Zouaves, Johnstown Zouave Cadets, Monroe Guards (Philadelphia), Negley Zouaves (East Liberty), US Zouave Cadets Co. A (Pittsburgh), Zouave Cadets (Altoona); *South Carolina:* Charleston Zouave Cadets; *Tennessee:* Harris Zouave Cadets (Memphis), Nashville Zouaves.

60. "The Zouaves and the Military," *Campaign Atlas and Bee* [Boston], July 28, 1860.

61. "The Zouaves Tactics," *NYH*, July 18, 1860; Whitfield B. East, *A Historical Review and Analysis of Army Physical Readiness Training and Assessment* (Fort Leavenworth, KS: Combat Studies Institute Press, 2013), 5–29.

62. Edgar M. Howell, *United States Army Headgear 1855–1902: Catalog of United States Army Uniforms in the Collections of the Smithsonian Institution*, II (Washington, DC: Government Printing Office, 1982), 12–18.

63. *NYDTr*, July 16, 1860.

64. Ellsworth, *Manual of Arms*, 157–92, reprints Ellsworth's plan for a skeleton regiment. "Illinois Militia Bill," *Military Gazette* 4 (February 1, 1861): 45, summarizes his Illinois legislation. "The Zouaves in Springfield," *NYH*, February 16, 1861 (quotation), details his plan for

a militia bureau. Gordon, "'Novices in Warfare,'" provides fuller discussion of Ellsworth's state and federal projects.

65. "New-York Zouaves," *NYDTr*, August 1, 1860 (great class); James H. Manning, *Albany Zouave Cadets: Fifty Years Young* (Albany: Weed-Parsons, 1910), 10–12 (circus), 16, 21, 42–44.

66. Miller, *American Zouaves*, 305–6; "Military Matters," *NY Leader*, August 11, 1860; "General City News," *NYT*, February 15, 1861 (manufactory).

67. George M. Whipple, *History of the Salem Light Infantry from 1805–1890* (Salem, MA: Essex Institute, 1890), 61–70.

68. Miller, *American Zouaves*, 24, 86; Robert E. Morsberger and Katharine M. Morsberger, *Lew Wallace: Militant Romantic* (New York: McGraw-Hill, 1980), 50–51.

69. Miller, *American Zouaves*, 246, 268–69, 294; Moses Mears Bagg, *Memorial History of Utica from Its Settlement to the Present Time* (Syracuse: D. Mason & Co., 1892), 301–2; Dwight H. Bruce, ed., *Memorial History of Syracuse from Its Settlement to the Present Time* (Syracuse: H. P. Smith & Co., 1891), part 2: 53–54; Jack Morgan, *New World Irish: Notes on One Hundred Years of Lives and Letters in American Culture* (New York: Palgrave Macmillan, 2011), 93.

70. Rufus Sibb Jones to Simon Cameron, May 13, 1862, in Ira Berlin, ed., *Freedom: A Documentary History of Emancipation*, series 2: *The Black Military Experience* (Cambridge, UK: Cambridge University Press, 1982), 83–84.

71. "The War and Its Lessons," *Weekly Anglo-African*, July 30, 1859.

72. "The Zouaves and the Military," *Campaign Atlas and Bee*, July 28, 1860.

73. "City Summary," *NYC*, September 8, 1860 (quotation); "Bryant's Minstrels," *NYH*, September 21, 1860; "Evening Ramble Sketches: Number Two," *NYC*, June 15, 1861. See Harald Kleinschmidt, "Using the Gun: Manual Drill and the Proliferation of Portable Firearms," *Journal of Military History* 63 (July 1999): 601–30; Harald Kleinschmidt, "The Military and Dancing: Changing Norms and Behaviour, 15th to 18th Century," *Ethnologia Europaea* 25, no. 2 (1995): 157–76.

74. "Hooley & Campbell's Minstrels—Niblo's Garden," *NYH*, December 30, 1860; "Zouave Fashions and Fancies," *Frank Leslie's Budget of Fun*, no. 24 (September 1, 1860): 8–9; see also "The Zouave Fever," *Comic Monthly* 2 (September 1860): 1.

75. Q. K. Philander Doesticks, "The Zouave Practice," *Yankee Notions* 10 (March 1861): 82–83; see also Q. K. Philander Doesticks, "Doesticks among the Zouaves," *Yankee Notions* 10 (February 1861): 54–55.

76. "The Military Furore," *NYT*, July 16, 1860.

77. "City Summary," *NYC*, December 8, 1860; "Behind the Scenes," *New-York Illustrated News* 2 (December 8, 1860): 78.

78. Cf. Robert Allen, *Horrible Prettiness: Burlesque and American Culture* (Chapel Hill: University of North Carolina Press, 1991), 105–8, 281–84; Faye E. Dudden, *Women in the American Theatre: Actresses and Audiences, 1790–1870* (New Haven, CT: Yale University Press,

1994), chap. 6; Ben Graf Henneke, *Laura Keene: A Biography* (Tulsa, OK: Council Oak Books, 1990), chap. 8; Elizabeth Reitz Mullenix, "From Carnival to Myth: Performing Nationhood in Pre–Civil War New York," *Journal of Dramatic Theory and Criticism* 18 (Fall 2003): 29–43.

79. "Wallack's Theater," *NYDTr,* July 31, 1860.

80. "Music and the Drama," *Wilkes' Spirit of the Times* 2 (August 25, 1860): 400; "Our London Correspondence," *New-York Illustrated News* 2 (September 15, 1860): 298.

81. "Music and the Drama," *Wilkes' Spirit of the Times* 3 (December 29, 1860): 272; "Amusements," *NYT,* January 7, 1861.

82. "Thoroughbred Heritage Portraits," www.tbheritage.com/Portraits/TheBaron.html; "The Yacht Squadron," *NYH,* August 11, 1860; "Base Ball," *Wilkes' Spirit of the Times* 4 (March 9, 1861): 5.

83. "Notes in Circulation," *New-York Illustrated News* 3 (February 23, 1861): 251; Thomas Wentworth Higginson, "Gymnastics," *Atlantic Monthly* 7 (March 1861): 297.

84. "Music and the Drama," *Wilkes' Spirit of the Times* 3 (March 2, 1861): 413; "Theatrical Record," *NYC,* March 2, 1861; "Personal," *Frank Leslie's Illustrated Newspaper* 11 (March 16, 1861): 267; "From Charleston," *NYT,* March 20, 1861.

85. "The Military Spirit on Saturday Last," *Sugar Planter,* December 8, 1860 (cooperationist); "Celebration of the Twenty-Second," *New Orleans Daily Crescent,* February 25, 1861 (fire-eater); "The Zouaves Are Coming!" *Sugar Planter,* March 16, 1861 (quotation).

86. "The Zouaves," *New Orleans Daily Crescent,* February 28, 1861.

87. "The Zouaves," *New Orleans Daily Crescent,* April 5, 1861; Ron Field, "The Inkerman Zouaves," *Military Collector and Historian* 66 (Summer 2014): 125–28 (quotation).

88. Michael Dan Jones, *1st Louisiana Zouaves: Jeff Davis' Pet Wolves* (Middletown, DE, 2015), 9–10, 38–39; Terry Jones, *Lee's Tigers Revisited: The Louisiana Infantry of the Army of Northern Virginia* (Baton Rouge: Louisiana State University Press, 2017), 4–6. We follow Civil War conventions in use of the apostrophe for Coppens' Zouaves and other instances.

89. John D. Hicks, "The Organization of the Volunteer Army in 1861 with Special Reference to Minnesota," *Minnesota History Bulletin* 2 (February 1918): 330; Richard Yates, inaugural address, *Journal of the Senate of the Twenty-Second General Assembly of the State of Illinois* (Springfield, IL: Bailhache & Baker, 1861), 68.

90. "Managerial Benefits—Last Night," *NYH,* May 31, 1858; "The Metropolitan Militia," *NYH,* April 17, 1861; "Military Movements in New York," *NYH,* April 19, 1861; "Col. Ellsworth's Zouaves Still in the City," *NYT,* April 29, 1861.

91. "Colonel Wilson," *HW* 5 (May 11, 1861): 289; "Wilson's Fighting Men," *HW* 5 (May 18, 1861): 311; Robert E. Cray, *A Notable Bully: Colonel Billy Wilson, Masculinity, and the Pursuit of Violence in the Civil War Era* (Kent, OH: Kent State University Press, 2021), 28.

92. Jones, *Lee's Tigers Revisited,* 27; Bela Estvàn, *War Pictures from the South* (2 vols., London: Routledge, Warne, and Routledge, 1863), vol. 1: 288–90.

93. Jones, *Lee's Tigers Revisited,* 7; "The De Kalb Regiment," *NYH,* May 8, 1861; "City News," *The Sun,* May 13, 1861.

94. Gerald Hawkins and Serge Nairsin, "Coppens' Zouaves: A Belgian Family in the Confederate Army," Confederate Historical Association of Belgium (1982), chab-belgium. com/pdf/english/Coppens%20Zouaves.pdf; Lee A. Wallace Jr., "Coppens' Louisiana Zouaves," *Civil War History* 8 (September 1962): 269–82; John McGrath, "In a Louisiana Regiment," *Southern Historical Society Papers* 31 (January-December 1903): 105. Jeffrey Zvengrowski, *Jefferson Davis, Napoleonic France, and the Nature of Confederate Ideology, 1815–1870* (Baton Rouge: Louisiana State University Press, 2019), 168, 174, which exaggerates the extent to which Zouaves were a specifically Confederate phenomenon, misidentifies Charles Dreux's battalion and the Washington Artillery as Zouave units.

95. Regiments included the units eventually numbered the 11th Indiana, the 8th Missouri, and the 5th, 6th, 9th, 10th, 11th, 62nd, and 73rd New York. Miller, *American Zouaves,* identifies the following Zouave companies organized and mustered into the Union or Confederate army during the ninety days after Fort Sumter. *Alabama:* Madison Rifles, Tuskegee Zouaves; *Connecticut:* Danbury Zouaves; *Illinois:* Chicago Light Infantry, Chicago Zouaves Co. A-D, Pekin Zouaves, Peoria Zouave Cadets; *Iowa:* Union Zouaves; *Kentucky:* Zouave Cadets; *Louisiana:* Louisiana Guards, New Orleans Zouaves, Tiger Rifles; *Maine:* Lewiston Zouaves; *Massachusetts:* Nim's Battery; *Michigan:* Tecumseh Volunteers; *Minnesota:* St. Paul Zouaves; *New Jersey:* Zouaves (Rahway); *New York:* Continental Zouaves (Schenectady), Duysing Zouaves, Flushing Zouaves, Independent Zouaves (Rochester), Seneca Falls Zouaves, Seward Volunteer Zouaves, Syracuse Zouaves (Thompson), US Zouave Cadets Co. B; *Ohio:* Cincinnati Zouave Guards (two groups), Giddings' Zouaves, Zanesville Zouaves; *Pennsylvania:* 1st PA Light Artillery Battery A, Gymnast Zouaves (Philadelphia), Pittsburg Fire Zouaves, US Zouave Cadets Co. C (Pittsburgh), US Zouaves (Pittsburgh); *Rhode Island:* Burnside Carbineers; *Tennessee:* Gotten Zouaves; *Virginia:* Richmond Zouaves; *Wisconsin:* Milwaukee Zouaves, National Zouaves. Non-mobilized units included companies awaiting Union or Confederate muster, militia and home-guard units, and college training corps.

96. Miller, *American Zouaves,* 239–42; "City News," *The Sun,* April 30, 1861.

97. "The Prince of Wales and the Firemen," *NYH,* August 31, 1860.

98. Richard M. Dorson, "Mose the Far-Famed and World-Renowned," *American Literature* 15 (November 1943): 293. See also Amy Greenberg, *Cause for Alarm: The Volunteer Fire Department in the Nineteenth-Century City* (Princeton, NJ: Princeton University Press, 1998), chap. 3; David L. Rinear, "F. S. Chanfrau's Mose: The Rise and Fall of an Urban Folk Hero," *Theatre Journal* 33 (May 1981): 199–212; Sean Wilentz, *Chants Democratic: New York City and the Rise of the American Working Class, 1788–1850* (New York: Oxford University Press, 1984). Burr Porter to Simon Cameron, April 16, 1861, OR, ser. 3, vol. 1: 77–78, independently urged recruitment of volunteer firefighters in major cities to form regiments comparable to French Zouaves.

99. Michael Burlingame and John R. Turner Ettlinger, eds., *Inside Lincoln's White House: The Complete Civil War Diary of John Hay* (Carbondale: Southern Illinois University Press, 1997), 21.

100. "The Ellsworth Zouaves and Mrs. Jno. J. Astor's Stand of Colors," *NYT,* April 29, 1861; "City News," *The Sun,* April 30, 1861; "War Movements in the Metropolis," *NYH,* April 30, 1861.

101. "Music and the Drama," *Wilkes' Spirit of the Times* 4 (April 27, 1861): 128; Charles A. Ingraham, "Colonel Elmer E. Ellsworth: 'The Knight Without Fear and Without Reproach,'" *Americana* 28 (July 1934): 315.

4. The Prettiest and Best Uniform in the Army

1. Bruce Catton, *The Coming Fury* (Garden City, NY: Doubleday, 1961), 390 ("amateurs," "destined"); Fred A. Shannon, *The Organization and Administration of the Union Army, 1861–1865* (Cleveland: Arthur H. Clark, 1928), vol. 1: 44 ("ridiculous"). Allan Nevins, *The War for the Union,* vol. 1: *The Improvised War, 1861–1862* (New York: Charles Scribner's Sons, 1959), 86; David Herbert Donald, *Liberty and Union* (Lexington, MA: D. C. Heath, 1978), 93, 97–98; and James M. McPherson, *Battle Cry of Freedom: The Civil War Era* (New York: Oxford University Press, 1988), 323, present similar views in influential syntheses. The erasure of Zouaves extends to scholarship that resists narratives of "maturation." The best recent work on the Civil War common soldier recognizes that the 5th New York (5NY) was an especially important unit because it illuminated conflicts over discipline within the New York City class structure and between the cultures of the regular army and the volunteers but does not mention that Zouave uniforms and drill were primary disciplinary instruments of the regiment. Lorien Foote, *The Gentlemen and the Roughs: Violence, Honor, and Manhood in the Union Army* (New York: New York University Press, 2010), 1–2, 133–35, 154.

2. H.J.W., "The Late Col. Ellsworth," *NYT,* May 29, 1861; Goodheart, *1861,* 286–92; Sarah J. Purcell, *Spectacle of Grief: Public Funerals and Memory in the Civil War Era* (Chapel Hill: University of North Carolina Press, 2022), chap. 2.

3. "Without Honor in their Own Country," *NYDTr,* August 12, 1861; R. L. Murray, *"They Fought Like Tigers": The 11th New York Fire Zouaves, 14th Brooklyn and the Irish 69th New York at First Bull Run* (Wolcott, NY: Benedum Books, 2005).

4. This approximation includes the 19IL, 11IN, 8MO, 33NJ, 35NJ, 5NY, 6NY, 9NY, 10NY, 11NY, 44NY, 53NY, 62NY, 73NY, 140NY, 146NY, 164NY, 165NY, 5NYVV (New York Veteran Volunteers), 17NYVV, 34OH, 54OH, 23PA, 72PA, 76PA, 95PA, 114PA, and 155PA. In addition to the regiments, some companies wore Zouave dress in otherwise non-Zouave regiments. Miller, *American Zouaves,* claims about two hundred mustered Union and Confederate units as Zouave, as well as many state militia and informal home guard units. Nine of the regular infantry regiments were oversized. Clayton R. Newell and Charles R. Shrader, *Of Duty Well and Faithfully Done: A History of the Regular Army in the Civil War* (Lincoln: University of Nebraska Press, 2011), 215–43; Frederick Phisterer, *Statistical Record of the Armies of the United States* (New York: Charles Scribner's Sons, 1883), 22–23.

5. Timothy J. Reese, *Sykes' Regular Infantry Division, 1861–1864: A History of Regular United States Infantry Operations in the Civil War's Eastern Theater* (Jefferson, NC: McFarland

& Co., 1990), 340; Mark W. Johnson, *That Body of Brave Men: The U.S. Regular Infantry and the Civil War in the West* (Cambridge, MA: Da Capo Press, 2003), 547–88. Zouave regiments in service from November 1864 through April 1865 included the 11IN, 33NJ, 35NJ, 62NY, 73NY, 140NY, 146NY, 164NY, 165NY, 5NYVV, 17NYVV, 76PA, 95PA, 114PA, and 155PA. The 8MO and 10NY were now battalions. The 33NJ and 35NJ no longer wore their original uniforms, but the 35NJ were issued new Zouave uniforms for their return home. Miller, *American Zouaves*, 195.

6. "Theatrical and Musical Matters," NYH, July 29, 1861. Abby Leighton succeeded Keene in the role of Diavoline.

7. "General Summary," NYC, August 24, 1861; "Dramatic," NYC, June 7, 1862; "Dramatic," NYC, July 18, 1863; "Theatrical Record," NYC, October 10, 1863; "Dramatic," NYC, June 11, 1864; "City Summary," NYC, June 3, 1865; J. E. McDonough, Playbill for *The Seven Sisters*, Washington Theater, December 9, 1861, WorldCat; Henneke, *Laura Keene*, 165; Kenneth A. Bernard, *Lincoln and the Music of the Civil War* (Caldwell, ID: Caxton Printers, 1966), 201n25 ("sauciest," quoting *Daily National Intelligencer*).

8. Frances M. Clarke, *War Stories: Suffering and Sacrifice in the Civil War* (Chicago: University of Chicago Press, 2012); Alice Fahs, *The Imagined Civil War: Popular Literature of the North and South, 1861–1865* (Chapel Hill: University of North Carolina Press, 2001). For arguments that the war led to realism and pragmatism, see especially George M. Fredrickson, *The Inner Civil War: Northern Intellectuals and the Crisis of the Union* (1965; Urbana: University of Illinois Press, 1993); Louis Menand, *The Metaphysical Club: A Story of Ideas in America* (New York: Farrar, Straus and Giroux, 2001); Edmund Wilson, *Patriotic Gore: Studies in the Literature of the American Civil War* (New York: Oxford University Press, 1962); and Peter S. Carmichael's application of Menand's framework in *The War for the Common Soldier: How Men Thought, Fought, and Survived in Civil War Armies* (Chapel Hill: University of North Carolina Press, 2018).

9. George C. Bradley and Richard L. Dahlen, *From Conciliation to Conquest: The Sack of Athens and the Court-Martial of Colonel John B. Turchin* (Tuscaloosa: University of Alabama Press, 2006), 31–37, 60; Miller, *American Zouaves*, 51–55, 243; "The Original Zouaves," NYH, July 17, 1861; "The Second Fire Zouaves of New York," HW (September 7, 1861): 572. The 73NY was also known as the Excelsior Zouaves. The 84NY continued to wear the *chasseur*-style uniform with wide red trousers that the regiment had adopted as the Fourteenth Brooklyn in the New York militia after the USZC tour. Observers often called the soldiers Zouaves, though the regiment did not use the designation.

10. On mid-nineteenth-century military spectacle see Robert E. Bonner, *Colors and Blood: Flag Passions of the Confederate South* (Princeton, NJ: Princeton University Press, 2002); Keller, *The Ultimate Spectacle*; Scott Hughes Myerly, *British Military Spectacle: From the Napoleonic Wars through the Crimea* (Cambridge, MA: Harvard University Press, 1996); Truesdell, *Spectacular Politics*, chap. 7.

11. Jones, *Lee's Tigers Revisited*, 178; Gary Schreckengost, *The First Louisiana Special Battalion: Wheat's Tigers in the Civil War* (Jefferson, NC: McFarland & Co., 2008), 88–91.

12. See, for example, "Army Supplies," *NYEP*, August 25, 1863; "Army Clothing and Equipment," *PP*, August 25, 1863.

13. Miller, *American Zouaves*, 180–82, 222–24, 353–56; Stephen D. Bosworth, *Lionel Jobert and the American Civil War: An Atlantic Identity in the Making* (Albany: State University of New York Press, 2021); Edward J. Hagerty, *Collis' Zouaves: The 114th Pennsylvania Volunteers in the Civil War* (Baton Rouge: Louisiana State University Press, 1997), 93. See also Michael J. McAfee, *Zouaves: The First and the Bravest* (Gettysburg, PA: Thomas Publications, 1991), and McAfee's many articles from 1979 to 2018 in *Military Images*.

14. Josiah Hazen Shinn, *Fort Jefferson and Its Commander, 1861–1862* (New York: Governor's Island, 1910), 20–21; "Personal," *NYEP*, February 7, 1885. See also "Domestic News," *Frank Leslie's Illustrated Newspaper* 13 (April 12, 1862): 366.

15. The regiments were the 44NY, 53NY, 34OH, 54OH, 23PA, 72PA, 76PA, and 95PA.

16. William J. Wray, comp., *History of the Twenty-Third Pennsylvania Volunteer Infantry, Birney's Zouaves* (n.p.: Survivors Association Twenty-Third Regiment, 1903-4), 34.

17. Gerald E. Wheeler and A. Stuart Pitt, "The 53rd New York: A Zoo-Zoo Tale," *New York History* 37 (October 1956): 416; Brian C. Pohanka, *Vortex of Hell: A History of the 5th New York Volunteer Infantry, Duryée's Zouaves* (Lynchburg, VA: Schroeder Publications, 2012), 506; Lew Wallace, *Lew Wallace: An Autobiography* (2 vols., New York: Harper & Brothers, 1906), vol. 1: 270.

18. Brian A. Bennett, ed., *An Unvarnished Tale: The Public and Private Civil War Writings of Porter Farley, 140th NYVI* (Wheatland, NY: Triphammer Pub., 2007), 153; Edward G. Longacre, ed., *From Antietam to Fort Fisher: The Civil War Letters of Edward King Wightman, 1862–1865* (Rutherford, NJ: Fairleigh Dickinson University Press, 1985), 133 (outlandish).

19. Miller, *American Zouaves*, 309; Brian C. Pohanka and Patrick A. Schroeder, eds., *With the 11th New York Fire Zouaves in Camp, Battle, and Prison: The Narrative of Private Arthur O'Neil Alcock in the New York Atlas and Leader* (Lynchburg, VA: Schroeder Publications, 2011), 114, 132–33.

20. "Letters from the War: No. VI," *Wilkes' Spirit of the Times* 6 (May 25, 1861): 180; "Letters from the War: No. XVI," *Wilkes' Spirit of the Times* 4 (July 6, 1861): 276; William Howard Russell, *My Diary North and South* (Boston: T. O. H. P. Burnham, 1863), 28.

21. "Military Movements in New York," *NYH*, July 9, 1861.

22. Longacre, ed., *From Antietam to Fort Fisher*, 104, 132; Miller, *American Zouaves*, 208–11; untitled cartoon, *Frank Leslie's Budget of Fun*, no. 44 (October 1861): 5; Patrick A. Schroeder, *We Came to Fight: The History of the 5th New York Veteran Volunteer Infantry Duryee's Zouaves, 1863–1865* (Brookneal, VA: Patrick Schroeder Publications, 1998), 107.

23. Wray, *History of the Twenty-Third Pennsylvania*, 33; Matthew J. Graham, *The Ninth Regiment, New York Volunteers (Hawkins' Zouaves)* (New York: E. P. Cody, 1900), 193. Earl Hess, *Civil War Infantry Tactics: Training, Combat, and Small-Unit Effectiveness* (Baton Rouge: Louisiana State University Press, 2015), 69–70, notes the difficulty of maintaining Zouave fitness standards.

24. "Theatrical Movements—At Home and Abroad," *Wilkes' Spirit of the Times* 6 (June 7, 1862): 213; "Letter from a Young Zouave," *Wilkes' Spirit of the Times* 6 (June 28, 1862): 259; Graham, *The Ninth Regiment*, 194–200; Charles F. Johnson, *The Long Roll: Being a Journal of the Civil War, As Set Down in the Years 1861–1863* (East Aurora, NY: Roy Crofters, 1911), 151–52.

25. Ron Field, *The Hampton Legion, part 2: Company Histories* (Gloucestershire, UK: Design Folio, 1995), 12–19.

26. Political general William O. Butler organized the largest review, which brought together two depleted divisions of volunteers after the end of the war. "Letter from Mexico," *Charleston Daily Courier*, May 13, 1848.

27. George B. McClellan, *McClellan's Own Story* (New York: Charles L. Webster, 1887), 97–98; "News from Washington," *NYH*, November 21, 1861; "The Grand Military Review Near Washington," *NYH*, November 21, 1861; "The Great Rebellion," *NYT*, November 21, 1861. George Meade to Margaretta Meade, November 21, 1861, grumbling that "altogether the affair as a 'spectacle' was a failure" represented an Old Army dissent from public approval of McClellan's innovation. dclawyeronthecivilwar.blogspot.com/2010/11/meade-reacts-to-grand-review.html.

28. Ernest D Spisak, *Pittsburgh's Forgotten Civil War Regiment: A History of the 62nd Pennsylvania Volunteer Infantry* (Tarentum, PA: Word Association Publishers, 2013), 45–46. See also Michael Schellhammer, *The 83rd Pennsylvania Volunteers in the Civil War* (Jefferson, NC: McFarland & Co., 2003), 38–42, 66.

29. "General News," *NYT*, March 18, 1864; Jeffrey L. Patrick, ed., *Three Years with Wallace's Zouaves: The Civil War Memoirs of Thomas Wise Durham* (Macon, GA: Mercer University Press, 2003), 157, 175.

30. "Army of the Cumberland," *PP*, December 13, 1862.

31. Schellhammer, *The 83rd Pennsylvania Volunteers*, 41; Eugene Arus Nash, *A History of the Forty-Fourth Regiment, New York Volunteer Infantry, in the Civil War, 1861–1865* (Chicago: R. R. Donnelley & Sons, 1911), 5, 22, 55.

32. Longacre, ed., *From Antietam to Fort Fisher*, 51; Charles W. Cowtan, *Services of the Tenth New York Volunteers (National Zouaves) in the War of the Rebellion* (New York: C. H. Ludwig, 1882), 181.

33. Pohanka, *Vortex of Hell*, 202, 471–72.

34. Brian A. Bennett, *Sons of Old Monroe: A Regimental History of Patrick O'Rorke's 140th New York Volunteer Infantry* (Dayton, OH: Morningside House, 1992), 337.

35. "Department of the Gulf," *NYT*, April 26, 1863, reported that the 165th New York's drill culture paralleled its "showy and distinctive uniform."

36. J. H. De Witt, *The Zouave's Light Infantry Tactics*, rev. John M. Gosline (Philadelphia: King and Baird, 1861); Ellsworth, *Manual of Arms*; Elmer Ellsworth, *Manual for the Recruit, in the Light Infantry Drill, Arranged for the U.S. Zouaves* (Philadelphia: King and Baird, 1861); Elmer Ellsworth, *Zouave Drill Book: French Bayonet Exercise, Skirmisher's Drill, Col.*

Ellsworth's Zouaves (Philadelphia: King and Baird, 1861); William J. Hardee, *Rifle and Light Infantry Tactics* (Philadelphia: Lippincott, Grambo, 1855), vol. 1: 64–65; "The Zouave Cadets of Chicago," *Frank Leslie's Illustrated Newspaper* 10 (July 28, 1860): 152–54; Nosworthy, *The Bloody Crucible of Courage*, 100. See also Paddy Griffith, *Battle Tactics of the Civil War* (New Haven, CT: Yale University Press, 1987), 154–56.

37. Griffith, *Battle Tactics*, 140–45, and Nosworthy, *The Bloody Crucible of Courage*, 268–71, 594–608, discuss the importance of bayonet charges. For causes of wounds see Thomas V. Moseley, "The Evolution of American Civil War Infantry Tactics," PhD diss., University of North Carolina, Chapel Hill, 1967, 209.

38. Charles Brandegee Livingstone, *Charlie's Civil War: A Private's Trial by Fire in the 5th New York Volunteers (Duryee Zouaves) and 146th New York Volunteer Infantry* (Gettysburg, PA: Thomas Publications, 1997), 19. See also Charles H. Banes, *History of the Philadelphia Brigade: Sixty-ninth, Seventy-first, Seventy-second, and One Hundred and Sixth Pennsylvania Volunteers* (Philadelphia: J. B. Lippincott & Co., 1876), 11; Pohanka, *Vortex of Hell*, 168.

39. "Bayonet Exercise at Dress Parade," *ANJ* 1 (March 5, 1864): 471.

40. Foster, *Letters from the Storm*, 7; Graham, *The Ninth Regiment*, 18–20; Longacre, ed., *From Antietam to Fort Fisher*, 97; Pohanka, *Vortex of Hell*, 296, 423, 465; Wallace, *Lew Wallace*, 348n2; Charles F. McKenna, ed., *Under the Maltese Cross, Antietam to Appomattox: The Loyal Uprising in Western Pennsylvania, 1861–1865* (Pittsburgh: 155th Regimental Association, 1910), 123; Robert C. Plumb, *Your Brother in Arms: A Union Soldier's Odyssey* (Columbia: University of Missouri Press, 2011), 176. On the wartime shift from commerce to industry within the New York elite, see Sven Beckert, *The Monied Metropolis: New York City and the Consolidation of the American Bourgeoisie, 1850–1896* (Cambridge, UK: Cambridge University Press, 2001).

41. Hagerty, *Collis' Zouaves*, 94, 269–70; Frank Rauscher, *Music on the March, 1862–'65, with the Army of the Potomac* (Philadelphia: W. F. Fell & Co., 1892).

42. "Grand Review of the Army of the Potomac," *PP*, May 24, 1865; "Grand Review of Gen. Sherman's Army," *PP*, May 25, 1865. Mary Genevie Green Brainard, *Campaigns of the 146th Regiment New York State Volunteers* (Lynchburg, VA: Schroeder Publications, 2000), 303, reports that the unit participated in the Grand Review although it did not appear in the parade list published in "Review of the Armies," *NYT*, May 24, 1865.

43. "Warlike Zeal," *New York Illustrated News* 6 (September 27, 1862): 332. The shadow of Mose is also a reminder that the association of Zouaves and firefighters extended well beyond the 11NY and 73NY. For example, firefighters comprised many of the volunteers in 5NY, Co. G; 72PA (Philadelphia Fire Zouaves); 19MA, Co. K (Boston Tiger Fire Zouaves); and 30MA, Co. I (Boston Fire Zouaves).

44. Celebration of anecdotes subverted the transformation of soldiers into data, charted by Stephen Berry, *Count the Dead: Coroners, Quants, and the Birth of Death as We Know It* (Chapel Hill: University of North Carolina Press, 2022).

45. Dorson, "Mose the Far-Famed," 294.

46. *History of the Second Battalion Duryee Zouaves* (1905), 13; "My Love He Is a Zou-Zu: Only 19 Years Old" (Boston: Horace Partridge, 1861); "The Zouave," *Yankee Notions* 11 (March 1862): 83.

47. Charles Dawson Shanly, "The Brier-Wood Pipe," *Vanity Fair* 4 (July 6, 1861): 5; William Cullen Bryant, ed., *A New Library of Poetry and Song* (New York: J. B. Ford, 1876), vol. 2: 475–76; Frank Moore, *Anecdotes, Poetry, and Incidents of the War: North and South* (New York: 1866), 381–82; Richard Grant White, ed., *Poetry, Lyrical, Narrative, and Satirical, of the Civil War* (New York: American News Co., 1866), 46–49.

48. "Santa Claus's Ball; or, A Plea for the Children," *HW* 7 (January 3, 1863): 13–14; see also "Our Christmas House," *PP*, December 25, 1861; "Santa Claus's Wish Council," *HW* 8 (December 24, 1864): 823.

49. Edward P. Kohn, "Teddy Roosevelt's Confederate Uncles," *NYT* Opinionator, June 25, 2014; Ross Barrett, *Rendering Violence: Riots, Strikes, and Upheaval in Nineteenth-Century American Art* (Berkeley: University of California Press, 2014), 118–19. "National Academy of Design," *NYT*, April 24, 1862, indicates that Nast's unlocated *Picketed Zouaves* depicted adult soldiers. See also Currier and Ives, *The Little Zouave* (1861).

50. "The Wounded Zouave in the Hospital at Washington," *HW* 5 (August 17, 1861): 513; Richard J. Powell, "*The Wounded Zouave* and the Cyrenian Paradigm," *The Civil War in Art and Memory*, ed. Kirk Savage (Washington, DC: National Gallery of Art, 2016), 66–78. Notable examples of dying Zouaves include "The Little Zouave," *Vanity Fair* 4 (October 5, 1861): 161; and Mary A. Denison, "The Dead Soldier's Dream," *New York Illustrated News* 7 (February 14, 1863): 235.

51. "Amusements," *NYH*, August 9, 1868; "Wood's Museum," *NYH*, September 18, 1868 ("touching"); M. R. Werner, *Barnum* (New York: Harcourt, Brace and Co., 1923), 307; Karen Halttunen, *Confidence Men and Painted Women: A Study of Middle-Class Culture in America, 1830–1870* (New Haven, CT: Yale University Press, 1982). Ward's painting is in the collections of the Metropolitan Museum of Art, www.metmuseum.org/art/collection/search/13131.

52. "Ballads of the War: Song of the Volunteer's Wife," *Vanity Fair* 4 (August 3, 1861): 60; Nina Silber, *Gender and the Sectional Conflict* (Chapel Hill: University of North Carolina Press, 2015), 20–22.

53. *Hooley's Opera House Songster* (New York: Dick & Fitzgerald, 1864), 17–18.

54. New-York Historical Society, *The Picket Guard*, emuseum.nyhistory.org/objects /14062/the-picket-guard;jsessionid=343F963873D8DB2E8A1B25F0EE4D9313; for sample adventure tales see Ledyard Bill, comp., *Pen-Pictures of the War* (New York: 1864), 116–23; D. M. Kelsey, ed., *Deeds of Daring by Both Blue and Gray* (Philadelphia: Scammell & Co., 1883), 30–42, 579–89. Fahs, *The Imagined Civil War*, provides thoughtful analysis of sentimental and sensational narratives.

55. William B. Styple, ed., *Writing and Fighting the Civil War: Soldier Correspondence to the New York Sunday Mercury* (Kearny, NJ: Belle Grove Publishing, 2000), 136–38; Walter George Smith, *Life and Letters of Thomas Kilby Smith: Brevet Major-General, United States*

Volunteers, 1820–1887 (New York: G. P. Putnam's Sons, 1898), 176; "Running the Block," *Southern Punch* 1 (September 26, 1863): 4.

56. "Miscellaneous Union News," *Frank Leslie's Illustrated Newspaper* 12 (August 10, 1861): 195; "The Zouave Boys," *Beadle's Dime Union Song Book* (New York: Beadle and Co., 1861), 66; "The Recruits' Catechism," *Vanity Fair* 3 (May 25, 1861): 252, rpt. as "Military Catechism," *Frank Leslie's Budget of Fun*, no. 79 (October 1864): 14; see also "How Beau Hackett Was Made a Zouave," *Nick-Nax* 8 (January 1864): 286, rpt. in Moore, *Anecdotes*, 13–14; McArone, "Civil War Correspondence," *Vanity Fair* 3 (June 22, 1861): 291; Peter McNeil, *Pretty Gentlemen: Macaroni Men and the Eighteenth-Century Fashion World* (New Haven, CT: Yale University Press, 2018).

57. Robert H. Newell, *The Orpheus C. Kerr Papers* (3 vols., New York: Blakeman & Mason, 1862), vol. 1: 42–49.

58. "The Fire Flags," *Frank Leslie's Illustrated Newspaper* 12 (October 5, 1861): 323; "Contrabands in Luck," *Weekly Anglo-African* (August 17, 1861).

59. Lesley J. Gordon, "'These Zouaves Will Never Support Us': Cowardice, Congress and the First Battle of Bull Run," in *Congress and the People's Contest: The Conduct of the Civil War*, ed. Donald Kennon and Paul Finkelman (Athens: Ohio University Press, 2018), 59–80.

60. Schroeder, *We Came to Fight*, 47–49; Iver Bernstein, *The New York City Draft Riots: Their Significance for American Society and Politics in the Age of the Civil War* (New York: Oxford University Press, 1990); Henry Morford, *The Days of Shoddy: A Novel of the Great Rebellion in 1861* (Philadelphia: T. B. Peterson & Brothers, 1863), 420; John Morris, *Wanderings of a Vagabond* (New York: The Author, 1873), 317; "Seeking the Bubble," *United States Service Magazine* 3 (April 1865): 353.

61. Carl Ehwa Jr., *The Book of Pipes and Tobacco* (New York: Random House, 1974), 104–34.

62. "Sporting," *NYH*, June 30, 1860, is a good summary with full set of New York rules; see also "Sporting," *NYH*, August 23, 1855; "Sporting," *NYH*, July 29, 1856; Sally Mills, "*Pitching Quoits*, 1865," in *Winslow Homer: Paintings of the Civil War*, ed. Marc Simpson (San Francisco: Fine Arts Museums of San Francisco, 1988), 208–15.

63. George Arnold, "Art Matters," *New York Leader*, June 3, 1865; Pohanka, *Vortex of Hell*, 474.

64. See generally Jonathan Levy, *Freaks of Fortune: The Emerging World of Capitalism and Risk in America* (Cambridge, MA: Harvard University Press, 2012); Richard Stott, *Jolly Fellows: Male Milieus in Nineteenth-Century America* (Baltimore: Johns Hopkins University Press, 2009), 223–47. Henry J. Morford, *Shoulder-Straps: A Novel of New York and the Army in 1862* (Philadelphia: T. B. Peterson & Brothers, 1863), illustrates the reputation of Duryea's Zouaves in the business community. Xanthus Smith, *Signal Station at Hilton Head* (1865), in the West Point Museum, situates the 76PA (Keystone Zouaves) in a highly modern location with commercial applications.

65. Homer also featured Zouaves in five of the twenty-four prints in his humorous collection *Life in Camp* (1864). Lucretia Giese, "Winslow Homer: Painter of the Civil War,"

PhD diss., Harvard University, 1985, 145–46, suggests comparison with Protais. *Pitching Quoits* is especially close to Protais's *Soldats Jouant aux Quilles* (1861), Musée de Grenoble. G. Tylden, "British and French Troops Off Duty in the Crimea," *Journal of the Society for Army Historical Research* 36 (September 1958): 93–95, discusses the version now in Cumbria's Museum of Military Life. On Protais's military genre paintings, see Thoma, *The Final Spectacle*, chap. 5. William R. Cross, *Winslow Homer: American Passage* (New York: Farrar, Straus and Giroux, 2022), 55–57, 81–84, notes Homer's particular interest in Zouaves, which the biographer attributes to Homer's presence at Ellsworth's fateful departure for Alexandria and the painter's connections to the Duryée Zouaves through regimental chaplain Gordon Winslow and officer Cleveland Winslow, the brother and nephew of the minister for whom Homer was named, but Cross does not explore Homer's interpretation of Zouaves' cultural significance.

66. "Music and the Drama," *Wilkes' Spirit of the Times* 4 (June 1, 1861): 208; "Canterbury Music Hall," advertisement, *NYH*, August 9, 1861; "Music and the Drama," *Wilkes' Spirit of the Times* 5 (October 12, 1861): 96; "New Bowery Theatre," advertisement, *NYH*, November 24, 1861; "The New York Concert Saloons," *NYEP*, December 24, 1861; "The Gaities," advertisement, *NYH*, February 9, 1862; "Varieties," *NYH*, October 26, 1864; "Music Halls," *NYC*, August 19, 1865; "Music Halls," *NYC*, October 28, 1865; "Dramatic," *NYC*, January 20, 1866; "City Summary," *NYC*, December 1, 1866; "Musical and Dramatic Notes," *NYH*, June 28, 1868; "Dramatic," *NYC*, September 4, 1869; "Dramatic," *NYC*, January 15, 1870; "Tony Pastor's Opera House," *NYH*, April 9, 1871; John Franceschina, *David Braham: The American Offenbach* (New York: Routledge, 2003), 20.

67. "Amusements," *Wilkes' Spirit of the Times* 9 (September 26, 1863): 64 (second quotation); "The Carter Zouave Troupe and the 'Critics,'" *NYH*, October 25, 1863 (first quotation); "Our Dramatic Portrait Gallery," *NYC*, May 14, 1864; "Excelsior Is Our Motto," advertisement, *NYC*, December 10, 1864; "The Early Days of the Carter Zouave Troupe," *NYC*, May 23, 1874; "Deaths in the Profession," *NYC*, March 7, 1891.

68. Ferdinand L. Sarmiento, *Life of Pauline Cushman, the Celebrated Union Spy and Scout* (Philadelphia: John E. Potter and Co., 1865), 53–67.

69. "Our City Theatres," *New York Illustrated News* 4 (August 5, 1861): 222 (behind); "Music and the Drama," *Wilkes' Spirit of the Times* 5 (October 12, 1861): 96; "Local and Other News," *Zanesville Daily Courier*, June 13, 1862 (Ellsworth). William Henry Wegner, "The Representation of the American Civil War on the New York Stage, 1860–1900," PhD diss., New York University, 1966, 30–37, traces the early development of this play. See also Daphne Brooks, *Bodies in Dissent: Spectacular Performances of Race and Freedom, 1850–1910* (Durham, NC: Duke University Press, 2006), 201, on Adah Isaacs Menken's performance as Jerusha Sparks in *Three Fast Women* (1861).

70. Jones, *Lee's Tigers Revisited*, 21–22.

71. Wray, *History of the Twenty-Third Pennsylvania*, 32; "Highly Important from the Upper Potomac," *NYT*, October 22, 1861; Elizabeth Leonard, *All the Daring of the Soldier* (New York: W. W. Norton, 1999), 150–51. Moore, *Anecdotes*, 166, narrates the wedding of a sergeant

and a *vivandière* in a Zouave regiment. See also "A Wedding in Camp," in John Truesdale, *The Blue Coats, and How They Lived, Fought and Died for the Union* (Philadelphia: Jones Brothers, 1867), 128–30.

72. Leonard, *All the Daring of the Soldier*, 148; Richard H. Hall, *Women on the Civil War Battlefront* (Lawrence: University Press of Kansas, 2006), 28.

73. Justin Jones, *Virginia Graham: The Spy of the Grand Army* (Boston: Loring, 1867), 6; Jane G. Austin, *Dora Darling; or the Daughter of the Regiment* (Boston: Lee and Shepard, 1864), 167.

74. Schellhammer, *The 83rd Pennsylvania Volunteers*, 42. Gayle V. Fischer, *Pantaloons and Power: A Nineteenth-Century Dress Reform in the United States* (Kent, OH: Kent State University Press, 2001), 89n35, notes that Zouave uniforms were a rare example of men wearing "harem" pantaloons identified with women. See also Jirousek and Catterall, *Ottoman Dress and Design in the West*, 202–8; Marr, *The Cultural Roots of American Islamicism*, 282–96.

75. Pohanka, *Vortex of Hell* (quoting letter of George Mitchell), 402; Dio Lewis, *The New Gymnastics for Men, Women, and Children* (Boston: Ticknor and Fields, 1862), 256; Louisa May Alcott, "The King of Clubs and the Queen of Hearts," in *On Picket Duty, and Other Tales* (Boston: James Redpath, 1864), 35; G. Norton Galloway, *The Ninety-fifth Pennsylvania Volunteers (Gosline's Pennsylvania Zouaves) in the Sixth Corps* (Philadelphia: Collins, 1884), 8. See also McGrath, "In a Louisiana Regiment," 120.

76. "Rebel Accounts of the Seizure of the St. Nicholas," *NYH*, July 8, 1861; "Another English Special Correspondent among the Rebels," *NYH*, August 18, 1861; Graham, *The Ninth Regiment*, 195; Linda Arden Foster, *Letters from the Storm: The Intimate Civil War Letters of Lt. J. A. H. Foster, 155th Pennsylvania Volunteers* (Chicora, PA: Firefly Publications, 2010), 229–30. See also "A Good Camp Story," *Pittsburgh Daily Post*, May 5, 1863, about a soldier who received a Zouave doll from female friends, igniting camp rumors that he was a woman and had given birth, for which he was granted a furlough. The tale circulated widely in newspapers and appeared as "Mother Corporal on a Ten Days' Furlough," in *The Pictorial Book of Anecdotes and Incidents of the War of the Rebellion*, ed. Frazar Kirkland [pseud. for Richard Miller Devens] (Hartford, CT: Hartford Publishing Co., 1866), 411–12.

77. Katharine Prescott Wormeley, *The Other Side of War with the Army of the Potomac: Letters from the Headquarters of the United States Sanitary Commission during the Peninsular Campaign in Virginia in 1862* (Boston: Ticknor and Co., 1889), 82–84, 125–31.

78. Wesley Bradshaw [pseud. for Charles Wesley Alexander], *Pauline of the Potomac, or, General McClellan's Spy* (Philadelphia: Barclay, 1862), 50–51. On Alexander see Fahs, *The Imagined Civil War*, 241–45.

79. Renée M. Sentilles, *Performing Menken: Adah Isaacs Menken and the Birth of American Celebrity* (Cambridge, UK: Cambridge University Press, 2003), 91–111. Examination of carte-de-visite photographs in the Harvard Theatre Collection confirms Sentilles's report that Menken wore a Zouave outfit in *Mazeppa* although *Performing Menken*, 234, incorrectly identifies the actress's costume in *The French Spy* as a Zouave uniform.

80. "The Amazons," *United States Service Magazine* 3 (February 1865): 162–63. Hall, *Women on the Civil War Battlefront*, 55–56, 130, cites an example in the 19th Illinois and suggests a possibility in the 114th Pennsylvania.

81. "Romantic Adventure—A Female Zouave," *NYT*, September 23, 1862; "The Female Suffrage Question in the Senate," *NYH*, December 13, 1866. See also W. O. Eaton, "A Female War Club—A Significant Sign of the Times," *Yankee Notions* 11 (May 1862): 138–41; Q. K. Philander Doesticks, "Martial Law in the Family—Women and War—Brigades of Belles and Beauties," *Yankee Notions* 11 (October 1862): 298–99.

82. "Another Great Card for Managers," *NYC*, November 7, 1863. "City Summary," *NYC*, August 8, 1868. Childers's name does not appear on the USZC tour roster in Ingraham, *Elmer E. Ellsworth*, 66. "Olympic Theatre—'The Lightning Drill,'" *NYH*, July 25, 1868, reported that Austin served in a Wisconsin regiment in the war. His biography does not match any of the three Charles Austins known to have served in Wisconsin regiments.

83. "Another Great Card for Managers," *NYC*, November 7, 1863; Campbell's Minstrels, advertisement, *NYC*, October 1, 1864; "City Summary," *NYC*, September 28, 1867 ("evolutions"); "The 'Skatorial Queen,'" *NYC*, February 29, 1868 (Moore); "Olympic Theatre—'The Lightning Drill,'" *NYH*, July 25, 1868 ("Amazon"); "Dramatic," *NYC*, February 17, 1872 (Ravel); "Dramatic," *NYC*, May 18, 1872 (rising); "Amateur," *NYC*, October 25, 1873 (Brownell).

84. "Olympic Theatre—'The Lightning Drill,'" *NYH*, July 25, 1868; "The Militia Competitive Drills," *NYT*, August 6, 1868; "City Summary," *NYC*, August 8, 1868; "Zouave Drill in Tompkins Square," *HW* 12 (August 15, 1868): 525–26.

85. "Dramatic," *NYC*, September 28, 1867. Sentilles, *Performing Menken*, and Dudden, *Women in the American Theatre*, assess the latitude of theatrical performance.

86. Brian Roberts, *Blackface Nation: Race, Reform, and Identity in American Popular Music, 1812–1925* (Chicago: University of Chicago Press, 2017), provides an overview of the large scholarship on minstrelsy.

87. Peter C. Luebke, "'Equal to Any Minstrel Concert I Ever Attended at Home': Union Soldiers and Blackface Performance in the Civil War South," *Journal of the Civil War Era* 4 (December 2014): 511, lists the 9NY, 165NY, and near-Zouave 84NY (14th Brooklyn) among twelve Union units that presented blackface shows. Regimental histories show that the 5NY, 6NY, 11NY, and 140NY also belong on that list.

88. Graham, *The Ninth Regiment*, 193–200; Longacre, ed., *From Antietam to Fort Fisher*, 147; Donald Yacovone, ed., *A Voice of Thunder: The Civil War Letters of George E. Stephens* (Urbana: University of Illinois Press, 1997), 214–15.

89. Luebke, "Equal to Any Minstrel Concert," 521.

90. "Practical Joke of a Chicago Fire Zouave," *CDT*, July 27, 1861.

91. "Practical Joke of a Chicago Fire Zouave," *The Liberator* 31 (August 9, 1861): 126; "Practical Joke of a Chicago Fire Zouave," *NYC*, August 10, 1861; "Our Soldiers and 'Contrabands,'" *Douglass' Monthly* 4 (September 1861): 517; "Practical Joke of a Chicago Fire

Zouave," *Washington Standard,* September 14, 1861; "Practical Joke of a Fire Zouave," *Yankee Notions* 10 (October 1861): 312; "An F. F. V. Outwitted by a Chicago Fire Zouave," T. R. Dawley, *Incidents of Camp Life: Being Events Which Have Transpired during the Present Rebellion* (2nd ed., New York: T. R. Dawley, 1862), 54–55.

92. "The Zouave and Slave Envelope," *Weekly Anglo-African,* August 17, 1861; "Miscellaneous Items," *Douglass' Monthly* 4 (September 1861): 527; Steven R. Boyd, *Patriotic Envelopes of the Civil War: The Iconography of Union and Confederate Covers* (Baton Rouge: Louisiana State University Press, 2010).

93. Giese, "Winslow Homer," 213–14; "A Bivouac Fire on the Potomac," *HW* 5 (December 21, 1861): 808–9; "The Arts," *Appleton's Journal* 114 (November 6, 1875): 603; "Academy of Design," *New-York Tribune,* April 8, 1876. *Our Jolly Cook* is in *Campaign Sketches* (Boston: L. Prang, 1863). See also Marc Simpson, *"The Bright Side: 'Humorously Conceived and Truthfully Executed,'"* in *Winslow Homer,* 46–63; "The Zouave and the Mule," in Moore, *Anecdotes,* 396–97.

94. Peter H. Wood and Karen C. C. Dalton, *Winslow Homer's Images of Blacks: The Civil War and Reconstruction Years* (Austin: University of Texas Press, 1988), 67–70, interprets *Contraband* as a picture of hierarchical paternalism without considering the distinctive relations of Zouaves and African Americans. The authors show that Homer subverted blackface minstrelsy stereotypes in *Taking a Sunflower to the Teacher* (1875) and *The Watermelon Boys* (1876), an insight that also applies to *Contraband.*

95. *New Bedford Republican Standard,* rpt. in "Wilson's Zouaves and the Colored Soldiers," *The Liberator,* April 16, 1863.

96. Robert J. Zalimas Jr., "A Disturbance in the City: Black and White Soldiers in Postwar Charleston," in *Black Soldiers in Blue: African American Troops in the Civil War Era,* ed. John David Smith (Chapel Hill: University of North Carolina Press, 2002), 361–90.

97. "Sketch of the Turcos of the French Army," *NYH,* June 24, 1859; "Uniforms of the 1st West India Regiment," *Illustrated London News* 34 (April 16, 1859): 372; "Barbaric Troops for the British Army," *NYH,* August 1, 1859; "The Emancipation Question," *HW* 3 (September 3, 1859): 562; Brian Dyde, *The Empty Sleeve: The Story of the West India Regiments of the British Army* (St. Johns, Antigua: Hansib, 1997), 148–50, 173–76; Rosalyn Narayan, "'Creating Insurrections in the Heart of Our Country': Fear of the British West India Regiments in the Southern U.S. Press, 1839–1860," *Slavery and Abolition* 39 (September 2018): 497–517.

98. "Barbaric Troops for the British Army," *NYH,* August 1, 1859; "Flag Raising in Albany," *NYH,* May 16, 1861; "The Great Naval Expedition," *NYEP,* October 26, 1861.

99. Sarah Weicksel, "The Fabric of War: Clothing, Culture and Violence in the American Civil War Era," PhD diss., University of Chicago, 2017, 159–60; "From South Carolina," *NYEP,* May 17, 1862; "The Situation," *NYH,* July 26, 1862; untitled squib, *Cleveland Morning Leader,* December 25, 1862; "Colored Soldiers and Contraband," *Douglass' Monthly* 5 (January 1863): 783–84.

100. Frank A. Rollin [pseud. for Frances Rollin], *Life and Public Services of Martin R. Delany* (Boston: Lee and Shepard, 1868), 141–44; "Colored Regiments," *Weekly Anglo-African,* October 12, 1861; "Black Regiments Proposed," *Douglass' Monthly* 3 (May 1861): 452; Rufus Sibb Jones to Edwin M. Stanton, May 13, 1862, in Berlin, ed., *Freedom: A Documentary History of Emancipation,* ser. 2: *The Black Military Experience,* 83–84; "The Tenth Regiment U.S. Colored Troops (Zouaves)," *Weekly Anglo-African,* November 19, 1863. Weicksel, "The Fabric of War," 164–67, thoughtfully characterizes Black discussion of Zouave uniforms as a debate over options to espouse or deny racial difference.

101. "From Washington," *NYDTr,* June 25, 1863. Alfred Woodhull, *A Medical Report upon the Uniform and Clothing of the Soldiers of the U.S. Army* (Washington, DC: Surgeon General's Office, 1868), 14, illustrates the persistence of this thinking after the war.

102. Richard Hill and Peter Hogg, *A Black Corps d'Elite: An Egyptian Sudanese Conscript Battalion with the French Army in Mexico, 1863–1867, and Its Survivors in Subsequent African History* (East Lansing: Michigan State University Press, 1995), 36.

103. "Negroes as Soldiers," *HW* 7 (March 14, 1863): 174; Christopher Looby, ed., *The Complete Civil War Journal and Selected Letters of Thomas Wentworth Higginson* (Chicago: University of Chicago Press, 2000), 99; Thomas Wentworth Higginson, *Army Life in a Black Regiment* (Boston: Fields, Osgood, and Co., 1869), 97.

104. S. B. Brague, ed., *Notes on Colored Troops and Military Colonies on Southern Soil* (New York: 1863), 5.

105. "The Negro at Home," *NYH,* June 18, 1865; "Foreign Military Affairs," *ANJ* 3 (February 3, 1866): 382; Melissa Bennett, "Picturing the West India Regiments: Race, Empire, and Photography c. 1850–1914," PhD diss., University of Warwick, 2018, chaps. 3–4.

106. Hendrik Kraay, "Patriotic Mobilization in Brazil: The Zuavos and Other Black Companies," in *I Die with My Country: Perspectives on the Paraguayan War, 1864–1870,* ed. Hendrik Kraay and Thomas L. Whigham (Lincoln: University of Nebraska Press, 2004), 61–80; Hendrik Kraay, *Bahia's Independence: Popular Politics and Patriotic Festival in Salvador, Brazil, 1824–1900* (Montreal: McGill-Queen's University Press, 2019), 120–22, 143–44.

107. "Our Colored Military Organizations," *Philadelphia Inquirer,* January 15, 1870; "The Wagner Zouaves," *Philadelphia Evening Telegraph,* May 14, 1870; "Our Citizen Soldiers," *CDT,* January 3, 1875; Miller, *American Zouaves,* 49, 314, 414–15, 418, 429. Black militia service as Zouaves, which Winslow Homer may have witnessed in Richmond, added to the interchangeability depicted in *Contraband.*

108. For illustrations, see Alexander Gardner, *Thaddeus Stevens Lying in State in the Rotunda of the Capitol at Washington,* www.metmuseum.org/art/collection/search/286388; "The Body of Thaddeus Stevens Lying in State at the Capitol, Washington—Photographed by Brady, Washington," *HW* 12 (August 29, 1868): 545.

109. "Sacramento Zouaves," *Stockton Daily Evening Herald,* August 1, 1871; Eleanor L. Hannah, *Manhood, Citizenship, and the National Guard: Illinois, 1870–1917* (Columbus: Ohio State University Press, 2007), 19–20.

110. Miller, *American Zouaves*, 404; "The Colored Troops," *Philadelphia Inquirer*, September 27, 1870; "Condensed Locals," *Washington Evening Star*, December 13, 1871.

111. "United States Troops in Chicago," *Chicago Tribune*, December 11, 1871; "The City," *CDT*, October 25, 1876.

112. "The Militia," *CDT*, November 26, 1876; Hannah, *Manhood, Citizenship, and the National Guard*, 66; W. T. Goode, *The "Eighth Illinois"* (Chicago: Blakely Printing, 1899), 5–6.

5. The Livery of Rome

1. Jean Guenel, *La Dernière Guerre du pape: Les Zouaves pontificaux au secours du Saint-Siège, 1860–1870* (Rennes: Presses universitaires de Rennes, 1998), 40.

2. For example, Henri Méhier de Mathuisieulx, *Les Zouaves pontificaux* (Tours: Alfred Mame et fils, 1914), 216, relates that one of Garibaldi's officers, an opponent of the Pontifical Zouaves, described them as *"i primi soldati del mondo!"*

3. Lucy Riall, *Risorgimento: The History of Italy from Napoleon to Nation State* (New York: Palgrave Macmillan, 2008).

4. David I. Kertzer, *The Pope Who Would Be King: The Exile of Pius IX and the Emergence of Modern Europe* (New York: Random House, 2018).

5. The most thorough account of the pontifical Zouaves is Guenel, *La Dernière Guerre*. In English, see Charles A. Coulombe, *The Pope's Legion: The Multinational Fighting Force that Defended the Vatican* (New York: Palgrave Macmillan, 2008).

6. Qtd. by Ferdinand Nicolas Göhde, "German Volunteers in the Armed Conflicts of the Italian Risorgimento, 1834–70," *Journal of Modern Italian Studies* 14, no. 4 (2009): 461–75, 469.

7. Elizabeth Leonard, *Lincoln's Avengers: Justice, Revenge, and Reunion after the Civil War* (New York: W. W. Norton, 2005), chap. 8; Laurent Gruaz, "Maximin Giraud, le berger de La Salette: de l'Apparition de la Vièrge aux soldats du Pape," *Chrétiens et sociétés* 17 (2010): 151–72; Florry O'Driscoll, "Confounding the Garibaldian Liars: The Letters of Albert Delahoyde, Irish Soldier of the Papal Battalion of St. Patrick and Papal Zouave in Italy, 1860–1870," *Studi irlandesi: A Journal of Irish Studies* 6 (2016): 49–63, 56; Simon Sarlin, "Mercenaries or Soldiers of the Faith? The Pontifical Zouaves in the Defense of the Roman Church (1860–1970)," *Millars. Espai i Història* 43 (2017): 189–218.

8. George Fitz-Hardinge Berkeley, *The Irish Battalion in the Papal Army of 1860* (Dublin: Talbot Press, 1929), 34, 69; Robert Doyle, "The Pope's Irish Battalion, 1860," *History Ireland* 18, no. 5 (2010), www.historyireland.com/the-popes-irish-battalion-1860/.

9. Simon Sarlin, "Henri de Cathelineau et l'expérience du volontariat armé contre-révolutionnaire dans l'Europe du XIXe siècle," *Collection de l'Ecole française de Rome* 454 (2011): 365–77.

10. *La Gazette de France*, July 5, 1860.

11. *L'Ami de la religion: journal politique, littéraire, universel*, October 13, 1860.

12. Cathelineau to Lamoricière, qtd. in Sarlin, "Henri de Cathelineau," 374.

13. See for example *La Gazette de France*, July 5, August 1, 1860; *La Gironde*, August 25, 1860.

14. Anatole de Ségur, *Les Martyrs de Castelfidardo* (Paris: A. Bray, 1861), 202.

15. René Hardy, *Les Zouaves: une stratégie du clergé québécoise au XIXe siècle* (Montreal: Boreal Express, 1980), 46.

16. Keller, *Le Général de la Moricière* 1: 482–84; Eugène de la Gournerie, *Notes biographiques sur le général de la Moricière* (Nantes: Forest et E. Grimaud, 1865), 17, 24–25.

17. Keller, *Le Général de La Moricière* 2: 159–61, 224–30, 272–73. On the personal and political debates surrounding the publication of Lamoricière's biography, see Luca Sandoni, "Un 'héros chrétien' anti-moderno? La memoria contesa del generale Lamoricière nel cattolicismo francese tardo-ottocentesco," in *Un mestiere paziente. Gli allievi pisani per Daniele Menozzi*, ed. Andrea Mariuzzo et al. (Pisa: ETS, 2017), 205–19.

18. Louis-Antoine de Becdelièvre, *Souvenirs de l'armée pontificale* (Paris: Jacques Lecoffre, 1867), 49 (quotation), 55–56; Keller, *Le Général de La Moricière* 2: 255 (turban); [Anatole de Saint Aulaire], *Henri de Verthamon, zouave pontifical, volontaire de l'ouest* (Périgueux, 1873), 51.

19. General Cugia, qtd. in Sarlin, "Mercenaries or Soldiers of the Faith?" 203; Guenel, *La Dernière Guerre*, 42–43.

20. E. Marquigny, "Les Zouaves hollondais de l'armée du pape," *Les Etudes religieuses, historiques et littéraires*, n.s., vol. 13 (1867): 874.

21. See for example the life of Alfège de Beaudiez in Ségur, *Les Martyrs de Castelfidardo*, 124–25; Attilio Vigevano, *La fine dell'Esercito pontificio* (Rome: Stabilimento Poligrafico per l'amministrazione della guerra, 1920), 137.

22. G. A. Cesana, "Corriere di Torino," in *Il mondo illustrato, giornale universale*, September 29, 1860.

23. Some examples: *Le Constitutionnel*, June 27, 1857; *Le Pays: journal des volontés de la France*, June 27, 1857; "Le Zouave trappiste," *Journal des villes et des campagnes*, June 30, 1857; "Nouvelles et faits divers," *L'Ami de la religion et du roi: Journal ecclésiastique, politique et littéraire*, June 30, 1857.

24. On Vernet's painting and its reproductions: Jules Verne, "Salon de 1857," in *Revue des Beaux-Arts: Tribune des artistes* 8, no. 6 (1857): 250; Louis Auvray, *Exposition des beaux-arts, Salon de 1857* (Paris: L'Europe artiste, 1857), 44–47; Isabelle Mancia, "Le Zouave trappiste d'Horace Vernet," *Le Journal des arts*, January 22, 2020. On the monastery, see the account of the Emperor and Empress's 1869 visit in Alfred Monbrun, *La Trappe de Staouëli* (Lille: J. Lefort, 1869), 93. The story of the Trappist Zouave appears in other media: Sidoine Baraguey, "Le Zouave trappiste, vers inspirés par la vue du tableau d'Horace Vernet," in *La Muse des familles: recueil de vers inédits des poètes contemporains* 2 (1858): 76; "Correspondance orphéonique," in *Le Grand Écho du Nord de la France*, December 2, 1903, advertised sheet music for "Le Zouave trappiste."

25. Eugène de Mirecourt, *Lamoricière* (Paris: Librairie des contemporains, 1871), 8.

26. Yves Marthot, "Première messe en Kabylie," www.cdha.fr/premiere-messe-en
-kabylie. The painting is currently in the Musée cantonal des Beaux-Arts in Lausanne,
Switzerland.

27. [Félix Dupanloup], *Oraison funèbre du Général de la Moricière, prononcée dans la
cathédrale de Nantes* (Paris: Douniol, 1865), 8; Henri de Riancey, *Le Général de Lamoricière*
(Paris: Victor Palme, [before 1865]), 7, 9; Sarah Curtis, "Emilie de Vialar and the Religious
Reconquest of Algeria," *French Historical Studies* 29, no. 2 (2006): 261–92.

28. "Les Diables du Bon Dieu": L. Defives de Saint Martin, *Pro Petri Sede ou nos zouaves
belges à Rome* (Mechelin: J. Thys, 1899), 144.

29. Oscar de Poli, *Souvenir du bataillon des zouaves pontificaux* (Paris, 1861), 245–47.

30. Frank Russell-Kilough, *Dix Années au service pontifical, récits et souvenirs* (Paris: Victor Palmé, 1871), 88–89.

31. Russell-Kilough, *Dix Années*, 63–68; Abbé Staub, *Historique de la Légion Franco-
Romaine ex-Légion d'Antibes devenue 47e régiment de marche* (Abbeville: C. Paillart, n.d.), 29.

32. Matteo Sanfilippo, "Documents et souvenirs romains des zouaves pontificaux," in
*Les Zouaves pontificaux en France, en Belgique, et au Québec: La mise en récit d'une expérience
transnationale (XIX–XXe siècles)*, ed. Bruno Dumons and Jean-Philippe Warren (Bern: Peter
Lang, 2015), 21–38; Guenel, *La Dernière Guerre*, 73.

33. Ségur, *Les Martyrs de Castelfidardo*. These memoirs form the basis for Carol E. Harrison, "Zouave Stories: Gender, Catholic Spirituality, and French Responses to the Roman
Question," *Journal of Modern History* 79, no. 2 (2007): 274–305.

34. *Oraison funèbre du Général de la Moricière*, 37.

35. Harrison, "Zouave Stories," 288–89.

36. Mizael le Mesre de Pas, described by Ségur, *Les Martyrs de Castelfidardo*, 74, and Jules
Delmas, *La Neuvième Croisade* (2nd ed., Paris: Bleriot frères, 1881), 86.

37. Félicité de Laville Leroulx writing to Mgr Richard, vicar general of the city of Paris,
about the death of her nephew, November 14, 1867 (Archives historiques de l'archidiocèse
de Paris, I DX7, folder A, letter 21a).

38. Identification of the figures in the painting is uncertain. Alexis Miranville puts
Louis in the center and identifies the third figure as a cousin, Robert Vetch (*Madame Des-
bassayns, le mythe, la légende, et l'histoire* [Réunion: Musée historique de Villèle, 2012], 170).
The collection of Zouave portraits available on Facebook at @ZouavesPontificauxVolont
airesDeLOuestPortraits-Community describes them, from left to right, as Gaston, Louis,
and Charles de Villèle. Gaston joined the Pontifical Zouaves in 1866 at age twenty; see
Adéodat et Emmanuel Dufournel, officiers aux Zouaves pontificaux (Lille: Desclée, de Brouwer
et Cie., 1898), 40. The nineteenth-century biographers of the artist, Jacques Pilliard, list the
subjects as Laurent Dugas and "the Villèle brothers": Jules Bouvier and Claude Bouvier, *Le
Peintre Jacques Pilliard (1811–1898)* (Vienne: E. J. Savigné, 1898), 165.

39. Facebook group: @ZouavesPontificauxVolontairesDeLOuestPortraits-Community.

40. Laurent Gruaz, *Les Officiers français des Zouaves pontificaux. Histoire et devenir entre*

XIXe et XXe siècle (Paris, Honoré Champion, 2017), part 1, addresses recruitment patterns among Zouave officers.

41. René Laurentin, *Bernadette Speaks: A Life of Saint Bernadette Soubirous in Her Own Words,* trans. John W. Lynch and Ronald DesRosier (Boston: Pauline Books, 2000), 469.

42. Qtd. by Claude Langlois, review of Gruaz, *Les Officiers français des Zouaves pontificaux,* in *Revue de l'histoire des religions* 236, no. 2 (2017): 637.

43. J. S. Allard, *Le Volontaire Joseph-Louis Guérin du corps des Zouaves pontificaux* (Nantes: Mazeau, 1860); Harrison, "Zouave Stories," 274–75, 298–304; Simon Sarlin, "Combattre et mourir pour la foi. Joseph-Louis Guérin (1838–1860), séminariste, soldat du pape et 'martyr,'" *Le Mouvement social* 264 (2018): 61–74; Laurent Gruaz, "L'extraordinaire chrétien chez les Zouaves pontificaux: Joseph-Louis Guérin (1838–1860) mort en odeur de sainteté," *Revue de l'histoire des religions* 234 (2017): 485–517.

44. Allard, *Le Volontaire,* 84; Delmas, *La Neuvième Croisade,* 291–92.

45. Sarlin, "Combattre et mourir" (canonization dossier); Delmas, *La Neuvième Croisade,* 335; and J. S. Allard, *Les Zouaves pontificaux, ou journal de Mgr Daniel, aumônier des zouaves, camérier secret de SS Pie IX et de SS Léon XIII* (Nantes: Bourgeois, 1880), 210 (prayer cards); Marcel Launay, *Le Diocèse de Nantes sous le Second Empire: Monseigneur Jacquemet, 1849–1869* (2 vols., Nantes: CID Editions, 1982), vol. 2: 738, 740; and Gruaz, "L'extraordinaire chrétien," 500–512 (hair); Laurent Bart-Loi, *Au service du pape et de la France: Catherin, 1861–1870* (Lille: Desclée, de Brouwer et Cie., 1901), 90–91 (bust).

46. Valerio Cardella, S.J., *Giulio Watts-Russell, Pontifical Zouave,* trans. William Tylee (London: John Philp, 1868), 4, 71–73. For another case of a family composing an argument for sanctity, see Harrison, "Zouave Stories," 299–301.

47. Rafaele de Cesare, *The Last Days of Papal Rome,* trans. Helen Zimmern (Boston: Houghton Mifflin, 1909), chap. 35; David I. Kertzer, *Prisoner of the Vatican: The Popes' Secret Plot to Capture Rome from the New Italian State* (Boston: Houghton Mifflin, 2004).

48. Laurent Gruaz and Patrick Nouaille-Degorce, "Des Zouaves Pontificaux aux zouaves du Sacré Cœur. Un exemple de la fidélité à Rome des Catholiques français sous la IIIe République," *Revue d'histoire ecclésiastique* 111, no. 102 (2016): 115–47. The press followed these negotiations: for example, *Le Courrier du Gard: journal politique, administratif et judiciaire,* October 7, 1870; the *Courrier* reprinted its story from the *Gazette de l'Ouest.* On recruitment patterns: Patrick Nouaille-Degorce, "Zouaves pontificaux et volontaires de l'ouest dans la guerre de 1870–1871. Présentation des matricules régimentaires," Mémoire de D.E.A., Université de Nantes, 2000.

49. Qtd. by Martin Simpson, "From Zouaves Pontificaux to the Volontaires de l'Ouest: Catholic Volunteers and the French Nation, 1860–1901," *Canadian Journal of History* 53, no. 1 (2018): 1–29, 11.

50. Patrick Nouaille-Degorce, "Des Zouaves pontificaux aux 'volontaires de l'ouest': la mutation d'un corps hétéroclite et peu expérimenté en une troupe d'élite," *Cahiers de la Pensée Mili-Terre* 44 (2016): 12–15.

51. Simpson, "From Zouaves Pontificaux," 3–4, 21–23.

52. Raymond Jonas, *France and the Cult of the Sacred Heart: An Epic Tale for Modern Times* (Berkeley: University of California Press, 2000).

53. *Henri de Verthamon.*

54. Mgr. Baunard, *Le Général de Sonis d'après ses papiers et sa correspondance* (4th ed., Paris: Poussielgue, 1890), 322, 328.

55. Baunard, *Le Général de Sonis,* 330–36.

56. Baunard, *Le Général de Sonis,* 541.

57. Robert Tombs, "Paris and the Rural Hordes: An Exploration of Myth and Reality in the French Civil War of 1871," *Historical Journal* 29, no. 4 (1986): 795–808, quotations from the *Journal official* (of the Commune), April 3 and 5, 1871, on pp. 795–96 (emphasis in the original).

58. Ruth Harris, *Lourdes: Body and Soul in the Secular Age* (New York: Viking, 1999), 216.

59. Gruaz and Nouaille-Degorce, "Des zouaves pontificaux aux zouaves du Sacré-Cœur"; Jonas, *France and the Cult of the Sacred Heart,* 177–97.

60. Etienne Fouilloux, "Le Sacré Coeur," in *Les Lieux de l'histoire de France,* ed. Olivier Wieviorka et al. (Paris: Perrin, 2017), 297–310. The elaborate monument to Lamoricière, erected in the cathedral in Nantes in 1878, was similarly an occasion to assert Catholic intransigence: Antoinette Le Normand-Romain, "Le monument au général de Lamoricière," in Jean Bouteiller et al., eds., *Nantes* (Strasbourg: La Nuée bleue, 2013), 247–49.

61. W. Jacob, *My Personal Recollections of Rome; a Lecture partly delivered on the 9th of February 1871 at the Town Hall, Pontypool* (London, 1871); *The Tablet,* April 15, 1871.

62. Diane Audy, *Les Zouaves de Québec au XXe siècle* (Quebec: Presses de l'Université Laval, 2003), 21–23.

63. Cécile Vanderpelen-Diagre, "Les soldats de la mémoire: les représentations des zouaves pontificaux en Belgique de 1862 à aujourd'hui," in *Les Zouaves pontificaux en France, en Belgique, et au Québec,* 141.

64. Hardy, *Les Zouaves,* 227.

65. Athanase de Charette, *Noces d'argent du régiment des zouaves pontificaux, 1860–1885* (Rennes: Oberthur, 1885), 40.

66. *Confrérie du Sacré-Cœur. Chapelle des Zouaves pontificaux, Basse Motte* (Saint-Malo: Bazouge, 1892).

67. See for example the obituary for Xavier von Schmising-Kerssenbrock in *L'Avant-garde,* January 15, 1911. My thanks to Ferdinand Nicolas Göhde for sharing his knowledge of German Zouaves.

68. Charles J. Esdaile, *Spain in the Liberal Age: From Constitution to Civil War, 1808–1939* (Oxford, UK: Blackwell, 2000), 129–33, 146–47; Edgar Holt, *The Carlist Wars in Spain* (London: Putnam, 1967), chaps. 21–22; Augustín Pacheco Fernández and Francisco Javier Suárez de Vega, *Wils y el batallón de zuavos carlistas. Guerra en Cataluña, 1869–1873* (Valladolid: Galland, 2019).

69. Gruaz, *Les Officiers français des Zouaves pontificaux*, 123; Pacheco and Suárez, *Wils*, 340–48.

70. Pacheco and Suárez estimate that there were between 70 and 100 foreign Carlist Zouaves: *Wils*, 344, 482. Of the roughly 100 Spanish Pontifical Zouaves, at least 31 joined the Carlist unit.

71. Alexandre Dupont, *Une Internationale blanche: histoire d'une mobilisation royaliste entre France et Espagne dans les années 1870* (Paris: Editions de la Sorbonne, 2020), 284.

72. Victor Balaguer, reporter for *El Telégrafo*, qtd. in Pacheco and Suárez, *Wils*, 327.

73. Pacheco and Suárez, *Wils*, 224–25.

74. Pacheco and Suárez, *Wils*, 459.

75. Pacheco and Suárez, *Wils*, 228–33, 518–22, 533.

76. The painting is reproduced in María de las Nieves de Braganza y de Borbón, *Mis memorias sobre nuestra campaña en Cataluña en 1872 y 1873 y en el centro en 1874* (Espasa-Calpe, 1938).

77. Fernando Durán López, *"Mis memorias*, de María de las Nieves de Braganza: una guerra para la Judit del siglo XIX," *Crítica hispánica* 37, no. 2 (2016): 41–69. A Carlist unit formed in the 1930s called itself the "María de las Nieves Regiment."

78. Louis Edmond Moreau, *Nos Croisés, ou histoire anecdotique de l'expédition des volontaires canadiens à Rome pour la défense de l'église* (Montreal: Fabre et Gravel, 1871), 16.

79. Edouard Lefebvre de Bellefeuille, *Le Canada et les zouaves pontificaux: mémoires sur l'origine, l'enrôlement, et l'expédition du contingent canadien à Rome pendant l'année 1868* (Montreal: Typographie du journal *Le nouveau monde*, 1868), reproduces the correspondence of the Catholic Committees.

80. René Hardy, "L'Origine des Zouaves pontificaux canadiens," in Hardy and Elio Lodolini, *Les Zouaves pontificaux canadiens* (Montreal: Musées nationaux du Canada, 1976), 41–66; Jean-Philippe Warren, "La diplomatie comme champ de bataille," *Le Devoir*, February 10, 2018. Julie Plourde, "Révolutions européennes et théâtre à la Congrégation de Notre-Dame, 1868–1871," *Etudes d'histoire religieuse* 85, no. 1–2 (2019): 77–90, describes community efforts to raise funds for Zouave recruits.

81. Moreau, *Nos Croisés*, 21.

82. J. I. Little, *Nationalism, Capitalism, and Colonization in Nineteenth-Century Quebec: The Upper Saint Francis District* (Montreal: McGill-Queen's University Press, 1989), chap. 6; Jean-Philippe Warren, "Piopolis: Une Colonie militaire des Zouaves pontificaux," in *Les Zouaves pontificaux en France, en Belgique, et au Québec*, 71–89.

83. Olivier Hubert, "Des jeunes gens comme il faut," in *Les Soldats du pape: les zouaves canadiens entre l'Europe et l'Amérique*, ed. Jean-Philippe Warren (Quebec: Presses de l'Université Laval, 2015), 23–30.

84. Until the Second World War, AZQ members were allowed to carry weapons in public: Audy, *Les Zouaves de Québec*, 21–26, 36, 54–55, 74–90. See the AZQ drill manual: *Exercises et manœuvres d'infanterie pour les Zouaves canadiens* (Quebec, 1909). French-Canadian

migration brought similar Catholic organizations to Massachusetts and New Hampshire. Miller, *American Zouaves,* 146–48, 193.

85. Qtd. by Sanfilippo, "Documents et souvenirs," 37.

86. Audy, *Les Zouaves de Québec,* 29–34.

87. Jean-François Lanier, "L'Eglise-nation canadienne-française au siècle des nationalités: regard croisé sur l'ultramontanisme et le nationalisme," *SCHEC, Etudes d'histoire religieuse* 81, nos. 1–2 (2015): 15–37.

88. Michael Gauvreau, *Catholic Origins of Quebec's Quiet Revolution, 1931–1970* (Montreal: McGill-Queen's University Press, 2005), 46–57; Audy, *Les Zouaves de Québec,* 94–98 (John Paul II).

89. Qtd. by Vanderpelen-Diagre, "Les soldats de la mémoire," 149.

6. Sounding the Retreat

1. Qtd. by Jess Tyre, "Music in Paris during the Franco-Prussian War and the Commune," *Journal of Musicology* 22, no. 2 (2005), 173–202, 176 (emphasis in the original). See also Mary Manning, "Bazille, Painter-Zouave: Friendship and Duty and the Dawn of the Franco-Prussian War," in *Male Bonds in Nineteenth-Century Art,* ed. Thijs Dekeukeleire, Henk de Smaele, and Marjan Sterckx (Leuven: Leuven University Press, 2021), 123–37.

2. Xavier Boniface, "La réforme de l'armée française après 1871," *Inflexions* 20, no. 3 (2012): 41–50; Rachel Chrastil, *Organizing for War: France, 1870–1914* (Baton Rouge: Louisiana State University Press, 2010), 38–49.

3. Lieutenant Théodore Burkard, *L'Epopée des zouaves. 4e zouaves et zouaves de la Garde* (2 vols., Paris: Flammarion, 1897), vol. 1: frontis.; vol. 2: 317.

4. Christina Carroll, "Imperial Ideologies in the Second Empire: The Mexican Expedition and the *Royaume Arabe,*" *French Historical Studies* 42, no. 1 (2019): 67–100; Xavier Yacono, "Kabylie: L'insurrection de 1871," in *L'Encyclopédie Berbère* 26 (2004): 4022–26; Mohammed Brahim Salhi, "L'insurrection de 1871," in *Histoire de l'Algérie à la période coloniale,* ed. Abderrahmane Bouchène et al. (Paris: La Découverte, 2014), 103–9.

5. Ernest Watbled, "Un épisode de l'insurrection Kabyle de 1871: L'Alma—Palestro," *Revue des deux mondes* 108, no. 3 (1873): 625–40.

6. François Chevaldonné, *Un Village d'Oranie: Les Ouled Mimoun jusqu'à 1914* (Paris: Non Lieu, 2016), 92–97.

7. For a detailed account of the movements of Zouave regiments, see "Les tirailleurs d'hier et d'aujourd'hui": www.les-tirailleurs.fr/.

8. Noulens, *Les Spahis,* 67–71; René Chartrand, *French Naval and Colonial Troops, 1872–1914* (Oxford, UK: Osprey, 2018).

9. Jacob: Lefrère and Berche, "Le Zouave Jacob," 571–77. Paper soldiers: Tom Quinn, "La Gloire guerrière et les images d'Epinal, *Irish Journal of French Studies* 3, no. 1 (2003): 78–93; Nicole Garnier-Pelle, *L'Imagerie populaire française,* vol. 2: *Images d'Epinal gravées sur bois* (Paris: Réunion des musées nationaux, 1996), 368, 404. ABC books featuring Zouaves

from the collection of the Bnf: *Mon ABC d'enfance avec lettres illustrées* (Rouen, 1873); Jérome Clamaron, *Alphabet militaire pour apprendre l'alphabet aux enfants, complété par un alphabet à l'usage des sourds-muets* (Paris: Librairie de l'Echo de la Sorbonne, 1873); *Alphabet des grandes lettres* (Epinal: Ch. Pinot, 1874); *Alphabet de fillettes* (whose Zouave is a *cantinière*) (Pont à Mousson: Imagerie de Pont à Mousson, 1880); *Alphabet des bonnes exemples* (Paris: Jules Lévy, 1885); E. de Liphart, *Album-alphabet illustré* (Paris: Quentin, 1885); Léon Vanier, *L'Armée française: Nouvel album militaire avec descriptions alphabétiques* (Paris, 1886); G. Gaulard, *Grand alphabet militaire* (Paris: Monrocq, 1889); F. Modelon, *Alphabet français* (Paris: 1887); *Alphabet de ma petite fille* (Paris: 1890); *Alphabet de la phosphatine Falières* (Paris: Chassaing, 1905).

10. Ad for a "composition Zouave" in *Le Constitutionnel,* June 9, 1851.

11. David Lebovitz, *Drinking French: The Iconic Cocktails, Apéritifs, and Café Traditions of France* (Berkeley, CA: Ten Speed Press, 2020), 98–99. Lucien Lefèvre's poster design for Absinthe Mugnier is an icon of *fin de siècle* advertising.

12. "The History of Zig-Zag," zigzag.com/pages/zz-history.

13. Brett Berliner, *Ambivalent Desire: The Exotic Black Other in Jazz-Age France* (Amherst: University of Massachusetts Press, 2002); Ann McClintock, *Imperial Leather: Race, Gender, and Sexuality in the Colonial Context* (New York: Routledge, 1995), chap. 5.

14. François Robichon, *L'Armée française vue par les peintres, 1870–1914* (Paris: Herscher, 2000).

15. Marc Morillon, "L'uniforme du Marsouin de Bazeilles," *Bulletin de l'Association des amis du Musée des Troupes de Marine* 33 (2016): 15–16. Méliès: www.youtube.com/watch?v =93G3_81dPQk/; Pathé: www.youtube.com/watch?v=wir_oEj3CNU. The third film, by the Lumière brothers: catalogue-lumiere.com/les-dernieres-cartouches/.

16. Alphonse Daudet, "Le Mauvais Zouave," in *Contes du Lundi* (Paris: Alphonse Lemerre, 1873), 53–60.

17. A very incomplete list: Alfred Assolant, *D'Heure en heure* (Paris: Michel Lévy frères, 1862); Charles Delsys, *Maître Guillaume* (Paris: Ch. Blériot, 1877); Delsys, "La Farandolière," in *L'Abime* (Paris: C. Marpon et E. Flammarion, 1888); Pierre Zaccone, *La Vivandière des zouaves* (Paris: Calmann-Lévy, 1880), building on his earlier novel *Les Zouaves* (Paris: A de Vresse, 1859); Paul de Sémant, *Merveilleuses Aventures de Dache, perruquier des Zouaves* (Paris: Flammarion, 1911). Some of this Zouave fiction focused on Pontifical Zouaves or was inflected with Catholicism: Sophie de Ségur, *Après la pluie, le beau temps* (Paris: Hachette, 1871); L. Gallen, *Hippolyte-René Bel-Kassem, enfant adoptif des zouaves* (Clerment-Ferrand: Imprimerie centrale, 1877); Frédéric Koenig, *Les Deux Zouaves* (Tours: Mame et fils, 1878).

18. Ouida, *Under Two Flags* (1867; London: Chatto and Windus, 1912), 200. The hero, whose most outstanding quality is his horsemanship, enlists in the *chasseurs algériens*. Ouida, *Cigarette: cantinière des zouaves* (2 vols., Paris: Plon, 1883). On the global success of *Under Two Flags,* see Celia Phillips, "*Under Two Flags:* The Publishing History of a Best-Seller, 1867–1967," *Publishing History* 3 (1978): 67–69.

19. Memoir: Louis Noir, *Campagne du Mexique. Puebla: souvenirs d'un zouave* (Paris:

Bureaux du "Siècle," 1872); *Campagne du Crimée. L'Alma: souvenirs d'un zouave* (Paris: A. Faiure, 1868); *Histoire de l'invasion, deuxième Empire: Wissembourg, Rorback, Reichshoffen, Borny, Gravelotte, Saint-Privat, Metz, Procès Bazaine, Sedan* (Paris: Claverie, 1875). Travelogue: *Grands jours de l'Afrique. Peuplades algériennes Mazagran* (Paris: Degorce Cadot, 1872). Zouave-themed novels include *Jacques La Hache* (Paris, 1868); *Jean Chacal* (Paris: Sceaux, 1876); *Alexandra la nihiliste: une martyre du Tzar* (Paris: 1880). *Les Martyrs de la Pologne* (Paris: 1865) ingeniously combines North African and Polish Zouaves. Jean-Marie Seillan, *Aux Sources du roman colonial (1863–1914): L'Afrique à la fin du XIXe siècle* (Paris: Karthala, 2006).

20. Bertrand Joly, *Déroulède: L'Inventeur du nationalisme français* (Paris: Perrin, 1998).

21. Edmond de Amicis, "Paul Déroulède," *Le Drapeau*, March 16, 1882, 5; Joly, *Déroulède*, 25–28.

22. Paul Déroulède, *Chants du soldat*, 116th ed. (Paris: Calmann Lévy, 1883), 58, 88.

23. Fernand Movel, "Galerie artistique: Mlle Amiati," *La Chanson: Journal de musique populaire*, December 5, 1880, 1–2; Charles Rearick, "Song and Society in Turn-of-the-Century France," *Journal of Social History* 22, no. 1 (1988): 45–63, 51.

24. Joly, *Déroulède*, 87–88. A survey of *Le Drapeau*'s first year of publication (1882) indicates that Zouaves were an important visual resource: Léon Couturier, "Officer de Zouaves, tenue de campagne," "Zouaves en marche," (both March 23, 1882); "Sergent de Zouaves" (March 30, 1882) and "Les Troupes coloniales: Zouave (tenue de campagne)," (April 20, 1882), and an untitled Zouave (November 25, 1882). An unsigned image of a Zouave smoking illustrates E. Duchiron, "Une campagne du 3e Zouaves," a story of the siege of Constantine (March 16, 1882), and Zouaves appear in du Paty, "Le Colonel de Suzzoni" (August 17, 1882); Horace Vernet's "La Prise de Constantine" illustrated another story about that exploit (October 14, 1882); and there are more Zouaves in Regamey's "L'Abbatoir, Inkermann" and Armand Dumarescq, "Pas Froid aux yeux (Un Zouave, guerre de Crimée)" (both November 18, 1882). Turcos appeared on the cover (Poilpot, "Un Turco," March 23, 1882) and in drawings by Marius Roy (February 9, 1882). Neuville's *Les Dernières Cartouches* ran in *Le Drapeau* on September 2, 1882. On the relationship between Déroulède's Ligue des patriotes and the art world, see François Robichon, "Representing the 1870–1871 War, or the Impossible Revanche," in *Nationalism and French Visual Culture, 1870–1914*, ed. June Hargrove and Neil McWilliam (Washington, DC: National Gallery of Art, 2005): 82–99, 89. Allison Matthews David notes that the combination of Déroulède's poetry and military art appeared in the fashion press as well: the first issue of *L'Art de la mode* in 1880 featured Déroulède's poem "Le Porte-Drapeau" (the flag bearer) and painter Edouard Détaille's image with the same title: "Decorated Men," 28.

25. "Paul Déroulède à Montbéliard," *Le Drapeau*, May 28, 1899; advertisement in *Le Drapeau*, June 1, 1899.

26. Maurice Barrès, "Paul Déroulède," *Les Annales politiques et littéraires*, February 8, 1914, 130–31. See also François Robichon, *Edouard Détaille, un siècle de gloire* (Paris: Bernard Giovanangeli, 2007), 130. The painting is in the Musée historique de Strasbourg.

27. Philippe-E. Landau, *Les Juifs de France et la Grande Guerre: un patriotisme républicain, 1914–1918* (Paris: CNRS Editions, 1999), 34.

28. Jacques de Biez, *Edouard Manet: Conférence faite à la salle des Capucines, le mardi 22 janvier 1884* (Paris: Ludovic Baschet, 1884), 59–60. Translation: Pierre Courthion and Pierre Cailler, eds., *Portrait of Manet: By Himself and His Contemporaries*, trans. Michael Ross (London: Cassell, 1953), 58.

29. Vincent van Gogh, letter to Theo van Gogh, Arles, June 21, 1888, in "Van Gogh's Letters, Unabridged and Annotated" (www.webexhibits.org/vangogh/letter/18/501.htm). J. B. de la Faille et al., *The Works of Vincent Van Gogh: His Paintings and Drawings* (Amsterdam: Meulenhoff, 1970), 196–97. One of the two paintings is in the Van Gogh Museum in Amsterdam; the other is in a private collection. The Metropolitan Museum of Art in New York owns a watercolor sketch of a Zouave that van Gogh sent to his friend, the painter Emile Bernard.

30. Bernadette Murphy, *Van Gogh's Ear: The True Story* (New York: Farrar, Straus and Giroux, 2016), 79, 98–99.

31. Van Gogh to Theo van Gogh, June 23, 1888 (www.webexhibits.org/vangogh/letter /18/502.htm); and to Emile Bernard, June 23, 1888 (www.webexhibits.org/vangogh/letter/18/B 08.htm).

32. Van Gogh to Theo van Gogh, ca. March 14, 1888 (www.webexhibits.org/vangogh/letter /18/469.htm); Murphy, *Van Gogh's Ear*, 60–61.

33. Venita Datta, "Buffalo Bill Goes to France: French-American Encounters at the Wild West Show, 1889–1905," *French Historical Studies* 41, no. 3 (2018): 535–55.

34. "The National Guard," *NYT*, April 15, 1866.

35. "New York City," *NYDTr*, August 8, 1884.

36. "Military Matters," *NYH*, December 13, 1865; "The National Guard," *NYT*, February 19, 1866; "The National Guard," *NYT*, October 23, 1866; "The National Guard," *ANJ* 7 (December 4, 1869): 248.

37. *Annual Report of the Adjutant General of the State of New York* (Albany: Argus Co., 1869), 34–36, 42.

38. Hess, *Civil War Infantry Tactics*, 206–11; Wallace, *Lew Wallace* 1: 273–74; Jeffrey A. Marlin, "The National Guard, the National Board for the Promotion of Rifle Practice, and the National Rifle Association: Public Institutions and the Rise of a Lobby for Private Gun Ownership," PhD diss., Georgia State University, 2013.

39. J. P. Clark, *Preparing for War: The Emergence of the Modern U.S. Army* (Cambridge, MA: Harvard University Press, 2017), 93–98. For examples of the Zouave presence in early postwar American discussion of tactics, see "Skirmishing," *ANJ* 3 (November 11, 1865): 185; "The Light Infantry of Europe," *ANJ* 3 (November 18, 1865): 197; and "Skirmishing and Improvised Earthworks," *ANJ* 4 (September 8, 1866): 40, all contributed by J. Watts De Peyster under the pseudonym "Anchor."

40. John P. Langellier, *Army Blue: The Uniform of Uncle Sam's Regulars, 1848–1873* (Atglen, PA: Schiffer Military History, 1998), 127–38, 183, 227–31.

41. "Our Special History of the War," *NYH*, August 18, 1870; "The Military Condition of France," *NYEP*, August 19, 1870 (signed "M"); "Sherman," *NYH*, September 17, 1872. The attacks cut deeper than the cracks in the Zouave reputation caused by French frustrations in Mexico. "Very Late from Mexico," *NYH*, June 14, 1862; "Mexico," *NYH*, March 10, 1865; "Mexico," *NYH*, June 18, 1865.

42. Miller, *American Zouaves*, lists militia affiliations for postwar Zouave units. On Illinois see Hannah, *Manhood, Citizenship, and the National Guard*, 25.

43. "Challenge Competitive Drill," *NYC*, July 15, 1871; "The National Guard," *ANJ* 8 (July 15, 1871): 773–74.

44. "The San Francisco Soldiers," *The Sun*, August 26, 1873; "The National Guard," *ANJ* 11 (August 30, 1873): 44–45.

45. "The Aborigines to Be Utilized," *San Francisco Examiner*, May 23, 1877; "What to Do with the Red Man," *Benton Weekly Record*, June 15, 1877; Jerry Wasserman, "Aboriginal Dance, Military Drill: Captain MacDonald's Trained Indians and Nineteenth-Century Variety Entertainment," in *A World of Popular Entertainments: An Edited Volume of Critical Essays*, ed. Gillian Arrighi and Victor Emiljanow (Newcastle upon Tyne: Cambridge Scholars Publishing, 2012), 3–17.

46. William P. Clarke, *Official History of the Militia and the National Guard of the State of Pennsylvania: From the Earliest Period of Record to the Present Time* (3 vols., n.p.: Charles J. Hendler, 1909), vol. 1: 52–53.

47. "The National Guard," *ANJ* 7 (August 13, 1870): 823–25; "The National Guard," *ANJ* 8 (September 17, 1870): 79–80; *Annual Report of the Adjutant-General, of the State of New York* (Albany: Weed, Parsons and Co., 1881), 4, 19; *Annual Report of the Adjutant-General of the State of New York for the Year 1881* (Albany: Weed, Parsons and Co., 1882), 4–9; *Report of the Adjutant-General of the State of New York for the Year Ending December 31, 1882* (Albany: Weed, Parsons and Co., 1883), 336; "Beginning Camp Life," *NYT*, June 22, 1884.

48. Hannah, *Manhood, Citizenship, and the National Guard*, 109. The Ellsworth Zouaves, local successor to the USZC, traded in their Zouave uniforms ten years earlier for the gray uniforms of the First Regiment of the Illinois National Guard ("the First Chicago"), an attempt to match the social prestige of the New York Seventh Regiment. "Our Citizen Soldiers," *CDT*, January 3, 1875.

49. "Must Give Up Their Uniforms," *NYT*, July 14, 1893; J. Madison Drake, *Historical Sketches of the Revolutionary and Civil Wars* (New York: Webster Press, 1908), 270–72.

50. "The Interstate Drill at Houston, Texas," *ANJ* 21 (May 24, 1884): 886–87 (maids); "Southern Competitive Drills," *NYT*, May 18, 1885 (superexcellence); "The Philadelphia Encampment," *ANJ* 22 (July 11, 1885): 1021 (monkey).

51. Miller, *American Zouaves*, 55, 182–88, 419–20; "Foreign," *Chicago Daily Inter Ocean*, October 4, 1882; "The State Troops," *ANJ* 32 (July 27, 1895): 797–98; "Winners at San Antonio," *NYT*, July 26, 1897. *Report of the Secretary of War*, Ex. Doc. 1, pt. 2; 49th Cong., 1st Sess. (Washington, DC: Government Printing Office, 1886), vol. 1: 243, 277, describes the Busch

Zouaves as a company in the Missouri National Guard at the interstate encampments held in Mobile and Philadelphia in 1885.

52. "The National Guard," *ANJ* 5 (February 22, 1868): 432; "Amusements," *NYH*, May 16, 1869 (quotation); "Major Burk," *NYC*, February 14, 1914.

53. "Variety Halls," *NYC*, October 11, 1873 (Sgt. Joseph H. Childers); "Sergeant W. H. L. Hamilton," advertisement, *NYC*, December 20, 1873; "Circuses," *NYC*, February 25, 1881 (Maj. Thomas); "Miscellaneous," *NYC*, March 20, 1882 (Elmer Ellsworth Hamilton); "City Summary," *NYC*, September 9, 1882 (Capt. Jack Smith); "Kohl, Middleton & Hagar," advertisement, *NYC*, March 24, 1883 (Sgt. Ahern); "Circus, Variety and Minstrel," *NYC*, January 8, 1887 (Lt. George Ellsworth); "Miss Esther Lyons' French Spy Company," advertisement, *NYC*, May 7, 1887 (Sgt. Latta); "Variety and Minstrel Gossip," *NYC*, June 15, 1889 (Major Kibble).

54. "What the Militia Needs," *CDT*, June 4, 1887.

55. "The Military King, Major Kibble, The Lightning Military Drill Artist," advertisement, *NYC*, June 1, 1889.

56. "The Great Kissell," advertisement, *NYC*, May 26, 1888; J. H. Haverly to William Foote, June 12, 1892, Minstrel Show Collection, Harry Ransom Center, University of Texas (thanks to Madeline Steiner for pointing out this letter). "Variety, Minstrel and Circus," *NYC*, January 22, 1887; "The Original Whirlwinds of the Desert," advertisement, *NYC*, October 25, 1890; Tahar may have been part of the 1886 international P. T. Barnum show discussed in Linda K. Jacobs, "Playing East: Arabs Perform in Nineteenth Century America," *Mashriq and Mahjar* 2 (2014): 79–110. See also Lhoussair Simour, "The Other History of Cultural Encounters through Performance Revisited: Shifting Discourses on Moroccan Acrobatic Entertainers in Nineteenth-Century America," *Cultural Studies* 34 (January 2020): 70–94. In 1894, William K. L. Dickson of Edison Motion Pictures filmed Hadj Lessik's gun-spinning routine: Charles Musser, *Edison Motion Pictures, 1890–1900: An Annotated Filmography* (Washington, DC: Smithsonian Institution Press, 1997), 106–7, 136–37. "Vaudeville and Minstrel," *NYC*, November 20, 1897, announced that Kissell and Lessik had dissolved their partnership and that Lessik would henceforth work alone. It seems likely that Kissell conducted shows in both guises before focusing wholly on his assumed stage identity.

57. "Inter-State Drill," *Kinsley Graphic* (Kansas), June 13, 1890; "Duties and Drills," *Indianapolis Journal*, July 6, 1891; "The Famous Aurora Zouaves," *NYC*, August 1, 1903; Joy S. Kasson, *Buffalo Bill's Wild West: Celebrity, Memory, and Popular History* (New York: Hill and Wang, 2000), 144–45.

58. Miller, *American Zouaves*, 65, 71–72, 85, 166–67; Richard O'Hara, *The Sensation of the Century: Streator's World Famous Zouaves* (n.p.: CreateSpace, 2019); "Observations by Joe Hepp," *NYC*, February 22, 1913; "Ewing's Zouave Band," *NYC*, December 19, 1914.

59. O'Hara, *The Sensation of the Century*, 18, 46; "Things at the Theater," *The Sun*, January 20, 1899 (quotation); "Theatrical Novelties," *NYT*, March 16, 1902.

60. Margaret Mitchell, *Gone with the Wind* (New York: MacMillan, 1936), 16, 169; Eliz-

abeth Young, *Disarming the Nation: Women's Writing and the American Civil War* (Chicago: University of Chicago Press, 1999), chap. 6.

61. André Billy, *La Muse aux bésicles* (Paris: La Renaissance littéraire, 1921), 25; Kathleen Antonioli, "Colette *française* (*et fille de zouave*): Colette and the French Singularity," *French Politics, Culture, and Society* 38, no. 1 (2020): 113–28.

62. Hervé Drévillon, *L'Individu et la guerre: Du Chevalier Bayard au soldat inconnu* (Paris: Belin, 2013), 13.

63. Colette, "Un Zouave" in *Les Heures longues*, in *Colette: Romans, récits, souvenirs* (*1900–1919*) (3 vols., Paris: Robert Laffont, 1989), vol. 1: 1238–41, originally published as "Le Journal de Colette" in *Le Matin*, May 27, 1915. The encounter between Captain Colette and the emperor also appears in Godchot, *Le 1er régiment* 1: 157–58.

64. Colette, "Blessés: l'aube" in *Les Heures longues*, 1206. In the same hospital ward she meets a man with a damaged face who repeats the Crimean-era joke about needing a double ration of coffee because he leaks through his wounds. Marieke Dubbelboer, "'Nothing Ruins Writers Like Journalism': Colette, the Press, and Belle Epoque Literary Life," *French Cultural Studies* 26, no. 1 (2015): 32–44.

65. Judith Thurman, *Secrets of the Flesh: A Life of Colette* (New York: Alfred A. Knopf, 1999).

66. *Histoire du 2e régiment de Zouaves* (Paris, 1921), 11.

67. The event was widely covered in the press: see for example Paul Ginesty, "Victor-Emmanuel III, caporal," in *Le Petit Parisien*, May 31, 1915.

68. *La Chéchia*, October 15, 1915.

69. Capitaine Fiori, Caporal Cabanne, and Sergent Clozier, *Au clair de la . . . dune* (n.p., 1915); *C'est à schlitter partout!* (n.p., 1916) and *Jamais deux sans trois* (n.p., 1916). "Schlittage": François Déchelette, *L'argot des poilus: dictionnaire humoristique et philologique des soldats de la grande guerre de 1914* (Paris: Jouve et Cie., 1918), 199–200. "Zouave Girls": *Jamais deux*, 49–50.

70. *La Chéchia* and *Le Zouzou* are both in the collection of the BnF. *La Chéchia*, June 1, 1915; July 30, 1915. See also *La Chéchia*'s "menu de guerre" from October 18, 1915. Stéphane Audoin-Rouzeau, *14–18, Les combattants des tranchées* (Paris: Armand Colin, 1986).

71. Guillot de Saix, "Le Théâtre au front: les revues sous l'obus," *La Rampe*, August 31, 1916, 10–11; Romain Piana, "L'étranger dans les revues de la guerre, 1914–1918," in *L'Altérité en spectacle, 1789–1918*, ed. Isabelle Moindrot and Nathalie Coutelet (Rennes: Presses universitaires de Rennes, 2019), 141–60.

72. *Le 1er régiment de marche de Zouaves dans la Grande Guerre, 1914–1919* (Marseille: Ferran jeune, 1920), 4–5. For a catalogue of consumer goods featuring the story, see "Rubrique 'des Zouzous par milliers'" (esmma.free.fr/mde4/tirez_ndd.htm) and "Tirez donc, nom de Dieu!" (www.letempsdeschansons.fr/partition/tirez-donc-nom-de-dieu/). The episode features on the cover of the regimental souvenir *Historique du 2e régiment de Zouaves* (Paris, 1921) even though the featured soldier was in the First Zouaves. It also reached the United States: "Zouave in Foe's Hands Told Comrades to Fire," *NYT*, November 24, 1914, 1.

73. René Clozier, "Tirez donc, nom de Dieu," chap. 5 in *Les Zouaves: Epopée d'un régiment d'élite* (Paris: Alexis Redier, 1931), 83–91, 85. Clozier's title parodies the official history of the Fourth Zouaves: Burkard, *L'Epopée des zouaves*.

74. *Reliquaire du 2me régiment de Zouaves* (Oran, n.d.), 7.

75. Emmanuelle Cronier, "Les Poilus," in *Histoire du poil*, ed. Marie-France Auzépy and Joël Cornette (2nd ed., Paris: Belin, 2014), 235–54.

76. See for example *Reliquaire*; Burkhard, *L'Epopée des zouaves*; *Historique du 2e régiment*; *Le 1er régiment de marche de Zouaves*; *Historique du 9e régiment de marche de zouaves dans la Grande Guerre, 1914–1918* (Algiers: Imprimerie Orientale, 1921); *Petit historique du 8e Zouaves pendant la Grande Guerre* (Paris: Chapelot, 1919). On the complexities of identifying "settler soldiers" and distinctions between *indigènes* and *poilus*, see Claire Eldridge, "'The Forgotten of this Tribute': Settler Soldiers, Colonial Categories, and the Centenary of the First World War," *History and Memory* 31, no. 2 (2019): 3–44.

77. Cronier, "Les Poilus."

78. David Murphy, "Representations of the *tirailleur sénégalais* and World War I," in *Visualizing Empire: Africa, Europe, and the Politics of Representation*, ed. Rebecca Peabody, Steven Nelson, and Dominic Thomas (Los Angeles: Getty Research Institute, 2021), 118–35, 130.

79. Richard S. Fogarty, *Race and War in France: Colonial Subjects in the French Army, 1914–1918* (Baltimore: Johns Hopkins University Press, 2008), 271; John Horne, "'L'impôt du sang': Republican Rhetoric and Industrial Warfare in France, 1914–18," *Social History* 14, no. 2 (1989): 201–23.

80. Fogarty, *Race and War in France*, 99–107.

81. Cribbs, "Campaign Dress of the West India Regiments," 174–88, 181–87; Bennett, "Picturing the West India Regiments," 216–18, 220, 267–72, 331.

82. Selwyn Hodson-Pressinger, "Khaki Uniform, 1848–49: First Introduction by Lumsden and Hodson," *Journal of the Society for Army Historical Research* 82 (2004): 341–47; Christopher Leach, "Uniforms and Commercial Culture: Constructing a Vision of Warfare in Pre–Great War Britain," *Cultural History* 10, no. 1 (2021): 31–60.

83. Sandra S. Swart, "'You were men in war time': The Manipulation of Gender Identity in War and Peace," *Scientia Militaria, South African Journal of Military Studies* 28, no. 2 (1998): 187–91, 196. See also Jane Tynan, *British Army Uniform and the First World War: Men in Khaki* (Houndmills, UK: Palgrave Macmillan, 2013).

84. Julien Villaume, *Les Zouaves dans la Grande Guerre* (Fiacre: Montceaux-les-Meaux, 2019), 30.

85. A.R., "Tenue de campagne," *Journal des sciences militaires* 86 (September 1, 1910): 98–108, 105, qtd. by Villaume, *Les Zouaves dans la Grande Guerre*, 28–29.

86. Aubagnac, "Le Camouflage et la grande guerre," 91–101, quotation on 97.

87. Charles Nordman, "Revue scientifique: la protection du soldat—le casque," *Revue des deux mondes* 44, no. 2 (March 1918): 445–56, 455, 453.

88. Bashford Dean, *Helmets and Body Armor in Modern Warfare* (New Haven, CT: Yale University Press, 1920), 66.

89. *C'est à schlitter partout!* 13.

90. Martin Evans, *Algeria, France's Undeclared War* (New York: Oxford University Press, 2012), chaps. 9 and 10.

91. The statue was repatriated in 1962 and reerected in 1969 in the Breton village of Saint-Philibert-de-Grand-Lieu, near the ancestral home of the Lamoricière family: "Monument au général de Lamoricière," anosgrandshommes.musee-orsay.fr/index .php/Detail/objects/3308. There have been recent demands to remove the statue: "Au sud de Nantes, la statue d'un général fait polémique," www.lefigaro.fr/actualite-france /au-sud-de-nantes-la-statue-d-un-general-fait-polemique-20220418.

92. Jan C. Jansen, "1880–1914: Une 'Statuomanie' à l'algérienne," in *Histoire d'Algérie à la période coloniale*, ed. Bouchène et al., 261–65; and Jansen, *Erobern und Erinnern: Symbolpolitik, öffentlicher Raum und französischer Kolonialismus in Algerien, 1830–1950* (Munich: Oldenbourg, 2013), 517–20.

93. Jan C. Jansen, "Fête et ordre colonial: Centenaires et résistance anticolonialiste en Algérie pendant les années 1930," *Vingtième siècle* 212 (2014): 61–75; Dónal Hassett, "A Tale of Two Monuments: The War Memorials of Oran and Algiers and Commemorative Culture in Colonial and Post-Colonial Algeria," in *Commemorating Race and Empire in the First World War Centenary*, ed. Ben Wellings and Shanti Mumartojo (Aix en Provence: Presses universitaires de Provence, 2018), 151–68.

94. Jean-Vincent Blanchard, *At the Edge of the World: The Heroic Century of the French Foreign Legion* (New York: Bloomsbury, 2017); David Slavin, *Colonial Cinema and Imperial France, 1919–1939: White Blind Spots, Male Fantasies, and Settler Myths* (Baltimore: Johns Hopkins University Press, 2001), chap. 7.

95. See for example the video of the Armée de terre honoring two men of the First Spahis killed in Mali in February 2018: "Hommage aux 2 soldats décédés du 1er Spahis," www. youtube.com/watch?v=nXHDGqHxxPA. On the Compagnons de la Libération: "Armée de terre," www.ordredelaliberation.fr/fr/armee-de-terre.

96. "'14-18': L'Afrique du nord dans la grande guerre. 1915 Les Hirondelles de la mort et les gas toxiques," 14-18-afriquenord.com/Guerre/Zones-de-Combats/1915-Les-Hirondelles -de-la-Mort-et-les-gas-toxiques.

97. "1er régiment de tirailleurs," fr.wikipedia.org/wiki/1er_r%C3%A9giment_de_tirail leurs.

98. Bruno Carpentier, *La Légende des Zouaves: De l'Afrique du nord au Massif ardennais* (Charleville-Mézières: Editions Sopiac, 2003), 153–72, 177–84.

Encores

1. Sara Catterall, "Women's Trousers and Such: The Ottoman Influence on Early Western Feminism," *Humanities* 41, no. 1 (2020), www.neh.gov/article/womens-trousers -and-such.

2. Bernardine Morris, "A Rousing Show by Saint Laurent—and Valentino, too," *NYT*, October 27, 1976. See also Elodie Nowinski, "Yves Saint Laurent et l'exotisme dans les années 1960: de l'exception insolente à la naissance du métissage dans la haute couture," in *La Mode des sixties: L'entrée dans la modernité*, ed. Dominique Veillon and Michèle Ruffat (Paris: Autrement, 2007), 131–53; "The New Zouave Silhouette," *NYT*, September 8, 1940; "Trends," *NYT*, January 7, 1945; "Display Ad No. 40," *NYT*, June 22, 1958; "Display Ad No. 138," *NYT*, March 17, 1968, 92; Sameer Reddy, "How Low Can You Go?" *NYT*, March 14, 2010, SM46A. Many thanks to Ava Gartman for her research assistance.

3. Christopher George Bates, "What They Fight For: The Men and Women of Civil War Reenactment," PhD diss., University of California at Los Angeles, 2016, is a useful point of entry into a large literature.

4. "In Memoriam: Terrence Lee (Terry) Daley, August 11, 1953–April 10, 2020," *Camp Chase Gazette*, July 23, 2020; Philip McBride, "Reenacting as a Zouave," *Camp Chase Gazette*, May 21, 2016.

5. *Shaun Grenan's Zouave Database*, www.zouavedatabase.com, and *Zouaves of the World*, zuaus.blogspot.com, provide information on most of these groups. See also "Anderson Zouaves Re-enactors in Germany," *Zouave!* no. 3 (March 2007): 3; "Camp of Instruction," *Zouave!* no. 12 (April 2008): 1. Gordon Jones, "Gut History: Civil War Reenacting and the Making of an American Past," PhD diss., Emory University, 2007, 212, 278, 338, notes the frequent appearance of Zouave uniforms in Civil War reenactments. A Zouave enthusiast's production of a general guidebook suffused with Zouaves typifies the disproportionate presence. Shaun C. Grenan, *So You Want to Be a Soldier: How to Get Started in Civil War Re-Enacting* (Lynchburg, VA: Schroeder Publications, 2003).

6. Pohanka, *Vortex of Hell*; Patricia Sullivan, "Brian Pohanka Dies; Civil War Historian, Film Adviser," *Washington Post*, June 17, 2005.

7. Dennis Hall, "Civil War Reenactors and the Postmodern Sense of History," *Journal of American Culture* 17 (September 1994): 9.

8. Stephen Gapps, "Mobile Monuments: A View of Historical Reenactment and Authenticity from Inside the Costume Cupboard of History," *Rethinking History* 13 (September 2009): 398.

9. *Remember Ellsworth 150th*, glwillard154.org/events/remember-ellsworth-150th.

10. Paolo Ventura, *Lo Zuavo Scomparso* (Rome: Punctum Press, 2012).

11. Francine Prose, "Paolo Ventura," in *Paolo Ventura: Photographs and Drawings*, ed. Walter Guadagnini (Milan: Silvana Editoriale, 2020), 25.

12. Prose, "Paolo Ventura," 31; Monica Poggi, "Interview with Paolo Ventura," in *Paolo Ventura*, ed. Guadagnini, 43–47.

13. Poggi, "Interview with Paolo Ventura," 59–61; see also "Civil War," in *Paolo Ventura*, ed. Guadagnini, 150–59.

14. Poggi, "Interview with Paolo Ventura," 57. Ventura's picture also spoofs Jacques Pilliard's painting of the Villèle brothers in Saint Peter's Square. (See fig. 39, above.)

15. "Le groupuscule d'ultradroite les Zouaves Paris dissous en conseil des ministres," *Le Monde,* January 5, 2022.

16. Pierre Plottu, "Les 'Zouaves,' nouveaux petits soldats de l'extrême droite radicale," *Libération,* January 20, 2020.

17. Pierre Plottu, Maxime Macé, "Qui sont les Zouaves, le 'groupuscule de combat' derrière le lynchage des militants de SOS Racisme," December 6, 2021, www.streetpress.com /sujet/1638808521-qui-sont-zouaves-groupuscule-neonazis-lynchage-militants-sos-racisme -meeting-zemmour-extreme-droite.

18. "How Extremists Weaponize Irony to Spread Hate," April 26, 2021, www.npr.org /transcripts/990274685.

19. Nadim Février, "Cartographie des groupuscules d'extrême-droite en France: tendances, bastions et modes d'actions," *L'insoumission,* May 10, 2022, linsoumission. fr/2022/05/10/cartographie-extreme-droite/.

20. Jean-Yves Camus, interviewed by Tristan Berteloot, "Ultradroite: 'La bagarre de rue est la raison d'être des 'Zouaves,'" *Libération,* February 1, 2019; Nicolas Lebourg, "L'Odyssée des rats noirs: voyage au cœur du GUD," *Fragments sur les temps présents,* February 6, 2010, tempspresents.com/2010/02/06/nicolas-lebourg-odyssee-des-rats-noirs-voyage -au-coeur-du-g-u-d/.

21. Caqueray-Valmenier family background and Action française membership have been widely reported: see for example Sébastien Bourdon and Marine Turchi, "Violences au meeting de Zemmour: deux militants d'ultradroite mis en examen," *Médiapart,* December 15, 2021; Livio Ferrero, "Marc de Caqueray-Valmenier, leader des Zouaves, condamné à un an de prison ferme'" *Paris Match,* January 21, 2022.

22. Marine Turchi and Sébastien Bourdon, "Un groupe héritier du GUD multiplie les attaques en plein Paris," *Médiapart,* June 9, 2020.

23. Lebourg, "L'Odyssée des rats noirs." See also Jean-Yves Camus, "La Nouvelle droite: bilan provisoire d'une école de pensée," *La Pensée* 345 (2006): 23–33.

24. Nicolas Lebourg, "Violence militante juvénile d'extrême droite: le cas du Groupe Union Défense (GUD)," in *Radicalités identitaires,* ed. Manuel Boucher (Paris: L'Harmattan, 2020), 219–42.

INDEX

Page numbers in *italics* refer to illustrations.

www.ingramcontent.com/pod-product-compliance
Lightning Source LLC
Chambersburg PA
CBHW020445100426
42812CB00036B/3457/J